KENYA'S QUEST FOR DEMOCRACY

CHALLENGE AND CHANGE IN AFRICAN POLITICS

KENYA'S QUEST FOR DEMOCRACY

TAMING LEVIATHAN

MAKAU MUTUA

LYNNE
RIENNER
PUBLISHERS

BOULDER
LONDON

Published in the United States of America in 2008 by
Lynne Rienner Publishers, Inc.
1800 30th Street, Boulder, Colorado 80301
www.rienner.com

and in the United Kingdom by
Lynne Rienner Publishers, Inc.
3 Henrietta Street, Covent Garden, London WC2E 8LU

Library of Congress Cataloging-in-Publication Data
Mutua, Makau.
   Kenya's quest for democracy : taming leviathan / by Makau Mutua.
      p. cm.
   Includes bibliographical references and index.
   ISBN 978-1-58826-590-6 (hardcover : alk. paper)
   1. Kenya—Politics and government—1963–1978.   2. Kenya—Politics and
government—1978–2002.   3. Kenya—Politics and government—2002–
4. Constitutional history—Kenya.   5. Political culture—Kenya.
6. Postcolonialism—Kenya.   I. Title.
   JQ2947.A58M85 2008
   320.96762—dc22

                                                            2007045124

British Cataloguing in Publication Data
A Cataloguing in Publication record for this book
is available from the British Library.

Printed and bound in the United States of America

       The paper used in this publication meets the requirements
∞   of the American National Standard for Permanence of
       Paper for Printed Library Materials Z39.48-1992.

   5   4   3   2   1

Contents

Acknowledgments

EVERY BOOK HAS a genesis. The origins of this work are located in my childhood in Kenya. Growing up in Kitui, and later in Nairobi, I became acutely aware of the political pathologies around me. But I could not understand then and I am still baffled today by the failure of the Kenyan political class to imagine a larger destiny for the country. Once I joined the centers of higher learning, I became more fascinated with this conundrum and vowed to unravel its hidden mysteries. I became, in essence, a student of the state, particularly its postcolonial variant. The entry points for my research and scholarship were human rights and international law because I felt that one had to critically understand the relationship between the state and the citizen, on the one hand, and the postcolonial state and international law, on the other. I still believe that to be the case.

This book is an attempt to understand the dysfunction of Kenyan political society and to gestate a renaissance. That is why the opportunity to spend the 2002–2003 sabbatical year in Kenya was a godsend. I would use my time there to study firsthand the climax of a decades-old struggle to remove from power the Kenya African National Union (KANU), the kleptocratic party that had ruled the country since independence from Britain in 1964. I planned to be the quintessential academic—doing primary research, incubating deep thoughts, collecting empirical data, digesting everything into analytical categories, and dreaming up high theory. Little did I know that academic abstraction and the pure seduction of ideas would not be my lot. My carefully crafted research plan unraveled quickly upon my return to Kenya, when I was drafted into practical politics. As a lifelong reformer, and as chair of the Kenya Human Rights Commission (KHRC), the country's leading NGO, I put on my hard hat and went to work to oust KANU. On December 27, 2002, we accomplished that historic mission.

Thus, this book is a personal journey for me that started in my early childhood but is still unfinished. Put in that context, the book would not have been possible but for all the people in my life who affected it, for good or ill. From all of them I have learned what the book documents. Obviously, it is impossible to mention everyone who has affected me in some fundamental way—nor would it be desirable—but I am compelled to name a few whose influence and help have been more immediate to this project. I do so with some reluctance, knowing that I will inevitably forget some individuals. From them, I seek forbearance. I hope they will take some solace in the recognition of an idea or question that they helped me develop or settle. But I also hope that they understand that all scholarship is social and is produced in an interactive context, even when the writer is seemingly oblivious to the world around him.

Crucial to the work has been the guidance of Willy Mutunga, now with the Ford Foundation in Nairobi. Willy is my earliest and most influential mentor. He is a man who lives his politics and knows how to nurture others. I know because he was my teacher at the University of Nairobi and a fellow cofounder of the KHRC. He served with me there for many years, all with exemplary distinction. Many were the days and nights that we sat and talked endlessly about this project. His political insights, ability to parse through complex ideas, and uncanny facility to marry theory and practice are legendary. I started writing this book in 2002, the year that the National Rainbow Coalition smashed KANU. I completed it six years later. Through it all, Willy was always there, urging me on and improving the book with his critiques of Kenyan politics.

The support of my friends at the Ford Foundation who generously backed the project has also been enormously important. It was Julius Ihonvbere in the foundation's New York office whose excitement about a project on constitutional reform in Kenya opened doors. He spoke with Joseph Gitari, then at the foundation's office in Nairobi, about my research. Both Joseph and Tade Aina, the representative in Nairobi, gave me the grant to support the work. My discussions with them, and especially Tade, helped me clarify many themes. I am also grateful to the KHRC, my own organization, for hosting the grant. I hope they all recognize their fingerprints on the book.

There are many Kenyans who have given a lot to this project in ways big and small. They include ordinary folks, politicians, state leaders, academics, clerics, journalists, professionals, civil society actors, and government functionaries. I will list some of them, but not in any order. They include James Orengo, Paul Muite, Raila Odinga, Betty Murungi, Kiraitu Murungi, Alamin Mazrui, Ali Mazrui, Betty Maina, Koki Muli, Pheroze Nowrojee, Kalonzo Musyoka, Michael Chege, Stephen Ndegwa, Charity Ngilu, John Munuve, Karuti Kanyinga, Davinder Lamba, John Githongo, Jane Kiragu, Katini Ombaka, Maina Kiai, Peter Anyang' Nyong'o, L. Muthoni Wanyeki, Vincent Musebe, Yash Ghai, Steve Ouma, Wanjiku Miano, Njeri Rugene, Judith Mbula Bahemuka, Micere Githae Mugo, Shadrack Gutto, James Gathii, Tirop arap Kitur, Gacheke Gachihi, Wambui Kimathi, Pius Mutua, Joseph Odindo,

Wangethi Mwangi, Mutuma Mathiu, Kivutha Kibwana, Nzamba Kitonga, Mutava Musyimi, P. L. O. Lumumba, and Mwai Kibaki.

A project of this magnitude cannot be accomplished without collegial mentorship and guidance. In this respect, the greatest influence on the book has been John Harbeson, the editor of the series in which this book appears and one of the fathers of the study of Kenya in the United States. He patiently read through several early drafts and provided detailed and structured comments that were critical to the project. Without him, I am not sure the book would have seen the light of day. John is an academic's academic, toiling in the background without demanding credit or attention. To him, I say thank you.

Frank Holmquist, whose work on Kenya can only be described as deeply penetrating and grounded in social reality, was an early and enthusiastic supporter of the book project. He read several drafts of the manuscript and offered insightful commentary that brings the work closer to the politics of resistance. Joel Barkan is another student of Kenyan politics who was a constant source of ideas that clarified many an issue in the book. These giants of scholarship on Kenya offered their time and advice without any limitations. Henry Steiner, one of my closest friends and a colleague with whom I worked at the Harvard Law School Human Rights Program, taught me human rights at Harvard. He has been a source of many clarifying conversations in my development as a scholar. Guyora Binder, my colleague at Buffalo Law School, has been a great source of insightful discussions on postcolonialism over the years.

Many other fellow academics and thinkers have been critical in helping me shape the views herein. They are Henry Richardson, C. Maina Peter, Joe Oloka-Onyango, Antony Anghie, Balakrishnan Rajagopal, Issa Shivji, Leila K. Hilal, Hope Lewis, Tom Wolf, Mahmoud Mamdani, Mohammad-Mahmoud Mohamedou, Obiora Okafor, Roberto Aponte-Toro, Randall Kennedy, Charles Ogletree, Jose Alvarez, Peter Rosenblum, Bill Alford, Martha Minow, Mary Ann Glendon, Ibrahim Gassama, David Kennedy, Adrien Wing, Leonard Reed, Muna Ndulo, Bereket Habte Selassie, Abdullahi Ahmed An-Na'im, and Joel Ngugi.

I owe a debt of gratitude to my research assistants in Buffalo and Nairobi. I am grateful for the work of Bhavjyot Kaur Singh, my brilliant summer intern from Cornell University. I must thank Davis Malombe of the KHRC and Tabitha Kilatya for their diligent and thorough research. Their work was essential to the primary study on which the book is based.

I have spent many fruitful and productive years at Buffalo Law School. Nils Olsen, the dean at Buffalo until December 2007, generously supported this project, as he did all my other work. I also cannot forget to mention the law school's Baldy Center for Law and Social Policy, which supported this project at the beginning. My work at the law school would have been difficult without the professional support of my diligent secretary, Sandra Conti.

I am indebted to Lynne Rienner for believing in this project. This work has been improved by the talents of Shena Redmond of Lynne Rienner Publishers, and Beth Partin, my superb copyeditor.

My family traveled with me to Kenya during my sabbatical year. Lumumba, Amani, and Mwalimu—my three boys—lived in Kenya with us for the year. They attended school there but also took in much of my political work. Athena, my wife, was incredible throughout the project. She read and discussed several drafts with me. In Kenya, she was engaged in the political struggle for reform. In particular, she helped form a women's coalition that became the leading voice for advancing the rights of women in the constitution-making process. Because of her work—and political insights—she has been an extremely important voice in this book. I am deeply indebted to her.

Finally, this book is a tribute to ordinary Kenyans, for whom and by whom the state must be reformed.

—*Makau Mutua*

1

Introduction

THIS BOOK ATTEMPTS to explain why Kenya has failed at reform and how its fortunes can be reversed. I argue that constitutional reform—an exercise that must fundamentally alter the raison d'être of the state—is critical to the reform of the African state. However, such reform will not be possible without the leadership of civil society, the only sector that can fundamentally renew the political class. For me, this book is the culmination of a personal journey. In August 2002, I left Buffalo, New York, to live in Kenya for a year during my sabbatical from Buffalo Law School, at the State University of New York. Fortuitously, 2002 was an election year in which the opposition would get one more crack at deposing the Kenya African National Union (KANU), the only ruling party the country had ever known. There was a fever for fundamental change over the land. A decades-long tumult over the state's stubborn dictatorship had reached a crescendo. For the first time, the opposition formed a united front against President Daniel arap Moi. KANU nearly imploded as key apparatchiks left it to form the National Rainbow Coalition (NARC), the opposition party that would end its reign over the country.

It was under these circumstances that I was swept up in the maelstrom and deposited right in the vortex of the struggle for regime change. As the chair of the Kenya Human Rights Commission (KHRC), the country's leading human rights group, my inclusion was not an accident. A decade earlier, the KHRC had led Kenya's civil society effort for constitutional reform. Under Willy Mutunga and Maina Kiai, the KHRC had been the first to produce a model constitution for Kenya in the mid-1990s.[1] The KHRC's leadership of the reform movement was evident even at the brink of the formation of NARC when KANU rebels joined the united opposition. Mutunga had been chair of the National Alliance for Change (NAC), the forerunner of the National Alliance Party of Kenya (NAK), itself the mother of NARC.[2] It was no wonder that in October 2002, Mutunga and I endorsed Mwai Kibaki and NAK for the elections.[3] The endorsement was a calculated risk that Kibaki and NAK stood the

1

best chance to steer Kenya onto the path to recovery. Our logic was that NAK had among its ranks a number of proven reform advocates. Although they were vastly outnumbered by old-style politicians, we pinned our hopes for a reformist government on them.[4]

But as soon as Kibaki moved into State House, NARC's calculations began to shift, although it seemed as though reformers might bring about change. Several cabinet ministers were celebrated reform advocates. Kibaki appointed John Githongo, the respected head of the Kenya chapter of Transparency International, to be the government's anticorruption czar. Some corrupt judges were dismissed. An official inquiry into the Goldenberg scandal, in which the Moi regime was suspected of having looted hundreds of millions of dollars from the treasury, was launched. NARC made good on its promise of free primary education. I was appointed chair of the Task Force on the Establishment of a Truth, Justice, and Reconciliation Commission to prepare the country for a truth commission. The Kenya National Commission on Human Rights, an official watchdog, was established under Kiai, one of the founders of the KHRC. The government restarted the National Constitutional Conference to write a democratic constitution. The first few months were a time of great hope. As an academic, I used the study of African constitutionalism as a practical opportunity to influence the recovery of the state from the inner sanctum of power. However, the euphoria was short-lived.

But once again, Kenya's political class betrayed the country. Kenyan ruling elites, like their counterparts elsewhere in Africa, have performed poorly. The continent will not emerge from its interminable crises unless a new political class emerges, or the elites undergo a radical conversion. The postcolonial African state is an albatross, a yoke that the West has spun around the neck of Africa. Over the decades, it has proven a Sisyphean problem. Many a reformer—and reformist movement—have fallen victim to its predatory proclivities. Books without number have been written to explain its pathologies.[5] The continent's malaise seems resistant to traditional prescriptions for state recovery and reform. The optimism that greeted the independent state and the democratization wave of the post–Cold War period has given way to cynicism. Externally, a scandalous international order fuels the ravage of Africa.

In this book, I argue that the redemption of the postcolonial African state must start with the writing of a broadly legitimate national charter that creates a new compact between the state and its citizens. Constitutional reform is the only framework on which the sinews of the democratic state will be constructed. I put forward a number of basic themes that are essential for the recovery of the state. Since the political class has been a catastrophe, I emphasize the role of civil society to act as the engine of change. The Kenyan experiment demonstrates the central role that civil society can play in democratizing the state. The Kenyan struggle shows the salience of ethnicity, religion, and gender as critical variables in the reform effort. These factors must be re-imagined for politics to be reconstructed. The renewal of the state will not be possible unless a reformed political class—in which civil society plays the key role—comprehends the larger national interest. Otherwise, the postcolonial state is likely to reach a point of no return.

The reclamation of the African continent must be driven by Africans. But Africa must comprehend a basic truism. Although many a society has failed with a visionary elite, not a single nation has ever prospered without one, since the beginning of recorded history. The spiritual, ideological, and political rebirth of the African elites is the condition sine qua non for the recovery of the state. But the persistent problem is that elites, even where political democracy has been implanted, remain beholden to political myopia and moral bankruptcy. It seems virtually impossible to prevail upon elites to imagine a larger national interest. Francis Kaparo, the speaker of Kenya's National Assembly, sharply put this point. "There is a clear lack of clarity, purpose, and vision in the behavior of our MPs. They no longer have any cause and do not espouse any ideology."[6] In a predictable response, the legislators sought his resignation or censure.[7] But Kaparo again warned them against their rapacious greed at the expense of the welfare of Kenyans.[8]

Kenya's renaissance, as elsewhere in Africa, can only start with the creation of a new political class. The most progressive political actors have been drawn from the ranks of civil society. Only from this sector can Kenyan politics be renewed. In the past, visionary civil society leaders have been content to influence the exercise of power, not seek its direct capture. This must change. Civil society leaders must become the vanguard of a new social movement for reform. The movement would be a grassroots one and address the most urgent needs of the Kenyan people in policy terms. Its agenda must be based on a new code of ethics for both members and leaders. Any persons who have been credibly implicated in atrocities and acts of pillage cannot hold leadership positions within the movement or run for any elective office under its auspices. Altruism, out of which grows self-fulfillment, is a key building block of any genuinely reformist movement, and Kenya's cannot be different. The social movement would become the basis for a political party that would contest for state power.

In the reform of society and politics, constitutionalism, as has been argued by Julius Ihonvbere, is critical.[9] There can be no doubt that the postcolonial African state does not stand a chance without the radical revision of its raison d'être, along with its legal and constitutional framework.[10] But such reformist exercises cannot be successful unless they draw support and legitimacy from a wider national audience.[11] Kenya's struggle over constitutionalism amply demonstrates that renewing the social contract is an arduous, if not impossible, task.[12] The experiences of most African countries have been equally daunting.[13] Even the more successful cases, such as South Africa's, are highly contested affairs.[14] But cleavages of postcolonialism must be squarely faced for a successful constitutional reform effort.[15] The constitutional reform process is supposed to lay the groundwork for the minimum conditions to institutionalize a free and popular state that includes shared democratic principles, an engaged and visionary middle class, and democratic leadership.[16] But it must go beyond the mechanical reordering of the state. Participatory inclusivity is essential for legitimacy and the inculcation of a culture of constitutionalism within the body politic.[17]

Kenya's constitutional reform effort—an exercise that goes back to the 1980s—has hit roadblocks at every turn. The political class has been unable to produce a broadly legitimate constitution in which the country could invest its loyalty. Political elites have played a zero-sum game with constitutional reform. Former president Daniel arap Moi and KANU did not want a democratic constitutional order because it could have written them out of power and into political oblivion.[18] President Mwai Kibaki was loath to give up the despotic powers vested in the executive by the constitution, even though he campaigned on a platform of reform.[19] The "opposition" wing of NARC led by Raila Odinga prevailed on the National Constitutional Conference to produce a draft constitution with a powerful premiership, a weak presidency, and a quasi-federalist state system.[20] That pushed Kibaki and his senior aides to derail the constitution-writing process. The Wako Draft, a government revision of the Bomas Draft constitution, retained the strong presidency, which was one of the main reasons for its defeat in the 2005 referendum by a joint Odinga-KANU alliance.

Students of African politics know that until December 2007, Kenya had been one of the more hopeful countries on the continent. It had shown promise at various points in its history. That is why one might ask why I have adopted what might be characterized as a pessimistic tone toward this so-called beacon of hope. The near genocidal violence since the December 2007 election is ample reason for pessimism. As Barkan demonstrates, the country has a checkered political history.[21] Some periods have been more hopeful than others. Clearly, the country reached its nadir under the twenty-four-year reign of President Moi. Ironically, however, it was during the Moi period that the reformist opposition movement took root and eventually forced the partial liberalization of the state. The post-KANU Kibaki state, in spite of its corruption, was a slight improvement over the dim past. The legislature became more autonomous of the executive. The press was more vigilant in spite of attacks on it by the state.[22] Civil society operated in a relatively open political environment. These were signs that democratic practices and a culture of accountability were being implanted in spite of government efforts to thwart reform. Unless Kenyan leaders agree to restore peace and reform the state, the postelection violence could start Kenya on an irreversible downward spiral.

Until December 2007, Kenya was only one of a handful of African states that had not experienced a coup d'état, a crippling civil war, or failure as a state. Except for the aborted coup by a section of the Kenya Air Force in 1982, the armed forces have stayed out of politics and have largely remained professional. Ethnic tensions, even when the state fanned the flames of intercommunal conflict, had failed to ignite a national conflagration. This resilience, and the refusal to submit to the pull of the primordial, suggested an incipient commitment by citizens and political institutions to the idea of Kenya as a viable state. Ironically, the prolonged constitution-writing project is evidence of that commitment.[23] The Kenyan people are neither incapable of nor opposed to reform. But the majority of the political elite lacks imagination about the purposes of leadership in a modern state. It is this political class about which I express despair—hence my contention that only a transformation of the political elite can lead to the genuine reformation of the state.

Kenya is not unique among African states. Its near collapse after the December 2007 elections and the gruesome interethnic pogroms are evidence of deep-seated historical grievances and social dysfunctions. Nor is it out of the bounds of the experiences of postcolonial states beyond Africa or even states in the industrialized world. In industrial democracies, however, institutions are often strong enough to resist the base proclivities of leaders. In contrast, where institutions are fragile and the norms of democratic government are not fully incubated, a single leader or a corrupted elite can easily overwhelm society. More than anywhere else, a visionary elite is indispensable in the reform of deeply distorted postcolonial states. The lessons that the Kenyan experience offers the world are both complicated and multiple. An obvious one is that reform is a long and arduous process. Its legitimacy requires broad political participation by elites and the general population. But elites, as the birth of the postapartheid South African state demonstrated, are key to political democracy. Those with moral and political leverage must use it to restrain ethnic exceptionalism and demagoguery. Ultimately, the society must be able to imagine a broad consensus that binds it and provides the largest opportunity for development. This consensus has proven elusive to the Kenyan political class.

In the spectrum of African states, Kenya had been far from a basket case. It had remained one of the more stable and hopeful countries on the continent. Even under the bungling regime of President Kibaki, the country made some minimal gains on several fronts. For one, the economy grew at 5.8 percent in 2005 and 6.1 percent in 2006, and was expected to top 6.9 percent in 2007.[24] Clearly, there was some resilience to the state because its basic institutions still functioned, albeit at highly insufficient levels. Nairobi, the capital city, is still by far the region's hub. Kenya's economy dominates the region, and the country played leading roles in mediating the civil war in Sudan and attempting, though unsuccessfully, to put the Somali state back together. With respect to this last endeavor, Kenya was playing the role of the stable regional power. The not-so-subtle message was that Kenya could get distressed African states to put their houses in order. And, as Barkan has argued, Kenya's performance earned it a leadership role in Africa: "Along with Nigeria and South Africa, Kenya is one of the three 'anchor' states in sub-Saharan Africa that is key to the stability of the region because of its location and resources. Egypt is the other anchor state in North Africa. As a result, Kenya has become the platform for U.S. operations in East Africa and the Horn."[25]

Why then, given Kenya's potential and its basic functionality, has the country not matured into a viable democracy? Why, even with its great promise, has the state not attained a fuller legitimacy within the populace and reached the stage of irreversibility in terms of democratizing its institutions? What are the ingredients of this promise and potential, or, put differently, what had kept Kenya from going the way of other failing African states? Perhaps it is those nubs of promise and potential on which a Kenyan renaissance can be launched. Here, one needs to look at the country through the lens of history and identify key moments that could have led to a consolidation of a modern, viable, and prosperous democracy. What factors conspired to limit Kenya's potential? Has the country's progress been hampered by accidents of history, the policy choices of its leaders, external factors, or a combination of all of the above?

The independence of Kenya in 1964 was greeted with enthusiasm both at home and abroad. In a few years, that euphoria was tempered by the challenges of nation building and some ill-advised decisions by the KANU regime of Jomo Kenyatta, the country's founding father. After Kenyatta's demise in 1978, the Moi KANU state embraced corruption and political repression as tools of governance. These choices by both leaders form part of the explanation for the malignant character of the Kenyan state today. Under Kibaki, the Kenyan state was unable to break with the debilitating legacies of the past. This book scans Kenyan history to identify key moments when the country could have gone in a different, more positive direction, but failed to do so. In so doing, the book seeks to answer one basic question: What can still be done on the ground—*empirically and realistically*—to move Kenya beyond these bottlenecks to secure its enormous potential as a modern, viable democracy?

Notes

1. Kenya Human Rights Commission, International Commission of Jurists, and Law Society of Kenya, *The Kenya We Want: Proposal for a Model Constitution* (Nairobi, 1994).

2. "The Troubled Search for Joint Opposition Platform," *Daily Nation*, February 3, 2002; "How to Settle on One Presidential Hopeful—Dr. Mutunga," *Daily Nation*, April 30, 2002.

3. Makau Mutua and Willy Mutunga, "Why and How to Bring About Regime Change in Kenya," Kenya Human Rights Commission, October 2, 2002.

4. Ibid.

5. Ali A. Mazrui, *The African Condition: The Reith Lectures* (London: Heinemann, 1979); Angelique Haugerud, *The Culture of Politics in Modern Kenya* (Cambridge: Cambridge University Press, 1995); Stephen N. Ndegwa, *A Decade of Democracy in Africa* (Leiden: Brill Academic Press, 2001); Claude Ake, *A Political Economy of Africa* (New

York: Longman, 1981); Basil Davidson, *Africa in Modern History: The Search for a New Society* (London: Allen Lane, 1978); Ali A. Mazrui, *The Africans: A Triple Heritage* (London: Little, Brown, 1986); Kwame Nkrumah, *Africa Must Unite* (Los Angeles: International Publishers, 1970); Kwame Anthony Appiah, *In My Father's House: Africa in the Philosophy of Culture* (London: Methuen, 1992); Robert H. Jackson and Carl Rosberg, *Personal Rule in Black Africa: Prince, Autocrat, Prophet, Tyrant* (Berkeley: University of California Press, 1982); Washington Okumu, *The African Renaissance: History, Significance, and Strategy* (Trenton, NJ: Africa World Press, 2002); Basil Davidson, *Can Africa Survive? Arguments Against Growth Without Development* (London: Heinemann, 1975); Wole Soyinka, *The Open Sore of a Continent: A Personal Narrative of the Nigerian Crisis* (New York: Oxford University Press, 1996); V. Y. Mudimbe, *The Invention of Africa: Gnosis, Philosophy, and the Order of Knowledge* (Bloomington: Indiana University Press, 1988); Keith Richburg, *Out of America: A Black Man Confronts Africa* (London: HarperCollins, 1997); I. William Zartman, ed., *Collapsed States: The Disintegration and Restoration of Legitimate Authority* (Boulder: Lynne Rienner Publishers, 1995).

6. "Most MPs Dishonest and Selfish, Says Kaparo," *Daily Nation*, June 24, 2005.

7. "Quit or Be Censored, MPs Rage at Kaparo," *Daily Nation,* June 25, 2005.

8. "Greed: Kaparo Warns MPs They Face Verdict at the Polls," *Daily Nation*, May 8, 2006.

9. Julius Ihonvbere, *Towards a New Constitutionalism in Africa* (London: Center for Democracy and Development, 2000).

10. See Kivutha Kibwana, ed., *Readings in Constitutional Law and Politics in Africa: A Case Study for Kenya* (Nairobi: Claripress, 1998).

11. Mahmood Mamdani, "Social Movements and Constitutionalism: The African Context," in *Constitutionalism and Democracy: Transitions in the Contemporary World,* ed. Douglas Greenberg, Stanley M. Katz, Melanie Beth Oliviero, and Steven C. Wheatley (New York: Oxford University Press, 1993); Issa Shivji, ed., *State and Constitutionalism: An African Debate on Democracy* (Harare: Sapes Trust, 1991).

12. Willy Mutunga, *Constitution-Making from the Middle: Civil Society and Transition Politics in Kenya, 1992–1997* (Harare: MWENGO, 1999).

13. Bereket Habte Selassie, *The Making of the Eritrean Constitution: The Dialectic of Process and Substance* (Trenton: Red Sea Press, 2003).

14. Siri Gloppen, *South Africa: The Battle over the Constitution (Law, Social Change, and Development)* (Burlington: Dartmouth Publishing, 1997).

15. Joe Oloka-Onyango, ed., *Constitutionalism in Africa: Creating Opportunities, Facing Challenges* (Kampala: Fountain Publishers, 2001).

16. Michael Chege, "Between Africa's Extremes," *Journal of Democracy* no. 6 (1995): 44.

17. H. W. O. Okoth-Ogendo, "Constitutions Without Constitutionalism: Reflections on an African Political Paradox," in *Constitutionalism and Democracy: Transitions in the Contemporary World,* ed. Douglas Greenberg, Stanley M. Katz, Melanie Beth Oliviero, and Steven C. Wheatley (New York: Oxford University Press, 1993).

18. Laurence Juma, "Ethnic Politics and the Constitutional Review Process in Kenya," *Tulsa Journal of Comparative and International Law* no. 9 (2002): 471.

19. Frank Holmquist, "Kenya's Anti-Politics," *Current History: A Journal of Contemporary World Affairs* 209 (April 2005).

20. Joel D. Barkan, "Kenya After Moi," *Foreign Affairs* 83 (January–February 2004): 87.

21. Ibid.

22. "Shut Down," *East African Standard,* March 2, 2006; "Angry Kenyans Condemn Raid on 'Standard' and KTN," *East African Standard,* March 3, 2006; "Police Shut Down Standard, KTN," *Daily Nation,* March 2, 2006.

23. Godwin R. Murunga and Shadrack W. Nasong'o, eds., *Kenya: The Struggle for Democracy* (London: Zed Books, 2007); Alicia L. Bannon, "Designing a Constitution-Drafting Process: Lessons from Kenya," *Yale Law Journal* 116 (2007): 1824.

24. Republic of Kenya, State House, "His Highness the Aga Khan Commends Kenya's Economic Growth," August 13, 2007, available at http://www.statehousekenya .go.ke/; Amos Kimunya [Minister for Finance], *Kenya Budget for Fiscal Year 2006–2007,* June 15, 2007; "Minister Targets Rich and Big Spenders," *Daily Nation*, June 16, 2006; U.S. Department of State (Bureau of African Affairs), *Background Note: Kenya*, available at http://www.state.gov/r/pa/ei/bgn/2962.htm, accessed August 2, 2006; Abu Namwamba, "Kibaki Economic Magic a Mirage," *East African Standard,* June 17, 2007; "MP Queries Growth as Budget Is Discussed," *East African Standard,* June 20, 2007.

25. Barkan, "Kenya After Moi," 87.

2

The Reconstruction
of the African State

THE CHALLENGES OF African statehood constitute much of the literature on the postcolonial African state.[1] Soon after the decade of independence—the 1960s—the short burst of enthusiasm was replaced by a long, almost unremitting, period of despair. Military coups, civil wars, repressive regimes, refugee flows, and economic stagnation soon came to define many an African state. Paradoxically, the achievement of political independence from colonial rule turned into a false start for the renaissance of the African continent. Even though the African state retained international legitimacy and its juridical status in legal, normative terms, there was no doubt that its empirical, domestic writ was wafer-thin.[2] It is remarkable that many African states did not collapse altogether, given the acuteness of internal illegitimacy. But in the late 1980s, as the Cold War came to an end, a confluence of factors awakened new hope in Africa.

The end of the reflexive support for African states by the key Cold War protagonists removed a huge barrier to political transformation on the continent. Almost overnight, many African regimes lost their automatic, clientelist relationships with Cold War hegemons. This erosion of international legitimacy severely diminished the resources available to the African state. It exposed the inability of the state to control the political realm without external military, diplomatic, political, and economic support. Nowhere was this vulnerability more visible than in Zaire, Somalia, Ethiopia, and Liberia. In the ensuing vacuum, long-suppressed demands exploded into the open. Bourgeoning political movements, usually couched in the language of reform, sought to capture central power with a vow to reform the state.[3] These upheavals came to be grouped under the heading of democratization, although some analysts feared another false start.[4]

Whatever the case, the political convulsions of the 1990s would irrevocably alter the political cultures of most African states. The protest coalitions of oppositionists, professionals, students, the press, and trade unions left an indelible mark on the African state. They forced long-serving autocrats to either relinquish power through open elections, overthrew them outright, or loosened the grip of the state over society through piecemeal reforms. Virtually no state was left untouched by the wave of change dubbed by many Africans as the "second liberation," suggesting an epochal shift of the magnitude of decolonization. Crawford Young identifies Libya and Sudan as the only holdouts, but even the latter acquiesced to "token gestures of liberalization."[5] With a few exceptions, gone were the Big Men who bestrode the African state like so many colossi. But did these transformations usher in the project of democracy or have most of the transitions been ill fated? What has the nature of these reforms been? Are they normative, conceptual, and structural? Or has the African state remained impermeable to real, meaningful reform?

The focus of conflict and social ferment in postcolonial Africa has been the struggle over the nature of the state. At the core of that question is how state power is organized, shared, and exercised. In other words, the constitution of the state—the sum total of its power and authority—lies at the center of the crises of the modern African state. That is why the most urgent question for reformers has revolved around the constitution as a normative document of values, objectives, and principles. Clearly, rewriting the constitution by itself will not suffice to cure the African malaise. But it is the essential starting point for political transformation and the reclamation of the state. In essence, a new consensus about the character and nature of the state must be forged so that groups and factions feel a meaningful inclusion. Without a redefinition of the meaning and the purpose of the state—and its relationship to individuals and groups in society—the political culture cannot be transformed for the better. But the constitution is just one of the many variables that the reconfiguration of state power in Africa must address. The nature of the African state—and its relationship with the international legal, political, and economic orders—must be reformed to bring the continent out of its abyss.

The focus of this book is the struggle to reform the Kenyan state through a new democratic constitution. That effort has stalled—and may even have been reversed—in several respects. But Kenya, like other African states, suffers from a script of normative and structural deficits that ostensibly defy fundamental reforms. Even so, the Kenyan state has progressively become more liberal since the early 1990s. Amid the despair, there have been rays of hope. For one, Kenyans are still committed to the idea of a viable country, even if the actions of the political elite seem to threaten that belief. These weaknesses of the African state are largely responsible for the stagnation and, in many cases, the failure of the democratic project. The question is whether Kenya can recognize these common fault lines and heal them in a way that responds to the needs of its population. In other words, what overarching themes or questions must be addressed in the reform of the African state, and Kenya, in particular? What broad lessons does Africa hold for Kenya? How can those lessons be applied to a specific country to tackle the problem of the viability of the African state? What are the compelling trends that have emerged from the experience of the wave of reforms that has swept Africa since 1989? Could the success—or stagnation and even failure—of the reform of the Kenyan state foretell the fortunes of other African states?

The crisis of the African state is an inability to create viable, legitimate, and democratic societies. Virtually every major thinker and political scientist concerned with Africa has identified this problem as the bane of the African state. Simply put, the African state suffers from a deficit of democracy. But that begs the question—why is there a deficit of democracy? Political democracy, as a normative and structural ideology, arises from liberalism. Liberalism, in turn, is distinguished from other traditions by its commitment to formal equality and abstract autonomy. In its contemporary expression, liberalism requires a constitutional state with limited powers. Such a state would be anchored in a political democracy under the genus of a system known as constitutionalism. Today, many of these values have been captured in the human rights corpus, a collection of norms and practices that bind the state to limited, prescribed conduct.[6]

One of the roots of liberal theory has been its attention to the risk of the abuse of the individual by the state. Hence the skepticism of liberal theorists about entrusting the state with power that is not subject to enforceable limitations. Translated into political terms, constitutionalism then requires a system of government with several incontestable features, albeit in varying configurations. The state must be based on a conception of popular sovereignty in which the constitution provides that the state is accountable to the people through a range of devices and techniques, the most critical of which is open, periodic, multiparty elections.[7] But the powers of the state would be curtailed through the system of checks and balances and the separation of the three arms of the state to ensure an independent judiciary. In this scheme, the judiciary is the guardian of legality and of the rule of law to safeguard individual rights through the judicial review of executive action. Otherwise, the executive or the legislature could run amok and impose tyrannical rule on the populace. But constitutionalism is not just a set of rules, procedures, devices, and techniques. To become meaningful, constitutionalism must empirically become a set of cultural norms and values subscribed to at the core by officialdom and the public at large. It must be part of their zeitgeist.

In emergent societies, as is the case in Africa, democracy cannot be merely a matter of procedures and rules. Democratic rule must be viewed as substantive, meaning that procedures and rules must have just and legitimate outcomes in the eyes of the populace. Otherwise, the experiment in open government will fail. That is why J. Schumpeter and Samuel Huntington, whose definitions of democracy are predominantly procedural, may not completely fit the African case.[8] For Africa, democracy cannot simply be a method; it must pay particular attention to outcomes. Otherwise, the state will not be able to gain allegiance from its people. Furthermore, outsider groups and interests will forswear the state and deny it legitimacy. Although, as Robert Dahl suggests, open elections are the critical difference in a democracy, the formal right to vote and stand for elections can be meaningless if political conditions restrict real choices and discourage participation.[9] Even though democracy is the single most important deficit in Africa—and the critical proxy for the legitimization of the state—it would be a mistake to treat it simply as a method of governance.

Scholars have, therefore, put forward several thematic categories that should be addressed in the recovery of the African state. There is unanimity neither on the number of categories nor on the emphasis to be placed on each. What is not in doubt, however, is the salience of each of the categories. Needless to say, the categories revolve around the viability and legitimacy of the state. One of the most important, and perhaps the only category on which there is universal agreement among the scholars of African politics, is democratization, which is a recurrent theme in the work of every scholar on African politics.[10] The subject appears in a variety of guises—as governance, electoral politics, and political participation, among others. Richard Joseph refers to this phenomenon as the reconstitution of political order.[11] Indeed, it is an exercise that requires a fundamental reconstruction of the state beyond the traditional panacea of holding multiparty elections, strengthening legislatures, or revitalizing political parties. The state cannot be reconstructed without a new constitutional dispensation. That is why a new democratic constitution—one that is popularly mandated—must be written.

The second key theme involves the centrality of civil society in the reconstruction and democratization of the state. It is not the purpose here to explore in any depth the conceptual meanings and definitions of civil society from John Locke or G. W. F. Hegel and their theory of the social contract.[12] Patrick Chabal has defined civil society as a "vast ensemble of constantly changing groups and individuals whose only common ground is their being outside the state and who have . . . acquired some consciousness of their externality and opposition to the state."[13] As Young correctly notes, given this definition, civil societies predated the imposition of the colonial state by the Europeans.[14] In any case, the modern state, including its postcolonial variant, is deemed incapable of self-restraint without a vigilant and vibrant civil society.[15] Thus civil society is an indispensable element in the push for democratization. An analysis of any political transition must, out of necessity, pay particular attention to the structure, philosophy, role, composition, size, and depth of civil society.

The third important variable in the reformation of the African state is the relationship between state power and ethnic groups that constitute the whole. The failure and tragic collapse of a number of states have been occasioned by their inability to accommodate group identities, whether precolonial or postcolonial, and forge a common national psyche and destiny. The dysfunction of

Nigeria, for example, is largely attributable to the failure of the state to devise a system of government that can adequately provide for the fruitful coexistence of its three major population groups—the Hausa, Ibo, and Yoruba.[16] In legal constitutional terms, that is ostensibly a problem of balancing group rights with the interests of the central state. Yet the calculus is more complex. It is more about forging a national character by absorbing precolonial and other group identities into the whole without establishing an informal hierarchy of groups or ethnicities. To be sure, doing so may include systems of devolution at the local level, but within a unifying, accommodating, and inclusive central authority.

Fourth, political parties occupy a central place in the governance of the modern state, particularly in Africa after the end of military dictatorships or one-party states. Political liberalization in the 1990s opened the door to the contestation for political power through the ballot.[17] But political parties per se have not necessarily been a force for democratization. As noted by Frank Holmquist, Kenyan political parties are not guided by ideological considerations and rarely, if at all, mobilize their members on the basis of coherent policies.[18] Regrettably, many parties in Kenya and other parts of Africa are either empty receptacles for ethnic barons or have no deep resonance in the population. As a result, the ability of political parties to deepen and incubate democratic discourse is sharply limited. Even so, the project of democracy requires competent and ideologically sound political parties. As the recent Kenyan experience demonstrates, the efforts to reform the state through the constitution-making process were shipwrecked partly because of the immaturity of the country's political parties.

Last, but not least, is the place and role of messianic religions—Islam and Christianity—in national political culture. In several countries, such as Nigeria and Sudan, religious and sectarian conflict has been a source of instability and dysfunction in the state. In both cases, secessionist wars have led to massive losses of life and untold destruction of the fabric of society. Among other factors, religious conflicts and intolerance have limited the state's ability to become viable and democratic. They have made it extremely difficult to tame political power and have wreaked havoc with institution building. The executives in such states have taken advantage of the deterioration of security to clamp down on reformers and contract whatever was left of the open political space. Even when not engaged in conflict with others, Islam and Christianity have tended to advocate public positions that either undermine or restrict a range of rights, most notably those related to gender. In Kenya, that occurred largely with respect to "hot-button" social questions, such as gender equality, family law, abortion, property ownership and inheritance, and privacy in the constitution-making process. The potential for the use of religion to entrench the subordination of women—and hence the retardation of the democratic project—in the patriarchal African states cannot be overstated.[19]

The Reconstitution of Political Order

The viability of the political order of the postcolonial state has been a central question since the dawn of independence from colonial rule. The immediate difficulties faced by African states soon after independence did nothing to dispel this fear. Could the African state stand on its own, shorn of colonial tutelage and guardianship? The answers to this question can only be found in the constitution—or construction—of the state and the relationship between it and those under its authority. Unfortunately, those under the authority of the state were often subjects, not citizens. Some analysts have argued that this was a deficit of "national consciousness" without which the nation could not securely exist.[20] Citizenship often meant the "right" of the state to command those under it. But viable democratic states must have a sound normative foundation on which political society rests. In other words, what pacts or binding agreements do elites and citizens share about the state? Is there an irreducible core of values, assumptions, and principles on which the state pivots?

The artificiality of most African states is not in doubt. Young has argued that the colonial state was not a "state" as such because it lacked three crucial elements of statehood—sovereignty, nationhood, and the ability to act externally.[21] Although these deficits applied to all colonial states, they were most acute in Africa, which to the European imperial powers was the extreme "alien other," far removed from civilization. As Young has argued elsewhere, "the colonial legacy cast its shadow over the emergent African state system to a degree unique among the major world regions."[22] The imposed nature of the colonial state, its extreme alienation from Africans, and the cruelty of its rulership created enormous challenges of legitimacy and viability for the postcolonial state. Even so, as Mwalimu Nyerere articulately put it, colonialism was a rallying point for nascent African nationalism: "Africans all over the continent, without a word being spoken, either from one individual to another, or from one African country to another, looked at the European, looked at one another, and knew that in relation to the European they were one."[23]

However, no matter the pull of pan-Africanism, it was insufficient to overcome the normative problems of the illegitimacy of the colonial state. In his study of the state in Africa, Pierre Englebert incorrectly discounts the importance of the moral legitimacy of the state and instead focuses on legitimacy per se.[24] In his view, legitimacy per se, which does not imply a just, democratic, or inclusive state, can come only from the endogenous creation of the state from local history, culture, and domestic power relations.[25] By that definition, few states could be said to be legitimate per se. However, in the African context, both the foreign or imposed genesis of the state and its cruelty toward the population have denied it any legitimacy, be it moral or political legitimacy per se. The difficulty and, in many cases, the failure of the African state is an absence of both forms of legitimacy, whose disaggregation is not really possible. A state that was conceived as a predator and run as such against the majority of its subjects—not citizens—lacks any rudimentary moral and political legitimacy. But that is not an argument against the recovery or legitimation of the African state. Indeed, several postcolonial African states have acquired varying degrees of both moral and political legitimacy since independence. It is the process through which such legitimacy has been acquired—or denied in other cases—that should concern thinkers about the African state. It must be submitted, however, that the reconstitution of the political order ranks very high among the factors that have led to such legitimation.

As the wave of democratization hit Africa in 1989, many analysts focused attention on the role of elections as one of the most important variables in the reconstitution of the political order.[26] Elections appeared to be an appropriate benchmark because they led to a change in leadership in many cases, and even regime change in others. The upheaval was fast and furious, a fact that made it difficult for analysts to fully appreciate or comprehend the magnitude, the scope, or even the nature of the shift and transformation under way. Predictions and analyses of the phenomenon ranged from the ecstatically optimistic to the very skeptical. Would it be another false start or a renaissance for the African state? Richard Joseph reflected these conflicting emotions and analyses when he captured the ebb and flow of the Africanist academy in the United States. Toward the close of the century, a sober and restrained perspective had formed.

> Hopes for a more democratic Africa were tentatively expressed in 1997, as they were in 1989, reflecting the fact that the euphoria of the 1990s had ebbed. On the eve of these transformations, there had been little confidence that viable structures of democracy would be installed in Africa in the near future, so students of the continent pinned their hopes on the revitalization of civil society, speculating that political reconstruction would germinate at the local level. By 1997, however, it was evident that even a vibrant civil society such as Nigeria's, or a nascent one such as Zambia's, could be suppressed by regimes determined to avoid democratization.[27]

It became clear that the reconstitution of the political order of the African postcolonial state would take more than mere elections or the hasty electoral transitions of the 1990s. Although it was true that the modalities for the transitions had a lot to do with the nature of the change, the challenges of legitimating the African state became a reality check. The stubborn autocracy and illegitimacy of the African state proved more resilient than some analysts wanted to allow. As noted by Zeleza, African states adopted three main pathways to political liberalization and incipient democratization.[28] The first involved countries where strong one-party states legalized a weak or fragmented opposition through an amendment to the existing constitutional and legal framework. Invariably, the incumbent regime would retain control of the state after elections and minimal reforms. External pressure, usually by the West, hastened the acquiescence of some regimes to the change. This was true, for instance, in Kenya. The second approach was the national constitutional conference in which the elites, by mobilizing mass pressure, substantially rewrote the political order and overthrew the incumbent state. The national constitutional conference seemed to work best in French-speaking states such as Benin, Mali, and Congo Brazzaville, among others. This model failed to gain traction in English-speaking states, including Kenya. The last model involved managed transitions by military oligarchies fatigued by years of misrule and loss of faith in the state. Nigeria typified this approach.[29] The depth of the reforms in each of these models depended almost entirely on the strength of social forces and the pacts struck between competing political interests and actors.

Five decades—roughly the time that most African states have been independent—is a blip on the screen of history. Even less significant is the nearly two decades of the current process of democratization and political transition. During that period, African states have responded in varying ways to the pressures of political liberalization and globalization. At the one extreme, the Somali state has completely collapsed.[30] On the other, postapartheid South Africa has by far carried out the most successful experiment in democracy.[31] In between, there are a variety of cases trending toward either extreme. In virtually every African country, the political landscape is in flux, as though in a permanent transition. The good news is that the transition is a contest between the forces of reform and those of reaction. Nowhere in Africa is autocracy or dictatorship accepted as the unquestioned norm. Even autocrats such as Omar Hasan Bashir in Sudan pay homage to democracy. But it is in the more invigorating cases, like South Africa, Tanzania, and Benin, that hope inheres. Despite the many challenges faced by the South African experiment, it appears to be instituting one of the most viable normative foundations for the postcolonial state in Africa. So, what is the secret to the reconstitution of the political order of the African state? What are the basic ingredients of such a transformation?

Allegiance by key sectors of the society to the state is central to its legitimacy. For the African state, it means that elites must enter into solid normative compacts that are backed by the populace at large. Such a compact must allow large segments of the population a sense of ownership, belonging, and loyalty to the state. This logic would, for now, reject the proposition by Jeffrey Herbst that one viable alternative is the creation of an entirely different geographic state as the panacea to the endemic crisis of the postcolonial Africa state.[32] Herbst argues that the failure of the imposed African state is partly geographical and might be cured by an abandonment of the African state system for more legitimate African-driven alternatives.[33] For now, however, the focus by both Africans and outsiders seems to be largely on rewriting the internal institutions of the state to legitimate them and produce a viable, democratic polity. In this regard, attention is focused on reengineering a new political order, starting with the redefinition of the constitutional framework of the state. But in fairness to Herbst, Eritrea demonstrated when it split from Ethiopia in 1993 that secession is not out of the question where it is a viable option. The explosive racial cauldron that is Sudan is another case where secession or separation may have a solid basis. Other large and incoherent states such as the Democratic Republic of Congo or Chad might conceivably benefit from geographic disaggregation. However, secession alone does not answer the challenge of the internal legitimacy of the state, as the problems of the Eritrean state under Isaias Afworki have amply demonstrated.

The obvious place to start the process of regenerating the political order is the constitution, the one document that defines the sum total of the powers of the state, their distribution, and the limitations imposed on the government. No fundamental reconstruction of the political order in an undemocratic, opaque, or largely illegitimate state is possible without the foundational revisiting of the constitution and the legal framework of the state. No substantive new pacts can be made without such a departure. Of course, the constitution is a proxy for the political order. It implies the actual document, although it is much more than a mere booklet of norms. In the case of South Africa, for example, the struggle over the postapartheid constitution was a proxy for the overhaul of the state from a racist dictatorship to a multiracial democracy.[34] Even though a new constitutional dispensation was the focus of regime change, it was understood that an entirely new society and state were being created to replace and discard the old order. The racial peace since the transfer of power to a democratic state in 1994 is but one of the symptoms of the success of the new compact.

The centrality of constitutional reform in the re-creation of the state has been the focus of reformist movements across the continent since 1989. In some cases, completely new constitutions were written. In others, important amendments were made to accommodate a new order. Yet in some, only minor changes were effected. All these variations were symptomatic of the balance of power within each country and the extent to which reform could be effected. In the case of Kenya, as in several other countries, the state resisted a substantial rewriting of the national charter, fearing that the ruling elite would be sent into political oblivion. But as the history of Kenya since the late 1980s has clearly shown, no viable political order can be put in place absent a new broadly acceptable constitution. Public discourse in the country is virtually unanimous that the political order must be reconstituted. The lesson of the Kenyan experience is that citizens regard a new constitution as the central tool for regaining political order. Otherwise, large segments of the population will continue to regard the state as illegitimate. The support for a new democratic constitution through a broadly participatory process is so deep and popular that it has transformed the way citizens view the state. They equate the legitimacy of the state with their ability to determine its character through a new constitution.

Civil Society and Democratization

Civil society has long been recognized as a bulwark of democracy.[35] Thinkers of most persuasions, including Antonio Gramsci and Karl Marx, believed that civil society had a great capacity to undermine the tyranny of the state and its control by exploitative ruling classes.[36] Today, civil society has acquired a broader meaning, encompassing the nonstate, nongovernmental, and private sectors that seek to influence how state power is exercised. It seeks to tame the exercise of state power, not capture it. In other words, civil society struggles to keep the state from occupying the entire political sphere and acts as a check on the arbitrariness of the state. In that sense, civil society is the buffer, the cartilage, between the state, or the official sphere, and the private or unofficial space. Ethical civil society holds an intrinsically skeptical or distrustful view of the state. Such skepticism does not rule out selective collaboration, but it recoils from cooptation that undermines the autonomy that is crucial to civil society.

There is a mistaken view among some scholars that there was an absence of civil societies in Africa prior to the advent of the colonial state. But as Young has correctly argued, the existence of states and other forms of centralized authorities in precolonial Africa implies their interaction and relationship with society.[37] However, colonialism changed the nature of African civil societies and their relationship with the state. The reconstructed African colonial state necessarily restructured communities and their consciousness. Ethnicity and group consciousness took on new meanings within the new colonial state under European rulership. New societal categories and tensions emerged as individuals and groups adjusted, opposed, or sought accommodation with the colonial state. New social stratification and class structures emerged as a result of novel economic, social, and power relations. In the colonial economy, villagers became peasant producers whose duty was to feed markets. A large number of Africans became workers and laborers in industries, mines, farms, and plantations. Mission and public schools produced a "modern" African elite who, together with precolonial ancestral "traditional" elites, became the petty bureaucrats and auxiliaries of the colonial state.[38] Out of these new configurations arose forces of contestation and accommodation with the new order. The first leadership of the independent African state was drawn from these new elites. Importantly, the new social relations laid the foundation for the modern African civil society.

As was often the case in postcolonial countries, African postcolonial states failed to establish enduring democracies. The paper-thin liberal constitutions imposed by departing colonial hegemons from London and Paris soon unraveled, allowing the colonial state to reassert itself under the guise of the postcolonial state.[39] What followed was an extremely tumultuous period for the African state—a number of states collapsed, many became deeply dysfunctional, and others atrophied.[40] But, as has been demonstrated by virtually every scholar on Africa, it was civil society that was at the forefront of the reformist wave that swept the continent starting in 1989. As noted by Harbeson, an effective and viable civil society is indispensable for democratic reform in Africa.[41] Even when they were organized as opposition political parties, often illegal under extant law, movements for political reform were driven by individuals and groups drawn from civil society. The success—or failure—of the ensuing political transitions has had a lot to do with the depth of the movements themselves. How deep did these movements reach in various societies? Did they transform themselves from elitist oppositionists to broader social movements? Did they articulate their reformist agendas as struggles for social justice, or were they concerned about the mere competition for political power? Were they narrow and elite-driven campaigns without viable roots in communities and groups outside urban centers?

Even though civil society had been largely forgotten before the last few decades of the Cold War, its rediscovery roughly coincided with the so-called third wave of democratization.[42] John Keane showed the resurgence of civil society discourse in Europe,[43] and Harbeson has argued that it was not a "passing terminological fad" but a "key to understanding and addressing effectively the political and socioeconomic crises in Africa and elsewhere, both on the ground and in contemporary theory."[44] Several writers have argued that civil societies in a number of African states are engaged in the fundamental reconstruction of politics. Michael Bratton suggests that in some cases, control of politics shifted from state elites to more popular forces because of the emergence of strong civil societies.[45] It is this shift—or lack of it—that explains the pace and depth of political reform. Fundamental change is more likely to occur in countries with stronger civil societies, such as South Africa or Kenya, although Nigeria's case has at times pointed in the opposite direction where a determined military elite could thwart or even suppress democratization, in spite of the presence of a vibrant civil society and an independent media.

Although the Kenyan reform process is far from complete, it bears out much of the theoretical analysis on the relationship between civil society and the state in the throes of the democratization and legitimation of the state. Since the onset of the current reform period in Kenya, civil society has been a key factor at almost every critical juncture. Many of the gains in civil and political liberties were forced on the regime of Daniel arap Moi and the Kenya African National Union by an activist civil society composed of religious organizations, human rights groups, the media, and professional associations working closely with opposition political parties and individual dissenters. But political parties—KANU when it was in power and the National Rainbow Coalition after it defeated KANU in 2002—resisted democratization and reform. The lesson of the Kenyan experience, which seems to be borne out by other countries, is that deep and transformative reform of the state cannot be secured without a vigilant and strong civil society.

The Ethnicization of Politics

The concept of citizenship lies at the heart of democratic government. It is the citizens on whose behalf the modern state rules over society. The notion of popular sovereignty, without which constitutional democracies would not exist, makes citizens the owners of the state. Yet in Africa citizenship is often a tortured concept because allegiance and loyalty to the state as ideas are tangential, absent, misplaced, or underdeveloped. That is not surprising, given the genesis of the African state. As Young points out, the only African states with a meaningful precolonial identity are Morocco, Tunisia, Egypt, Zanzibar, Swaziland, Lesotho, Ethiopia, Burundi, Rwanda, Madagascar, and Botswana, out of fifty-three.[46] That means not only are the majority of African states recent creations, but also their citizenries have recently been manufactured or invented. Whether and when identities have been transferred from precolonial repositories are questions that bear heavily on the legitimacy of the state. Citizenship is complicated by the evolution of and distortions in the identities of groups as they position themselves within and against the state. This disjuncture in citizenship—between the precolony and the colony—raises unavoidable questions about group rights and nation building.[47]

Often, though not always, the colonial state corrupted and poisoned relations between African groups and sowed the seeds for the modern phenomenon referred to as tribalism. Colonial rule rallied Africans to liberation, but in many cases it was insufficient to overcome the legacy of the divide-and-rule strategies fostered to sustain it. At the dawn of independence, many African nationalities within the colonial state found themselves at loggerheads over the control of the emergent independent state. Since colonialism did not forge a common citizenship, it fell on the postcolonial state to build a national psyche from multiple nationalities. However, the challenges of the vast geographies of many African states, weak and illegitimate bureaucracies inherited from the colonial state, scarcity of resources, irrational borders, and resilient precolonial identities conspired to retard nation building.[48] It is this fractured political society that today still teeters between failure, dysfunction, and recovery.[49]

African ruling elites have been reluctant to acknowledge the centrality of ethnic subnationalism beyond ritualistic and hypocritical denunciations of tribalism as a cancer on the body politic. In fact, virtually every African ruling elite, usually drawn from one group or a coalition of groups, cynically manipulates ethnicity to consolidate and keep a stranglehold on power. This has caused ethnic group psychosis where some groups consider themselves either insiders or outsiders to the state, given the vantage point of a particular ethnic group in relation to the state. An insider group would typically be the one whose elite controls the state, whereas the outsider group would be the one that is not at the center of power. Outsider psychology is often the basis for the denial of state legitimacy by a group. It reflects the struggle over resources, because groups associate the control of the state by a fraction of their elite with the control of national resources. It is important to note, however, that the group as a whole never benefits from the control of the state by its elite. In Kenya, for example, the Kikuyu still had the largest number of landless squatters during Jomo Kenyatta's rule. Similarly, the majority of the Kalenjin remained destitute under Daniel arap Moi. Nevertheless, although African states are severely underdeveloped, they remain the largest source of resources and employment for most inhabitants of Africa. Hence the death-and-life struggles by ethnic elites to capture and control the state in the name of their groups.

Marina Ottaway argues that many African states are artificial constructs, made up by imperial powers.[50] However, she does overstate the artificiality of African ethnic identities, even though she is right that they are not fixed and frozen in time.[51] Nelson Kasfir argues that "ethnic identity is both fluid and intermittent."[52] What matters, however, is not whether African ethnic identities are primordial, artificial, or invented—the fact is that they are real and living constructs that exercise enormous influence on politics.[53] One does not have to essentialize African ethnic communities to give them reality. They are simply factual. They can neither be wished away nor minimized. What is clear is that group identities have become an irresistible force in national political discourses across the continent. In certain cases, such as in Zambia and Côte d'Ivoire, political actors have even attempted to denationalize their opponents in order to deny them legal standing within the state.[54] Rather than hypocritically suppress ethnic identities, as many regimes in Africa have done, it makes more sense to address them within a legal and constitutional framework that permits local autonomy where necessary in the context of democracy without compromising the internationally guaranteed human rights of others, including women and minority groups.[55]

But the challenges of managing ethnic and group identities in the reconstitution of the political order of the African state will not be easy. The advent of open political competition and multipartyism has given vent to ethnic expression, much of it negative. Since the emergence of multipartyism in Africa in the 1990s, politicized ethnicity has found a home in most new political parties.[56] In fact, no other factor, with the possible exception of the personality cult, exerts a stronger influence on political parties. The call of nativism is so intense in many cases that even political parties, which were initially founded on broad civic nationalism, have retreated into ethnic cocoons. This trend toward the ethnicization of political parties has had a deleterious effect on democratization.

Ethnic groups have such a strong distrust of the African state that they have been reluctant to transfer their loyalties and sense of citizenship to it.[57] That is hardly surprising since the postcolonial state has in most cases done very little to win the allegiance of African populations. If anything, the state has been such an ogre and predator that individuals and groups have virtually no reason to embrace it. Add this alienation to the inability of the state to perform even the most basic functions of statehood—providing security, protecting life and property, and guaranteeing justice and the rule of law—and there is virtually no reason to expect broad sections of Africans to identify with the state and its rulers. This deep-seated illegitimacy of the state, and the disillusion, if not outright revulsion, that many Africans feel for it is one of the major bottlenecks to building a civic national democratic culture.

In Kenya, which has escaped the worst excesses of tribalism, these pathologies have been on naked display. Although Kenya has a sizable African middle class, ethnic cleavages have more often than not stifled the reformist agenda. The opening of the political space frequently raises the ugly specter of negative ethnicity. Political parties have been in the grip of tribal barons. Ethnic political demagogues roam the country preaching an ethnic-based political agenda. Campaigns for office openly appeal to ethnic allegiances. Political parties seem only able to mobilize their ethnic constituencies based on tribal myths, distorted histories, and perceived grievances against other groups. All the major political leaders draw most of their support from their particular ethnic strongholds. Needless to say, this dynamic has diminished the importance of both ideology and social questions as bases on which to distinguish between one party (and its leader) and another party.

The reality on the ground is that most African political parties are not communities of political ideology or philosophy; rather, they are vehicles of ethnic nativism. The identity of most political parties is a result of demagogic manipulation by ethnic elites. Ostensibly ethnic-neutral ideologies such as human rights, social democracy, or even classic liberal democratic ideas have been trumped by narrow tribalism. In the face of a corrupt and repressive state, which most view as lacking legitimacy, refuge in ethnic group identity is often a cloak of security and group pride. Groups also perceive such parties as offering the best opportunity for one of their own—and vicariously themselves by extension—to either capture state power or bargain for a share of power and national resources. The pull of the tribe is evident during every election cycle.

Kenya offers a classic example of these pathologies. Although a vibrant public debate is now a feature of Kenyan political life, its myopia and bankruptcy can at times be stunning. The stalled remaking of the constitution was in part brought about by the corrosive ethnicization of the process. The democratization of the state was hostage to ethnic politics and greed for power, both of which were driven by ethnic-based group interests. Even though the outlines of a democratic constitution were not in dispute, political elites refused to strike a pact for a new constitution because of ethnic pressures. The process came unglued on two fronts. First, ethnic barons insisted on a share of executive power in which central authority would be split among the three or four most powerful ethnic leaders. Second, some ethnic groups demanded steep devolution of power from the center to the regions. In response, a Kikuyu ethnic cabal, the group from which President Mwai Kibaki came, was determined to stall the constitution-making process unless it retained executive authority in his person.

Kenya's stranded reform process has fallen victim to the centralization of ethnicity in politics, but that is nothing new. Former presidents Jomo Kenyatta and Daniel arap Moi ruled by cobbling together ethnic coalitions or manipulating ethnic groups against each other, even as they railed against tribalism. Because of the contracted political space dominated exclusively by KANU, both Kenyatta and Moi wielded enormous power through the patronage system of neopatrimonial rule. Tribal field trips to State House, in which the tribal baron would lead his or her community in a pledge of allegiance to the head of state, were the hallmark of both leaders. Every one of Kenya's forty-two ethnic communities fought to outdo the others in this test of personal loyalty to the "father" of the Kenyan nation. As heads of state, Kenyatta and Moi were rarely challenged until the latter's powers were increasingly curtailed by the multiparty crusade and KANU was voted out of power in 2002.

In contrast to the Kenyatta and Moi eras, enlarged political space emboldened Kibaki's opponents and limited his ability to wield untrammeled power over the country's ethnic groups. Many leaders were able to cobble their own "counterhegemonic" tribal coalitions. Kibaki's opponents, particularly those who sought to succeed him, proved adept at playing the ethnic card. Major leaders like Raila Odinga and Kalonzo Musyoka put together countervailing tribal coalitions to undercut the advantage of Kibaki's incumbency. Genuine political competition opened a Pandora's box in which ethnicity led to greater demands for group rights within the state and the further fragmentation of the political landscape. Ironically, associational and speech rights were manipulated by demagogic ethnic leaders to arrest the democratization of the state. In this ethnic-dominated landscape, smaller ethnic groups—and their leaders—stood virtually no chance of successfully vying for the country's top leadership. That meant that leaders and communities from the five most populous groups—Kikuyu, Luhya, Kamba, Kalenjin, and Luo—dominate the country's politics.[58] This reality ensures the further marginalization of the smaller groups, many of which live in the periphery of the state. Without a doubt, this dynamic adds another layer of complication to the legitimacy and democratization of the state.

Even though ethnicity has been used to undermine democratic practices and to erode the legitimacy of the Kenyan state, identities are not static. Indeed, to the extent that identities are artificial in nature, their very permanence must remain in doubt. For example, under colonial rule, identities were used or fostered by the British for divide-and-rule politics. Colonial rulers demonized the Kikuyu, for example, to tamp down any cross-ethnic sympathies for the Land and Freedom Army, the armed expression of resistance to colonial rule. This liberation army was formed by the Kikuyu and related ethnic groups

(Meru, Embu, and Kamba) as a response to the violence of the colonial state. The freedom fighters believed that violence was the only language the colonialists would understand and that repossessing stolen lands was the condition sine qua non for independence. However, in urban areas where many ethnicities cohabited, some identity barriers broke down through intermarriage, socialization, and cultural proximity. For Kenyans born and bred in large urban areas, such as Nairobi or Mombasa, ethnic identities tend to be less prominent than in mono-ethnic rural areas. Nevertheless, one should not overstate the process of detribalization as a cultural phenomenon. Ethnicity is still very much alive, even in the large metropolitan melting pots. People still largely congregate and socialize with "their own." As a political matter, candidates for elective office, particularly the Parliament (also known as the National Assembly) in Nairobi and other urban areas, still pull most of their support from their ethnic kin. That is why Nairobi continues to elect largely Kikuyu legislators because of the large number of that community in the city. Thus "electable" candidates usually come from the largest ethnic groups in the city; a candidate without an ethnic base is virtually unelectable in Kenya.[59] This seems to contrast with Tanzania, where the fortunes of candidates have not generally depended on their ethnicity. Ethnicity will remain a formidable force in politics unless the state is seen as more than a feeding trough for individuals and groups.[60]

Religion and Political Liberalization

A cursory review of African history shows that imported religions have complicated politics in Africa. John Mbiti has written, perhaps with a little hyperbole, that Africans are "notoriously religious."[61] Perhaps that is why the two messianic faiths—Christianity and Islam—have spread like wildfire on the continent.[62] But African religions still hold some sway, even with the predominance of the imperial faiths.[63] However, the destructive effects of imported religions cannot be underestimated. Imperial faiths delegitimized indigenous religions and customs in a process akin to cultural genocide.[64] Throughout the continent, Islam and Christianity have been presented as the superior and more desirable spiritual cosmologies. They were associated with modernization and civilization.[65] Even Pope John Paul acknowledged the destructive effects of Christianity on the cultures and faiths of the global South.[66] This unusual admission of guilt by the conservative head of the Catholic Church was a rare acknowledgment of the damage done to so-called native peoples by Catholics, among others. The civilizing mission, particularly through the colonial state, would have been that much more difficult without the pacifying effects of Christian spiritualism. There is no doubt that Christianity, along with merchant interests, colluded with European political hegemons to impose the colonial state on Africa.[67] With the exception of the progressive role played by clerics in the post-1989 push for multipartyism, religion has generally been permissive of authoritarianism. That was true in the colonial period and much of the postcolonial era.

The fierce competition for souls between Christianity and Islam—and the struggle by each to gain preeminence within the state—have created new social cleavages, tensions, and conflicts.[68] In some cases, such as Nigeria or Sudan, these conflicts have either exploded into periodic spasms of sectarian violence or have contributed to civil war and the collapse of the state. Denominational conflicts and tensions have led to exclusionary and discriminatory practices, even in countries that are predominantly Christian. African constitutions have been one of the important sites for these intra-religious and inter-religious chasms.[69] At the one extreme, such as in Côte d'Ivoire and Sudan, religion has been a source of political fragmentation and untold suffering. On the other, such as in Benin, reformers deployed religion positively in 1990 to midwife a transition to democracy.[70] There, political leaders used the moral authority of religious leaders to imbue the process of transition with an atmosphere of divinity.

The cases of Benin, Kenya, and South Africa indicate the positive role that clerics can play in the transition from a dictatorship to a more open society. In Benin, the election of Archbishop Isidore de Souza to chair the national conference led to the ouster of Mathieu Kerekou and set the stage for the nonviolent transition to democracy. It gave the process a solemn and sanctified aura.[71] The coming together of Muslim, Vodum (an African religion, also practiced by Haitians, and referred to pejoratively as Voodoo in the West), Catholic, and Protestant clerics endowed the conference with a religious dimension that immunized it from political sabotage by the state. Because of the largely spiritual nature of Africans, woe unto the leader who shows an open defiance of popular clerics. In Kenya, for example, both the Conference of Catholic Bishops and the National Council of Churches of Kenya, the umbrella organization for the mainline Protestant congregations, played leading roles in prying open the opaque and undemocratic state constructed by KANU under Kenyatta and perfected by Moi. Their voices were instrumental in the crusade for multipartyism and the writing of a new democratic constitution. Without them, the transition to a more open society would have been extremely difficult.

In spite of the positive role of religion in the reform process in countries as different as South Africa and Benin, faith-based political activism requires a complex balancing act in Africa. Even though clerics may support the transition from an autocratic, oppressive system to a liberal democracy, they may constrain political discourse and push for a more conservative normative foundation for the state. On women's issues, the clergy in Africa have generally adopted a restrictive interpretation of the rights language in the constitution as well as general statutory law. For instance, both Muslim and Christian clerics sought to impose rigid understandings of reproductive rights, including abortion, in the Kenyan constitution reform debate. Athena Mutua has illustrated how religion sought to retard advocacy of women's rights in the Kenyan constitutional process.[72] Clerics viewed abortion as murder and made it uncomfortable, if not impossible, to have an open debate on the matter.[73] Nor were they any more liberal on general questions of family law. Most Christian and Muslim leaders espouse a very strict, patriarchal reading of religious doctrine.

Religious fundamentalism, hyper-religiosity, and the proclivity of the church and the mosque to be permissive of authoritarianism have often retarded the democratic project. Hyper-religiosity among Muslims and Christians in Kenya has often heightened political temperatures and chilled a robust constitutional discourse on matters critical to reform in the post-Moi era. Christian fundamentalism has had the effect of holding hostage the constitutional review process. After the ouster of KANU in 2003, the dominant churches in Kenya played two key roles with respect to reform. First, they tended to be protective of Kibaki's incumbent authority and not particularly keen to reform the executive. Second, they assumed mostly reactionary positions on gender in the constitutional debate. Given the power of the patriarchy in both the public and private spheres in Africa—and the subordination of women in virtually every facet of life—full-blown transitions to democracy are not possible if one-half of the population is hamstrung by traditionalist, conservative, and even misogynistic beliefs cloaked in religion.

Looking Ahead

Africa's postcolonial history falls into four distinct phases: the immediate postindependence period, which was marked by great optimism; the dim era of the one-party autocratic states and military juntas; the euphoria of multipartyism in the early 1990s; and the current, often chaotic, uneven, and painful transitions to more open societies.[74] The lessons from the last phase—political transition from autocracy—are decidedly mixed.[75] While nakedly despotic regimes are generally a thing of the past, reform has been slow and marked by many reversals.[76] Since colonial rule, there has been a persistence and stubbornness to the crises facing the continent. The problem lies not in the diagnoses of the malaise, but in the prescription to overcome them. There is a general consensus among analysts that two related variables are at the center of these crises. The first, and perhaps the most important, is the African state itself. The illegitimacy and resistance of the African state to democratization are without question the key denominators in its dysfunction. Whether it is the repressive nature of the state, its disdain for civil society, its inability to perform the basic functions of statehood, or its proclivity for corruption, the African state stands at the center of the crisis. The second variable is Africa's relationship with the international legal, political, and economic order. International institutions, hegemonic states, and the culture of international law have at best been negligent and at worst destructive.

Obviously, fundamental change will not come overnight. That is why the expectations of what the reformist transitions can accomplish in the near term must be tempered by reality. South Africa, one of the most hopeful cases, offers a sobering lesson about the difficulty of reform.[77] The experiments in Kenya and Zambia demonstrate how political transitions from autocracy can fail to germinate a true democracy. Both cases underline the slow, if arduous, process of transformation.[78] How do African states become effective and enabling actors in the lives of their citizens, instead of objects of charity and pity by the West and the rest of the world? In other words, how does the continent move from a humanitarian wasteland to functional democratic states? The suggestion is that the process of transformation has to be foundational and thoroughgoing. It is no longer tenable to simply prescribe cautious, band-aid, and unimaginative programs, the type that donors and multilateral organizations have historically promoted. Instead, African states must be reengineered from the bottom up.[79] This is a task that must begin at home, with Africans themselves. The citizenry of each state must create more viable and legitimate political societies. Without such reform, the African state cannot be redeemed. Internationally, Africa needs debt relief, direct foreign investment, aid, and better terms of trade to couple political reforms with economic renewal.

But there are no shortcuts for Africa. African states must reconstruct their political orders, address ethnicity and group rights in political transitions, grow and nurture a vibrant civil society that is national in character, and expand the commitment of religious institutions to the full democratic project. In some countries, such as Kenya, the constitution-writing framework provides the perfect opportunity to begin the political renaissance of the state on all these fronts at once. There will no doubt be different entry points for a variety of states. And each variable will require contextual emphasis depending on the particulars of the state in question. This book looks at each of the five issues identified at the start of the chapter and analyzes them in the light of Kenya's constitution-making process.

Notes

1. See, for example, Crawford Young, *Ideology and Development in Africa* (New Haven: Yale University Press, 1982); I. William Zartman, ed., *Collapsed States: The Disintegration and Restoration of Legitimate Authority* (Boulder: Lynne Rienner Publishers, 1995); Richard Joseph, ed., *State, Conflict, and Democracy in Africa* (Boulder: Lynne Rienner Publishers, 1999); John Harbeson and Donald Rothchild, *Civil Society and the State in Africa*, ed. Naomi Chazan (Boulder: Lynne Rienner Publishers, 1994); Michael Bratton and Nicolas van de Walle, *Democratic Experiments in Africa: Regime Transitions in Comparative Perspective* (New York: Cambridge University Press, 1997); Robert Fatton, *Predatory Rule: State and Civil Society in Africa* (Boulder:

Lynne Rienner Publishers, 1992); John W. Harbeson and Donald Rothchild, eds., *Africa in World Politics* (Boulder: Westview Press, 1991).

2. Robert H. Jackson and Carl G. Rosberg, "Why Africa's Weak States Persist," *World Politics* 35 (1982): 1.

3. Paul Tiyambe Zeleza, "Introduction: The Struggle for Human Rights in Africa," in *Human Rights, the Rule of Law, and Development in Africa*, ed. Paul Tiyambe Zeleza and Philip J. McConnaughay (Philadelphia: University of Pennsylvania Press, 2004).

4. Richard Joseph, "State, Conflict, and Democracy in Africa," in Joseph, *State, Conflict, and Democracy in Africa*, 3.

5. Crawford Young, "The Third Wave of Democratization in Africa: Ambiguities and Contradictions," in Joseph, *State, Conflict, and Democracy*, 15.

6. Louis Henkin, *The Age of Rights* (New York: Columbia University Press, 1991).

7. Henry J. Steiner and Philip Alston, *International Human Rights in Context: Law, Politics, Morals* (New York: Oxford University Press, 2000).

8. J. Schumpeter, *Capitalism, Socialism, and Democracy*, 3rd ed. (New York: Harper and Row, 1950); Samuel Huntington, *The Third Wave: Democratization in the Late Twentieth Century*, 6th ed. (Norman: University of Oklahoma Press, 1990).

9. Robert Dahl, *A Preface to Democratic Theory* (Chicago: University of Chicago Press, 1956).

10. See, for example, Jennifer Widner, ed., *Economic Change and Political Liberalization in Sub-Saharan Africa* (Baltimore: Johns Hopkins University Press, 1994); Marina Ottaway, ed., *Democracy in Africa: The Hard Road Ahead* (Boulder: Lynne Rienner Publishers, 1997); Richard Joseph, ed., *The Democratic Challenge in Africa* (Atlanta: Carter Center, 1994); Larry Diamond, A. Kirk-Greene, and O. Oyediran, eds., *Democracy in Developing Countries: Africa*, vol. 2 (London: Adamantine Press, 1988); Joel Barkan, ed., *Beyond Capitalism vs. Socialism in Kenya and Tanzania* (Boulder: Lynne Rienner Publishers, 1994); Bratton and van de Walle, *Democratic Experiments in Africa*; Claude Ake, *Democracy and Development in Africa* (Washington, DC: Brookings Institution Press, 1996); Claude Ake, "Rethinking African Democracy," *Journal of Democracy* 2 (1991): 32.

11. Joseph, "State, Conflict, and Democracy in Africa," 3.

12. John Locke, *Two Treatises of Civil Government* (London: J. M. Dent and Sons, 1955); Z. A. Pelczynski, ed., *The State and Civil Society: Studies in Hegel's Political Philosophy* (New York: Cambridge University Press, 1984); John Keane, ed., *Civil Society and the State* (London: Verso, 1988).

13. Patrick Chabal, "Introduction," in *Political Domination in Africa: Reflections on the Limits of Power*, ed. Patrick Chabal et al. (Cambridge: Cambridge University Press, 1986).

14. Crawford Young, *The African Colonial State in Comparative Perspective* (New Haven: Yale University Press, 1994).

15. John W. Harbeson, Donald Rothchild, and Naomi Chazan, eds., *Civil Society and the State in Africa* (Boulder: Lynne Rienner Publishers, 1994); Bratton and van de Walle, *Democratic Experiments in Africa*, 147–149.

16. Wole Soyinka, *The Open Sore of a Continent: A Personal Narrative of the Nigerian Crisis* (New York: Oxford University Press, 1996).

17. See Zeleza, "Introduction: The Struggle for Human Rights in Africa," in Zeleza and McConnaughay, eds., *Human Rights, the Rule of Law, and Development in Africa*.

18. Frank Holmquist, "Kenya's Antipolitics," *Current History: A Journal of Contemporary World Affairs* (May 2005): 209; Makau Mutua, "Identity Crisis Weighs

Down Political Class," *Sunday Nation,* July 2, 2006; see also "Political Parties to Get Cash," *Daily Nation*, September 28, 2007, reporting on the Kenyan National Assembly's passage of the Political Parties Bill.

19. Federation of Women Lawyers (FIDA), Institute for Education in Democracy (IED), Kenya Human Rights Commission (KHRC), and League of Kenya Women Voters (LKWV), *Safeguarding Women's Gains Under the Draft Constitution: Parliamentary Handbook* (2003).

20. Art Hansen, "African Refugees: Defining and Defending Their Human Rights," in *Human Rights and Governance in Africa,* ed. Ronald Cohen, Goran Hyden, and Winston P. Nagan (Gainesville: University of Florida Press, 1993).

21. Crawford Young, *The African Colonial State in Comparative Perspective*, 43.

22. Crawford Young, "The Heritage of Colonialism," in Harbeson and Rothchild, eds., *Africa in World Politics*, 20.

23. Quoted in ibid., 30.

24. Pierre Englebert, *State Legitimacy and Development in Africa* (Boulder: Lynne Rienner Publishers, 2000).

25. Ibid., 5.

26. See, generally, Thomas Carothers, *Critical Mission: Essays on Democracy Promotion* (Washington, DC: Carnegie Endowment for International Peace, 2004); Thomas Carothers, *Aiding Democracy Abroad: The Learning Curve* (Washington, DC: Carnegie Endowment for International Peace, 1999); Richard Joseph, "Africa: The Rebirth of Political Freedom," *Journal of Democracy* 2 (1995): 11.

27. Richard Joseph, "State, Conflict, and Democracy in Africa," 3.

28. Zeleza, "Introduction: The Struggle for Human Rights in Africa," 2–3.

29. For a further discussion of African political transitions, see Mahmood Mamdani and Ernest Wamba dia Wamba, eds., *African Studies in Social Movements and Democracy* (Dakar: CODESRIA Books, 1995); Bratton and van de Walle, *Democratic Experiments in Africa*.

30. Ahmed I. Samatar, "Somalia: Statelessness as Homelessness," in *The African State: Reconsiderations*, ed. Abdi Ismail Samatar and Ahmed I. Samatar (Portsmouth: Heinemann, 2002).

31. Yvonne Muthien and Gregory Houston, "Transforming South African State and Society: The Challenge of Constructing a Developmental State," in Samatar, *The African State: Reconsiderations*, 53.

32. Jeffrey Herbst, *States and Power in Africa: Comparative Lessons in Authority and Control* (Princeton: Princeton University Press, 2000); see also Makau wa Mutua, "Why Redraw the Map of Africa? A Moral and Legal Inquiry," *Michigan Journal of International Law* 16 (1995): 1113; Makau wa Mutua, "Putting Humpty Dumpty Back Together Again: The Dilemmas of the Post-Colonial African State," *Brooklyn Journal of International Law* 21 (1995): 505.

33. Herbst, *States and Power in Africa,* 260–261.

34. Siri Gloppen, *South Africa: The Battle over the Constitution* (Aldershot: Ashgate, 1997).

35. Alexis de Tocqueville, *Democracy in America* (New York: Library of America, 2004).

36. Antonio Gramsci, *The Modern Prince* (London: Lawrence and Wishart, 1957); Karl Marx, *The German Ideology* (New York: International Publishers, 1970).

37. Young, *The African Colonial State in Comparative Perspective*, 222.

38. Ibid., 230–231.

39. Bill Freund, *The Making of Contemporary Africa* (Boulder: Lynne Rienner Publishers, 1984).

40. Leonardo A. Villalón and Philip A. Huxtable, eds., *The African State at a Critical Juncture: Between Disintegration and Reconfiguration* (Boulder: Lynne Rienner Publishers, 1998).

41. John W. Harbeson, "Civil Society and Political Renaissance in Africa," in *Civil Society and the State in Africa*, ed. John W. Harbeson, Donald Rothchild, and Naomi Chazan, 1–2.

42. Huntington, *The Third Wave.*

43. Keane, *Civil Society and the State.*

44. Harbeson, "Civil Society and Political Renaissance in Africa," 2.

45. Michael Bratton, "Civil Societies and Political Transitions in Africa," in Harbeson, Rothchild, and Chazan, eds., *Civil Society and the State in Africa,* 51–52.

46. Young, "The Heritage of Colonialism," 19.

47. Makau Mutua, "Ethnicity Is the Bane of Kenyan Politics," *Sunday Nation,* September 23, 2007; Mutua, "Why Redraw the Map of Africa?"

48. See, generally, Herbst, *States and Power in Africa*; Nelson Kasfir, *State and Class in Africa* (London: Cass, 1984); Tom Mboya, *Challenge of Nationhood* (New York: Praeger Publishers, 1970); Makau Mutua, "How to Build the Kenyan Nation," *Sunday Nation,* July 15, 2007.

49. Donald Rothchild, "Ethnic Insecurity, Peace Agreements, and State Building," in Joseph, *State, Conflict, and Democracy in Africa,* 319–337.

50. Marina Ottaway, "Ethnic Politics in Africa: Change and Continuity," in Joseph, *State, Conflict, and Democracy in Africa,* 301.

51. Ibid.

52. Nelson Kasfir, "Explaining Ethnic Political Participation," in *The State and Development in the Third World,* ed. Atul Kohli (Princeton: Princeton University Press, 1986), 88.

53. Naomi Chazan, Robert Mortimer, John Ravenhill, and Donald Rothchild, *Politics and Society in Contemporary Africa* (Boulder: Lynne Rienner Publishers, 1988).

54. Joseph, "State, Conflict, and Democracy in Africa," 7.

55. See Thomas Carothers, ed., *Promoting the Rule of Law Abroad: In Search of Knowledge* (Washington, DC: Carnegie Endowment for International Peace, 2006).

56. Ottaway, "Ethnic Politics in Africa: Change and Continuity," 311.

57. See, generally, Donald Rothchild, *Managing Ethnic Conflict in Africa: Pressures and Incentives for Cooperation* (Washington, DC: Brookings Institution Press, 1997).

58. Makau Mutua, "Raila Odinga: Nelson Mandela or Idi Amin?" *Sunday Nation,* May 6, 2007; Makau Mutua, "Raila Is His Own Worst Enemy," *Sunday Nation,* July 8, 2007; "Kenya," in *The World FactBook,* available at https://www.cia.gov/cia/publications/factbook/geos/ke.html, visited on August 1, 2006.

59. Makau Mutua, "Raila and Kalonzo Had No Opponents, Just Political Escorts" ["ODM: The Real Losers"], *Sunday Nation,* September 2, 2007; Makau Mutua, "Kalonzo a Reformer? Give Me a Break!" *Sunday Nation,* August 19, 2007; Stephen Brown, "Theorising Kenya's Protracted Transition to Democracy," *Journal of Contemporary African Studies* 22 (September 2004): 325, 334.

60. Jean-François Bayart, *The State in Africa: Politics of the Belly* (London: Longman, 1993).

61. John S. Mbiti, *African Religions and Philosophy* (London: Heinemann, 1969).

62. Ali A. Mazrui, "Africa and Other Civilizations: Conquest and Counterconquest," in Harbeson and Rothchild, eds., *Africa in World Politics.*

63. Ambrose Moyo, "Religion in Africa," in *Understanding Contemporary Africa,* ed. April A. Gordon and Donald L. Gordon (Boulder: Lynne Rienner Publishers, 1996).

64. Makau wa Mutua, "Limitations of Religious Rights: Problematizing Religious Freedom in the African Context," in *Religious Human Rights in Global Perspective: Legal Perspective,* ed. Johan D. van der Vyver and John Witte, Jr. (The Hague: Martinus Nijhoff, 1996).

65. Makau Mutua, "Returning to My Roots: African 'Religions' and the State," in *Proselytization and Communal Self-Determination in Africa,* ed. Abdullahi Ahmed An-Na'im (Maryknoll: Orbis Books, 1999); Elizabeth Isichei, *A History of Christianity in Africa: From Antiquity to the Present* (Grand Rapids: Eerdman's Publishing, 1995); Noel King, *Christian and Muslim in Africa* (New York: Harper and Row, 1971).

66. Alessandra Stanley, "Pope Asks for Forgiveness for Errors of the Church over 2,000 Years," *New York Times,* March 13, 2000.

67. Denys Shropshire, *The Church and Primitive Peoples* (New York: Macmillan, 1938); Chinua Achebe, *Things Fall Apart* (New York: Ballantine Books, 1959); R. L. Tignor, *The Colonial Transformation of Kenya: The Kamba, Kikuyu, and Maasai from 1900 to 1939* (Princeton: Princeton University Press, 1976); Makau Mutua, "Proselytism and Cultural Integrity," in *Facilitating Freedom of Religion or Belief: A Deskbook,* ed. Tore Lindholm, W. Cole Durham, Jr., and Bahia G. Tahzib-Lie (Leiden: Martinus Nijhoff Publishers, 2004),

68. Lamin Sanneh, *Encountering the West: Christianity and the Global Cultural Process: The African Dimension* (Maryknoll: Orbis Books, 1993); John S. Pobee, "Africa's Search for Religious Human Rights Through Returning to the Wells of Living Water," in *Religious Human Rights in Global Perspective: Legal Perspectives*, ed. Johan D. van der Vyver and John Witte, Jr. (The Hague: Martinus Nijhoff, 1996).

69. See, generally, Abdullahi Ahmed An-Na'im, ed., *Proselytization and Communal Self-Determination in Africa* (Maryknoll: Orbis Books, 1999).

70. Bruce A. Magnusson, "Testing Democracy in Benin: Experiments in Institutional Reform," in Joseph, *State, Conflict, and Democracy in Africa,* 217–237.

71. Ibid.

72. Athena Mutua, "Gender Equality and Women's Solidarity Across Religious, Ethnic, and Class Difference in the Kenya Constitutional Review Process," *William and Mary Journal of Women and Law* 13 (2006): 1.

73. Makau Mutua, "Time to Lift the Lid on Abortion Debate," *Sunday Nation,* June 25, 2006.

74. See, generally, John Mukum Mbaku and Julius Omozuanvbo Ihonvbere, eds., *The Transition to Democratic Governance in Africa: The Continuing Struggle* (Westport: Praeger Publishers, 2003).

75. Bratton and van de Walle, *Democratic Experiments in Africa.*

76. Jibrin Ibrahim, *Democratic Transition in Anglophone West Africa* (Dakar: CODESRIA Books, 2004); Bamidele A. Ojo, *Contemporary African Politics: A Comparative Study of Political Transition to Democratic Legitimacy* (Lanham: University Press of America, 1999).

77. Hein Marais, *South Africa: Limits to Change: The Political Economy of Transition* (New York: Palgrave Macmillan, 2001).

78. Shadrack Wanjala Nasong'o, "Political Transition Without Transformation: the Dialectic of Liberalization Without Democratization in Kenya and Zambia," *African Studies Review* 50 (April 2007): 80; Godwin R. Murunga and Shadrack W. Nasong'o, eds., *Kenya: The Struggle for Democracy* (London: Zed Books, 2007).

79. Heinz Klug, *Constituting Democracy: Law, Globalism, and South Africa's Political Reconstruction* (Cambridge: Cambridge University Press, 2000).

3

Africa and Postcolonial Trauma

IT IS AN incontestable truth that the modern African state has been an abysmal, often catastrophic failure.[1] The crises of the African postcolonial state are so intrinsic and endemic that they seem, even to the untrained eye, completely pathological. In the recent history of many an African state, brief periods of hope have usually been doomed by long spells of despair. It is a vicious cycle that has become virtually inevitable. To many Africans, optimism about fundamental change or reform is often guarded because the danger of disappointment lurks in the background. Even so, Africans yearn for liberty, freedom, and prosperity. Given the mirth that characterizes African cultures, one might be forgiven for thinking that Africans are oblivious to their pain. That is why, in spite of the pogroms of history, the continent is very much alive. The indomitable spirit and eternal hope belie the cruel history and misfortune that have befallen Africans. Yet they soldier on and, like Sisyphus, are heartbroken. Watching the plight of the continent, one cannot help but ask: Are Africans forever condemned by history, or is there hope? Once a part of the ubiquitous Third World, Africans now live in a lower substratum of that world, or even worse. Today they are segregated in something akin to a Fourth World. Whatever the case, contemporary Africa is the forgotten continent, a sad and pathetic afterthought to most of the world.

But Africa cannot be understood unless resort is had to its tormented history.[2] Three pivotal epochs have indelibly redefined the psychology and identity of the continent. All inflicted incalculable traumas on Africans. The first is modern slavery, in which Africa lost millions of its people to the European, American, and Arab slave raids and trades. The second is the European colonial conquest, known in history books as the scramble for Africa. The third is the investiture of the postcolonial state. These three eras have forever traumatized, humiliated, disfigured, and transformed Africa. It is in their ruins that the secrets of African misery are buried. However, there seems to be a rush of amnesia, a deliberate forgetfulness that wants to wish away barbaric history.

33

The purpose of this new absolutionist trend is to locate African suffering elsewhere, perhaps in Africans themselves or in the continent's inability to cope with modernity. In the meantime, the future of an entire continent hangs in the balance, a place from whence it seems to stare hopelessly and plaintively at the abyss. Whither Africa?

Although the three epochs have deeply damaged Africa, evidence suggests that the colonial state, reproduced under the guise of the independent state, has been responsible for the worst distortions of design, character, and purpose. This condition is here referred to as postcolonial trauma. Simply stated, colonialism has been the single most important variable in determining the future of Africa. As noted by Crawford Young, the "colonial legacy cast its shadow over the emergent African state system to a degree unique among the major world regions."[3] In fact, so totalizing was the colonial experience that the mentalities, routines, and referential points for Africa became deeply Eurocentric. But it was a perverse Eurocentrism, a phenomenon of self-denial, an attempt to produce dark-skinned Europeans, in essence dumb copies of the original. It was as though Africa did not exist prior to colonization. Its political institutions, borders, and culture were either extinguished or substantially rewritten under the unforgiving European hand. Arguably, no other region of the world has ever undergone such complete transformation in so quick a time.

Yet, what was the nature of colonization, and why has it been so cancerous in the African context? To be sure, Africa is not the first region to be subjected to colonialism. Most political societies of the world have at various historical points fallen prey to alien conquest. In the last 600 years, Europeans have subjected virtually the entirety of the globe to direct colonialism. But the depth and violence of European penetration and subjugation of Africa may very well explain its exceptional postcolonial trauma. With the exception of Morocco, Tunisia, Egypt, Ethiopia, Burundi, Rwanda, Madagascar, Swaziland, Lesotho, and Botswana, the majority of present-day African states do not have a coherent precolonial identity.[4] And even those states were themselves subjected to colonialism and are now postcolonial states, much like other African states. Virtually all of Africa was divided up among several European imperial powers between 1875 and 1900, during the phenomenon commonly referred to as the scramble for Africa. By the start of the twentieth century, every inch of African soil was either partitioned or bounded for colonial exploitation and domination. The continent's political landscape, previously home to thousands of nations, was now reduced to a few dozen European-style states.

Needless to say, precolonial African societies were governed by norms, institutions, and processes internal to them. It is also clear that precolonial Africa was home to hundreds of independent political, ethnocultural societies. For example, the territory known as Kenya today may in all likelihood have housed more than forty different, completely independent nations or political societies. But European colonialism either abolished these political societies or forcibly merged them with others, ending their independent existence overnight. Thus in what became Kenya, for instance, the approximately forty independent nations were taken over, amalgamated into a single state, and forced to live under the thumb of the newly minted British colonial state. The way in which the British and other European powers went about creating new states in Africa is completely stunning.

The typical examples of the creation of Kenya and Uganda will suffice to demonstrate the logic of colonial boundary delimitation, which can only be described as callous and arbitrary. The area today known as Kenya was declared a British "sphere of influence" in 1886, proclaimed the East African Protectorate in 1896, and became the Kenya Colony in 1920.[5] The area now known as Uganda also became a British "sphere of influence" in 1886 and was named the Uganda Protectorate in 1894, but its precise borders remained uncertain for a while because the British could not immediately determine the status of the kingdoms of Buganda, Toro, and Ankole.[6] But soon thereafter, the British stripped these precolonial African kingdoms of their sovereignty and made them part of the new Ugandan colonial state. For a moment, from 1900 to 1902, the British even contemplated combining the Kenyan and Ugandan colonial protectorates into one political entity.[7] In 1902, a large tract of eastern Uganda, consisting of its "Eastern Province, the southern part of the Elgon district of central Uganda and the southern portion of Rudolf Province," was transferred and became the Kisumu and Naivasha provinces of Kenya.[8] These transfers survived into the postcolonial state, but in 1976 became a subject of tension between Kenya and Uganda when Idi Amin, the late Ugandan military ruler, laid claim to them.[9]

It is clear that European imperial cartographers gave little or no consideration to precolonial dynamics between different African nations or societies. The new mapmakers proceeded as though Africa was a blank slate, no-man's-land, uninhabited. As noted by C. M. Peter, at the famous Berlin Conference where Africa was shared out among European imperial powers, the continent was "regarded as terra nullius, subject to the possession of the European powers exercising effective authority. They never took into account that there were people of vastly different backgrounds and cultures living on the continent."[10] Comments by European imperial overlords provide some powerful insights into how they perceived their cartography. Joseph C. Anene notes, mirthlessly, that "the manner in which boundaries were made was often a subject for after-dinner jokes among European statesmen."[11] In 1890, for example, Lord Salisbury, the British prime minister, remarked at a dinner at Mansion House after the conclusion of the Anglo-French Convention at which West Africa was divvied among European states, that "we have been engaged in drawing lines upon maps where no white man's foot ever trod; we have been giving away mountains and rivers and lakes to each other, only hindered by the small impediment that we never knew exactly where the mountains and rivers and lakes were."[12] Another senior British official who was involved in creating the boundary between Nigeria and Cameroon was quoted making similar remarks.

> In those days we just took a pencil and a rule, and we put it down at Old Calabar, and drew that line to Yola. . . . I recollect thinking when I was sitting having an audience with the Emir [of Yola], surrounded by his tribe, that it was a good thing that he did not know that I, with a blue pencil, had drawn a line through his territory.[13]

The most important variables in creating new borders were imperial rivalries, competition among European trading companies, and in many cases the scramble for new souls by rival Christian denominations.[14] In most instances, independent African nations, some of which had a history of tension between them, were lumped into the same state. In others, the new frontiers split political societies and nations and located them in different colonial states.[15] Some of the more famous examples include the Maasai, who were separated between Kenya and Tanzania, and the Ewe, splintered in Togo and Ghana.[16] Ian Brownlie has captured the arbitrariness of the process of European colonial mapmakers.

> Boundary making in the period of European expansion in Africa took place in circumstances that generally militated against reference to tribal or ethnological considerations. Political bargaining involved the construction of parcels of territory upon broad principles evidenced graphically by liberal resort to straight lines and general features such as drainage basins and watersheds. Within a framework of overall political bargaining, the accidents of prior exploration and military penetration were often to determine delimitation as between Britain, France and Germany. Thus the map of West Africa was drawn. In any case lines were commonly drawn on maps at a stage when there was no great knowledge of the region concerned. The boundaries that emerged were generally based upon geographical features, especially rivers and watersheds, and astronomical and geometric lines.[17]

European ignorance of and disregard for precolonial African nations determined the physical contours of colonial states. Only in a very few cases were ethnology and existing African societies a factor. In creating Nigeria, for example, extant boundaries were followed in the north and the west to simplify administration. But even here, previously independent nations were forcibly put together. Precolonial borders were also followed in the cases of Burundi, Rwanda, and some areas of North Africa, among others.[18] Even so, the final outcome was the creation of an entirely different state. The newly contrived state represented for many Africans the physical symbol of the loss of independence and sovereignty over their societies. The manner in which the colonial state was created after long periods of resistance and so-called pacification, a euphemism for the brutal suppression of resistance, combined with the purpose for which it was brought into existence and the way in which it was governed, produced a sick instrumentality at the outset. It is against this backdrop that Africans began their contest with the modern state.

The Curse of Colonialism

The colonization of Africa was motivated by the economic exploitation of the continent by Europe.[19] In fact, the first substantial forays into Africa by Europeans were for the capture of Africans for sale as slaves into the Americas. Portugal, one of the earliest colonial powers in Africa, had for many centuries been a slave trader in Africans.[20] Morally, racism and Christian bigotry were the justifications for colonization. After the decision to take Africa, Europe then employed all means to make colonization real. Wars of conquest and fraudulent treaties with African rulers were the principal means for effecting colonization. Even so, European control over the continent met with stiff resistance from Africans. German brutalities in Tanzania and Namibia, for example, were not isolated incidents.[21] Even where conquests of such severity were not attempted, effective colonial rule was imposed through "treaties of protection" between African rulers and European powers, usually after a war, by coercion, deceit, fraud, intimidation, or any combination thereof.[22] It is this genesis of the modern African state that made it, at least initially, an imposed falsehood. T. O. Elias, the distinguished African jurist, identifies the violent meeting between Africa and Europe as the basis for the dysfunction of the African state.

> In 1884–1885, the European imperial powers met in Berlin and without the consent or the participation of the African people, demarcated the Continent of Africa into colonies or spheres of influence. In many cases, kingdoms and tribes were split into colonies with such reckless abandon that they came under two or three European imperial powers. This event was the genesis of many present-day conflicts and virtually insoluble problems in the African Continent.[23]

The argument that colonialism is to blame for Africa's economic, political, and social woes is not new.[24] The performance of the African postcolonial state, even after the surge of reform, human rights, and democratic movements since the end of the Cold War, has been abysmal, if not catastrophic.[25] Until the end of the 1980s, military dictatorships and opaque, oppressive, and kleptocratic one-party states were the rule, not the exception. As Paul Zeleza points out, at the "beginning of 1990, all but five of Africa's 54 countries were dictatorships, either civilian or military."[26] But the hopes of Africans were not always dim. Early in the life of the postcolonial state, soon after the end of direct European colonial rule, optimism filled the air. In virtually every African state, political independence was initially perceived as the end of one era and the beginning of another. It was assumed, as a matter of course, that the postcolonial African-led state would be a material and normative departure from its illegitimate, predatory colonial predecessor.[27] But in 1963, soon after it was born, the postcolonial state started to come apart, as Togo experienced Africa's first military coup. From then on, African postcolonial states imploded from shore to shore and from one capital city to the next.[28]

The transition from colonialism to independence—if it can be called that—lasted a split second. As noted by Michael Bratton, the apparatus of the postcolonial state began to "crumble before it has been fully consolidated."[29] The collapse of several states in the last three decades of the twentieth century drove Mazrui to term the African state a "political refugee."[30] According to him, such a state cannot perform what he calls the functions of statehood: exercise sovereign control over its territory; have sovereign oversight and supervision over the nation's resources; exercise the effective and rational collection of revenue; maintain adequate national infrastructure, such as roads and telephone systems; and have the capacity to govern and maintain law and order.[31] These elementary functions have long eluded the postcolonial state. The African state, as a professional bureaucracy, has largely been unable to exercise meaningful sovereignty over people and territory, let alone deliver services with any modicum of consistency, efficiency, and ability. At the heart of the problem is a basic disconnection between the state, defined as the ruling elites, and the ordinary citizen.

Yet states are living organisms. The character of a state is generally a reflection, at some level, of its elites and citizenry. That is why the contrived and artificial citizenry of the African state is at the center of the crises wracking the continent. Although the struggle against colonial rule within the borders of the colonial state created unity among the different nations within it, such unity was shallow and insufficient to form a cohesive national identity. In any case, the irony of the forced "unity" of precolonial African nations under the roof of the colonial state is best understood in the context of the "disunity" fostered by its divide-and-rule policies. In other words, beyond race and oppression, African nations within the colonial territory did not have much else in common. That is why the new African elites, as well as the masses, faced a loyalty crisis once political power was ostensibly transferred to them at independence. To whom did they owe their loyalty—their precolonial nation or the postcolonial state? Could they, in fact, owe their loyalty to the postcolonial state, an ogre born out of the colonial state, the instrumentality that had been created for the sole purpose of colonial exploitation? Or, would they now view the state as their own and fully identify with it as their basic political home? Was the euphoria generated by the installation of black African governments sufficient to coalesce a new affinity for the postcolonial state?

The nagging question is whether African states are nation-states in the sense of their counterparts in other parts of the world. That is not a trivial matter because precolonial national identities and subnationalism continue to inflame politics and hinder the process of nation building. Although certainly not unique to Africa, as experiences in the former Soviet bloc have demonstrated, the illegitimacy of both the colonial and postcolonial African states has alienated the citizenry to a degree that is unique in historical terms. Art Hansen puts the blame squarely on the failure of elites to transform the colonial state.[32] He argues that, though formally independent, African states are still conceptually colonial entities that are heavily dependent on the norms and structures of the colonial state. The most significant change at independence was not the transformation of the state, but the transfer of politics from the imperial capitals in London and Paris to Nairobi or Dakar, as the case may be. Thus, the changing of the guard, the replacement of white faces by black ones at State House, was the most palpable change. Hansen has sharply criticized the conservation of the colonial state under the guise of the independent state. He has argued that African leaders have adopted and continue to utilize as guides norms and precedents based on the European experience.[33]

It fell on the leaders of the postcolonial African state to indigenize—indeed Africanize—and legitimize it. But the legitimization of the state meant rewriting almost entirely its internal structures and the norms governing it. For one, different African nations within the state would have to cohere into one supernation, an entity that would claim their primary loyalty and give them a shared identity. But that could only happen if the populace saw the state as a nurturer, not a predator. Except for a few states, the overwhelming majority of African states have failed to make this critical transition. Tanzania, arguably one of the most successful cases, owes much of its coherence and national identity to the late Mwalimu Nyerere, its founding president. A selfless pan-Africanist, Nyerere developed Kiswahili into the dominant language and used mass political movements to inspire an overriding national identity and consciousness. Even with an anemic economy, Tanzania, with the exception of Zanzibar, its island enclaves, cohered to a degree that is unique among African postcolonial states. The difference between Nyerere and other independence-era African leaders is that he was genuinely committed to the creation of a viable state out of the collection of precolonial nations. Equally important was his ability to conceptualize Tanzania as an intellectual project in nation building. Nyerere, the philosopher-ruler, had few intellectual peers among leaders on the continent. But the task of creating nations out of colonial states has elsewhere been arduous.[34]

But what does the disconnection of the people from the state mean? How would public officials and citizens understand their duties to the state and to each other? No state can successfully exist, and carry out its core functions, without some form of popular legitimacy. Since the African state has often lacked internal legitimacy, that is, loyalty from its officials and citizens, its survival has largely been ensured by external factors and interests.[35] The most important of these factors was the grant of the political right of self-determination to the colonial state. In other words, the international order conferred upon the colonial state the privilege of juridical statehood.[36] Other key factors included the logic of the Cold War and the necessity of protecting the viability of the international state system, with its center at the United Nations and the Bretton Woods institutions. The rapid deterioration or collapse of several African states in the aftermath of the Cold War was proof that absent international guarantees, the African postcolonial state was a house of cards. Robert H. Jackson argues that the pathology of the state, which was located in the absence of a national consciousness, could not be cured by juridical statehood. A state in law—absent a citizenry that identifies with it—is not necessarily a state in fact.[37]

Clearly, the disconnection of the people from the state is a relative phenomenon; that gulf is wider in some African countries than in others. Yet what is undeniable is the persistence of the chasm and the inability of various actors and normative approaches, including the democracy and human rights projects, to fully legitimize the state. What has exacerbated the situation since the 1970s is the loss of faith in the state by huge majorities of Africans. The persistence of the inability of most states to protect citizens and provide economic meaning to their lives has produced a cynical population. Coming on the heels of the caprice of the colonial state, the alienation of the postcolonial state from the populace only serves to deepen public disillusion with the state. Can such faith be reclaimed? If so, what are the pathways to change? There is neither a magic formula that every state can mimic nor a blueprint. Each situation will require its own solutions. The question, however, is whether there are broad principles that can be tailored to specific contexts. Even so, it must remain an open question whether it is possible—at all—to re-create and legitimize most African states.

Taming Leviathan

The invention of the African state by colonialism, and the subsequent misapplication of the right to self-determination, stand at the root of the crisis of the postcolonial state. The denial of the right of self-determination to precolonial nations and communities is one of the fundamental reasons for the failure of the state to develop into a cohesive, effective, and functional apparatus. In the context of other aggravating factors, the multinational character of the African state has become a deforming Achilles' heel. As a response, political elites have made numerous efforts, some serious, others cynical, to address these basic flaws. Until the early 1990s, the instrument of choice to deal with the malaise was the imposition of the one-party state.[38] Its proponents argued that it would promote national unity and foster nation building.[39] But the one-party state failed dismally; in most cases, it was a demented bandit, looter, and terrorist, although in the case of Tanzania, it did forge a national identity. But in general, the political monopoly of the single party was merely a tool for the exclusive stranglehold on state power by a single leader and his chosen elite.

Not surprisingly, single-party despotism in Africa was either engineered or supported by both the West and the Soviet bloc.

Two other dominant constitutional models have been tried in a bid to re-cover the African postcolonial state. Federalism, the first, was expected to ab-sorb and contain competing subnationalist rivalries. It did not suffice. Since the end of the Cold War, the second model, the liberal democratic state, has been promoted as the antidote to the crisis of postcolonialism. On this, the early signs are troubling, although the jury remains out.

Federalism was one of the earliest devices employed to confront the prob-lem of multinationalism within the state and the perversion of the right to self-determination for precolonial nations. In general, federalist designs lacked a proper balance between the center and the regions and suffered from the lack of a culture of civil political bargaining among elites. Most often, leaders at both loci of power did not fully appreciate the subtleties of federalism. Though noble, federalism was also an admission of the contradiction that was the post-colonial state. It is an unavoidable fact that every "nation" within the African state is a "state in embryo," an entity that could have been entitled to exercise its right to self-determination.[40] However, federalism was meant to create unity within the postcolonial state through the assimilation of all the nations within it, and thereby extinguish their claims of self-determination. Propo-nents for the retention of the multicultural, postcolonial African state argue that these opposing faces can be reconciled if the right to self-determination is "exercisable within, as well as through, the nation state."[41]

However, Africa's experience with federalism has largely proven a disap-pointment. Some of the countries in which federalism has been tried include Kenya, Uganda, the former Zaire, and Nigeria.[42] Although it was motivated by specific reasons in each case, federalism was not always the popular choice of the elites that controlled state power. The continent's leading nationalists, includ-ing Kwame Nkrumah, Milton Obote, Jomo Kenyatta, and Mwalimu Nyerere, viewed it as a ploy by the West to weaken newly independent African states through balkanization. To them, federalism was inefficient, wasteful of scant re-sources, and bound to exacerbate ethnic differences. They argued that it would impede decisionmaking and nation building. It is not difficult to understand their arguments against federalism, given the artificiality of the colonial state and the dangers of secession and irredentism. For a continent that was emerging from centuries of foreign occupation and domination, the temptation of strong, cen-tralized states was a natural response. To make matters worse, the support for federalist structures by the British and other former colonial powers only served to confirm the fears of the nationalists.[43] Benjamin Neuberger has correctly ar-gued that federalism offered a middle course between separatists and national-ists, or those who advocated strong unitary states.[44]

Several experiments among postcolonial states offer some clues about the failure of federalism. Kenya, the focus of this book, offers a symptomatic pathology.[45] The genesis of federalism in Kenya was the fear of the white minority settler class and the Luhya, Kalenjin, and several other nations that the Kikuyu-Luo-Kamba alliance would deny them their share of the spoils of independence. The Kenya African National Union (KANU), the nationalist party, was controlled by an alliance of the Kikuyu, Luo, and Kamba, whereas the British-backed Kenya African Democratic Union (KADU) was the preserve of the Luhya, Kalenjin, and coastal communities. In reality, both KANU and KADU represented only the political and economic interests of the elites in the respective communities. Further, the British thought that KADU was more likely to protect settler land and commercial interests. A major bone of contention was who would control the distribution of land in central Kenya, the so-called White Highlands and the Rift Valley, formerly reserved for white settlers. Both parties adopted positions that would enhance their chances of retaining or seizing control of the fertile lands. In this matrix, a federal government would vest the weaker KADU communities with power over land redistribution and deny the Kikuyu-Luo-Kamba alliance domination of the new state.[46]

KADU, the proponent of federalism, equated regional autonomy with self-determination and access to or ownership of land. Peter Okondo, a leading Luhya politician, argued that basic individual and group rights could only be guaranteed under a federal constitution, not a unitary state.[47] KADU differed with KANU over regional boundaries and pushed for a federal constitution in which regional legislatures would regulate land. These fears, which were acknowledged by Julius G. Kiano, a leading Kikuyu politician, were provoked by the power of the Kikuyu-Luo alliance.[48] The fearful groups hoped to mobilize support to dilute the influence of the Kikuyu-Luo bloc. The British settlers and commercial interests were also jittery about a unitary state and supported a federal state for fear of losing access to land and other resources if the more "radical" KANU, the party that led the country to independence, prevailed on the centralized state. In 1963, the British government forced through the "Majimbo Constitution," which provided for a quasi-federal structure as the condition for independence and the assumption of power by KANU.[49] From the start, the Lancaster (Majimbo) Constitution lacked legitimacy among the dominant elite because the British imposed it on them as a condition for liberation. Neuberger captured the crux of the matter, although with some hyperbole:

> In Kenya, the quasi-federal "Majimbo Constitution," which divided the country into Regions with their Regional Assemblies, Regional Civil Service and regional powers, was designed to protect the small backward ethnic groups from the Kikuyu-Luo alliance. It had strong support in KADU, which represented the Coastal, Baluhya and Kalenjin tribes. One of its leaders, Masinde Muliro, saw in federalism the ideal solution for Africa—because it provides for "free association" and prevents "imposed unity." The dominant

Kenya African National Union (KANU) opposed federalism, which it regarded as a colonial device to strengthen those tribes that did not participate
in the anti-colonial movement, and to weaken the position of the "radical"
Kikuyu. *KANU accepted the "Majimbo Constitution" because that was the
British condition for independence. It very soon eroded and then abolished
the federal system, and imposed a unitary regime strongly dominated by the
Kikuyu bureaucracy.*[50] [emphasis added]

The Kenyan experiment with federalism was doomed because the Kikuyu-
Luo-Kamba alliance substantially "owned" the new postcolonial state with superior numbers and the most prominent anticolonial nationalist leaders. KADU,
however, suffered from its association with the colonial order, an image that
KANU used to its political advantage. Nevertheless, KADU's fears were realized once Kenya achieved full independence. In 1964, when Kenya became a
republic, one of KANU's first acts was the immediate abolition of the quasi-
federal system.[51] It was replaced by a highly centralized state with power concentrated in an executive presidency. Even though the experiment in federalism suffered a sudden death, the federalist aspirations of the original KADU
communities have never been fully extinguished. They reemerged in the National Constitutional Conference in 2003 and contributed, in part, to the failure
of the constitution-writing project. In fact, the problem over the "ownership"
of the Kenyan state remains one of the banes of its existence. In the 2003 constitutional talks, *devolution* replaced *federalism* as the language of choice for
the conflict between the center and the regions. But *devolution* sought the identical arrangements of a federal structure.

Uganda's postindependence flirtation with federalism was equally short-
lived. The precolonial kingdoms of Buganda, Bunyoro, and Ankole were
granted a type of federal status by the British. Under the 1962 Ugandan independence constitution, the kingdoms retained substantial regional autonomy—
self-government, *lukiko,* or Parliament, and their own civil services within the
federal structure of the Ugandan postcolonial state.[52] In 1959, the Buganda,
the most numerous group, constituted 16.3 percent of the population—hence
its successful push for regional autonomy.[53] Less powerful groups, such as the
Acholi and Lango of northern Uganda, the dominant groups in the Uganda
People's Congress (UPC), the leading nationalist party, opposed federalism
because they resented the commanding position enjoyed by the Buganda
Kingdom. In the end, Milton Obote, the UPC leader who became Uganda's
first prime minister, was forced to accept a federal system to avoid the secession of Buganda, in effect the loss of the country's pivot.[54]

But this tenuous status quo did not last long. In 1966, barely four years after
independence, Obote violently destroyed the Buganda Kingdom, abolished the
federal structure, and concentrated power into his own hands.[55] The 1966
Uganda Constitution eliminated the autonomous powers of districts and federal
states, merged the office of the president with that of the prime minister, stripped

the Buganda Kingdom of any special privileges, and authorized the president to legislate when Parliament was not in session. In this respect, Uganda followed Kenya's suit. But on May 20, 1966, the Buganda Kingdom rejected the new constitution and ordered the central government to leave Buganda. Four days later, the government of Uganda captured the *lubiri*, the palace of the *kabaka*, the Buganda monarch, following a fierce battle. Kabaka Mutesa II fled to the United Kingdom, where he died in 1969.[56] With his departure, the postcolonial state rejected a political accommodation of precolonial political identities in a federal structure. Once again, an African state had failed to reconcile nation building with subnationalism and ethnic self-determination through federalism.

In Congo, the irreconcilable tensions among separatists, unitarists, and federalists, coupled with US and Belgian interference, almost resulted in the collapse of the state soon after independence in 1960.[57] Patrice Lumumba, the legendary anticolonial leader and his party, the nationalist Mouvement National Congolais (MNC), scored a narrow victory in the first open elections over Joseph Kasavubu's more conservative Alliances des Bakongo (ABAKO), a party of the historic Kongo people.[58] Lumumba advocated a strong unitary state, whereas Kasavubu and Moise Tshombe, the Katangese leader, called for either federalism or secession. Katanga was blessed with enormous deposits of diamonds and other precious minerals. In 1960, the failure among the three to agree on the structure of government led to a constitutional crisis, a mutiny, a Belgian-led effort for the secession of Katanga, and the murder of Prime Minister Lumumba in which Mobutu Sese Seko, the army chief of staff, and the US Central Intelligence Agency were implicated.[59] After a prolonged period of political instability and chaos, Mobutu formally took power in a military coup in 1965, banned all political activity, and created a highly abusive police state with power concentrated in his hands. With the patronage and unwavering support of the United States, France, and Belgium, Mobutu erected one of the most malignant kleptocracies in the world.[60] In 1997 Laurent Kabila ousted Mobutu through an armed insurrection. Kabila was assassinated in 2001. His son, Joseph Kabila, replaced him as head of state and won the 2006 elections. It remains to be seen whether the 2006 presidential and general elections—the first democratic vote since 1960—will start a process of recovery.[61]

Federalism has also been tried in Ethiopia, with Eritrea,[62] and in the Cameroons.[63] In 1964, Tanganyika and Zanzibar formed Tanzania, a federal republic known as the "United Republic of Tanzania."[64] Since then, the "union" has been under constant stress from Tanzanian strong-arm tactics, Zanzibari nationalists, and separatists.[65] But perhaps the most enduring, though largely unsuccessful, attempt at federalism has been undertaken in Nigeria, Africa's most populous and complex country. Federalism found many adherents in Nigeria because diverse communities saw it as the only viable option if the country was to attain independence as one. In a rare show of support for federalism, all three major Nigerian nations—the northern Hausa-Fulani, the eastern Ibo-dominated areas, and the western Yoruba region—all supported some form of a federal government, even though such an arrangement favored the populous but largely less developed north. But the Ibo- and Yoruba-dominated south pushed for the creation of many ethnolinguistic states to counterbalance the predominance of the north. It was the inability of the federal government to balance the ethnic groups with the states that brought Nigeria to the brink of disintegration in 1966.

The impatience of the south with the reluctance of the north to fully federalize and share power, political dissension and electoral violence in the west, and official corruption combined to cause fundamental fissures in the state. In January 1966, Ibo military officers took advantage of the crisis to stage the country's first military coup, in which leaders from the north were killed.[66] This act ended the country's fragile democracy. Major General Aguiyi Ironsi, an Ibo and head of the new national military government, issued a decree replacing the federal structure with a military government.[67] Northerners vigorously protested the coup and massacred many Ibos in the north. In a countercoup on July 29, 1966, Ironsi was abducted while on a tour of the north and killed by northerners, along with the Ibo officers accompanying him. The leader of the coup, Colonel Yakubu Gowon, a northerner, immediately rescinded the decree abolishing federalism, although the act did not stop the mass slaughter and expulsion of Ibos from the north. Fearful of northerners and because of the pogroms, the easterners, under Lieutenant Odumwengu Ojukwu, the military governor of Eastern Nigeria, declared the secession of the region as the Republic of Biafra on May 30, 1967. Federal troops rushed in to crush the rebellion, but a prolonged war, in which hundreds of thousands died, did not end until January 12, 1970. Biafra was crushed and returned to Nigeria.[68]

Since those coups in the 1960s, Nigeria has undergone contradictory periods, some hopeful, others more precarious. Brief intervals of political democracy have punctuated long reigns of military dictatorships. Corruption has become a way of life. In the meantime, Nigeria remains largely dysfunctional, unable to create a viable democratic, internally legitimate state out of its federal system. Competing ethnic, religious, regional, and class interests threaten the country's survival to this day. In 1999, when Olusegun Obasanjo was popularly elected as head of state, the country's young democracy raised hopes, but his rule was marred by corruption and dysfunction.[69] The election in April 2007 of Umaru Musa Yar'Adua, Obasanjo's handpicked successor, was marked by vote rigging and fraud.[70] Even so, it was the first peaceful transition of power between civilians.[71] The period since 1999 has been the longest continuous period of civilian rule since independence in 1960. Nigeria's experiment with federalism remains tenuous, however, and it is an open question whether this democratic transition will be entrenched in the political culture.

Except for large urban areas, nationality and ethnicity usually correspond with ancestral lands, a fact that tends to congregate groups in particular regions of the postcolonial state. Although this is a general rule, throughout Africa there

are regions that for different reasons have attracted settlers or migrants from ad-
jacent or even faraway regions. The structures of colonial economies, demands
for labor, or forced colonial relocations may also account for population movements of groups away from their ancestral areas. Even so, most regions in
African states are usually identified and claimed by particular groups and communities. The exceptions usually occur in highly urbanized centers or regions
that have attracted migrants from diverse groups. Under the circumstances, it
would seem that federalism was the magic solution for meeting the demands of
self-determination within the postcolonial state. Yet, ironically, federalism has
failed in virtually every country wherever it has been attempted. The cynical
manipulation of ethnic identities aside, federalism has not been viable in Africa
because the postcolonial state does not offer an open, free, and unfettered forum
for mediating the fears and aspirations of different nations within the state.

Quite often, African elites saw each other as enemies, not political opponents. Because of the youth of the postcolonial state, the fragility of most
economies, and the scarcity of other loci for power, elites treated the capture of
the state as a life-and-death matter. Those in power, usually drawn largely from
one ethnic group or a coalition of groups, saw federalism as an attempt to weaken
their grip on power, while those on the outside, vying for power, saw federalism
as an equalizer, a tool to prevent domination and retain autonomy over their affairs. The logic of federalism, which is the decentralization of power, was lost.
That was certainly the experience with federalism in the post-Mengistu period of
Ethiopia. The pretense by Prime Minister Meles Zenawi that different ethnic
groups could govern themselves turned out to be a perversion of federalism
wherein a stronger central state was instead instituted.[72] Perhaps the federalist
option would have had a new lease on life had postapartheid South Africa used
it as the model for accommodating competing ethnic, racial, and economic interests. Instead, South Africa decided to create a strong central state hemmed in by
an individual rights regime, separation of powers, checks and balances, entrenched oversight institutions, and limited devolution to the regions.[73] Groups
in postcolonial African states have seen politics as a zero-sum game in which all
the spoils belonged to the victor. Most saw the capture of state power as the vehicle through which they would exercise their right to self-determination at the
exclusion and often expense of other groups. Internal or local colonialism—as
opposed to European colonialism—has very often resulted from exclusionary
practices. It is this conundrum that has doomed federalism.

At independence, many outgoing colonial powers left the machinery of
the colonial state intact, even though the new African elite was supposed to
rule through the imposed liberal constitution. But as history would have it, the
pathology of the postcolonial state quickly overcame the liberal constitution
and replaced it with the one-party state or military dictatorship, quite often at
the instigation of either the West or the East, the Cold War protagonists. Ironically, the end of the Cold War unleashed a fever for the liberal constitution as

the panacea for dictatorships in general and the postcolonial state in particular.[74] Since the early 1990s, a new global consensus has put political democracy at the center of cultural, political, social, and economic renaissance. Key to this consensus is the reconstruction of the state into a liberal-democratic, pluralistic, market-oriented, open society. In this exercise, no other document is more important than the constitution. That is why reformers demand either a new constitution or a rewrite of the existing one to provide the normative basis for liberal democracy.

For Africa, the question is whether the new consensus will deliver society from damnation, and if so, what type of norms, processes, and institutions will be necessary. Will a return to the liberal democratic arrangements adopted or imposed at independence suffice? Does Africa have to re-imagine new forms and structures of the state to recover the postcolonial state? Will political democracy itself be enough to reclaim the state, or does Africa have to imagine radical economic and social reforms to complement political freedom? Are African elites equal to the challenge of state reformation, or will they first have to be fundamentally transformed for the continent to get a fighting chance? What will the role of the West, Africa's historical tormentor, be in the process of reclamation? Although this chapter has focused attention on the difficulties—and in most cases failures—of federalism as a probable cure for the dysfunction of the postcolonial state, the book seeks to evaluate, through the lens of the Kenyan experience, the viability of various constitutional devices to address the malaise of the postcolonial state. Is political decentralization the answer? Would a strong civil society make the difference? The book reflects on the roles of elites, the psychosis of postcolonialism, and the roadblocks posed by the international order. It argues that recovery may be possible, but only if new domestic and international scripts are written. The book seeks to identify moments of hope and possibility by mining Kenya's history and forecasting the future. The book is therefore a search for what—empirically and practically—could revitalize the state and turn it into a legitimate crucible for human empowerment and development.

Notes

1. William Zartman, ed., *Collapsed States: The Disintegration and Restoration of Legitimate Authority* (Boulder: Lynne Rienner Publishers, 1995); Scott Peterson, *Me Against My Brother: At War in Somalia, Sudan, and Rwanda* (New York: Routledge, 2002); Philip Gourevitch, *We Wish to Inform You That Tomorrow We Will Be Killed with Our Families: Stories from Rwanda* (New York: Picador, 1998); Tony Avirgan and Martha Honey, *War in Uganda: The Legacy of Idi Amin* (Westport: L. Hill, 1982); Howard W. French, *A Continent for the Taking: The Tragedy and Hope in Africa* (New York: Vintage, 2004).

2. See Thandika Mkandawire, *African Intellectuals: Rethinking Politics, Language, Gender, and Development* (Dakar: CODESRIA, 2006); Ali A. Mazrui, *The Africans: A Triple Heritage* (London: Little, Brown, 1986).

3. Crawford Young, "The Heritage of Colonialism," in *Africa in World Politics*, ed. John W. Harbeson and Donald Rothchild (Boulder: Westview Press, 1995), 19, 20; Kamuti Kiteme, *We, the Panafrikans: Essays on the Global Black Experience* (New York: Edward W. Blyden Press, 1992).

4. Young, "The Heritage of Colonialism," 19. Even these surviving precolonial states were themselves subjected to direct colonial rule or occupation.

5. Ian Brownlie, *African Boundaries: A Legal and Diplomatic Encyclopedia* (London: C. Hurst, for the Royal Institute of International Affairs, 1979), 775.

6. Kenneth Ingham, *The Making of Modern Uganda* (London: George Allen and Unwin, 1958), 41–85.

7. Brownlie, *African Boundaries*, 941.

8. Ibid., 942.

9. Ibid.

10. Chris M. Peter, "The Proposed African Court of Justice—Jurisprudential, Procedural, Enforcement Problems and Beyond," *East African Journal of Peace and Human Rights* 1 (1993): 124–125.

11. Joseph C. Anene, *The International Boundaries of Nigeria, 1885–1960: The Framework of an Emergent African Nation* (New York: Humanities Press, 1970), 1.

12. Ibid.

13. Ibid., 2–3 (quoting the *Geographic Journal*, vol. 28, *Proceedings*, March 9, 1914).

14. Roland Oliver, *The African Experience* (New York: Icon-Harper Publishers, 1991), 179–180.

15. Kenneth Barbour, "A Geographical Analysis of Boundaries in Inter-Tropical Africa," in *Essays on African Population,* ed. Kenneth M. Barbour and R. M. Protero (New York: Praeger Publishers, 1961), 30.

16. Brownlie, *African Boundaries*, 277, 938.

17. Ibid., 6.

18. Ibid., 6–7.

19. Walter Rodney, *How Europe Underdeveloped Africa* (Dar-es-Salaam: Tanzanian Publishing House, 1973).

20. S. E. Crowe, *The Berlin West African Conference* 11 (Westport: Negro Universities Press, 1970); for a fuller account of the European trade in Africans for slavery, see Basil Davidson, *Africa in History: Themes and Outlines* (New York: Collier Books, 1991).

21. Oliver, *The African Experience*, 198. The brutalization of the Congo stands out even by the savage standards of pillage and killing within the colonial project. See Adam Hochschild, *King Leopold's Ghost: A Story of Greed, Terror, and Heroism in Africa* (New York: Mariner Books, 1999); Tim Jeal, *Stanley: The Impossible Life of Africa's Greatest Explorer* (London: Faber and Faber, 2007).

22. U. O. Umozurike, "International Law and Colonialism in Africa," *East African Law Review* no. 3 (1970): 47.

23. T. O. Elias, *Africa and the Development of International Law* (Dobbs Ferry, NY: Oceana Publications, 1988).

24. Ali A. Mazrui, "The African State as a Political Refugee: Institutional Collapse and Human Displacement," *International Journal of Refugee Law* (July 1995): 21, Special Issue; Kwame Nkrumah, *Neo-Colonialism: The Last Stage of Imperialism* (New York: International Publishers, 1965); Mahmood Mamdani, *Citizen and Subject: Contemporary Africa and the Legacy of Late Colonialism* (London: Fountain Publishers, 1996).

25. See, for example, Human Rights Watch, *World Report: Events of 2004* (New York: Human Rights Watch, 2005), 95–182; Peter Anyang' Nyong'o, ed., *Thirty Years of African Independence: The Lost Decades?* (Nairobi: Academy Science Publishers, 1992); Eddy L. Harris, *Native Stranger: A Black American's Journey into the Heart of Africa* (London: Viking, 1992).

26. Paul Tiyambe Zeleza, "Introduction: The Struggle for Human Rights in Africa," in *Human Rights, the Rule of Law, and Development in Africa,* ed. Paul Tiyambe Zeleza and Philip J. McConnaughay (Philadelphia: University of Pennsylvania Press, 2004), 1 .

27. Caroline Elkins, *Imperial Reckoning: The Untold Story of Britain's Gulag in Kenya* (New York: Henry Holt, 2005).

28. Makau wa Mutua, "Putting Humpty Dumpty Back Together Again: The Dilemmas of the Postcolonial African State," *Brooklyn Journal of International Law* 505, no. 21 (1995): 505.

29. Michael Bratton, "Beyond the State: Civil Society and Associational Life in Africa," *World Politics* 41 (1989): 407.

30. Mazrui, "The African State as a Political Refugee," 21.

31. Ibid., 23.

32. Art Hansen, "African Refugees: Defining and Defending Their Human Rights," in *Human Rights and Governance in Africa*, ed. Ronald Cohen et al. (Gainesville: University of Florida Press, 1993), 139–167.

33. Ibid., 161.

34. Ibid., 161–162.

35. Robert H. Jackson, "Juridical Statehood in Sub-Saharan Africa," *Journal of International Affairs* no. 46 (1992): 1.

36. Ibid., 2.

37. Ibid., 1.

38. Peter Anyang' Nyong'o, "The One-Party State and Its Apologists," in Nyong'o, *Thirty Years of African Independence*.

39. Ibid., 3.

40. Abdullahi Ahmed An-Na'im, "The National Question, Secession, and Constitutionalism: The Mediation of Competing Claims to Self-Determination," in *State and Constitutionalism: An African Debate on Democracy,* ed. Issa Shivji (Harare: SAPES Trust, 1991), 101, 103.

41. Ibid.

42. Benjamin Neuberger, "Federalism in Africa: Experience and Prospects," in *Federalism and Political Integration*, ed. Daniel Judah Elazar (Lanham, MD: University Press of America, 1979), 171, 172–175.

43. Ibid., 180–182.

44. Ibid., 173.

45. See, for example, Mary L. Dudziak, "Working Toward Democracy: Thurgood Marshall and the Constitution of Kenya*,*" *Duke Law Journal* no. 56 (2006): 721.

46. Jennifer A. Widner, *The Rise of a Party-State in Kenya: From Harambee to Nyayo!* (Berkeley: University of California Press, 1992), 53–54.

47. Peter J. Okondo, "Prospects of Federalism in East Africa," in *Federalism and the New Nations of Africa,* ed. David P. Currie (Chicago: University of Chicago Press, 1964), 29, 34; Simiyu Wandabba, *Masinde Muliro* (Nairobi: East African Educational Publishers, 1996).

48. Julius G. Kiano, "The Emergent East African Federation," in Currie, *Federalism and the New Nations of Africa*, 74.

49. "Majimbo," the Kiswahili plural for "province," connotes the federal character of the 1963 Constitution of Kenya under which the country became independent. Yash P. Ghai and J. P. W. B. McAuslan, *Public Law and Political Change in Kenya* (Nairobi: Oxford University Press, 1970).

50. Neuberger, "Federalism in Africa," 175.

51. Art. 1, *Kenya Constitution* (Constitution Act, 1964).

52. Art. 2(2), *Uganda Constitution* (1962).

53. Nelson Kasfir, "Cultural Sub-Nationalism in Uganda," in *The Politics of Cultural Sub-Nationalism in Africa,* ed. Victor A. Olorunsola (New York: Anchor Books, 1972), 51, 82.

54. Arnold Rivkin, *Nation Building in Africa* (New Brunswick: Rutgers University Press, 1969), 89.

55. Kasfir, "Cultural Sub-Nationalism in Uganda," 112–113.

56. Ibid.

57. Kwame Nkrumah, *The Challenge of the Congo* (New York: International Publishers, 1967).

58. Neuberger, "Federalism in Africa," 176.

59. Makau wa Mutua and Peter Rosenblum, *Zaire: Repression as Policy* (New York: Lawyers Committee for Human Rights, now Human Rights First, 1990), 15–17; Stephen Weissman, "The CIA and US Policy in Zaire and Angola," in *American Policy in Southern Africa,* ed. Rene Lemarchand (Washington, DC: University Press of America, 1978).

60. Georges Nzongola-Ntalaja, *The Congo: From Leopold to Kabila: A People's History* (London: Zed Books, 2002); Adam Hochschild, *King Leopold's Ghost: A Story of Greed, Terror, and Heroism in Colonial Africa* (New York: Mariner Books, 1999); Howard W. French, *Continent for the Taking: The Tragedy and Hope of Africa* (New York: Vintage, 2005).

61. "After Violent Decades, Congo Finally Installs Elected Leader," *New York Times,* September 7, 2006, A15; "Congo Votes in Its First Multiparty Elections in 46 Years," *New York Times,* July 31, 2006, A3.

62. Established by Italians in 1889 as they sought to colonize Ethiopia, Eritrea was taken over by the British from 1941 to 1952, when it was joined with Ethiopia by a federation engineered by the United Nations. United Nations General Assembly Res. 390(V), UN Doc. A/1605 (1950), "Eritrea: Report of the United Nations Commission for Eritrea," December 2, 1950.

63. The two halves of the Cameroons, one colonized by the French, the other by the British, became the Federal Republic of Cameroon upon independence. Rivkin, *Nation-Building,* 97–99.

64. Neuberger, "Federalism in Africa," 177.

65. Human Rights Watch, *Tanzania: "The Bullets Were Raining": The January 2001 Attack on Peaceful Demonstrators in Zanzibar* (New York: Human Rights Watch, April 2001).

66. Olorunsola, "Nigeria," in *The Politics of Cultural Sub-Nationalism,* 5, 32.

67. Uma O. Eleazu, *Federalism and Nation-Building* (Illfracombe: Stockwell, 1977).

68. David Ijalaye, "Was Biafra at Any Time a State in International Law?" *American Journal of International Law* 65 (1971): 551.

69. Human Rights Watch, *"They Do Not Own This Place": Government Discrimination Against "Non-Indigenes" in Nigeria* (New York: Human Rights Watch, 2006); Human Rights Watch, *Testing Democracy: Political Violence in Nigeria* (New York: Human Rights Watch, 2003).

70. "A First in Nigeria: A Peaceful Succession of Power," *New York Times,* May 30, 2007.

71. Ibid.

72. Edmund Keller, "Remaking the Ethiopian State," in *Collapsed States*, 125–139; Makau wa Mutua, "The Regionalization Controversy," *Africa Report* (September–October 1993): 30–31.

73. A. M. Faure and Jan-Erik Lane, eds., *South Africa: Designing New Political Institutions* (London: Sage, 1996); *Constitution of South Africa* (1996).

74. Samuel P. Huntington, *The Third Wave: Democratization in the Late Twentieth Century* (Norman: University of Oklahoma Press, 1990).

4

The Constitutional History
of Kenya

WHAT IS TODAY the state of Kenya did not exist prior to the last two decades of the nineteenth century. Even so, there lived within its current borders dozens of nations and political societies, each separate and generally independent of the others. Scholars have divided these nations into three broad linguistic categories. They are the Bantu, which is the largest and includes the Kikuyu, Kamba, Luhya, Embu, Meru, Kisii, and Mijikenda; the Nilotic, which comprises the Luo, Kalenjin, and Maasai; and the Cushitic, which includes the Somali, Rendille, Orma, and Borana.[1] At the coast, a trading African civilization, largely of the Swahili, had long interacted with the Arabian Peninsula and the Indian subcontinent.[2] These coastal communities were overcome first by the Portuguese in the sixteenth century, then taken over by the Sultan of Oman, and finally fell to British colonial rule in the nineteenth century.[3] In the late nineteenth century, the British extended their reach into the interior as they sought control over Lake Victoria, the source of the Nile. Thus began British colonial rule over what are today the states of Kenya and Uganda, and later Tanganyika.

The Birth of the Kenyan State

In 1896, the British declared the region of Kenya the East African Protectorate, the first effective step toward the creation of the colonial state. In 1901, the British completed the construction of the Uganda Railway from Mombasa on the Kenyan coast to Kisumu on the shores of Lake Victoria. Although African communities fiercely resisted the building of the railroad, the British used force to establish effective control over the interior. Early colonial administrators decided that Kenya would be turned into a white man's settler country, much like South Africa, Rhodesia, and Australia.[4] Consequently, large tracts of land occupied by African groups were alienated for white settlement.[5] Africans were pushed out of fertile lands and into less productive areas. European farmers and white South African settlers were lured into the territory by cheap concessions on land. As noted by Africa Watch, "European settlement in Kenya arose out of ruthless suppression of indigenous people."[6] Indeed, "local resistance was overcome by a series of violent massacres, communal punishment, and confiscation of livestock—the most valued asset of both farming and pastoral groups."[7]

Almost overnight, African nations were abolished as independent political societies. Land was now placed under the control of the new colonial state, and nations that had previously been independent of each other were forcibly lumped into one administrative state under white European leadership. At the same time, Christian missionaries were involved in a relentless drive to convert Africans.[8] African spiritualities were demonized and reconstructed as savage, evil, and subhuman.[9] Missionaries quickly established schools, churches, and health centers that they used to both lure and coerce Africans into rejecting their cultures. Faced on the one hand by the new colonial state structures and pressed on the other by Christian zealots, Africans slowly succumbed to the new order. That is how the Kenyan state was born.

Two colonial measures served to underscore the subjugation of Africans to the new colonial state. The first was the promulgation of laws and decrees expropriating African lands in large areas of Kenya, in which many Maasai, Kikuyu, Embu, Meru, Kamba, Giriama, Luo, Kisii, and Luyha lost their livelihoods. But perhaps the most unfortunate were the Maasai, a pastoralist community that grazed their livestock over large distances within Nairobi, later the capital city of Kenya, and the Rift Valley. The British deemed the grazing areas terra nullius and seized them from the Maasai, sharply reducing their seasonal pastures. To add insult to injury, the British duped and coerced Maasai leaders into two fraudulent agreements through which they "gave up" most of their land.[10]

The second measure was the introduction of the annual hut tax, which served two related purposes. It raised revenue from Africans to run the colonial state and forced Africans to work on settler European farms, the only place where they could earn enough money to pay the tax.[11] Other oppressive measures included pass laws, or the "kipande" system, in which Africans had to carry a passbook, similar to the ones in racist South Africa, to allow travel between "native reserves" and European farms and settlements.[12]

While Africans lost sovereignty, the colonial state established a Legislative Council (LEGCO) in 1907, which catered solely to the interests of the European settlers. However, Asians, then a sizable community, demanded representation in the country's political processes. It was the Asian challenge to exclusive European supremacy that in 1923 resulted in the Devonshire Declaration that proclaimed Kenya an African country.[13] But in reality, nothing changed—Africans continued to be exploited, abused, and humiliated. Throughout the new country, the British invented, imposed, or manipulated African "chiefs." Alternatively, they co-opted or coerced existing precolonial ruling elites to work for the colonial state. These local rulers were responsible for enforcing colonial laws and implementing forced labor. Floggings and beatings of Africans by Europeans were commonplace. But land alienation, spiritual dispossession, forced labor, and oppressive treatment gave rise to nationalist sentiment among Africans. Starting in the 1920s, nationalist organizations such as the Kikuyu Central Association (KCA), Akamba Members Association, the Luo Kavirondo Taxpayers Association, and the Taita Hills Association galvanized opposition to colonial rule.

By the early 1950s, African resistance led to the Mau Mau movement, or the Kenya Land and Freedom Army (KLFA), among the Kikuyu, Meru, Embu, and Kamba. From 1952 to 1959, the British colonial government waged a scorched earth policy against the Mau Mau. In 1952, it declared a state of emergency and detained over a million Kikuyu, Embu, Meru, and Kamba in concentration-camp villages. In 1953, Jomo Kenyatta, the leader of Kenya African Union, a nationalist organization, was convicted on fabricated evidence in the trial of the Kapenguria Six for their alleged involvement with the Mau Mau.[14] In October 1956, the British captured Dedan Kimathi, the legendary Mau Mau leader, and reportedly hanged him at Kamiti Maximum Prison in February 1957.[15] Despite the blow of Kimathi's murder, the KLFA movement sputtered on. At the end of the Mau Mau war of liberation in 1959, at least 11,000 Africans had been killed, while many more had been imprisoned, tortured, and maimed.[16] The Mau Mau killed dozens of European settlers and colonial administrators. But the Mau Mau war had not only been costly to Africans; it also convinced the British that they had to grant Kenya independence. Without the Mau Mau struggle, Kenya would not have attained its independence as early as it did. Slowly, the British legalized the resumption of independent African political activity as a ploy to alienate Africans from the Mau Mau. In 1955, the Swynnerton Plan, a land reform program, gave Africans land titles for the first time in the formerly exclusive White Highlands, a move that was intended to defuse support for the Mau Mau and engender an African elite close to the state.

In 1960, nationalist leaders formed the Kenya African National Union (KANU), which Kenyatta headed upon his release from jail in 1961. KANU had the overwhelming support of the Kikuyu, Luo, and Kamba. Its other leaders included Paul Ngei, who had been detained with Kenyatta, Oginga Odinga, and Tom Mboya. In the same year, the Kalenjin, the Luhya, and some of the coastal communities formed the Kenya African Democratic Union (KADU) with Daniel arap Moi, Ronald Ngala, and Masinde Muliro as its key leaders. KADU, which had the support of the settler community, was seen as a counterweight against the more radical KANU. It was pitched as a vehicle for the protection of smaller ethnic groups against the Kikuyu-Luo-Kamba alliance. In 1963, however, KANU swept the first democratic elections and Kenyatta became prime minister. He assumed the presidency in 1964, when Kenya became a sovereign republic. Within eighty years, the British had managed to set up an entirely new political society, a brand new state, by abolishing and merging previously independent African nations. The region was transformed forever.

Mau Mau: Resistance and Civil War

The history of Kenya is deeply bound up with the legacy of the Mau Mau, the valiant liberation movement that waged a fierce guerrilla campaign against the British colonial state in Kenya. Even today, this indigenous anticolonial revolt continues to shape the politics of the country. That is why it is imperative to understand the effect of the Mau Mau on the colonial and postcolonial states in Kenya. The fissures engendered by the anticolonial struggle, the most significant expression of which was the Mau Mau, left an indelible mark on Kenya. Furthermore, the manner in which the insurgency was defeated and how the emergent postcolonial state treated the KLFA fundamentally affected the legitimacy of the state. Particularly within the Kikuyu and related peoples, and in the country in general, sharp cleavages and class divisions formed because of colonialism and the response of the Mau Mau to it. The failure of the postcolonial state to address these cleavages and to embrace the Mau Mau as a watershed movement in Kenya's liberation continues to divide society.

That the Mau Mau was a nationalist, anticolonial movement has never been in doubt.[17] Dedan Kimathi, its iconic leader, is valorized in Kenya as the epitome of nationalism.[18] The Mau Mau movement was a reaction to British imperialism in Kenya.[19] But so controversial was the movement that the early literature demonizes and distorts this vital indigenous liberation organization.[20] At the outset, the resistance confounded the British overlords and their African collaborators. What followed was a fierce anti-insurgency campaign that was characterized by gross human rights violations and atrocities never before witnessed in Kenya. Extrajudicial killings, concentration camps, torture, and forced labor were the norm under the state of emergency declared by the colonial state to put down the rebellion.[21] The ferocity of the war against the suspect African populations was chilling.[22] The West and its African collaborators in Kenya characterized the Mau Mau freedom fighters as terrorists.[23] The war and the state of emergency heightened and polarized racial, ethnic, economic, social, political, and class divisions between whites and Africans, among different African communities, and within African groups to a degree that was unprecedented.

Analysis of the Mau Mau war reveals several distinct but interrelated struggles within the context of liberation and counterinsurgency. The overarching contest, that of the political liberation of Kenya, pitted the KLFA nationalists against the British colonial rulers. This primary conflict was the raison d'être of the Mau Mau uprising. But neither side could wage this larger struggle without vying for the sympathy of Africans. On the one hand, an African population drawn from the colonial civil service, the "native" wings of the police and military, a growing local elite minted by the European mission schools, and collaborationist sections of the African traditional ruling classes supported the British. On the other, the Mau Mau fighters swelled their ranks from the alienated, landless, oppressed Africans. Koigi wa Wamwere has written that this chasm among Africans constituted a bitter intra-African struggle.[24] It is this division between the two African populations—those for and those against the Mau Mau—that would endure into the postcolonial state.

The violent conflict—war—that ensued between the Mau Mau and the British divided the Kikuyu, Embu, Meru, and even the Kamba right down the middle. Families were torn apart because of conflicting loyalties. Even though the Mau Mau was a war of liberation, it also became a civil war, particularly among the Kikuyu. Betrayals, killings, and other acts of violence came to define the nature of the conflict among the Kikuyu.[25] These brutalities took on a class character as the more educated propertied among the Kikuyu, Meru, Embu, and Kamba—those with a stake in the colonial state—joined in a full-scale campaign with the British to hunt down, eliminate, and neutralize the Mau Mau and their sympathizers.[26] The so-called African home guards—colonial collaborators whose fate was bound up with their masters—brutally repressed their fellow Africans on behalf of the British Empire.[27] Although Jennifer A. Widner is right to identify the class character of the KLFA struggle among Africans—as a conflict over land and other economic resources—she fails to appreciate its scope and depth in the wider Kikuyu, Meru, and Embu communities.[28] The effect of the Mau Mau on the formative postcolonial state cannot be underestimated.

The problem of landlessness in Kenya is largely traceable to dispossession by the colonial state and the failure of the Kenyatta regime to institute an appropriate land reform policy. John W. Harbeson has argued that equitable land reform is necessary for nation building and the legitimation of the state.[29] Since the 1960s, one of the consequences of this landlessness has been the rise in property crimes. Even ethnocultural social movements, such as Mungiki, the self-styled political movement of the "sons and daughters of the Mau Mau," have developed a criminal aspect because of social alienation and manipulation by influential state officials.[30] The Mungiki, which claims a neo–Mau Mau identity, is but one example of the failure of the state to address colonial era class schisms. The lack of land reform was identified by the Task Force on the Establishment of a Truth, Justice, and Reconciliation Commission as one of the most urgent issues facing the country.[31] This recommendation was voiced universally throughout the country, but particularly in the Central, Coast, Eastern, and Rift Valley provinces.[32] Similarly, the land question was one of the more sensitive issues at the constitutional conference. It is improbable that the Kenyan state can gain substantial legitimacy without resolving the volatile problem of land and the atrocities and distortions of the colonial era, including the depiction of Mau Mau. However, the Kibaki regime has refused to establish a truth commission to address some of these problems.[33] In 2007, the Kibaki government erected a statue of Dedan Kimathi in

Nairobi in a belated effort to reclaim the Mau Mau as a heroic nationalist movement.[34] But it is not clear whether it was a political ploy or a genuine attempt to honor Kenya's history of resistance. For instance, the government has failed to support the Kenya Human Rights Commission as it seeks to institute legal proceedings in London against the British government for its colonial era atrocities in Kenya.[35] The erasure of the Mau Mau from the national psyche by the ruling elites continues a legacy of deliberate amnesia over the sharp disagreements about the nature of the Kenyan state. The reclamation of the country's nationalist history—including that of Koitalel arap Samoei,[36] the Kalenjin anticolonial leader Mekatilili wa Menza,[37] and others—is essential for the construction of a national identity. These questions of land, identity, culture, and history were central to Kenya's constitutional debates.

The Legacy of Executive Despotism

Constitutionalism is a genre of state culture that is essential for a liberal democracy built on the rule of law and individual rights. An independent judiciary, the key guardian of the rule of law, is the linchpin of the system of checks and balances through which the separation of powers is ensured.[38] Otherwise, there is no guarantee that the executive will respect the rule of law and act within established legal norms and processes. This view of the rule of law assumes that the notion is value-laden—that at its core lies the essence of democratic values. The constitution is not merely a hortatory document but must be seen as the fundamental and basic law, a real and living document that defines, guides, and permits all actions by the state. The sum total of all the powers of the state reside in the constitution; no more, no less. But the law and the actions it authorizes must be fair and just. In this logic, no individual or official of the state is above the law or can act in defiance of constitutional prescriptions. But it strains credulity to argue that this idealized definition of a democratic, rule of law state could have become directly applicable on the day after the colonial state passed into postcolonialism. Kenya is one of the many examples that amply demonstrate this skepticism.

Since its creation in 1886, the Kenyan state has undergone several transformations, all marked by either illiberalism, massive human rights violations, or corruption. Not much more need be said about the colonial state, an instrumentality that was specifically organized for the purposes of political repression to facilitate economic exploitation of human and physical resources. But in 1963, Kenya attained internal self-government, the penultimate step to ending direct European colonial rule.[39] As the British Union Jack was lowered and the flag of an independent Kenya hoisted, the machinery of the ancien regime was left intact. Conceptually, the foundation of the postcolonial state was Eurocentric. Owing to this legacy, Kenya's postindependence history has been marked by sharp contradictions between the state, its citizens, and civil society, in spite of the country's image cultivated in the West during the Cold War, that the East African nation was a beacon of hope in a sea of chaos. Not even the reintroduction of multipartyism in 1991 or the contested elections in 1992, 1997, 2002, and 2007 banished illiberalism, corruption, and human rights violations, abominations that had become the trademark of the Nairobi government.[40] Since 2003, however, the Kibaki regime has presided over respectable economic growth and has permitted more freedom, although corruption has remained endemic and reforms have been either gradual or nonexistent in key sectors.

The constitutional order imposed on Kenya by the British in 1963 was a result of protracted negotiations between various political and economic interests at Lancaster House in London.[41] The nationalists, led by Kenyatta and Odinga, sought a strong unitary state, while the more conservative elements, including white settler interests, pushed for a federal system of government with a strong bill of rights that would protect private property interests, particularly land.[42] Although the KANU nationalists wanted a transfer of land without compensation to whites, the final constitutional settlement provided enough safeguards to protect settler property interests. Ironically, Thurgood Marshall, the African American civil rights leader, and an adviser to KANU at the 1960 Lancaster constitutional talks, had pushed for these protections for the white minority.[43] Odinga, however, was not happy with Marshall's role, seeing him as a mole for US interests.[44] Be that as it may, the 1963 Lancaster Constitution contained elaborate protections for property rights, including compensation to white settlers for the return of land to indigenous Africans. The white settlers and the British government had sought these protections as a condition for granting independence.[45] The outcome was a highly complex document that lacked singularity of purpose or identity, and to which none of the protagonists were particularly wedded.[46] It was a classic political compromise with just enough carrots and sticks for each of the parties, but devoid of a centralizing theme for the new Kenyan state.[47] Colin Leys has offered several possible explanations for KANU's acceptance of the land compensation scheme and other property protections in the Lancaster Constitution.

> The moderating influence of Kenyatta; the fear of independence being delayed; the hope of changing things after independence; a lack of interest in the detail of the negotiations; a fear that the rival party, the Kenya African Democratic Union (KADU), for whose supporters the land issue was less vital . . . , might agree to the proposed scheme first and perhaps manage to get KANU excluded from the transitional government; and finally, the risk of alienating the former forest fighters if they were not provided with land quickly.[48]

The 1963 Constitution provided for a multiparty democracy, a freely elected bicameral parliament, and guaranteed individual rights. The most important feature of the new constitution was its decentralization of power, even though it retained a strong executive in the office of the governor-general, who exercised executive power on behalf of the Queen, the British monarch.[49] In fact, the governor-general was only answerable to the Queen because Kenya remained a dominion of the United Kingdom. In addition to a robust bill of rights,[50] the Westminster model constitution created a relatively weak prime ministerial office answerable to the governor-general and the National Assembly.[51] Yet, it was clear that real political power lay with KANU and Kenyatta, the nationalists who enjoyed the support of the majority of the black African population. In retrospect, it should have been predictable that KANU would use its enormous popularity to revise the legal order. Paradoxically, it was this contradiction in the Lancaster Constitution—between law and fact—that would later provide Kenyatta with an opportunity to sow the seeds of dictatorship.

The Lancaster Constitution curtailed the powers of the centralized state by including a quasi-federal system of autonomous regional governments in its framework.[52] Of the two houses of Parliament (also referred to as the National Assembly), the Senate, or upper house, was the guarantor of the quasi-federal system, popularly known as "Majimboism," or regionalism. The House of Representatives, or lower house, was the main legislative body. Although it had a critical role to play in constitutional amendments, the Senate was secondary to the House of Representatives. The Bill of Rights and the elaborate system of checks and balances would presumably curb the power of any future African government to disturb the privileges of the European minority settler elite or even the Asian community, the position advocated by Marshall, the first black American on the Supreme Court of the United States.[53] But it was also the position favored by African groups who were ostensibly opposed to the dominance of larger communities. Other safeguards included an independent judiciary that enjoyed security of tenure, an independent attorney general as the chief legal adviser to the government, and a civil service insulated from routine politics. But the entire constitutional framework, including the difficult and cumbersome relationship between the center and the regions, the virtual impossibility of making amendments, and the lack of commitment to it by the protagonists, virtually doomed it from the start. It was largely an unworkable document for such a young state without any experience—or history—with democracy. The 1963 Constitution would be repeatedly revised, but each time with devastating consequences for the rights of Kenyans.

Paradoxically, the independence constitution was meant to both preserve the colonial order and at the same time give legitimacy to the emergent African ruling elite. In this process, akin to delivering a baby while choking it at the same time, a severe deformation occurred. The colonial state survived, but it morphed into a postcolonial variant, only too ready to continue tormenting its subjects. Put differently, the colonial state could not be transformed through a piece of paper that superimposed values and structures over a machinery that was oppressive, alien, and illegitimate. Nor could the imperial overlords relinquish direct control and reasonably expect their handiwork to remain intact without readjustment and substantial reordering by the new African elite. What happened was the reversion of the postcolonial state to its true form, the colonial predecessor. Strangely, or perhaps not, the Africans trusted that the new state would not take on the personalities and the powers of the colonial rulers, filling the buildings and state structures left vacant by the departing British. In hindsight, it seems foolish to have expected anything different from the postcolonial state, absent some transformative events to dismantle and repudiate the colonial state and establish a normatively different state. Not surprisingly, that is not what happened, or what could have happened, at Lancaster House in 1963. The Kenyan Independence Constitution, like those of other African postcolonial states, was not homegrown and lacked the contextual authenticity to make it work. Perhaps the outcome would have been markedly different had the dominant African elites come to a genuine agreement on the identity of the independent state.

The Centralization of Power

Perhaps the greatest weakness of the Independence Constitution was the insecurity it created in KANU, the largest and most dominant African political party. Kenyatta, KANU, and its senior leadership knew that they could not easily consolidate their power under the new constitution. So long as the constitution split executive power between the head of government (Kenyatta, the prime minister) and the head of state (the Queen of England, represented by the governor-general), KANU could not consolidate its power.[54] Odinga's disdain for the constitution was plain. He argued that it was "called a constitution of checks and balances, but I would say there were more checks than anything else."[55] No sooner was the constitution agreed upon than KANU publicly attacked it, making a case for its revision. During the 1963 elections, KANU proposed the amendments that it would push for once elected—to create a republic and to abolish regionalism—thus portraying the elections as a referendum on the Lancaster Constitution. KANU's overwhelming victory in those elections was seen as a public endorsement of the proposed constitutional changes.

In December 1963, as soon as Kenyatta was sworn in as the first African prime minister, he embarked on a mission to change the country's constitutional order. In 1964, using political pressure and promises of jobs and power sharing, Kenyatta prevailed upon Daniel arap Moi and other leaders to voluntarily dissolve KADU and join KANU, effectively crippling the fledgling opposition and setting the stage for a party-state. In the first amendment to the 1963 constitution, KANU declared Kenya a republic in which an executive president would be head of state and government as well as commander in chief of the armed forces.[56] It abolished the office of the prime minister and took back many of the powers reserved for the regional governments. On December 12, 1964, Kenya became a republic with Kenyatta as its first president. From then, Kenyatta and Moi, his successor, embarked on a frenzy of constitutional amendments, the effect of which was to dismantle the entire Lancaster Constitution, personalize power, and prevent the emergence of resilient, accountable, and transparent institutions of the state. Political convenience and survival would henceforth dictate the constitutional development and evolution of the Kenyan state.

The disappearance of KADU paved the way for a despotic executive run by a de facto one-party state. Even though the constitution still permitted multipartyism, political elites preferred to take their chances under the populist Kenyatta-led KANU as the trouble-free option for sharing out the spoils of independence. From 1964 to 1969, a period during which Kenyatta consolidated his personal power, KANU quickly passed a raft of amendments to make it easier to amend the constitution; declare a state of emergency; abolish the right of appeal to the Privy Council, the last court of appeal for extant and former British colonies; require members of Parliament to seek reelection if they defected from the party on which they were elected; grant the president power to detain individuals without judicial review; abolish the bicameral Parliament; completely abolish regionalism; and provide that presidential elections would be direct, but that the candidate had to be nominated by a political party.[57] This last amendment gave KANU, of which Kenyatta was the unquestioned leader, the preserve on the presidency, since it was the only effective political party in the country. It also ensured that Kenyatta would be reelected president without any competition. Within a few years of independence, the postcolonial state had rejected the constitution imposed on it by the British, as Kenyatta and KANU established their supremacy over the state. The rejection of the imposed constitution, however, did not have to lead to executive despotism and the tight political control that Kenyatta and KANU sought. Many of the constitutional amendments served no other purpose than to contract political space.

Even as Kenyatta worked to consolidate power and impose his authority on the emergent state, Kenya was rocked by an irredentist movement of Somalis in its Northern Frontier District, a region that bordered Somalia and had been subjected to pogroms and harsh colonial policies by the British. The postcolonial state failed to treat the region any differently, hence the push to secede and join Somalia. The Kenyan military responded harshly, committing widespread massacres, a pattern of gross human rights abuses that would last well into the 1990s.[58] The Somali secessionist movement only served to convince Kenyatta and KANU that regionalism should be a dead letter. But trouble was brewing within KANU, even though it had absorbed KADU. Originally, KANU was a coalition of diverse nationalist interests, some more radical than others. Odinga and Bildad Kaggia, who had been imprisoned with Kenyatta and the Kapenguria Six, led the more "radical" wing. This populist faction sought more radical economic policies, including redistributive land reforms to resettle squatters, the landless, and the poor.[59] Many former Mau

Mau fighters backed this faction. The conservative and more powerful wing was led by Kenyatta and Tom Mboya, the labor leader, and was allied with the emergent business and landed African elites.[60] KADU's dissolution and merger with KANU served to reinforce the conservatives and make KANU more acceptable to European and Asian commercial interests. Odinga, who had worked for the merger, later admitted it was a miscalculation.[61]

But Kenyatta's accommodationist politics should not have been unexpected. Once a fiery anti-imperialist radical, Kenyatta had started to moderate his political views even before he was detained in 1952.[62] Once he was released from detention in 1961, Kenyatta's public statements were calculated to assure the settler community and foreign investors that a future African government would obey the rule of law, respect property rights, and refrain from vengefulness.[63] The man whom the British had accused of masterminding Mau Mau, the "terrorist" organization, came out of prison to embrace a pro-business, free market philosophy and calm the fears of local whites, Western investors, and African entrepreneurs. He would safeguard their property because he would not run "a gangster government."[64]

The struggle between the competing ruling factions to define the economic and political ideology of KANU quickened the pace of the centralization of power by Kenyatta. In 1965, KANU pushed through Parliament the famous Sessional Paper No. 10, the government's pro-business economic blueprint that had been drafted by Mboya.[65] The policy document, which supported a mixed capitalist economic system, was a major blow to the aspirations of the Odinga "radicals," and signaled their decline and impotence within KANU. Odinga, who had established the Lumumba Institute, an ideological school for KANU, with the help of some socialist countries, was now on a warpath against his party.[66] But it was Sessional Paper No. 10 that became the tipping point. The nascent Kenyan state had come to a fork in the road and decided to go right.

> The regime's ideology was embodied in the remarkable policy statement *African Socialism and Its Application to Planning in Kenya*, which was introduced by Mboya and passed unanimously by the National Assembly in May 1965. Kenyatta described it as Kenya's economic "Bible." It was a pure statement of "bourgeois socialism" (i.e., focused on "redressing social grievances in order to ensure the continued existence of bourgeois society"), skillfully adapted to the interests of the comprador elements in a neo-colonial situation. According to people who should know, it was largely drafted by an American economist in Mboya's Ministry, but it does not really matter who drafted it in considering the contributions of Western technical-assistance experts to comprador administrators.[67]

In 1966, Kenyatta moved to crush the "radicals" at the KANU conference in Limuru, at which Moi's role was to neutralize Odinga. Ostensibly, the party conference was called to reorganize KANU and streamline its operations. But, as it turned out, "reorganization" meant getting rid of Odinga and his band of "radicals." The party constitution abolished the office of vice president, which Odinga held, and replaced it with seven provincial vice presidencies.[68] Since the party and the state were becoming increasingly indistinguishable, the removal of Odinga and other outspoken critics was evidence that dissent would no longer be tolerated. It also confirmed that no substantive reforms would be carried out to legitimize the state in the eyes of those who had been hardest hit by colonial policies. Instead, a new class of African entrepreneurs, together with the established European and Asian commercial interests, would use the state to solidify their grip on power and resources.

Soon after the Limuru conference, Odinga and a large section of KANU legislators resigned to form the Kenya People's Union (KPU), which became the official opposition in Parliament. But Kenyatta decided to use Parliament to forestall any further defections from KANU and to punish those who had left it. He forced through the fifth amendment to the 1963 Constitution, which stripped members of Parliament (MPs) of their seats if they defected from the party from which they were elected.[69] The effect was to force defectors to seek a fresh mandate from the electorate, and to scare off others who might contemplate defection. Several days after the adoption of that amendment, Kenyatta prorogued Parliament, making the dissidents lose their seats. In the ensuing election, KANU won more seats than KPU.[70] But more was in store. Parliament soon passed the sixth amendment to the 1963 Constitution, by which it enlarged the government's emergency powers, transferring them to the president without parliamentary oversight. The Preservation of the Public Security Act (PPSA), the detention law, was amended to give the president wide powers to detain individuals indefinitely without judicial review.[71] In 1969, the government banned the KPU and detained its leaders, including Odinga, following an anti-Kenyatta demonstration in Kisumu, Nyanza Province, and Odinga's home region. At least ten people were fatally shot by the security forces as Kenyatta fled the scene.[72] From 1969 until Kenyatta's death in 1978, the state became increasingly repressive. Human rights were denied across the board. Outspoken critics were detained, and some, like J. M. Kariuki, the vocal populist MP, were assassinated. In effect, Kenya became a police state. This period witnessed the crumbling of parliamentary supremacy.

It took just six years to dismantle the 1963 Lancaster House Constitution (the Independence Constitution), a process that indigenized executive despotism and tore down the constitutional order imposed on the postcolonial state by the British. A revealing fact is the ease with which Kenyatta used KANU to create a rubber-stamp Parliament, pass far-reaching constitutional amendments and laws, centralize power, stifle dissent, and construct a near-monarchical personality cult. During this period, Kenyatta's title of "Mzee," or elder in Kiswahili, came to mean "Father of the Nation," an eerie coincidence given the fact that his name was Kenyatta while the country was Kenya, suggesting his ownership of the nation. This play on words gave him a mythic and legendary stature and implied his "ownership" of the country. In a very short time, Kenyatta had become a Big Man, an authoritarian figure without any equal in the state. Several factors account for these stunning developments. First, the normative and institutional arrangements of the Lancaster House Constitution lacked a deep social base in Kenya and did not fall within the experience of the state and its new African political elite. Second, the African negotiators at Lancaster, especially KANU, were not fully committed to the compromise imposed on them by the British. Third, since Kenyatta and KANU essentially inherited the repressive colonial state intact, it was tempting—even natural—to manipulate it and consolidate power. Simply put, the Lancaster House Constitution was no more than a paper foisted on a tiger, a beast whose true colors could not long be suppressed. Could Kenyatta and KANU have made different choices that would have transformed the postcolonial state and democratized it? Possibly, but the temptation of power was too great.

The Personalization of Power

By the time Kenyatta died in 1978, most Kenyans had come to expect an authoritarian and unaccountable state. Its power was ubiquitous, and those who dared oppose its policies or leading personalities were ruined or marginalized. The African ruling elite had quickly normalized the culture of subservience and impunity first cultivated under the colonial state. During the 1970s, Kenyans knew that Kenyatta was in poor health, yet the matter of succession was taboo. Because open competition for the presidency was not permitted, leading political figures instead resorted to succession intrigues and plots. The most prominent was a scheme by Kenyatta's kitchen cabinet to amend the constitution to prevent Moi, then vice president and a member of the Kalenjin community, from automatically assuming the presidency upon Kenyatta's demise.[73] The plot, hatched by the powerful members of the Gikuyu, also written as Kikuyu, Embu, and Meru Association (GEMA), was thwarted by Charles Njonjo, the powerful attorney general who supported Moi's constitutional right to ascend to the presidency for ninety days upon the death of the president. Njonjo, a close confidant of both Kenyatta and Moi, killed the GEMA plot by issuing a stern warning: "It is a criminal offence for any person to encompass, imagine, devise, or intend the death or deposition of the President."[74] Kenyatta backed this threat, which was draconian and legally overbroad. As a result, the so-called Change the Constitution group, which sought to retain power in the hands of the Kikuyu, promptly folded. That is how Daniel arap Moi, the lackluster former KADU leader, assumed the presidency when Kenyatta died suddenly in 1978.[75]

Except for the constitutional guarantees of the office of the vice president, Moi was presumed to be the least likely person to succeed Kenyatta. Kenyatta had chosen him as deputy because he posed no apparent threat to the charismatic and scheming nationalist leader. It was inconceivable that an openly ambitious deputy would have been appointed. Kenyans perceived Kenyatta as above the law, an icon against whom no challenge could be fathomed. His legend stretched far back to the years he spent in the United Kingdom, where he was for many years one of the leading pan-Africanists, along with George Padmore, Kwame Nkrumah, and other black luminaries of the day. Upon his return to Kenya in the 1940s, Kenyatta quickly became an important nationalist leader, for which the British detained him in 1952. Doubts have been raised that Kenyatta was even a member of, let alone a senior leader within, the Mau Mau. Even so, lore and legend had replaced facts by the time he was released from detention in 1960. As a man, he had become the single most important symbol of Kenya's cry for freedom. Moi, a former schoolteacher with little formal education, could never hope to inspire the awe of the erudite Kenyatta.

Insecure at first, President Moi took a number of steps to establish a power base of his own and create a political class loyal to him. Together with Njonjo, the attorney general, and Mwai Kibaki, the new vice president, Moi's faction took control of KANU in preparation for the 1979 presidential and general elections, the first without Kenyatta at the helm. Those elections were a watershed, giving Moi the opportunity to exploit the centralized, personalized state created by Kenyatta. He was able to sideline his opponents, play the powerful Kikuyu political and commercial interests against each other, and project himself as the country's unquestioned leader. This he did with a combination of flair, a flurry of activity, populism, and deft manipulation. In December 1978, as an act of mercy calculated to endear himself to Kenyatta's opponents, Moi released from incarceration twenty-six of the most famous political prisoners and detainees, including Ngugi wa Thiong'o, the celebrated author. Then he set about reorganizing KANU and the government and placing his cronies in strategic positions. Almost from the start, he played potential challengers against one another and undercut those whose loyalty was in question.[76] He had learned well under Kenyatta.

But new challenges to Moi's increasingly centralized rule emerged from university students, government critics, and opposition politicians. In May 1981, student leaders at the University of Nairobi, including myself, organized massive demonstrations to demand open political competition, a broad range of human rights, and an end to executive despotism. In retaliation, the government arrested and expelled student leaders and forced many into exile. In May 1982, George Anyona, a former outspoken MP, and Odinga, the veteran opposition leader, announced the formation of the Kenya African Socialist Alliance (KASA), the first opposition party in the country since the banning of the KPU in 1969. In June 1982, Moi rammed through Parliament a constitutional amendment, the infamous Section 2A, which outlawed all political opposition and made Kenya a de jure one-party state.[77] When KANU became the sole legal political party in the country, even the pretense of political democracy was officially outlawed. From then on, the government became increasingly intolerant of dissent. It frequently detained its critics, including Willy Mutunga, Al Amin Mazrui, Kamoji Wachira, George Mkangi, Mukaru Ng'ang'a, and Edward Oyugi—all university lecturers accused of teaching political subversion.

The failed coup attempt by the Kenya Air Force in August 1982 became the perfect excuse for Moi to clamp down on his critics. The coup attempt was triggered by increased autocracy and corruption, as well as Moi's inability to carry out redistributive policies to redress ethnic imbalances.[78] In its wake, hundreds of people were arrested and convicted of treason, sedition, and other related charges. Raila Odinga, the scion of Oginga Odinga, was detained without charge on suspicion of being one of the coup's authors.[79] After the coup attempt, Moi moved pitilessly to consolidate his personal power in the party-state. Between 1982 and 1990, the government became increasingly repressive, and the country was characterized by waves of arrests, detentions, phony trials and convictions of government opponents, and severe restrictions on basic rights. Some of the most severe measures, including torture and killings, were carried out starting in 1986 in connection with Mwakenya, a clandestine organization committed to the overthrow of the KANU state.[80] Many lawyers, including Gibson Kamau Kuria, John Khaminwa, Paul Muite, Martha Karua, James Orengo, Gitobu Imanyara, Wanyiri Kihoro, and Mirugi Kariuki, were either detained, harassed, or forced to flee the country.[81]

Moi took other legal and constitutional measures to seal off any remaining avenues for dissent. In 1988, he abolished the secret ballot and introduced queue voting, a procedure that openly exposed voters by requiring them to line up behind the candidates of their choice. Few voters dared line up behind government critics.[82] In the same year, he amended the constitution, extending the period during which suspects could be held without judicial scrutiny from twenty-four hours to fourteen days. He also abolished the constitutional guarantee of tenure for judges, in effect removing one of the last vestiges of an independent judiciary.[83] In 1990, under intense domestic and international pressure, Moi restored judicial tenure, although the damage had already been done.[84] The judiciary remained beholden to the executive in politically sensitive cases. Particularly vulnerable were expatriate, non-Kenyan judges who served on contract, presumably at the pleasure of the president.[85] Civil society, or whatever fledgling nongovernmental organizations existed, the churches, and the press all operated under great strain and threat from the state. By the close of the 1980s, even as various groups sought to open up political space, the KANU state was determined to extinguish it.

The Repeal of Section 2A

The 1980s closed with winds of change blowing across the globe. Military, civilian, and one-party regimes were on the retreat as the Soviet bloc unraveled and the pro-democracy movements in Eastern Europe and Africa gained momentum. These pressures did not spare the Moi-KANU state, as both domestic and Western calls for an open political system increased.[86] The success of multiparty advocates in Benin, Mali, Zambia, and Malawi greatly emboldened Kenyan reform advocates. Cadres of lawyers, clergymen, politicians, and civil society openly attacked the party-state and called for multipartyism. The political assassination in 1990 of foreign minister Robert Ouko further raised political temperatures. Not even the detention of Kenneth Matiba and Charles Rubia, two prominent politicians, could quell the calls for change. Muite summed up the mood of the country when in 1991 he called on the government to end persecution and permit the registration of opposing political parties. "The Government," he stated:

> must continue to be told by us lawyers that the greatest threat to public security is not us the lawyers, when we speak out . . . the greatest danger to public security is the Kenya Government itself. It can remove that danger by adhering to the constitution, both in theory and in practice. By faithfully subscribing to the Rule of Law, democracy and respect for human rights, "threat to public security" will become a thing of the past.[87]

However, Amos Wako, the new attorney general and onetime member of the United Nations Human Rights Committee, stunned Kenyans by declaring that "a characteristic of the rule of law is that no man, save the president, is above the law."[88] So powerful had Moi become that even an attorney general with some claim to human rights credentials could declare him above the law. In August 1991, pressure mounted on the state when veteran politicians and pro-democracy advocates formed the Forum for the Restoration of Democracy (FORD), an opposition political party. Moi threatened dire consequences. But Mwai Kibaki, a former vice president who was then a minister in the Moi cabinet, opposed the repeal of Section 2A. He argued that ending KANU's monopoly would destroy Kenya. He said that opposition calls for the repeal were "akin to cutting a fig tree [*mugumo*] with a razor blade."[89] Kalonzo Musyoka, another KANU stalwart, argued that multipartyism would release ethnic animosities and tear Kenya apart. According to him, the choice was "between KANU and violence."[90] International pressure picked up in November 1991, when the influential Paris Club of donors suspended aid to Kenya pending political and economic reforms. Barely a week later, on December 2, President Moi, in a dramatic reversal, announced the repeal of Section 2A and legalized political opposition.[91]

Paradoxically, by repealing Section 2A, the postcolonial state had come full circle. Unable to resist a return to the political liberalism of the 1963 Lancaster House Constitution, the KANU state had acquiesced to multipartyism at the start of the 1990s. A bevy of political parties was registered in the wake of political liberalization. The most prominent were FORD-Kenya, led by Oginga Odinga and Paul Muite; FORD-Asili, led by Matiba and Martin Shikuku; and the Democratic Party (DP), led by Mwai Kibaki. Even though Kibaki had opposed the repeal of Section 2A, he left KANU in 1991 and formed DP once it became clear that his political ambitions could not be realized under the Moi-controlled KANU. In the run-up to the 1992 general elections, the first openly contested national vote since independence, KANU employed its control of the state machinery to disorganize, persecute, and manipulate the elections. The opposition, divided by ethnic and personal agendas, failed to unseat Moi and KANU, even though its combined tally was over two-thirds of the vote.[92] Although it had succumbed to the demands for change, KANU's triumph would ensure that although Kenya was formally a democracy, it would remain an illiberal, undemocratic state, trapped in the culture of executive despotism.[93]

Between 1992 and the next general elections in 1997, the culture of governance did not change much, even with substantial opposition representation in Parliament. The state continued to be opaque and undemocratic, although the 1997 elections increased the number of opposition legislators in Parliament. The consensus among reform advocates in Kenya was that political democracy could not be achieved so long as KANU remained in power. Regime change—meaning the ouster of KANU—was seen as the only salvation. But these advocates also believed that constitutional reform, by which they meant the writing of an entirely new constitution, was necessary to oust KANU and reform the state before the 2002 general elections. In any event, Moi would be constitutionally barred from standing for another term since the clock on presidential term limits had started to run in 1992. In the remaining years of the Moi era, from 1997 to 2002, reformers focused on the creation of a new constitutional order as the only avenue for reforming the postcolonial state.

Notes

1. E. K. Mburugu and F. Ojany, "The Land and the People," in *Kenya: An Official Handbook*, ed. Richard Ndirango (Nairobi: Ministry of Information, 1988), 8–10.

2. Africa Watch, *Kenya: Taking Liberties* (New York: Africa Watch, 1991), 1.

3. Ibid.

4. Duncan Ndegwa, *Walking in Kenyatta's Struggles: My Story* (Nairobi: Kenya Leadership Institute, 2006); Elspeth Huxley, *White Man's Country: Lord Delamere and the Making of Kenya* (London: Macmillan, 1935); *Black Man's Land: Images of Colonialism and Independence in Kenya*, 1973, VHS, directed by David Koff and Anthony Howarth (Van Nuys, CA: Anthony David Productions, distributed by Bellweather Group, 1979). For a description of the most serious attempt thus far, later abandoned, to create a Zionist state for persecuted European Jews in Kenya, see also Robert Weisbord, *African Zion: The Attempt to Establish a Jewish Colony in the East Africa Protectorate, 1903–1905* (Philadelphia: Jewish Publication Society of America, 1968).

5. M. Dilley, *British Colonial Policy in Kenya* (London: Frank Cass Publishers, 1967); Bruce J. Berman, *Control and Crisis in Colonial Kenya: The Dialectic of Domination* (Athens: Ohio University Press, 1999); J. B. Carson, *The Administration of Kenya Colony and Protectorate: Its History and Development* (Nairobi: Noia Kuu Press, 1945);

George Bennett, *Kenya, a Political History: The Colonial Period* (London: Oxford University Press, 1963).

6. Africa Watch, *Kenya: Taking Liberties*, 1.

7. Ibid., 1–2.

8. Robert W. Strayer, *The Making of Mission Communities in East Africa: Anglicans and Africans in Colonial Kenya, 1875–1935* (Albany: State University of New York Press, 1978); Ngugi wa Thiong'o, *The River Between* (London: Heinemann, 1990); Ngugi wa Thiong'o, *A Grain of Wheat* (London: Heinemann, 1988).

9. Makau Mutua, "Proselytism and Cultural Integrity," in *Facilitating Freedom of Religion or Belief: A Deskbook*, ed. Tore Lindholm, W. Cole Durham, Jr., and Bahia G. Tahzib-Lie (Leiden: Martinus Nijhoff Publishers, 2004), 651.

10. See James Thuo Gathii, "Imperialism, Colonialism, and International Law," *Buffalo Law Review* 54 (2007): 1013; Lotte Hughes, *Moving the Maasai: A Colonial Misadventure* (New York: Palgrave Macmillan, 2006).

11. Africa Watch, *Kenya: Taking Liberties*, 3.

12. Caroline Elkins, *Imperial Reckoning: The Untold Story of Britain's Gulag in Kenya* (New York: Henry Holt, 2005).

13. A. I. Salim and K. K. Janmohamed, "Historical Development," in *Kenya: An Official Handbook*, 22.

14. Montagu Slater, *The Trial of Jomo Kenyatta* (London: Secker and Warburg, 1965).

15. Koigi wa Wamwere, *I Refuse to Die: My Journey for Freedom* (Seven Stories Press, 2002), 133; Tabitha Kanogo, *Dedan Kimathi: A Biography* (Nairobi: East African Educational Publishers, 1992); Ian Henderson and Philip Goodhart, *The Hunt for Kimathi* (London: H. Hamilton, 1958).

16. Elkins, *Imperial Reckoning*.

17. Waruhiu Itote, *"Mau Mau" General* (Nairobi: East African Institute Press, 1967); Josiah Mwangi Kariuki, *"Mau Mau" Detainee: The Account by a Kenya African of His Experience in Detention Camps, 1953–1960* (New York: Oxford University Press, 1963); Bildad Kaggia, *Roots of Freedom, 1921–1963: The Autobiography of Bildad Kaggia* (Nairobi: East African Publishing House, 1975); Gakaara wa Wanjau, *Mau Mau Author in Detention* (Nairobi: Heinemann Kenya, 1988); E. S. Atieno and John Lonsdale, eds., *Mau Mau and Nationhood: Arms, Authority, and Narration* (Athens: Ohio University Press, 2003).

18. Ngugi wa Thiong'o and Micere Mugo, *The Trial of Dedan Kimathi* (London: Heinemann, 1977); Maina wa Kinyatti, *Kenya's Freedom Struggle: The Kimathi Papers* (London: Zed Books, 1988); Kanogo, *Dedan Kimathi*; Samuel Kahiga, *Dedan Kimathi: The Real Story* (Nairobi: Longman, 1990).

19. David Throup, *Economic and Social Origins of the Mau Mau* (Athens: Ohio University Press, 1988); Frank Furedi, *The Mau Mau War in Perspective* (London: James Currey, 1989); Wunyabari O. Maloba, *Mau Mau and Kenya: An Analysis of a Peasant Revolt* (Bloomington: Indiana University Press, 1998); Tabitha Kanogo, *Squatters and the Roots of Mau Mau, 1906–1963* (Athens: Ohio University Press, 1987); Don Barnett and Karari Njama, *Mau Mau from Within: Autobiography and Analysis of Kenya's Peasant Revolt* (New York: Monthly Review Press, 1966).

20. Carl Roseberg and John Nottingham, *The Myth of the "Mau Mau": Nationalism in Kenya* (New York: Praeger, 1966, published for the Hoover Institution on War, Revolution, and Peace, Stanford, CA); Robert B. Edgerton, *Mau Mau: An African Crucible* (New York: Free Press, 1990); Louis S. B. Leakey, *Mau Mau and the Kikuyu* (London: Methuen, 1953).

21. Elkins, *Imperial Reckoning in Kenya;* David Anderson, *Histories of the Hanged: The Dirty War in Kenya and the End of Empire* (New York: W.W. Norton, 2005).

22. Antony Clayton, *Counter-Insurgency in Kenya, 1952–1960: A Study of Military Operations Against the Mau Mau* (Nairobi: Transafrica Publishers, 1976); L. S. B. Leakey, *Defeating Mau Mau* (London: Methuen, 1954).

23. W. W. Baldwin, *Mau Mau Manhunt: The Adventures of the Only American Who Has Fought the Terrorists in Kenya* (New York: Dutton, 1957).

24. Wamwere, *I Refuse to Die*, 106–154.

25. Ibid., see generally.

26. See, generally, Elkins, *Imperial Reckoning in Kenya.*

27. Wamwere, *I Refuse to Die*, 124–133.

28. Jennifer A. Widner, *The Rise of a Party-State in Kenya: From Harambee to Nyayo!* (Berkeley: University of California Press, 1992), 41.

29. John W. Harbeson, *Land Resettlement and Development Strategy in Kenya* (Nairobi: Institute for Development Studies, University College, 1967); Harbeson, *Nation Building in Kenya: The Role of Land Reform* (Evanston, IL: Northwestern University Press, 1974).

30. Mutuma Ruteere, "Evolution of Organized Criminal Gangs and Why It's Hard to Control Them," *Sunday Nation*, June 24, 2007; Makau Mutua, "We Must Address Social Causes of Crime," *Sunday Nation*, June 17, 2007; John Mulaa, "Mungiki Actions Echo Events in Central Kenya During Emergency," *Sunday Standard*, June 3, 2007; "Mungiki: Tracing the Roots of a Mysterious Sect," *Sunday Nation*, February 19, 2006; "Mungiki Are Back with a Vengeance," *Daily Nation*, July 31, 2006.

31. Republic of Kenya, *Report of the Task Force on the Establishment of a Truth, Justice, and Reconciliation Commission* (Nairobi: Government Printer, 2003).

32. Ibid.

33. Makau Mutua, "Cleansing the Country of Past Evils," *Sunday Nation*, September 30, 2007; Makau Mutua, "Court Erred in Giving Blanket Immunity," *Sunday Nation*, August 6, 2006, stating that the political class in Kenya has blocked a truth commission.

34. Wanyiri Kihoro, "Kimathi's Battle for Recognition Finally Won," *East African Standard*, March 14, 2007; "National Heroes to Be Honoured," *Daily Nation*, August 11, 2006.

35. "Mau Mau Lawyers Still Need Sh5m [five million Kenya shillings], Says Don," *Daily Nation*, July 11, 2005; "There Is Urgent Need to Recognize the Surviving Mau Mau Fighters," *Daily Nation*, February 18, 2005.

36. "Nandis Sue Britain for Samoei's Head," *Sunday Nation*, April 16, 2006; "Nandi Leader Samoei Kit Found in UK," *Daily Nation*, January 31, 2006.

37. Elizabeth Mugi-Ndua, *Mekatilili wa Menza: Woman Warrior* (Nairobi: Sasa Sema Publications, 2000); "National Heroes to Be Honoured," *Daily Nation*, August 11, 2006.

38. Henry J. Steiner and Philip Alston, *International Human Rights in Context: Law, Politics, and Morals* (New York: Oxford University Press, 2000), 990.

39. *Kenya Independence Constitution, 1963.*

40. James Orengo, "Only Keen Vigilance Will Halt Graft," *Daily Nation*, June 10, 2005.

41. See, for example, Mary L. Dudziak, "Working Toward Democracy: Thurgood Marshall and the Constitution of Kenya," *Duke Law Journal* 56 (2006): 721.

42. Keith Kyle, *The Politics of the Independence of Kenya* (New York: St. Martin's Press, 1999); see also "Kenya Constitutional Conference, 1960: Report on the Conference," *Kenya Gazette*, February 25, 1960.

43. Dudziak, "Working Toward Democracy."

44. Oginga Odinga, *Not Yet Uhuru: The Autobiography of Oginga Odinga* (New York: Hill and Wang, 1967), 177.

45. "Protection of Fundamental Rights and Freedoms of the Individual," Chapter 2, *Kenya Independence Constitution,* 1963.

46. B. A. Ogot and W. R. Ochieng', eds., *Decolonization and Independence in Kenya, 1940–93* (Athens: Ohio University Press, 1995).

47. Colin Leys, *Underdevelopment in Kenya: The Political Economy of Neo-Colonialism* (Berkeley: University of California Press, 1975).

48. Ibid., 56.

49. *Kenya Independence Constitution,* Art. 72(1).

50. Ibid., Chapter 2.

51. Ibid., Chapter 5.

52. Ibid., Chapter 6.

53. Juan Williams, "Marshall's Law," *Washington Post (Magazine),* January 7, 1990; Juan Williams, *Thurgood Marshall: American Revolutionary* (New York: Times Press, 1998).

54. Odinga, *Not Yet Uhuru,* 233–234.

55. Ibid., 233.

56. *The Constitution of Kenya (Amendment) Act,* No. 28 of 1964.

57. Yash Ghai, "Constitutions and Governance in Africa: A Prolegomenon," in *Law and Crisis in the Third World,* ed. Sammy Adelman and Abdul Paliwala (London: H. Zell, 1993), 50, 61–63.

58. Makau Mutua, "The Age-Old Folly of Neglecting Northern Kenya," *Sunday Nation,* July 16, 2006.

59. Odinga, *Not Yet Uhuru,* 253–269.

60. Zarina Patel, *Unquiet: The Life and Times of Makhan Singh* (Nairobi: Zand Graphics, 2006); Tom Mboya, *Freedom and After* (Boston: Little, Brown, 1963); Edwin Gimode, *Tom Mboya* (East African Educational Publishers, 1996); Widner, *The Rise of a Party-State in Kenya,* 56–59.

61. Odinga, *Not Yet Uhuru,* 283–284.

62. Jeremy Murray-Brown, *Kenyatta* (New York: Dutton, 1979); Jules Archer, *African Firebrand: Kenyatta and Kenya* (New York: J. Messner, 1969).

63. Journal of African Marxists, *Independent Kenya* (London: Zed Books, 1982), 82.

64. Jomo Kenyatta, *Suffering Without Bitterness* (Nairobi: East African Publishing House, 1968).

65. Republic of Kenya, *African Socialism and Its Application to Planning in Kenya,* Sessional Paper No. 10 (Nairobi: Government Printer, 1965).

66. Odinga, *Not Yet Uhuru.*

67. Colin Leys, *Underdevelopment in Kenya,* 221.

68. Odinga, *Not Yet Uhuru,* 297–300.

69. *The Constitution of Kenya (Amendment) Act,* No. 17 of 1966.

70. John W. Harbeson, *The Kenya Little General Election: A Study in Problems of Urban Political Integration* (Nairobi: Institute for Development Studies, University College, 1967).

71. *The Preservation of the Public Security Act,* Chapter 57, Laws of Kenya.

72. Leys, *Underdevelopment in Kenya,* 237.

73. Widner, *The Rise of a Party-State in Kenya,* 112–117.

74. Ibid., 116.

75. Ndegwa, *Walking in Kenyatta's Struggles*; Joseph Karimi and Philip Ochieng, *The Kenyatta Succession* (Nairobi: Trans-Africa Books, 1980).

76. Widner, *The Rise of a Party-State in Kenya,* 110–129.

77. *The Constitution of Kenya (Amendment) Act,* No. 7 of 1982. Section 2A provided: "There shall be in Kenya only one political party, the Kenya African National Union."

78. James Dianga, *Kenya 1982—The Attempted Coup: The Consequence of a One-Party Dictatorship* (London: Pen Press, 2002).

79. Babafemi A. Badejo, *Raila Odinga: An Enigma in Kenyan Politics* (Nairobi: Yintab Books, 2006).

80. Makau Mutua, "Justice Under Siege: The Rule of Law and Judicial Subservience in Kenya," *Human Rights Quarterly* 23 (2001): 96, 102.

81. Drew S. Days, *Justice Enjoined: The State of the Judiciary in Kenya* (New York: Robert F. Kennedy Memorial Center for Human Rights, 1992), 58–61.

82. Africa Watch, *Kenya: Taking Liberties,* 18–20.

83. *The Constitution of Kenya (Amendment) Act,* No. 4 of 1988.

84. *The Constitution of Kenya (Amendment) Act,* No. 17 of 1990.

85. Days, *Justice Enjoined,* 23.

86. David Gillies and Makau wa Mutua, *A Long Road to Uhuru: Human Rights and Political Participation in Kenya* (London: Westminster Foundation for Democracy, 1993), 18.

87. Acceptance Speech by Paul Muite, Law Society of Kenya, March 9, 1991, quoted in Days, *Justice Enjoined,* 61.

88. Amos Wako, "The Rule of Law Will Prevail," *Weekly Review,* July 12, 1991, 26.

89. Andrew Morton, *Moi: The Making of a Statesman* (London: Michael O'Mara, 1998), 245.

90. David W. Throup and Charles Hornsby, *Multiparty Politics in Kenya: The Kenyatta and Moi States and the Triumph of the System in the 1992 Election* (Athens: Ohio University Press, 1998), 87.

91. Joel D. Barkan, "Kenya After Moi," *Foreign Affairs* 83 (January–February 2004): 87, 89.

92. National Elections Monitoring Unit, *The Multiparty General Elections in Kenya: 29 December 1992* (Nairobi: NEMU, 1993).

93. Joel A. Solomon and James Silk, *Failing the Democratic Challenge: Freedom of Expression in Multiparty Kenya* (Washington, DC: Robert F. Kennedy Memorial Center for Human Rights, 1993).

5

The Liberal Democratic Consensus

SINCE THE BRITISH founded Kenya in the nineteenth century, it has been a graveyard for radical, progressive, leftist, or transformative politics. Virtually every revolutionary political, economic, or social cause has been either rejected or crushed. Only gradualist or accommodationist political projects have achieved any measure of success. By the same token, opposition political actors who sought fundamental change have either been marginalized or have met with grief. Both the colonial and postcolonial states have been pitiless in meting out grim fates to radical visionaries and change agents. In the country's history, ruling elites have defined the state's interests so restrictively that quite often they even mistook their friends for foes. Principled debate and the honest exchange of information have never been cultivated as important values in statecraft. The result has been a culture of governance that rewards sycophancy, loyalty, and subservience and punishes innovation, merit, and critical analysis.

The predatory and conservative nature of the Kenyan state is related to the purposes for which it was made. Because it was established as an instrument to facilitate economic exploitation of the majority by a tiny, exclusive minority, the Kenyan state has remained distrustful of individuals and causes that have sought to fundamentally alter its mission. As early as 1896, at the dawn of the state, the British faced stiff resistance to their penetration of the interior when Koitalel arap Samoei, the legendary Nandi leader, led his people in disrupting the construction of the Kenya-Uganda railroad.[1] Eventually, the British tricked him into a meeting, only to murder him. In 1914, the British exiled Mekatilili wa Menza, the Kenyan heroine, when she led her Giriama people in opposition to the British campaign to capture their land and destroy their culture and shrines.[2] From the 1930s to the 1940s, opposition by various Taita, Kamba, Kikuyu, and Luo movements to colonial rule and its punitive policies was suppressed through detentions, deportations, and other harsh measures.[3] But the atrocities committed by the British against the Mau Mau movement were the apex of colonial repression and demonstrated the determination of the state to quash any efforts aimed at its radical transformation.[4]

The logic and rationale of the postcolonial state have been equally unforgiving to radical politics. This seamless turnover at independence was possible because Jomo Kenyatta and KANU saw the liberation project in purely racial terms, as a contest between Europeans and Africans, and not a struggle about the class interests of the state. Although race is a powerful category for the mobilization of nationalist politics, it is woefully inadequate as a tool for contesting other forms of subordination. Indeed, no race-based analysis can by itself constitute a cogent theory of antisubordination. That is why KANU's most important achievement was the Africanization or indigenization of the state, which was strictly understood as the replacement of European rulers and bureaucrats by Africans. The fundamental character of the state, which was extractive and exploitative, was never seriously questioned. Kenyatta and his allies in KANU viewed the state as an enabler of a free market economy without legalized racial barriers. Early attempts by Oginga Odinga, Bildad Kaggia, and other militant leaders within KANU to re-create the state were thwarted by the Kenyatta faction as it took an increasingly pro-business, antireformist stance.[5] Pio Gama Pinto, a leader with a redistributive agenda, was assassinated in 1965.[6] Odinga suggested that Pinto had died at the hands of the Kenyatta faction because of his Communist sympathies.[7] The subsequent trial strongly hinted at a government cover-up.[8]

The Pinto murder was but one indication that the Kenyatta state would wage a full-scale assault on its ideological enemies on the left. From the time Odinga and his supporters formed the KPU in 1966, they were hounded to their detention in 1969. Their departure ended any serious attempt to use Parliament as a tool to reform the state. It also capped the end of parliamentary supremacy and marked the emergence of Kenyatta as a dictator. In the 1970s, lone members of Parliament who questioned the failure of the state to transform society were every time met with an iron fist. One such politician, J. M. Kariuki, a former Mau Mau detainee and populist polemicist, was brutally assassinated by government agents in 1975.[9] In the 1980s and 1990s, the state under President Moi did not hesitate to eliminate, persecute, detain, and exile any Kenyan who dared question the class character of the state.[10]

The Rise of a Liberal Opposition

The politics of postcolonial states usually involve contests for power between different factions of the elite classes. The exception was during the era of the coup d'état—the 1960s to the 1980s—when a number of lower-ranking, sometimes uneducated military men ascended to power. Generally, however, elites have played a game of musical chairs to control the state. Rarely have grassroots movements outside elite classes ever produced senior leadership. Kenya has not been an exception, even though Moi had a very limited education. Still, he was considered a member of the African elite cultivated during the colonial period and catapulted to national leadership in the first African government. Ideologically, the Kenyan political elite has not been diverse. Even so, different iterations of the elite held the monopoly on power in KANU from 1969 to 1991. But opposition to KANU by various factions of the elite was often not based on ideology or a competing social vision.

To be sure, there was a small cadre of intellectuals, civil society activists, church leaders, politicians, and lawyers that sought to make Kenya a political democracy in principle. These reform-minded thinkers and activists believed that only a liberal democratic state could ensure the rule of law, human rights, and good government free of the endemic corruption that KANU had made into a culture. They deplored the caprice and arbitrariness of the one-party Kenyatta and Moi regimes. But the demands for an open political system were neither altruistic nor principled by many who jumped on that bandwagon. Many were driven by ethnic considerations and the quest for personal power. Kenyatta had packed the civil service with fellow Kikuyu elites and used the state to give them a large share of the economy, but Moi quickly removed the Kikuyu from many state positions and whittled down their access to and control of economic resources. In their place, he created a Kalenjin-dominated state bureaucracy to edge out elites in other groups in key economic sectors. Thus among certain elites, opposition to Moi and KANU was inspired more by economics and ethnicity rather than by politics. Elites had increasingly come to see the control of the state, the largest economic sector, as a zero-sum game. For the groups that had been shut out by KANU, the most viable route to political power and economic opportunity was through open political competition. Multipartyism was thus the only sure ticket back to power.

By the close of the 1980s, a consensus developed among many disaffected non-KANU political activists that Kenya had to lift the ban on open, competitive elections. Although these "outsider" elements spanned the political spectrum, they were brought together by their desire to end KANU's monopoly on politics and retire President Moi. They formed a broad coalition and exploited popular discontent among a general population that had become increasingly marginalized. Official corruption had skyrocketed to new levels, unemployment was out of control, infrastructure had nearly collapsed, schools and hospitals had sharply deteriorated, and an air of doom and gloom hung over the land. It was relatively easy for government critics to marshal public support for reforms under such dire circumstances. But precisely because of the unpopularity of the Moi regime, the opposition was not forced to articulate a coherent reformist agenda or an ideologically defensible platform. Membership in the opposition ranks had a low threshold and came cheap: distaste for Moi and KANU and loose rhetoric supportive of democracy, the rule of law, and human rights.

Once Section 2A was repealed in 1991, government opponents formed a number of political parties. The largest and most credible was the Forum for the Restoration of Democracy (FORD).[11] It brought together well-known opposition members, such as Odinga and Paul Muite, the chair of the Law Society of Kenya. But it was a loose receptacle for those opposed to the regime, whatever their political orientation. Haunted by its coalition nature, FORD soon splintered into two competing parties, substantially reducing the threat the opposition posed to KANU. Out of it was born FORD-Kenya and FORD-Asili, each headed by a major opposition figure. The third major party was the Democratic Party of Kenya (DP). The three would carry the hopes of the opposition to the general election against KANU on December 29, 1992. Other minor opposition political parties were also registered, including the Social Democratic Party (SDP), the Kenya National Democratic Alliance (KENDA), the Labor Party Democracy (LPD), the Party of Independent Candidates of Kenya (PICK), the Kenya Social Congress (KSC), and the Kenya National Congress (KNC). Some smaller parties, such as the Islamic Party of Kenya (IPK), were refused registration. The emergence of a legalized opposition signaled a sea change in Kenya's political landscape.

External factors played a large role in opening up Kenya's political system. In addition to domestic pressure, the reintroduction of competitive politics had been made possible by pressure exerted on Kenya by the West, especially the United States, which had downgraded Kenya's strategic importance after the Cold War.[12] The United States seemed to believe that the opposition that Smith Hempstone, the U.S. ambassador in Nairobi, had come to champion would serve its interests.[13] Although the United States and its European allies, particularly the United Kingdom, had largely been silent about abuses by both the Kenyatta and Moi regimes during the Cold War, the 1990s brought a more critical policy from the West. For the first time in Kenya's postcolonial history, Western governments and official institutions, including multilateral donor agencies, started to show some sympathy for the Kenyan reform movement. Before then, the only concern outside the country for Kenya's appalling human rights record had come solely from Western human rights groups such as Amnesty International, Human Rights Watch, the Lawyers Committee for Human Rights (later renamed Human Rights First), and the International Commission of Jurists. According to Joel D. Barkan, changed strategic interests led to a more positive policy by the West.[14]

An array of Western agencies and groups heightened their support for pro-democracy and human rights groups in Kenya.[15] Civil society organizations in Kenya, which arose in a climate of repression, found support in Western agencies and charities.[16] Mutahi Ngunyi has emphasized the crucial role played by bilateral and multilateral donors in promoting the civil society governance and human rights sectors.[17] Musambayi Katumanga captured the importance to civil society of donors' changing interests in Kenya.[18] The bottom line is that, although donors clearly pursued their own interests—usually consistent with the foreign policies of Western governments—they were a critical factor in enabling dissenting voices in Kenya. In turn, these voices became the impetus for the country's political opening. Nevertheless, one cannot lose sight of the agenda pushed by donors. They mostly supported elitist, middle-class groups in Nairobi. Such groups lacked a broad, deep base among the poor or the majority at the grassroots. Furthermore, the civil society engendered by these outsiders tended not to confront globalization and the privation wrought by market forces. Instead, it focused on political despotism. Donors thus generally incubated a conservative civil society in Kenya.

Multiparty politics in Kenya were deeply affected by the mixed fortunes of the original FORD. Prior to the legalization of independent political activity in 1991, opponents and critics of the government frequently spoke out against state repression. Much of the early criticism centered on the regime's appalling human rights record, particularly its contraventions of the rule of law. But among these critics, a cadre of young lawyers called the "Young Turks" captured the imagination of African constituencies in the West and gave the nascent reform movement international legitimacy. The focus of the youthful lawyers on liberal ideals such as judicial independence and the rule of law endeared them to leading Western international human rights organizations and lawyers' groups mentioned above. These groups frequently paraded the lawyers before American audiences, including the U.S. Congress, bar associations, and universities, and turned them into mini-celebrities.[19]

After these youthful political critics had demonstrated the vulnerability of the KANU government, a number of notable older ex-KANU politicians joined the growing chorus for multipartyism. Many of the newcomers had high profiles, owing to the notoriety of their service in the Kenyatta and Moi regimes. It was these two groups—the young and the old—that combined to form FORD. But FORD's senior leadership was drawn largely from the old guard because it was thought that they could provide the movement with instant credibility and legitimacy: Odinga, Martin Shikuku, and Masinde Muliro, all former cabinet ministers. Its brain trust was composed of lawyers Muite, Gitobu Imanyara, and James Orengo; Raila Odinga, the son of Oginga Odinga; Mukhisa Kituyi; and Peter Anyang' Nyong'o, a political scientist. The only common denominator among FORD members was their determination to remove President Moi and KANU from office.

However, FORD was soon wracked by ethnic, personal, and generational differences. Strangely, ideology was not a point of contention. Even so, the youth seemed more committed to liberalism, to which the old guard appeared only to pay lip service.[20] Instead of spending time putting together a comprehensive party platform and popularizing it across the country, FORD seemed to be more concerned with the pecking order of its leadership. A bitter power struggle, the central focus of which was picking the candidate for the presidency, ensued among the old men on top. The squabbling and narrow political ambitions sapped the party's energy, stunting political discourse. It prevented the development of a philosophy of reform beyond a rough and hazy outline of a liberal democracy with a free market system. The FORD Constitution provided, without any elaboration, its commitment to "serve as a political party with a view to establishing constitutional government, pluralist democracy, good governance, accountability and transparency in public affairs in Kenya."[21] It contained the kind of vacuous rhetoric those opposed to the autocracy of the one-party state under the Moi-KANU regime could easily accept. It was a bare statement of the central features of a liberal democracy, but without any hint of a social vision or any mention of how FORD would address the class character of the state.

In early 1992, it seemed as though FORD would stampede KANU at the polls. But its leadership, increasingly transfixed by the allure of power, was about to implode. The leadership wrangle pitted Kenneth Matiba, a wealthy businessman and a former cabinet minister under Moi, against Oginga Odinga, the grand doyen of opposition politics and FORD's interim chairman at the time. Matiba, detained in 1990 for advocating an open political system and released in 1991, had suffered a stroke, been sent to London for medical treatment, and returned to Kenya in May 1992. The rivalry between the two developed ethnic dimensions, with some of Matiba's Kikuyu supporters pressing for him over Odinga, a Luo. None of them appeared to be in good enough health to withstand the rigors of a presidential campaign in Kenya's rough-and-tumble politics. Odinga was an octogenarian, and Matiba could hardly read or write because of the debilitating stroke.

By June 1992, two distinct camps had emerged within the party. Odinga, Muite, and other so-called Young Turks led the key faction. Matiba and Shikuku, the interim FORD secretary-general, led the other. The jockeying for power dissipated public morale and eroded public confidence in the opposition. In September, the Matiba faction boycotted FORD's party congress, at which Odinga and Muite were elected chair and vice chair, respectively. In October, the Matiba faction held its own party congress, at which he was elected chair and Shikuku secretary-general. After a long delay, the government registered Odinga's faction as FORD-Kenya and Matiba's group as FORD-Asili. The division clearly benefited KANU and dampened public hopes for a formidable and united opposition against the Moi regime.

The bifurcated FORD now shared the opposition stage with Mwai Kibaki, the former minister of health who for a decade had served as vice president under Moi. Kibaki, a respected economist, had caused consternation and underlined the unpopularity of the KANU regime when he abruptly resigned in December 1991 to form the Democratic Party. DP was the largest ethnic-based party, attracting its support largely from the Kikuyu and kindred communities in Central Province and parts of Eastern Province. DP promised to restore investor confidence, rebuild the economy, and put the country back on track if elected. Of the opposition parties, the DP was the most vocal about its pro-market, growth-oriented party blueprint. In this respect, it appealed to large sections of the Kikuyu business elite who had suffered ignominiously under Moi and who now hungered for a return to the good old days of the Kenyatta regime.

Even though party platforms were rudimentary, the opposition was at the very least committed to competitive politics, the only avenue through which they could oust the Moi-KANU regime. Political elites had come to an agreement, even though reluctantly on the part of KANU, that access to the spoils of the state would henceforth be controlled through the ballot. Although there was little experience with open political competition or the role of a legalized opposition in the state, the right to govern would now be obtained by seeking legitimacy from citizens. Although it was clear that translating this formal normative commitment to liberalism into an institutional framework would be an arduous task, the political classes had agreed that legalized dictatorship could not be sustained. The pro-democracy movement had shown Kenyans that the state was not all-powerful and that popular pressure could dramatically influence public policy. A sense of people power had entered the political discourse, starting the process of transforming the relationship between the state and its citizens.

The Institution of Civil Society

Modern political democracies are not possible without vibrant, free, and activist civil societies.[22] In Africa, civil societies have arisen as a response to the dysfunction and despotism of the postcolonial state.[23] In Kenya, civil society organizations played an important role from the 1980s onward, as the state's inability to fulfill its functions increased. These organizations sought to reverse social decay, fight corruption, provide social services, and defend civil liberties. It is almost certain that Kenya would have been pushed to the edge of collapse without its civil society. But Kenya's civil society is a very recent phenomenon, an institution that is still seeking to define itself. Even so, it has not departed from the historical script identified by scholars elsewhere. Like its Western counterparts, Kenya's civil society is the large cartilage "between the simple world of the patriarchal household and the universal state."[24] Azzedine Layachi has called it the "independent eye" whose absence would ultimately mean that "those in power can turn into despots."[25] Civil society in Kenya has had to constantly fight for the right to exist while at the same time leading the movement for political democracy and human rights.

Since the late 1980s, a wave of democratic change has swept the African continent. Paul Tiyambe Zeleza notes that "at the beginning of 1990, all but five of Africa's 54 countries were dictatorships, either civilian or military."[26] Most African publics were totally excluded from effective political participation. But by 2004, most African states had succumbed to some form of political and economic reforms. In most cases, this period of political liberalization resulted in illiberal democracies. The process saw many reversals but also an upsurge in the formation of nongovernmental organizations (NGOs). Kenya had largely prevented the emergence of effective NGOs until the early 1990s, when open political activity was permitted. The majority of NGOs that the KANU state allowed to operate before had been nonpolitical, development, or women's groups that were largely co-opted by KANU.[27] Before 1991, the few vocal civil society organizations were the Law Society of Kenya; the university community; clerics; Wangari Maathai's Greenbelt Movement, an environmental activist group; and sections of the press. But they operated under constant persecution. Predictably, it was not until the early 1990s that a human rights movement emerged in Kenya, and became part of the open political landscape. It was both a Kenyan and continental phenomenon.[28]

The crucible of the Kenyan human rights movement has defined its identity and philosophical biases. The emergent human rights movement has been a rump extension of the so-called international human rights movement, which is based in the political capitals of the West. The conceptual bases, mandates, methods of work, and funding for Kenyan NGOs have largely been influenced by the "parent" organizations in the global North. Even though some local NGOs demonstrate originality in some areas, the influence of Amnesty International, Human Rights Watch, and the International Commission of Jurists (ICJ) remains evident. In that sense, they are miniature replicas. Even the Kenya Human Rights Commission (KHRC), the most prominent human rights group in Kenya, largely hewed to the traditional human rights format until its more recent campaigns in the areas of globalization, workers' rights, women's rights, economic and social rights, and grassroots mobilization in marginalized communities.

Like their counterparts in the West, human rights groups in Kenya tend to be lawyer-led and -driven. For example, in the 1970s lawyers founded the Legal Advice Centre, or Kituo Cha Sheria, literally the first human rights NGO in Kenya, to provide legal aid to the indigent. The KHRC, the Federation of Women Lawyers (Federacion International d'abogadas or FIDA), ICJ-Kenya, and the Institute for Education in Democracy have all been the preserve of lawyers. The symbiotic relationship between lawyers and human rights NGOs is not mysterious. Human rights are associated with the law and the discourse of rights, an idiom that is perceived to be the most effective tool for containing state despotism. More importantly, human rights groups in Kenya have generally focused on civil and political rights, the genre of entitlements that best secures a political democracy. Kenyan human rights groups have been largely formed as a response to state despotism.

In terms of a social base, the leadership of human rights groups in Kenya is drawn from the elite and middle classes, within either the intelligentsia or the professions. Human rights NGOs have attracted reform-minded activists who seek a democratic state. Although some have flirted with various models, including Marxism, the majority appear to have settled on political democracy as the system of choice. They regard political parties and basic civil rights as essential to a society. Although they are formally nonpartisan—not affiliated with a political party—there is little doubt that they support the emergence of a political democracy. These groups work to promote civil and political rights, particularly political participation rights such as the rights to assemble, associate, speak, publish, and organize, as well as due process, equal protection, and antidiscrimination norms. These rights are essential to an open democratic process, especially a free and fair election, which is the cornerstone of a political democracy.[29]

Civil society organizations often worked in tandem with opposition political parties to force KANU to adopt legal and political reforms and unlock its exclusive hold on political power. NGOs also served as a training ground for young politicians who later ran for public office. Civil society groups were instrumental in opening up the political space and pushing for reforms to level the playing field. Many, such as the Kenya Human Rights Commission, were influential in fostering the political coalition that eventually ousted the Moi-KANU regime from power in the pivotal 2002 general elections.[30] In a departure from tradition, the KHRC issued a lengthy statement in October 2002 endorsing Mwai Kibaki and the National Alliance Party of Kenya (NAK), the main opposition party, for the elections.[31] The endorsement, which was signed by me, as chair of the KHRC, and Willy Mutunga, its executive director, served to underline the extent of the involvement of civil society in the transition, as well as its unequivocal opposition to KANU.

Competitive Politics

Until 1990 KANU's supremacy in the country was unchallenged, and any attempts to question government policy or raise doubts about any of its leaders were taken as an act of disloyalty, or worse, a lack of patriotism. Moi, like his predecessor, did not hesitate to use the party machinery to sideline his critics or destroy their political careers.[32] He could do that because KANU enjoyed a monopoly on power, and lacked strong structures and internal democracy. Elections within KANU, which were rarely held, only ratified Moi's wishes and served to either strengthen those loyal to him or punish those suspected of harboring hostile intentions. KANU was so opaque and undemocratic that it did not know how to separate the party from the state or conform its behavior to the rules of open political competition. As a consequence, even though it had formally agreed to compete for power, for the next ten years until the National Rainbow Coalition (NARC) ousted it, KANU never abandoned its dictatorial culture, structures, and practices. Not surprisingly, KANU failed to fully grasp, accept, or embrace political democracy. Until the bitter end, KANU fought fiercely for a decade to retain power by attempting to destroy whatever seeds had been planted for a democratic dispensation.

Moi repeatedly warned that multipartyism would create tribalism, ethnic chaos, and civil war, an image that was meant to remind Kenyans of the relative calm they enjoyed compared to the bloodletting in several neighboring states.[33] The Moi-KANU government took a number of steps to hobble the opposition. The president liberally used his constitutional powers to appoint and dismiss officials, including judges, civil servants, and members of high-level commissions.[34] Repressive laws included the Preservation of the Public Security Act, under which the president could detain anyone without trial; the Chief's Authority Act, a relic of the colonial period that could be used to deny the rights to speech, assembly, and association; the Public Order Act, under which government administrators could deny permits for public gatherings; Kenya's penal code that broadly defined sedition and allowed the proscription of any publication on a wide variety of grounds; and the Societies Act, under which all associations, including political parties, had to be registered but could be refused registration or deregistered without any accountability.[35] In short, KANU was armed with a formidable arsenal of repressive tools with which to stall democratization.

Prior to the 1992 elections, opposition political parties and other critics called for constitutional and legal reforms to remove the overwhelming advantages enjoyed by KANU. The political transition required consultation and agreement between political and civil society stakeholders to gain legitimacy with the broad public. But it was clear that Moi and KANU were not interested in such consultations. However, several constitutional, legal, and institutional impediments were a matter of grave concern. First, it was crucially important that repressive constitutional provisions and laws that gave the government enormous powers to curtail basic freedoms be revised. Second, institutional structures such as the Electoral Commission of Kenya (ECK), which had never conducted a democratic election, and which was packed with KANU stalwarts who would now organize and oversee the multiparty elections, should have been reformed to make them nonpartisan. But Moi rejected all the proposals by the opposition and by civil society to enact needed reforms. Instead, the government unilaterally decided to effect minimal changes, many designed to insulate KANU from defeat.[36]

Several unilateral constitutional amendments prior to the election deserve mention. The most significant changed the matrix for electing the president. In addition to securing a plurality of the votes cast, the winning candidate had to garner at least 25 percent of the vote in at least five of the country's eight provinces.[37] The rationale behind the rule was to ensure that future presidents enjoyed broad national support, an important factor in a fractious multiethnic society. On the face of it, the rule was a plausible attempt to strengthen national consciousness and to avoid electing a president supported by merely the more populous regions and ethnic groups. But critics saw a sinister motive in the rule.[38] Opponents charged that it was meant to stop a candidate like Matiba or Odinga, who might win a plurality or even a majority of the vote but fail to meet the 25 percent rule in five provinces. After all, only KANU, with its established state machinery, resources, and the benefit of three decades of unchallenged supremacy, had the networks and the wherewithal to reach every nook and cranny of the country.[39] Critics also charged that the rule would compromise the one-person-one-vote principle since some provinces, such as the Northeastern Province, had fewer voters than some districts. But Moi wanted to blunt the advantage of his opponents in the densely populated opposition strongholds in Central, Nyanza, and Western provinces.[40] To ensure that he would remain president even if KANU lost the elections, the new constitutional amendment provided that the president must form the government from his party, even if that party was the minority in Parliament.[41]

The government sought to mollify the opposition by reforming the ECK but not ceding complete control of the electoral body. It eventually revised the constitution by formally separating the ECK from the attorney general's office, making it the sole institution responsible for the entire electoral process.[42] Although election laws were amended to give effect to these changes, the ECK was still headed and run by Moi appointees, which made it inaccessible to the opposition and hostile to their demands for a fair process.[43] Whereas previously the government had financed party nominations for elections, revisions to electoral laws now placed this expense with the parties themselves, a change that hamstrung opposition parties that did not have adequate resources or machinery to marshal funds.[44] Only KANU, with its control of the state and government structures, stood to benefit from the change. The National Elections Monitoring Unit (NEMU), a coalition of NGOs formed to monitor the 1992 elections, denounced KANU for these maneuvers.[45]

The registration of voters and campaigns took place in a climate of fear, mayhem, and intimidation. In March 1992, Moi banned opposition political rallies for two weeks while KANU operated unimpeded and imposed stringent conditions for permits even after the ban was lifted.[46] The Rift Valley, Moi's stronghold, was declared a "KANU only" zone, unleashing an open season of murder and pillage on members of the Kikuyu, Luo, and Luhya groups by government agents posing as members of the Kalenjin community.[47] Over 1,000 people deemed supportive of the opposition were killed in these so-called ethnic clashes. Many more were maimed, and their property was destroyed or confiscated.[48] In 1993, Moi reminded the country that he had "said in the past that when a multiparty system is introduced, it will create tribalism, divisions, and so on."[49] Even though the Moi-KANU party-state had acquiesced to multipartyism, it employed both legal and extrajudicial means, including the murder of innocents under the guise of ethnic conflict, to retain power.

The government took other measures to suppress basic freedoms in areas it perceived as opposition strongholds. Voter registration was slow in opposition zones, and at least a million young people were either not registered or experienced serious difficulties because they were denied the required national identity cards.[50] Droves of journalists were arrested in 1992, and tens of thousands of copies of independent publications, usually critical of KANU and the government, were confiscated by the state.[51] The persecution of the few independent publications was devastating to the opposition because the government held a monopoly on the electronic media and used the Kenya Broadcasting Corporation, the official media, to campaign for KANU and disparage the opposition. The government also dramatically expanded the supply of money to buy votes and purchase voters' cards, which are required in Kenya in addition to national identity cards, in opposition zones for destruction.[52] On December 29, 1992, Election Day, widespread irregularities were reported, including suspiciously high vote counts in government strongholds.[53] In short, the normative and institutional framework for multipartyism did not exist in 1992. As laid out in Table 5.1, the election results were not a surprise: Moi was returned to power with 36 percent of the vote; Matiba received 26 percent; Kibaki 19.5 percent; and Odinga 17.5 percent.[54] The opposition captured 88 seats in the 200-member chamber. NEMU, the coalition of domestic observers, declared that the elections had been neither free nor fair.[55]

Other observer groups, including the British Commonwealth and the International Republican Institute, concurred with NEMU, but they nevertheless accepted the election results.[56] Analysts offered three reasons for the Moi victory: that "Moi and KANU rigged it; that Moi and KANU had won it; or that the opposition lost it by splitting up."[57] The conclusion, even among Kenyans, was that all three were true.[58] The numbers seemed to bear them out. The tally for Matiba, Kibaki, and Odinga was 63 percent of the vote, a total that would have easily beaten Moi's 36 percent had they fielded one opposition candidate. But an immature opposition, wracked by narrow ethnic and petty agendas, had faced a dictatorial adversary in Moi and KANU and had come up empty. Even more important, the opposition lacked a galvanizing social vision, political

Table 5.1   Presidential Election Results, 1992

Name and Party	Number of Votes	Percentage of Total Vote
Moi, KANU	1,927,640	36.91
Matiba, FORD-A	1,354,856	25.95
Kibaki, DP	1,035,507	19.83
Odinga, FORD-K	903,886	17.31
Total	5,221,889	100.00

Source: Electoral Commission of Kenya, Nairobi, Kenya.

philosophy, and economic blueprint beyond undigested and vacuous notions about political democracy and free markets. Although there was consensus on political competition as a floor and on the need to remove Moi and KANU from power, the philosophical foundation of the reform movement was underdeveloped. Divided and faced by a deflated populace, the opposition could not mount a credible challenge to the results. Moi's victory was unassailable once election observers accepted the results. As two scholars put it, "popular disgust over the disunity and inflated egos of the opposition leaders that prevented a united opposition against Moi, made it virtually impossible for those leaders to mobilize the population in a rejection of the results."[59]

The 1992 elections exposed the underbelly of ethnicity in Kenyan politics and its stubborn persistence as an obstacle to nation building and democratization. One of the most irrepressible themes in Kenya is precolonial ethnic identity, understood here as postcolonial subnationalism or ethnicity, and its unquestioned ability to influence politics. It is a theme that dogged the Kenyatta presidency and that he deployed to great effect in constructing the postcolonial state, a tradition that Moi seemed to perfect. Tribalism, as the phenomenon is known in colonialist idiom, had become such a powerful currency in national politics that it robbed Kenya of a democratic transition in 1992. The parliamentary and presidential votes show the triumph of ethnic ideology over political liberalism.[60] These voting patterns will hamper the reform of the postcolonial state unless they are altered or accommodated in a constitutional order that takes the poison out of them.

All political parties, including KANU, arguably the most "national" of them, drew their support along ethnic lines. FORD-Asili was led by Matiba, a Kikuyu, and drew its largest support in Central and Nairobi provinces, two areas with large Kikuyu populations. Odinga, a Luo, led FORD-Kenya, the more national faction of the original FORD, but even it too drew most of its support from Nyanza, a province dominated by the Luo. DP, which was led by Kibaki, also a Kikuyu, drew most of its support from Central and Eastern provinces, areas inhabited by the Kikuyu, Meru, Kamba, and Embu, a cousinage of culturally and linguistically related peoples. Even though Paul Muite, a Kikuyu, was FORD-Kenya's vice president, Odinga's presidential bid fared poorly in Kikuyu-dominated areas. KANU, led by Moi, had its home base in the Rift Valley, the Kalenjin-dominated province, where it garnered overwhelming numbers. Moi then sneaked through by either rigging the vote in provinces without large "opposition" ethnic groups or relying on party and government machinery to coerce votes from four other provinces to meet the five-province, 25 percent rule. Not surprisingly, Moi only managed a scant 2 percent of the vote in Kikuyu-dominated Central Province.[61]

In spite of these questions, Kenyans and foreigners accepted flawed results for pragmatic reasons. Some took the philosophical view that a perfect political democracy could not be wished on Kenya overnight. Norms, institutions, and processes that engender and support democracy take time and hard work to construct as well as internalize in a populace. Elites, political parties, and citizens must learn democracy. Kenyans found that it was one thing to yearn for democracy but quite another to practice it. The elections also made clear that KANU would remain an impediment to democratization. Even so, the elections provided a political opening that could be expanded. As noted by Frank Holmquist and Michael Ford, the "expanded public voice provided everyone, and not just the middle class opinion-makers, with a well-earned sense of dignity and even confidence."[62] NEMU put a positive spin on the elections, seeing in them the most important step Kenya had ever taken toward the creation of a political democracy. It cited the large number of opposition MPs, the "open" nature of the elections compared to past KANU-only affairs, and the lessons taught by the electoral problems as critical milestones in the fragile process of nursing a democracy.[63] KANU's monopoly on power had been broken and demystified, and Kenya would never be the same again.

In spite of the significance of the 1992 elections, the proclivity of the state for violence and alienation from the populace continued unabated and, in some instances, got even worse. From 1993 to 1997, when multiparty general elections were held again, the Moi-KANU regime attempted to reverse the gains of the 1992 elections and turn back the clock, but to little avail. The opposition had engaged the KANU government in an incessant struggle to pry power from it, but more often than not it shot itself in the foot. Even so, Moi and KANU remained the greatest obstacle to constitutional, legal, political, and economic reforms. During the five-year span until 1997, there were notable developments, even though none of them normatively altered the character of the state. The most significant were the resurgence of political violence against government critics, the failure of the economy, and the increase in official corruption. Although formally now a democracy, the KANU-led postcolonial state was illiberal at its core, conceding the form but not the substance of political democracy.

The so-called tribal clashes, which had been orchestrated by the KANU party-state in 1991 to crush proponents of multipartyism, continued without pause into 1995. They reignited in 1997, with the second multiparty general elections just around the corner. This unprecedented wave of political violence, which was couched in ethnic terms, hit the Rift Valley, Western, Nyanza, and Coast provinces the hardest. In virtually all cases, it was directed toward "foreigners," a euphemism for African groups that had settled outside their precolonial ancestral areas. Much of the mayhem was directed at those areas and peoples perceived to be in the opposition. For no apparent reason, groups that had lived with each other relatively violence-free turned against each other in a murderous rage, inflicting heavy casualties on each other.[64] Investigations into these acts of pillage and death exposed senior government officials as key suspects, although no one was held to account.[65]

In 1993, the Goldenberg scandal, the largest case of official corruption in Kenyan history to that date, was exposed.[66] It involved a fraudulent scheme in which the public coffers were bilked of hundreds of millions of dollars in taxpayer funds. In the scheme, Kamlesh Pattni, a businessman, purported to export gold and diamonds, neither of which Kenya possessed. Pattni then presented fabricated export compensation claims for payment to the Central Bank of Kenya. Credible evidence linked the fraud to President Moi and his cronies, a fact that prompted Western donors led by the International Monetary Fund to suspend funding.[67] But Goldenberg was only one of several corrupt deals that were exposed; most were unknown to the public. As 1997 approached, the government stepped up its campaign of repression against opposition leaders and cadres, the press, human rights groups, and pro-reform organizations. Again, the government rejected any major constitutional, legal, or electoral reforms before the 1997 elections.

Even in 1997, the opposition still could not form a united front against KANU. Moi's opponents were even more splintered than in 1992. Opposition parties had multiplied; others had further split, creating a dizzying plethora of opposition voices. As in 1992, it seemed that they had decided to hang not together, but separately. The opposition was robbed of its dean when Oginga Odinga succumbed to a heart attack in 1994.[68] Odinga's death unleashed a power struggle within FORD-Kenya. Since there were no strong party structures and procedures, skullduggery took over; when the dust settled, Michael Kijana Wamalwa, a former law-lecturer-turned-politician, emerged at the helm. Importantly, Wamalwa, a Luhya, had prevented Raila Odinga, the veteran's son, from succeeding his father. His ambitions dashed, Raila Odinga decamped from FORD-Kenya with a large contingent of Luo politicians and took over the National Development Party (NDP), which he turned into the "Luo" party. Oginga Odinga's death decimated whatever pretensions FORD-Kenya still clung to of being a national party. It turned into an ethnic, Luhya party; the only prominent outsiders left in it were James Orengo, a Luo with a national outlook, and Gitobu Imanyara, a Meru human rights crusader and an original Young Turk. Muite, another original Young Turk and the presumptive opposition heir apparent to Oginga Odinga, left FORD-Kenya and founded Safina.

Safina was an offspring of the Mwangaza Trust, a collaborative effort of civil society and FORD-Kenya opposition politicians. Both groups were disaffected by the squabbles and petty ethnic politics that had gripped the opposition. Mwangaza was formed in 1993 to carry forward some of the more progressive ideals in the original FORD. Its trustees were Paul Muite, Peter Anyang' Nyong'o, Kiraitu Murungi, Richard Maore, Oki Ooko Ombaka, Farah Maalim, Joe Ager, Adelina Mwau, Wanjiku Kabira, Muturi Kigano, Willy Mutunga, Makau Mutua, Maina Kiai, Stanley Ngaithe, Agnes Chepkwony, Khadija Abdalla, Robert Shaw, and Ibrahim Mohamed. But the Moi regime deregistered

Mwangaza in 1995 when it got wind of its political agenda. However, Muite used its shell to form and register Safina in 1997 just before the elections.[69] But he was unsuccessful in getting his fellow Mwangaza trustees to join Safina, as many of them found refuge in ethnic-based parties.

In 1997, Moi faced fourteen opposition candidates. Charity Ngilu, a courageous DP opposition MP from Ukambani, left and took over the Social Democratic Party (SDP), a party with pretensions of social democracy, whose main ideologue was Peter Anyang' Nyong'o, a Luo academic who had been a leading figure in FORD-Kenya before its transmutation. Matiba, the FORD-Asili leader, boycotted the election, making himself and the party irrelevant in the process. Moi faced four serious "tribal" presidential candidates: NDP's Odinga for the Luo; SDP's Ngilu for the Kamba; FORD-Kenya's Wamalwa for the Luhya; and DP's Kibaki for the Kikuyu, Embu, and Meru. The election results were not a surprise. As illustrated in Table 5.2, Moi took 40.5 percent of the vote and 25 percent in the same five provinces he had won in 1992: Rift Valley, Coast, Eastern, Northeastern, and Western.[70] Kibaki received 31 percent of the vote, Odinga 10.9 percent, Wamalwa 8.2 percent, and Ngilu 8 percent.[71] Except for Moi, the other candidates performed dismally outside their ethnic bases. The 1997 election appeared to be a step backward for Kenya and did not represent a normative shift in the country's politics.

> Moi prevailed in Kenya's first two multiparty elections, held in 1992 and 1997, but with only a plurality of the vote. KANU won a narrow majority of seats in the National Assembly but not a majority of the votes cast. Both elections were characterized by unprecedented levels of communal violence and foul play. Neither could be described as free and fair, despite the presence of domestic and international observers. The main reason for the opposition defeat, however, was its failure to unite behind a single slate of candidates. In both elections, the opposition split its vote among three major ethno-regional parties and several smaller ones.[72]

The humiliating defeat of the opposition in 1997 had to do largely with the myopia of its leaders. It was a bitter lesson. In 2002, the opposition finally decided to come together in a united front against the Moi-KANU regime. Even then, the unity was forged out of luck, bungling by Moi, and public pressure. Barred by the constitution from running for another term, Moi chose Uhuru Kenyatta, a political novice but the scion of Jomo Kenyatta, Kenya's first president, as his heir apparent. The choice irreparably split KANU and caused a walkout by Raila Odinga, the popular Luo politician whom Moi had co-opted into KANU and the cabinet to save it from opposition defeat. Odinga, Kalonzo Musyoka, Moody Awori, William Ole Ntimama, and Vice President George Saitoti—arguably the most valuable KANU leaders—left the party to protest the slight. They had expected one of their own—Musyoka, Odinga, Saitoti, or Musalia Mudavadi—to be named KANU's presidential candidate.

Table 5.2   Presidential Election Results, 1997

Rank	Candidate	Votes	Percentage
1	Daniel arap Moi (KANU)	2,500,856	40.51
2	Mwai Kibaki (DP)	1,911,472	30.97
3	Raila Odinga (NDP)	667,886	10.82
4	Michael Wamalwa (FORD-Kenya)	505,704	8.19
5	Charity Ngilu (SDP)	488,600	7.91
6	Martin Shikuku (FORD-Asili)	36,512	0.59
7	Katama Mkangi (KNC)	23,554	0.38
8	George Anyona (KSC)	16,428	0.27
9	Kimani Wanyoike (FORD-People, an offshoot of the original FORD)	8,306	0.13
10	Koigi wa Wamwere (KENDA)	7,745	0.13
11	Munyua Waiyaki (United People's Party of Kenya, UPPK)	6,194	0.10
12	Godfrey Mwereria (Green African Party, GAP)	4,627	0.07
13	Wangari Maathai (Liberal Party of Kenya, LPK)	4,196	0.07
14	Stephen Oludhe (Economic Independence Party, EIP)	3,691	0.06
15	Joseph Ng'ethe (UPPK)		
Total		6, 185, 771	

Source: Institute for Education in Democracy (Kenya).

In November 2002, the KANU rebels, under the Liberal Democratic Party (LDP), joined NAK and formed the National Rainbow Coalition (NARC), a united opposition coalition with Kibaki as its flag bearer. NARC brought together the leading elites from four of the five major ethnic groups—Kikuyu, Luhya, Kamba, and Luo. Left only with the Kalenjin as their principal backers, KANU and its candidate Uhuru Kenyatta, a Kikuyu, could not overcome public resentment against the Moi-KANU regime and the public euphoria over NARC. On December 27, 2002, Kibaki and NARC overwhelmingly trounced Kenyatta and KANU at the polls. Kibaki captured 62 percent of the vote, and NARC won 125 seats, whereas KANU, Kenya's ruling party for four decades, managed only 64 seats.[73] Table 5.3 shows the overwhelming national vote for Kibaki, and Table 5.4 is the breakdown of the national vote by province. Table 5.5 is a tabulation of legislative seats by party, and Table 5.6 shows legislative seats by province. For the first time in Kenya's postcolonial history, regime change had been effected through the power of the ballot.

It took three elections—and ten years—for the Kenyan opposition to temporarily put aside its divisions and unite against KANU. NARC had campaigned on a reformist, democratic, and market-oriented agenda. It was expected to carry out sweeping reforms, end blatant official corruption, write a

Table 5.3   Presidential Election Results, 2002

	Party	Total Valid Votes
Mwai Kibaki	NARC	3,646,409
Uhuru Kenyatta	KANU	1,828,914
Simeon Nyachae	FORD-P	345,378
James Orengo	SDP	24,537
Waweru Ng'ethe	CCU	10,038
Total		5,855,276

Source: Institute for Education in Democracy (Kenya).

Table 5.4   Presidential Election Results by Province, 2002 (percentage of votes received)

	Kibaki	Uhuru	Nyachae	Orengo	Ng'ethe
Nairobi	76.5	20.8	2.4	0.2	0.1
Central	69.0	30.3	0.4	0.1	0.2
Eastern	72.5	26.2	0.8	0.3	0.2
Northeastern	28.1	67.1	4.6	0.2	0.1
Coast	62.8	33.4	3.2	0.4	0.2
Rift Valley	43.4	53.0	3.2	0.3	0.1
Western	76.3	21.5	1.4	0.5	0.3
Nyanza	61.4	7.6	29.8	1.1	0.1
Total	62.3	31.2	5.9	0.4	0.2

Source: Institute for Education in Democracy (Kenya).

Table 5.5   Legislative Seats by Party, 2002 Elections

	Candidates			Elected		
Party	Male	Female	Total	Male	Female	Total
NARC	195	13	208	117	8	125
KANU	207	2	209	63	1	64
FORD-People	178	7	185	14	0	14
FORD-Asili	37	4	41	2	0	2
Safina	56	3	59	2	0	2
Sisi Kwa Sisi	10	1	11	2	0	2
Shirikisho	16	1	17	1	0	1
All others	292	13	305			
Total	991	44	1,035	201	9	210

Source: Institute for Education in Democracy (Kenya).

Table 5.6 Legislative Seats by Province, 2002 Elections

	Nairobi	Central	Eastern	NEP[a]	Coast	R/Valley	Western	Nyanza	Total
NARC	8	21	22	1	11	18	22	22	125
KANU	0	6	9	10	7	30	2	0	64
FORD-P	0	0	1	0	2	1	0	10	14
SDP	0	1	0	0	0	0	0	0	0
Safina	0	0	1	0	1	0	0	0	2
Shirikisho	0	0	0	0	0	0	0	0	1
FORD-Asili	0	1	2	0	0	0	0	0	2
Sisi Kwa Sisi	0	1	1	0	0	0	0	0	2
Total	8	29	36	11	21	49	24	32	210

Source: Institute for Education in Democracy (Kenya).

Notes: a. NEP stands for Northeastern Province.

new constitution, institute transitional justice processes such as a truth commission, and revive the economy. However, nearly five years later, virtually the entire reform agenda has either been abandoned or repudiated. Grand corruption returned, and domestic and international support for the NARC state evaporated.[74] In February 2005, John Githongo, the respected anticorruption czar, resigned and went into exile, fearing for his life and unable to stop graft within government and among Kibaki's senior ministers.[75] Factional power struggles within NARC between the Odinga-led LDP faction and Kibaki's NAK took on ethnic dimensions.[76] These struggles finally killed NARC in 2005, when Kibaki sacked Odinga and his allies from the cabinet.

Notes

1. "Nandi Resistance Hero Caught in Political Wars of Today," *Sunday Nation,* October 23, 2005.

2. Elizabeth Mugi-Ndua, *Mekatilili wa Menza: Woman Warrior* (Nairobi: Sasa Sema Publications, 2000.

3. Zarina Patel, *Unquiet: The Life and Times of Makhan Singh* (Nairobi: Zand Graphics, 2006), 81–83.

4. Caroline Elkins, *Imperial Reckoning: The Untold Story of Britain's Gulag in Kenya* (New York: Henry Holt, 2005).

5. Oginga Odinga, *Not Yet Uhuru* (New York: Hill and Wang, 1967).

6. Patel, *Unquiet,* 449.

7. Odinga, *Not Yet Uhuru,* 287–288.

8. Ibid.

9. "Another Witness Goes to the Grave with Secrets of JM Murder," *Sunday Nation,* August 13, 2006; Africa Watch, *Kenya: Taking Liberties* (New York: Africa Watch, 1991), 7.

10. Human Rights Watch, *Playing with Fire: Weapons Proliferation, Political Violence, and Human Rights in Kenya* (New York: Human Rights Watch, 2002); Human Rights Watch, *Divide and Rule: State-Sponsored Violence in Kenya* (New York: Human Rights Watch, 1993); Koigi wa Wamwere, *Conscience on Trial: Why I Was Detained: Notes of a Political Prisoner* (Trenton, NJ: Africa World Press, 1993); Ngugi wa Thiong'o, *Barrel of a Pen: Resistance to Repression in Neo-Colonial Kenya* (Trenton, NJ: Africa World Press, 1988).

11. Eruch Nowrojee, "Kenya: Political Pluralism, Government Resistance, and United States Responses," *Harvard Human Rights Journal* 5 (1992): 149, 156.

12. Ibid.

13. Smith Hempstone, *Rogue Ambassador: An African Memoir* (Sewanee, TN: University of the South Press, 1997); Makau Mutua, "Why Hempstone Cannot Be My Hero," *Sunday Nation,* March 25, 2007.

14. Joel D. Barkan, "Kenya After Moi," *Foreign Affairs* 87, 89, no. 83 (2004).

15. Wachira Maina, "Kenya: The State, Donors and the Politics of Democratization," in *Civil Society and the Aid Industry,* ed. Alison Van Rooy (London: Earthscan Publications, 1998), 134; Maria Nzomo, "Civil Society in the Kenyan Political Transition: 1992–2002," in *The Politics of Transition in Kenya: From KANU to NARC,* ed. Oyugi Walter, Peter Wanyande, and C. Odhiambo-Mbai (Nairobi: Heinrich Böll Foundation, 2003).

16. Karuti Kanyinga, "The Socio-Political Context of the Growth of NGOs in Kenya," in *Economic Liberalization and Social Change in Africa,* ed. Peter Gibbon (Uppsala: Nordic African Institute, 1993).

17. Mutahi Ngunyi, "Civil Society and the Challenge of Multiple Transitions in Kenya," in *Civil Society and Democratic Development in Africa: Perspectives from Eastern and Southern Africa,* ed. Julius Nyang'oro (Harare: MWENGO, 1999), 117; Ngunyi, *Democracy and the Aid Industry in Kenya: An Assessment of Grantmaking to the DG Sector of Civil Society in Kenya* (Leeds: University of Leeds/SAREAT, 1999).

18. Musambayi Katumanga, *Cascading Donor Interest and the Democratic Transition in Kenya* (Nairobi: IPAR, 1998); Makau Mutua, ed., *Human Rights NGOs in East Africa: Political and Normative Tensions* (Philadelphia: University of Pennsylvania Press, forthcoming).

19. One of the lawyers, Gibson Kamau Kuria, was the recipient of the 1988 Robert F. Kennedy Human Rights Award; see Drew S. Days, *Justice Enjoined: The State of the Judiciary in Kenya* (New York: Robert F. Kennedy Memorial Center for Human Rights, 1992), xiv.

20. David Gillies and Makau wa Mutua, *A Long Road to Uhuru: Human Rights and Political Participation in Kenya* (London: Westminster Foundation for Democracy, 1993), 19–20.

21. Forum for the Restoration of Democracy, Draft Constitution, Section 2(b), August 1992.

22. Jean L. Cohen and Andrew Arato, *Civil Society and Political Theory* (Cambridge, MA: MIT Press, 1992).

23. Claude E. Welch, Jr., *Protecting Human Rights in Africa: Strategies and Roles of Non-Governmental Organizations* (Philadelphia: University of Pennsylvania Press, 1995), 43.

24. John Keane, "Despotism and Democracy: The Origins and Development of the Distinction Between Civil Society and the State Since 1750–1850," in *Civil Society and the State,* ed. John Keane (New York: Verso, 1988), 35, 50.

25. Azzedine Layachi, "Algeria: Reinstating the State or Instating a Civil Society," in *Collapsed States: The Disintegration and Restoration of Legitimate Authority,* ed. I. William Zartman (Boulder: Lynne Rienner Publishers, 1995), 171, 172.

26. Paul Tiyambe Zeleza, "Introduction: The Struggle for Human Rights in Africa," in *Human Rights, the Rule of Law, and Development in Africa,* ed. Paul Tiyambe Zeleza and Philip J. McConnaughay (Philadelphia: University of Pennsylvania Press, 2004).

27. Between 1975 and 1985, the number of NGOs in Kenya grew from 100 to 400. Alan Fowler, "The Role of NGOs in Changing State Society Relations: Perspectives from Eastern and Southern Africa," *Development Policy Review* no. 9 (1991): 80.

28. Stephen Ndegwa, *The Two Faces of Civil Society: NGOs and Politics in Africa* (Bloomfield, CT: Kumarian Press, 1996); Makau wa Mutua, ed., *Human Rights NGOs in East Africa: Political and Normative Tensions* (Philadelphia: University of Pennsylvania Press, 2008); Mutua, "African Human Rights Organizations: Questions of Legitimacy and Context," in Zeleza and McConnaughay, *Human Rights, the Rule of Law, and Development in Africa*, 194.

29. Makau wa Mutua, "The Ideology of Human Rights," *Virginia Journal of International Law* 36 (1996): 589.

30. Athena Mutua, ed., *Eyes on the Prize* (Nairobi: Kenya Human Rights Commission, 2003).

31. Kenya Human Rights Commission, "Why and How to Bring About Regime Change in Kenya," ibid., 25.

32. Jennifer Widner, *The Rise of a Party-State in Kenya: From Harambee to Nyayo!* (Berkeley: University of California Press, 1992).

33. Joel A. Solomon, *Failing the Democratic Challenge: Freedom of Expression in Multi-Party Kenya* (Washington, DC: Robert F. Kennedy Memorial Center for Human Rights, 1994), 8.

34. Maina Kiai, *The Legitimization of Repressive Laws and Practices in Kenya* (Nairobi: Kenya Human Rights Commission, 1994).

35. Ibid., Appendices 1–6.

36. National Elections Monitoring Unit, *The Multi-Party General Elections in Kenya, 29 December 1992* (Nairobi: NEMU, 1993), 23.

37. Section 3, *The Constitution of Kenya (Amendment) Act*, 1992.

38. Makau wa Mutua, "Roadblock to Democracy in Kenya," *Boston Globe* (October 26, 1992); Brian Atwood, "Kenya's Rigged Election," *Christian Science Monitor,* September 2, 1992.

39. National Elections Monitoring Unit, *The Multi-Party General Elections in Kenya,* 23.

40. Mutua, "Roadblock to Democracy."

41. Section 4, *The Constitution of Kenya (Amendment) Act*, 1992.

42. Section 42A, *The Constitution of Kenya.*

43. David Gillies and Makau wa Mutua, *A Long Road to Uhuru: Human Rights and Political Participation in Kenya* (London: Westminster Foundation for Democracy, 1993), 8–9.

44. *Elections Laws (Amendment) Act*, 1992.

45. National Elections Monitoring Unit, *The Multi-Party General Elections in Kenya,* 21.

46. Solomon, *Failing the Democratic Challenge*, 14.

47. See National Council of Churches of Kenya (NCCK), *The Cursed Arrow: A Report on Organized Violence Against Democracy in Kenya* (Nairobi: National Council of Churches of Kenya, 1992); National Assembly, *The Report of the Parliamentary Select Committee to Investigate Ethnic Clashes in Western and Other Parts of Kenya* (Nairobi: National Assembly of Kenya, 1992).

48. Africa Watch, *Divide and Rule: State-Sponsored Ethnic Violence in Kenya* (New York: Human Rights Watch, 1993).

49. "President Moi Defends Kenya's Human Rights Record," FBIS-AFR-93-189, October 1, 1993, 3, from Kenya Broadcasting Corporation Television, September 29, 1993.

50. Frank Holmquist and Michael Ford, "Kenya: State and Civil Society the First Year After the Election," *Africa Today* 41 (1994): 7–8.

51. Committee to Protect Journalists, *Attacks on the Press* (New York: Committee to Protect Journalists, 1992), 47.

52. Holmquist and Ford, "Kenya: State and Civil Society," 7–9.

53. Ibid., 8.

54. Solomon, *Failing the Democratic Challenge,* 14–15.

55. National Elections Monitoring Unit, *The Multi-Party General Elections in Kenya,* 90.

56. Holmquist and Ford, "Kenya: State and Civil Society," 8.

57. Ibid.

58. Ibid.

59. Ibid., 9.

60. Joel D. Barkan, "Kenya: Lessons from a Flawed Election," *Journal of Democracy* 4 (1993): 85, 88; Githu Muigai, "Ethnicity and the Renewal of Competitive Poli-

tics in Kenya," in *Ethnic Conflict and Democratization in Africa,* ed. Harvey Glickman (Atlanta: African Studies Association Press, 1995).

61. Barkan, "Kenya: Lessons from a Flawed Election," 97.

62. Holmquist and Ford, "Kenya: State and Civil Society," 9.

63. National Election Monitoring Unit, *The Multi-Party General Elections in Kenya,* 90–91.

64. Republic of Kenya, *Report of the Task Force on the Establishment of a Truth, Justice, and Reconciliation Commission* (Nairobi: Government Printer, 2003), 22.

65. Law Society of Kenya, *Impunity: Report of the Law Society of Kenya on the Judicial Commission of Inquiry into Ethnic Clashes in Kenya* (Nairobi: Law Society of Kenya, 2000); Republic of Kenya, *Report of the Judicial Commission of Inquiry into Ethnic Clashes in Kenya* (Akiwumi Report) (Nairobi: Law Society of Kenya, 2002).

66. Republic of Kenya, *Report of the Judicial Commission of Inquiry into the Goldenberg Affair* (Bosire Report) (Nairobi: Government Printer, October 2005); Catherine Gacheru, "Goldenberg: It Goes to the Top," *Daily Nation,* October 5, 2000.

67. Joel D. Barkan, "Leakey Saved Elephants: Now the Public Purse?" *Christian Science Monitor,* August 11, 1999; Human Rights Watch, *World Report 2000: Events of 1999* (New York: Human Rights Watch, 2000), 50.

68. "Odinga Is Dead," *Daily Nation,* January 21, 1994, 1.

69. Willy Mutunga, *Constitution-Making from the Middle: Civil Society and the Transition Politics in Kenya, 1992–1997* (Harare: MWENGO, 1999), 140.

70. Charles Hornsby, "Election Day and the Results," in *Out for the Count: The 1997 General Elections and the Prospects for Democracy in Kenya,* ed. Marcel Rutten, Alamin Mazrui, and François Grignon (Kampala: Fountain Publishers, 2001), 135, 139.

71. Ibid., 140.

72. Joel D. Barkan, "Kenya After Moi." See also J. Harbeson, "Guest Editor's Introduction: Political Crisis and Renewal in Kenya: Prospects for Democratic Consolidation," *Africa Today* 45 (1998): 161–184; Frank Holmquist and M. Ford, "Kenyan Politics: Toward a Second Transition?" *Africa Today* 45 (1998): 22–58.

73. Institute for Education in Democracy, *Enhancing the Electoral Process in Kenya: A Report on the Transition General Elections 2002* (Nairobi: Institute for Education in Democracy, 2003).

74. Makau Mutua, "NARC Has Rejected the Path of Reforms," *East African Standard,* September 4, 2004.

75. Mugumo Munene, "Why Githongo Is Not Likely to Return Soon," *Daily Nation,* February 14, 2005.

76. Makau Mutua, "End of Reforms in Kenya," *Boston Globe,* August 14, 2004.

6

The Quest for a
Democratic Constitution

SINCE THE LATE 1980s, Africa has seen a gradual repudiation of one-party civilian and military dictatorships. Political transitions from closed to more open societies have been the norm. There are three basic avenues through which political liberalization has taken place, although in each case the political opening was brought about by a combination of domestic and international pressure. Incumbent regimes either have legalized the political opposition through constitutional amendments, have been forced to cede power through national conferences, or have carefully managed reforms to permit minimal change.[1] In the case of Kenya, it seemed as though the opposition would stampede Kenya African National Union (KANU) out of power immediately after the prohibition on multipartyism was lifted in 1991. But through the deft and ruthless use of the extensive apparatuses and resources of the state, President Daniel arap Moi quickly recovered from the gathering political storm, took back the initiative, and started to dictate both the pace and content of reforms. Until the late 1990s, Kenya's transition was largely dominated by the state.

The Coalition for a National Convention

The political transition from an authoritarian, illiberal state to a more open society in Kenya has centered on the constitution. The Lancaster Constitution, which was imposed on Kenyans by the British and mutilated by the Kenyatta and Moi regimes, failed to create an open society. The members of the emergent ruling class did not defend or protect the Lancaster Constitution because they did not believe in it and needed to neutralize it to consolidate their power. Starting in the 1980s, two schools of thought emerged in Kenya with respect to the democratic transformation of the state. The first, whose adherents advocated for the legalization of the opposition, argued for minimum legal and constitutional reforms to level the playing field. Its main objective was the capture of state power. The second school, prevalent within the emergent civil society organizations, called for a constitutional overhaul of the state and a basic reformulation of the purposes of political society. Although the two schools formed the opposition to the Moi-KANU regime until 2002, their visions of reform sharply diverged beyond a certain point because of these fundamental differences.[2]

The pressure for reforms markedly increased after 1990. Government critics called for a national conference to introduce political democracy.[3] One argued, in a widely held view, that the national debate was not simply about multipartyism but about the "most appropriate political system that would create the politically suitable conditions within which Kenyans can meaningfully pursue and achieve their social, cultural, economic, and other related societal goals."[4] The government did not create any enabling conditions for reform, however, beyond the repeal of the ban on political parties. The nascent opposition political parties did not seem enthusiastic about key reforms before the elections. It fell on civil society, including religious groups, to lead the charge for reforms to make sure that the elections would be free and fair at a minimum. To this end, the National Council of Churches of Kenya (NCCK), a critic of the KANU, organized two national meetings to debate the transition. But the agenda was limited to opposition unity and the narrow rules governing the staging of an open election.[5] The second meeting, however, took on a broader agenda, including the need for a national convention to debate a new constitution. The pressure for this more comprehensive agenda came from the Kenya Human Rights Commission (KHRC) and Release Political Prisoners (RPP), two advocacy human rights organizations that would play critical roles in the transition. In June 1992, both the KHRC and RPP led advocacy groups and minor political parties in forming the Coalition for a National Convention (CNC), a pressure group that sought the fundamental restructuring of the state, instead of a narrow focus on elections and the transfer of political power from one faction of the political class to another.[6]

The CNC's agenda for a national convention prior to the 1992 elections was complex. Among its key planks were the dissolution of Parliament, the readoption of the 1963 Lancaster Constitution, and the creation of a transitional government.[7] The CNC called for the boycott of the 1992 elections, including voter registration. However, the push for a national convention, which the CNC saw as the only tool for the fundamental reformation of the state, did not gain broad support among Kenyan political and religious elites. The main opposition political parties only paid lip service to it, whereas religious organizations, such as the NCCK, did not actively promote it. As Willy Mutunga writes, "opposition political parties were horrified by the proposals for a transitional government" because they believed that they would beat KANU at the polls and take over the state.[8] They had no real interest in any project that would delay their assumption of power, although they, like the establishment religious groups, did not publicly distance themselves from the idea of a national convention. But Western donors who had committed political clout and resources to the electoral process did not support a national convention either and instead focused on the elections. To them, the political opening was a significant advance for Kenya. But the CNC urged a boycott, warning that the elections would be neither free nor fair and that Moi and KANU would rig themselves back to power absent serious reforms.[9] Even so, Kiraitu Murungi, then a leader in FORD-Kenya, argued that the allure of power was too great for the opposition to resist.

> The issue of constitutional reform and creation of a sound legal framework for multi-party and free and fair elections had been raised by a section of opposition politicians, civil society and religious organizations prior to the 1992 elections. The mainstream opposition parties, however, decided to "win" the elections first and then change the constitution once they got to State House. The feeling was that since we were winning the elections anyway, the reforms could wait until the opposition came to power. An attempt to boycott the voter registration exercise in 1992 was abandoned when the consensus on the issue collapsed.[10]

As the CNC had predicted, the opposition lost the 1992 elections to Moi and KANU. There was a consensus that the elections had been neither free nor fair, although observers accepted the results because the divisions in the opposition contributed to the loss. FORD-Kenya, FORD-Asili, and DP—the three major opposition political parties—tried but failed to reject the elections because they could not agree on the modalities for the challenge. The CNC rejected the calls for a fresh election and instead urged the opposition to push for a national convention, which it saw as the only midwife for reform. The defeat demoralized the opposition and created further rifts within it. Although it was clear that the main political parties had been their own worst enemy—by failing to demand reforms before the elections—they now sought to blame others for their loss. Inexplicably, they placed the blame not on themselves but on religious organizations and donors. As Murungi said, "We blamed the churches and the donors for not supporting the boycott and urging the opposition to participate in the flawed elections."[11]

The 4Cs and the Model Constitution

The disappointment of the 1992 elections deflated the political opposition and propelled its leadership into petty squabbles. Struggles for power erupted within the parties themselves. Virtually all the parties took an ethnic identity as the leadership was reshuffled. As Murungi notes, "During this period, constitutional reform had taken a back seat and was only addressed by individual politicians on an ad hoc basis."[12] But the betrayal of the reformist project of the CNC by the political and religious elites only served to invigorate the civil society's determination for fundamental constitutional change. The period from 1993 to 1997 was a high-water mark for the young advocacy human rights and rule of law organizations. For the first time in the history of the country, the most important political initiative was driven not by the state or the opposition, but by emergent human rights groups. The most important of these groups was the KHRC, which took over the agenda of the CNC. Formed and registered in 1991 in the United States, the KHRC relocated to Kenya in 1992, where it became the country's first human rights organization with a broad agenda.[13] In 1993, the KHRC started work on a draft constitution that was the impetus for a new national effort on constitution making. Murungi correctly acknowledges that it was "only the legal and human rights NGOs which kept the agenda for constitutional reform alive."[14]

By the mid-1990s, the leadership of the human rights NGOs formed the Citizens' Coalition for Constitutional Change, better known as the 4Cs, its acronym. The 4Cs core comprised the KHRC, the Kenya branch of the International Commission of Jurists (ICJ-Kenya), and the Law Society of Kenya (LSK) and was led by Willy Mutunga, Maina Kiai, Paul Wamae, and Christopher Mulei—all lawyers from those organizations.[15] It was later expanded to include a wide range of stakeholders, most from civil society, but was also supported by religious organizations and opposition politicians. The call for a new constitution by the Catholic Church gave more legitimacy to the efforts to produce a draft constitution. In 1994, the 4Cs officially published a draft constitution entitled *Proposal for a Model Constitution.*[16] The launch of the draft constitution drew participation from a wide cross-section of institutions, including the clergy and the opposition. Their endorsement gave new impetus to the growing demands for a democratic constitution and fired the public's imagination.[17] While feuds, schemes, and plots for power paralyzed leaders in the opposition, the civil society had taken the upper hand in the initiative to reform the state.

The Model Constitution was an ambitious document that sought to rewrite the basis of political power while radically altering the relationship between the state and its people. Its central purpose was to fundamentally re-create the normative and structural edifices of the state and to transform the rationale of the predatory postcolonial state. The Model Constitution sought to introduce a new constitutional order to salvage the postcolonial state. Its key principles were the introduction of genuine multipartyism with an accountable executive; separation of powers; creation of a national, as opposed to an ethnic, consciousness; reconstitution of citizenship; respect for human rights; an autonomous legislature; representation and political participation; an independent judiciary; reform and democratization of the executive; fiscal accountability; and land reform.[18] This menu was meant as a guide for the questions that broad cross-sections of Kenyans should debate as they wrote a new constitution. It was not itself a constitution. Nevertheless, it was a radical departure from the extant constitutional order that protected the interests of a narrow kleptocracy. It was remarkable that a tiny but vocal section of civil society could transform the terms of the political debate in an illiberal, closely controlled postcolonial state. Mutunga, the political and intellectual leader of the civil society constitutional reform effort, has written that the 4Cs had to adopt cautious and reassuring tactics to assuage the fears of those who were likely unhappy with a process they deemed radical and threatening.

> The 4Cs needed to survive the slippery terrain of Kenyan politics. It had to address the diversionary politics of the regime that clearly did not want a constitution-making project that it did not control. It had to negotiate and co-exist with an opposition that was interested in a narrow project in constitution making, namely, constitutional reforms that guaranteed free, fair and peaceful elections. It had to persuade the international community of the stabilizing effect of its mission . . .
>
> The issue of the identity of the 4Cs was quickly disposed of. A logo was chosen: a flying white dove in a background of black, green, and turquoise. This logo represented an emphatic mission of an active, non-violent, legal, moral, and peaceful constitution-making project.[19]

How did the political class squander the reformist moment made possible by multipartyism? Growing pains in the official opposition were partially responsible for the disarray and myopia within it and could have explained its lack of strategic vision. However, more serious problems may have been at work. Peter Anyang' Nyong'o, a founding member of the Forum for the Restoration of Democracy (FORD), has written that the opposition was held back by old-style, independence-era political leaders. He has argued that the leaders and "their strong ethnic constituencies were specialists in the zero sum game of politics and were averse to the politics of compromise to achieve goals greater than their individual egos and ambitions."[20] Amplifying this theme, Anyang' Nyong'o has cautioned that "one thing that the pro-democracy forces have had to contend with is how to build democracy where tribalism and fascism are both popular—where political parties, in order to build a popular base, find it easy to advocate tribalistic and fascistic ideologies."[21] But Anyang' Nyong'o is too quick to absolve the so-called Young Turks who were an integral part of the opposition leadership from any responsibility. Most lined up behind their "tribal barons." It was clear that the quest for political power alone, especially in an ethnically tormented society, is not sufficient to cohere a democratic political movement.

The Model Constitution proposed by the 4Cs caught the attention of the government and the opposition political parties. Sensing a political threat from the public momentum created by the Model Constitution, President Moi moved quickly to seize the initiative for constitutional reform from civil society. On New Year's Eve in 1995, he shocked the nation when he stated that Kenya needed a new constitution and outlined a hazy process for it.[22] In Moi's scheme, foreign experts would collect the views of Kenyans, draft a constitution, and hand it over to Parliament for discussion and ratification—a top-down, government-driven process.[23] It was a classic Moi maneuver: hijack, repress, demonize, quash, ignore, or sidestep democratic and popular reformist initiatives. But Kenyans across the board found his call for foreign experts particularly insulting, and that alone helped coalesce opposition to his initiative and give unexpected impetus to demands for a "people-driven" constitutional review process. Unwittingly, Moi had further galvanized the country and put constitutional reform at the center of public discourse. The 4Cs saw Moi's statement as an opportunity to energize its base.

> Ordinary Kenyans did not participate in the Lancaster House constitutional conferences. The constitution that emerged as the Independence Constitution was as foreign as the place where it was made [London]. The Steering Committee [of the 4Cs] stated clearly that there was adequate local expertise and resources to carry out the exercise and, moreover, that calling in foreigners to draft the constitution was unpatriotic. The Steering Committee stated that it was clear that the President's announcement meant that he alone had decided on the process on behalf of 25 million Kenyans. He had devalued the citizenship of all Kenyans.[24]

Collaboration, Conflict, and Betrayal

By 1994, opposition political parties had realized that government harassment would consign them to irrelevance if they did not develop an agenda for reform. The exercise of arbitrary power by the executive continued in spite of the introduction of multipartyism.[25] It was in this atmosphere that the opposition started to organize parliamentary caucuses to fight back. Still, many of these forums lacked clarity and did not properly diagnose the nation's malaise. Although they appeared to be driven by noble ideals, narrow agendas threatened to derail them. Murungi, the opposition politician whose tent was pitched between the opposition political parties and civil society, stated the need for these caucuses eloquently.

> Some of us in the opposition were feeling frustrated that personal ambitions, ethnic suspicion, and intra-party rivalry were paralyzing the opposition and depriving Kenyans of a chance to have a clean democratic government. By mid-1994, various opposition caucuses were holding meetings to discuss ways and means of fielding a single opposition presidential candidate and creating a level electoral playing field through constitutional and legal reforms. There was a common feeling that the opposition needed a new initiative along these lines if it was to avoid an electoral disaster in 1997.[26]

But participants in the forums soon realized that they lacked the ability, time, resources, and logistical support to produce a coherent agenda for reform.

It took them a while to realize that civil society could be used to their advantage. Before then, only a handful of politicians, among them Muite, Murungi, and Anyang' Nyong'o, had an appreciation for the central place of civil society in the reform process. Anyang' Nyong'o alluded to this hostility between civil society and political parties when he accused Mutunga of treating political parties shoddily in the book Mutunga had written on constitution-making. He wrote that Mutunga had treated political parties "as a nuisance in the process of change: meddlesome, not to be trusted, opportunistic."[27] This distrust between civil society and political parties is a natural reflection of the tension between the two sectors. Political parties are essentially governments in waiting because they seek to capture political power. Historically, however, civil society has not sought the capture of power but rather has striven to influence the exercise of power.[28] This mutual suspicion existed when the opposition and civil society shared a common foe in the KANU state and will persist in perpetuity.

Distrust between the opposition and civil society notwithstanding, the two sectors intensified consultations on reforms in late 1995. That year, Moi and KANU had gone back on an earlier promise to give Kenyans a new constitution, arguing that there was no crisis to warrant a new basic law. However, in October 1996 Moi announced that Kenya needed comprehensive constitutional reform, but that such an enormous task could not be carried out until after the 1997 elections. Moi had calculated that he would most likely lose elections under a new constitutional order. The president's chicanery convinced the 4Cs and the opposition that he was intent on stealing the election. The government's intransigence only served to drive the opposition and civil society into each other's arms, their distaste for each other notwithstanding. Their most important collaboration was the 4Cs-inspired National Convention Assembly (NCA), the national forum that sat on three separate occasions, in April, August, and October 1997. At the second sitting, irreconcilable differences of vision and strategy about the nature of reforms emerged between the opposition political parties and civil society.

The first session of the national convention took place in Limuru, just outside Nairobi, and was attended by over 500 delegates from every sector of society except KANU and the government. The delegates included opposition political parties, religious organizations, civil society, professional associations, women's groups, and the media. The convention agreed on a menu of minimum constitutional and legal reforms to make the 1997 elections free and fair, including constitutional amendments to reduce the powers of the president, public funding of political parties, and the barring of defections of MPs to other parties. Repressive laws would be repealed, and other measures, including affirmative action, would be implemented to create a fair and level playing field.[29] The convention resolved that its participants would boycott the elections if the government refused to enact the minimum reforms. But the NCA, at least from the view of civil society, saw these minimum reforms simply as a precursor to a more comprehensive constitutional overhaul after the elections.

The NCA created the National Convention Executive Council (NCEC), its executive arm, to advocate for the implementation of the minimum reforms.

KANU rejected the minimum reform agenda on the pretext that the country needed comprehensive constitutional review, not a patchwork of reforms, but the NCEC had captured the imagination of the Kenyan public. In the words of Anyang' Nyong'o, it had become a "potentially formidable mass movement once it got opposition political parties backing it."[30] The NCEC organized mass rallies from May to October 1997 to promote the agenda for minimum reforms. The "mass action" rallies drew large crowds. Kenyans, including the cautious professional classes, came in droves to the rallies. The KANU government responded to the rallies with savage brutality, killing at least thirteen people on Saba Saba, named for the rally on July 7, 1997. It even used private militias to attack peaceful demonstrators. The Moi regime was determined to stop the constitutional reform movement by any means necessary. Senior government officials insisted that the state did not recognize the NCEC and rebuffed its overtures.

The NCA took place amid a deteriorating political and security climate in the country. Positions hardened on all sides. The NCEC felt that the Moi-KANU regime was hell-bent on violently crushing the pro-democracy movement to perpetuate itself in power. The broad base of the NCEC, as well as the national convention, which included political parties, was to prove its undoing. Although it was necessary for the NCEC and the national convention to be as inclusive as possible, particularly of the opposition political parties, there was competition for supremacy between the political parties and civil society and conflict among various sectors because of the class interests they represented. One poignant question concerned the depth and reach of the reform agenda. Some of the senior leaders of the political parties were apprehensive of the radicalization of NCEC by its civil society leadership and the youth. "Old guard" opposition politicians, such as Mwai Kibaki of the DP, Martin Shikuku of FORD-Asili, and Michael Kijana Wamalwa of FORD-Kenya, grumbled that the convention was biased in favor of James Orengo, Paul Muite, and Raila Odinga, who were regarded as more youthful and radical. Wamalwa publicly stated that Safina, the party headed by Muite, had hijacked the convention.[31] As told by Mutunga, students at the convention were scathing in their attack on political leaders, whom they accused of wavering on the minimum reform agenda.

> The students read their list of "antireformists." Mwai Kibaki, Kenneth Matiba, Kijana Wamalwa, Martin Shikuku, and Charity Ngilu were named as violators of the NCA's [National Convention Assembly] resolution that there would be no elections before the facilitative or minimum reforms were enacted. The students claimed that the political leaders had by their actions or utterances violated the word and spirit of the resolution.[32]

In this charged atmosphere, the national convention contemplated the assumption of political power by establishing a parallel government, in effect a civilian coup. Delegates were very much aware of the phenomenon of sovereign national conferences that earlier in the decade deposed dictatorships and introduced more open governments in a number of states, including Benin, Mali, and Congo.[33] There was substantial support for continued mass action to force reforms on the KANU regime or sweep it aside by setting up a government of national unity. But the nuclear option was abandoned because political parties, religious organizations, and many in the middle classes did not favor it. Some argued that a parallel government could have provoked massive retaliation by the KANU state, precipitating a civil war. The delegates had come to the brink and chose not to tempt fate. Instead, they agreed on what many considered a less risky alternative. Mutunga has written that the "compromise, which seemed to be a relief to the convention, was that in the event Parliament was dissolved before the enactment of the minimum or facilitative reforms, the NCA would constitute itself into a Constituent Assembly."[34] For one, Mutunga has dismissed as exaggerated the possibility of a civil war and argued that the softer option reflected the cautionary posture of the middle class, which in effect bought the Moi-KANU regime a new lease on life.[35] But Anyang' Nyong'o, a politician himself, has differed, arguing that Moi could have gone to any length to keep power.

> Willy [Mutunga] says that the danger of civil war was exaggerated. I do not think so. Especially noting the steps the regime eventually took to rig the elections. If they could keep power through rigged elections, they would have maintained the same by keeping elections away through a regime coup. The NCEC was planning a civilian coup; what type of coup was the regime expected to plan? Of course both a civilian and military coup.[36]

To the surprise of civil society at the national convention, it was revealed that opposition politicians were involved in parallel secret negotiations with KANU on another minimum reform agenda. Moi, an astute political animal, knew that the political crisis over reforms could not be wished away, that, in fact, it could cost him political power. But he did not want to succumb to the popular pressure of the NCEC. Instead, he reached out to the opposition political parties, hoping to take the steam out of the NCEC. Thus was born the Inter-Parties Parliamentary Group (IPPG) talks, a conclave of KANU and the parliamentary opposition, whose mandate was to agree on a set of minimum reforms before the elections. Suddenly, there was a "rational" and "less threatening" alternative to the NCEC's "radical" agenda. Murungi, an architect of the IPPG, expressed his trepidation about the NCEC's nuclear option and rationalized the support of the IPPG by most of the opposition MPs.

> There were those [at the national convention] who felt that it was time to remove KANU through more radical strategies, the "Kabila Option" [Laurent Kabila removed President Mobutu Sese Seko from power in Zaire through a

guerilla war]. The convention discussed controversial matters like creating a Constituent Assembly—a parallel parliament to deal exclusively with matters of constitutional reform. The implication of this option was not clear and left many questions unanswered . . . I felt that the academics leading NCEC [Mutunga, Kivutha Kibwana, Gibson Kamau Kuria] were getting carried away from political realities. I didn't see why we could not open up negotiations with KANU, which didn't mind NCEC participating in the negotiations together with MPs. NCEC was deliberately taking a hard-line stance to create a revolutionary situation.[37]

Murungi and other leading opposition politicians, in essence the government-in-waiting, needed some reforms to ensure a free and fair election, which they hoped to win. From this narrow perspective, unlike their civil society counterparts, they did not have a stake in a comprehensive constitutional reform agenda. Nor did they seem to comprehend, or at least want to entertain, the necessity of the total reformation of the state—a conclusion that sections of the civil society now saw as the only antidote to despotism in Kenya. But at the same time, the opposition was in a bind. On the one hand, they could not simply sit back and do nothing, allowing civil society to drive them into political irrelevance. A bonfire for reform had been stoked in the general populace by the NCEC, and the political parties, who claimed to represent the masses, had to find a way to tap into this political capital or risk marginalization. On the other hand, a caucus with KANU on reforms was tricky and could result in the betrayal of the entire reform agenda, including even its minimalist iteration. A nod by religious leaders and pressure from donors for MPs to join the IPPG sealed the fate of the NCEC reform effort, although the IPPG talks would use the minimum reform package developed by the national convention of NCEC as the baseline for negotiations. According to Mutunga, the IPPG initiative was a "relief to many of the stakeholders, the foreign interests, the political parties and, of course, the religious organizations."[38] Although most MPs jumped the NCEC ship to join the IPPG, many others, including Muite, Odinga, and Orengo, did not. Anyang' Nyong'o, who enjoyed the respect of the NCEC, shuttled between the two but eventually voted against the IPPG package.[39] Murungi, in an account that has been contested, argued that the NCEC drove MPs from the national convention and into KANU's IPPG arms.

The perennial struggle between civil society and politicians had finally caught up with NCEC. The NCEC was informed that MPs who were talking to KANU were traitors. Inter-Parties Parliamentary Group talks were dismissed as a ploy to destroy NCEC. They were exposed to ridicule. NCEC had become a formidable political institution. No opposition politician could fight it without digging his own political grave. Now MPs didn't care. They could not tolerate the ridicule and insults any longer . . . The negotiations could now take place directly between KANU and parliamentary opposition parties. NCEC was no longer the solo voice of all pro-democracy voices in Kenya. NCEC was dying from its own internal hemorrhage.[40]

Mutunga contested Murungi's analysis and dismissed it as "rationalization to argue that politicians of the caliber of Kiraitu Murungi defected to the IPPG because they were booed in the plenary of the NCA."[41] Mutunga argues that, since 1992, political parties had squandered every opportunity to lead the reform agenda. Their failure to form a united front, agree on a single presidential candidate, and work together was a "history of seeking opportunities to rejoin KANU."[42] Mutunga suggested that the leadership of the opposition was largely ex-KANU and therefore did not have any fundamental normative differences with KANU, except its drive to capture state power.[43] As such, the opposition's vision of constitutional reform did not materially depart from that of KANU. It was against this backdrop that most of the opposition joined KANU in the IPPG and agreed to minor constitutional changes as well as the review of several dozen repressive laws that had been used to improve KANU's chances in the electoral process.[44] By a stroke of political genius, KANU had taken the initiative for minimum reforms from the NCEC. In a telling statement, Murungi notes that some KANU leaders, such as the hawkish Kipkalya Kones, were even more "radical" than many opposition MPs.[45] It would not take him long to find out why democracy had so quickly found zealous "converts" within KANU. Soon after the reform package was passed, Moi dissolved Parliament and called elections, in effect preventing the implementation of the minimum reforms. Murungi's bitterness was obvious.

> After the IPPG reforms had been enacted into law, we [IPPG] had worked late into the night with Phares Kuindwa, the Head of the Civil Service, on the sessional paper for the implementation of the IPPG reforms. To our surprise and disbelief, Moi dissolved Parliament and rushed us into elections before the sessional paper was debated by Parliament. KANU had behaved in a hawkish and Machiavellian manner.

The NCEC had denounced the IPPG efforts and warned that Moi and KANU could not be trusted to deliver on the reform agenda. The folly of opposition complicity in the IPPG was exposed in what Anyang' Nyong'o called the "civilian coup" by the regime.[46] He conceded that "some of us [opposition MPs] who were in it realized this was the game—but too late."[47] He even admitted that "without the NCEC within the IPPG, we could not stem the tide."[48] Moi had seized the initiative and now forced the opposition, which was still fragmented, to face him at the polls where he still could—and did—manipulate the process to his advantage. Before the passage of the IPPG reforms, the third session of the national convention had taken place in October 1997 and adopted the call of "no reforms, no elections."[49] However, after the dissolution of Parliament, most politicians—even those who had stuck with the NCEC, including Odinga, Muite, and Orengo—decided to participate in the elections.

Duplicity: Safari Park to Ufungamano

The bitter struggles between civil society and opposition politicians over the extent and depth of reforms prior to the 1997 elections broke the guarded trust and alliance that the two sectors had forged since the late 1980s. After the electoral debacles of 1992 and 1997, civil society became ever more circumspect about joint reform projects with the opposition. The opposition appears to have decided that it was unwise to cede so much political space to civil society. In 1998, even though Moi had deceived it, the opposition nevertheless decided to restart negotiations with KANU on the constitutional review process. The NCEC did not let up on its demands for a comprehensive "people-driven" constitutional reform agenda. The church reasserted itself as a more independent player in the reform process. To Moi's chagrin, the quest for a democratic constitution had not been squelched by either the IPPG or the 1997 elections. Attention was now focused on the Constitution of Kenya Review Act, which had been enacted in the 1997 IPPG reforms.[50]

The year 1998 opened in an atmosphere of deep suspicion, hatred, and hostility between NCEC and what its members called the "political class." The immediate bone of contention was the Constitution of Kenya Review Commission Act, which had been amended and passed by Parliament as part of the IPPG package. The act was intended to provide a framework for comprehensive review of the constitution after the 1997 elections. NCEC rejected the act as fundamentally flawed and dismissed the commission created thereunder as "illegitimate," "ill-advised," and "unworkable." It correctly observed that President Moi could easily manipulate the commission and the Parliament to adopt a "doctored" constitution that did not represent the wishes and aspirations of Kenyans. NCEC also argued that Parliament was ill suited to review the constitution because most MPs had been elected through a flawed electoral process.[51]

The clergy—Muslims, Catholics, and the NCCK—as well as the Women's Political Caucus, an influential group of women, rejected the government's road map to a new constitution. Individual clerics such as Timothy Njoya, Henry Okullu, Alexander Muge, Manasses Kuria, Lawford Imunde, and David Gitari of the NCCK, the umbrella organization for Protestant churches, and Ndingi Mwana Nzeki of the Conference of Catholic Bishops had been outspoken critics. Muge's 1990 death in an auto collision had raised suspicion of government complicity.[52] Only the evangelical African Inland Church, to which Moi belonged, was solidly pro-KANU.[53] After 1997, the church played a pivotal role in the reform process. These groups, together with civil society, were adamant that constitutional reform could not be successful or acceptable to Kenyans if it was conducted under the aegis of the state by the rules and within institutions imposed on the country by the KANU regime. Murungi later conceded these criticisms, but admitted that the legislators' "focus at IPPG was on minimum pre-election reforms" and not on the "detailed examination" of the constitutional review law.[54] Interestingly, the opposition still thought that the KANU state could be a broker for a democratic constitution. But after 1997, Moi divided the opposition again when he established an alliance with Raila Odinga's National Development Party (NDP). The KANU-NDP alliance gave Moi a solid majority in Parliament and allowed him to thwart democratization and dictate the future of constitutional reform.[55]

The parliamentary opposition joined KANU in 1998 to form the Inter-Parties Parliamentary Committee (IPPC), a forum to craft the path for constitutional reform. In October 1998, the IPPC convened a series of public meetings of key stakeholders known as the Safari Park talks to agree on the norms, institutions, and processes for constitutional reform. The central point for debate was the Constitution of Kenya Review Act, the law to authorize the process. But KANU sought to exclude the NCEC and other independent civil society groups. It wanted to include compliant NGOs such as Maendeleo Ya Wanawake, the national women's organization that had long been a virtual department of KANU.[56] Then KANU relented and allowed outspoken civil society organizations to be part of the negotiations. The Safari Park consensus, which was regarded as legitimate because it involved all key stakeholders, agreed on amendments to the Constitution of Kenya Review Act, the most important of which were (1) making the composition of the Constitution of Kenya Review Commission (CKRC)—the body that would oversee the writing of a new constitution—more representative and (2) allowing ordinary Kenyans to participate.[57] But the euphoria of the moment was short-lived.

The bane of the Safari Park compromise was the composition of the CKRC. Although the forum agreed that the CKRC would be composed of twenty-five commissioners—thirteen from parliamentary parties and twelve from stakeholders outside Parliament—the formula for doling out the slots among the political parties was not written into the law. In May 1999, as each party pushed to have more appointees than the other, the IPPC initiative collapsed when KANU and the opposition failed to agree on a formula. Moi instead announced in a public rally that Parliament, not *wanjiku,* the female Kikuyu name commonly used to denote an ordinary Kenyan citizen, would write the new constitution.[58] Moi said, "If you went to Wanjiku and asked her what should be changed in the current constitution, she will tell you she has an MP whom she voted for and who should do the work for which he was elected."[59] He added that the 4.5 billion in Kenya shillings (KShs) set aside for the review process could be used for poverty eradication programs and argued that two good constitutional lawyers could draft the constitution and submit it to Parliament for debate and adoption, saving the country the expenditure for a process in which *wanjiku* did not want to participate and for which she was not qualified.[60] Moi's rejection of Safari Park was true to character—despotic and contemptuous of the citizenry. He would rely on Parliament, controlled by his party, to dictate the process. Murungi analyzed the situation thus: "As far as KANU was concerned, Safari Park was a mistake. It went too far and progressed to a point where it threatened the status quo. The Safari Park process had to be sabotaged and deadlocked. It had to be re-organized and re-arranged to ensure control of the process and its outcome by KANU."[61]

The opposition, even after the Moi-KANU IPPG deception, had once again taken Moi's bait. But Safari Park was an opportunity for civil society to experience the treachery of the KANU elite. KANU felt that the Safari Park process left too much up in the air—it could easily lose control of the process. There was no guarantee what the constitution-making process would yield if it were opened up to popular participation. It might bring about far-reaching reforms, many of which could adversely affect the political, economic, and social structures of an elite that had committed mass atrocities, looted the state, and broken the law with impunity.[62] The failure of Safari Park convinced civil society and religious organizations that Kenya would not undergo a comprehensive and popularly legitimate constitution-making exercise unless they took charge and led the process. They condemned President Moi's constitutional review road map.

> We totally reject Parliament as the only forum for constitution making. We do not recognize it as representative of all the voices in Kenya. We do this appreciating that there already is a stated national consensus that the constitution properly belongs to all the people of Kenya. We unequivocally state that the constitutional review process is irreversible and must be people-driven.[63]

On December 15, 1999, the Ufungamano Initiative, a clergy-led constitutional review process that included all other key stakeholders except KANU and the NDP, was launched. The Ufungamano Initiative, whose convener was Mutava Musyimi, the outspoken cleric and secretary-general of the NCCK, established the NGO People's Commission of Kenya (PCK) to write the constitution in lieu of the Moi-Odinga-driven parliamentary process. The PCK followed the script of the 1997 Constitution of Kenya Review Act that had been agreed upon at the Safari Park talks. The chair of the PCK, with over twenty commissioners drawn from various sectors, was Oki Ooko Ombaka, a respected jurist and former legislator. The PCK was mandated to conduct a people-driven constitutional review process by traveling around the country to collect the views of Kenyans from all walks of life and produce a draft constitution. The PCK's mandate was identical to that of the Safari Park–conceived CKRC before it was killed by the KANU-NDP alliance.

Parliament, controlled by KANU and the NDP, moved to implement its own constitutional review process. On December 15, 1999, the same day that the Ufungamano Initiative was launched, the Parliamentary Select Committee on Constitutional Review (PSC) was established to collect the views of Kenyans and propose amendments to the Constitution of Kenya Review Act. Not surprisingly, Raila Odinga, who was deeply involved with Moi in intrigues against the Ufungamano Initiative, assumed the chairmanship of the PSC. In 2000, the Parliament adopted the recommendations of the Odinga committee that the CKRC be composed of fifteen commissioners and two ex-official members, all nominated by the PSC but formally appointed by President Moi.[64] In 2000, in what analysts viewed as a public relations coup, President Moi appointed Yash Ghai, the widely respected Kenyan and renowned University of Hong Kong law professor, as chairman of the CKRC. Ghai's appointment followed months of courtship by Amos Wako, the long-serving attorney general and key adviser on many of KANU's repressive measures.[65] But Ghai knew that the CKRC would never attain legitimacy unless it was reconstituted to include the PCK, a feat that he accomplished in 2001.

The struggle to control the constitutional review process pitted reformers against KANU loyalists. The KANU elite was opposed to reforms for obvious reasons. The influential key stakeholders in the reforms were all part of the middle classes—whether in opposition parties, intelligentsia, professional associations, religious organizations, elite women's groups, or civil society. Within the opposition, there were clearly many intriguers, ethnic demagogues, and power mongers. But as a whole, the pro-reform middle class wanted reforms to introduce a responsive political democracy with a transparent and accountable government in which the rule of law was paramount. This group defined Kenya's problem simply as one of bad governance, a condition that could be excised by the creation of accountable institutions. Even among this group, there was trepidation about how thorough the reforms needed to be, given that most of them were beneficiaries of the largesse of the KANU state. It is these material and other moral, religious, and social interests that rendered much of Kenya's middle classes politically conservative.

The radical wing of civil society, represented by elements within the KHRC and the NCEC, sought a more penetrating reform that would alter social and economic relations, including a vigorous program of land reform and poverty alleviation. The quest for a democratic constitution was definitely a clash between these political ideals. The leadership of the latter group had a history of radical politics, whether from academic institutions or nationalist, antisubordination politics that can be traced back to anti-imperialist, Marxist, nationalist Third World liberation discourses, or the Mau Mau and other Kenyan anticolonial movements and struggles. Although employing a language of human rights and political democracy, this group sought a "people-driven" process as a window to a more wholesome empowerment. The agitation for constitutional reform for them was an opportunity to rethink the raison d'être of the Kenyan state and make it more responsive to the country's impoverished masses.

Notes

1. Paul Tiyambe Zeleza, "Introduction: The Struggle for Human Rights in Africa," in *Human Rights, the Rule of Law, and Development in Africa*, ed. Paul Tiyambe Zeleza and Philip J. McConnaughay (Philadelphia: University of Pennsylvania Press, 2004), 1–3, 5.

2. Willy Mutunga, *Constitution-Making from the Middle: Civil Society and Transition Politics in Kenya, 1992–1997* (Harare: MWENGO, 1991).

3. Makau Mutua, "A Call for a National Dialogue," *Nairobi Law Monthly*, September 1991, 25.

4. Odindo Opiata, "Of Phrase-Mongering and Political Debate," *Nairobi Law Monthly*, September 1991, 41.

5. Mutunga, *Constitution-Making from the Middle*, 27.

6. Ibid., 30–35.

7. Ibid., 32.

8. Ibid., 35.

9. Ibid., 30–37.

10. Kiraitu Murungi, *In the Mud of Politics* (Nairobi: Acacia Stantex Publishers, 2000), 72.

11. Ibid.

12. Ibid., 73.

13. Makau Mutua, Maina Kiai, Willy Mutunga, Kiraitu Murungi, and Peter Kareithi formed the KHRC in the United States in 1991 and registered it in Washington, DC, in 1992. Willy Mutunga and Alamin Mazrui, "Rights Integration in an Institutional Context: The Experience of the Kenya Human Rights Commission," *Buffalo Law Review* 123, no. 8 (2002).

14. Murungi, *In the Mud of Politics*, 73.

15. Mutunga, *Constitution-Making from the Middle*, 68.

16. Kenya Human Rights Commission, International Commission of Jurists, and Law Society of Kenya (Kenya Section), *The Kenya We Want (Kenya Tuitakayo): Proposal for a Model Constitution* (1994).

17. Mutunga, *Constitution-Making from the Middle*, 60–61.

18. Kenya Human Rights Commission, International Commission of Jurists, and Law Society of Kenya, *The Kenya We Want (Kenya Tuitakayo): Proposal for a Model Constitution* (1994).

19. Mutunga, *Constitution-Making from the Middle*, 71.

20. Peter Anyang' Nyong'o, "Preface," in Murungi, *In the Mud of Politics*, xii.

21. Peter Anyang' Nyong'o, "Comments on Constitution-Making from the Middle: Civil Society and Transitional Politics in Kenya," in Mutunga, *Constitution-Making from the Middle*, 284.

22. Mutunga, *Constitution-Making from the Middle*, 61.

23. Ibid.

24. Ibid.

25. International Commission of Jurists, *Democratization and the Rule of Law in Kenya: ICJ Mission Report* (Geneva, 1997).

26. Murungi, *In the Mud of Politics*, 73–74.

27. Anyang' Nyong'o, "Comments on Constitution-Making from the Middle," 284.

28. John W. Harbeson, Donald Rothchild, and Naomi Chazan eds., *Civil Society and the State in Africa* (Boulder: Lynne Rienner Publishers, 1994); John Keane, ed., *Civil Society and the State* (London: Verso, 1988).

29. National Convention Assembly, Resolution 1/NCA/April 1997, Act of Establishing and Constituting the National Convention Assembly, Declaration and Resolutions of the National Convention Assembly's First Plenary Sitting [Session] at Limuru Conference and Training Center, April 3–6, 1997.

30. Anyang' Nyong'o, "Comments on Constitution-Making from the Middle," 284.

31. Murungi, *In the Mud of Politics*, 79.

32. Mutunga, *Constitution-Making from the Middle*, 201–202.

33. Makau wa Mutua, "Democracy in Africa: No Easy Walk to Freedom," *Reconstruction* 39, no. 2 (1992).

34. Mutunga, *Constitution-Making from the Middle*, 202.

35. Ibid., 203.

36. Anyang' Nyong'o, "Comments on Constitution-Making from the Middle," 285.

37. Murungi, *In the Mud of Politics*, 78.

38. Mutunga, *Constitution-Making from the Middle*, 149.

39. Ibid., 217.

40. Murungi, *In the Mud of Politics*, 79–80.

41. Mutunga, *Constitution-Making from the Middle*, 217.

42. Ibid., 215.

43. Ibid.

44. *The Statute Law (Repeals and Miscellaneous Amendments) Act*, 1997; *The Constitution of Kenya Review Commission Act* (Nairobi: Government Printer, 1997).

45. Murungi, *In the Mud of Politics*, 81.

46. Anyang' Nyong'o, "Comments on Constitution-Making from the Middle," 285.

47. Ibid.

48. Ibid.

49. National Convention Assembly, Resolution 9/NCA/August 1997, Declarations and Resolutions of the National Convention Assembly's Second Plenary Sitting [Session] at Ufungamano, Nairobi, August 25–28, 1997.

50. *The Constitution of Kenya Review Act, 1997*, No. 13 (Nairobi: Government Printer, 1997).

51. Murungi, *In the Mud of Politics*, 83.

52. Africa Watch, *Kenya: Taking Liberties* (New York: Africa Watch, 1991), 223.

53. Bishop H. Okullu, "Church, State and Society in East Africa," in *Thirty Years of Independence in Africa: The Lost Decades*, ed. Peter Anyang' Nyong'o (Nairobi: Academy Science Publishers, 1992), 25.

54. Murungi, *In the Mud of Politics*, 83.

55. Raila Odinga quickly accepted the results of the 1997 elections after a meeting with President Moi, a move that killed any attempts by the opposition to challenge them. Ibid., 82.

56. David Gillies and Makau wa Mutua, *A Long Road to Uhuru: Human Rights and Political Participation in Kenya* (London: Westminster Foundation for Democracy, 1993), 29.

57. *The Constitution of Kenya Review Commission (Amendment) Act*, 1998.

58. "Send Law Review to Parliament," *Sunday Nation*, May 23, 1999, 1–3.

59. Ibid.

60. Ibid.

61. Murungi, *In the Mud of Politics*, 86.

62. Republic of Kenya, *Report of the Task Force on the Establishment of a Truth, Justice, and Reconciliation Commission* (Nairobi: Government Printer, 2003).

63. "Leaders Dismiss Moi's Prescription for Constitutional Review," *Daily Nation*, May 24, 1999; "Moi Reform Plea Is Unacceptable," *Daily Nation*, May 26, 1999.

64. "House Adopts Raila's PSC Report," *East African Standard*, April 27, 2000, 8.

65. Makau Mutua, "Justice Under Siege: "The Rule of Law and Judicial Subservience in Kenya," *Human Rights Quarterly* 96, no. 23 (2001).

7

The Institution of
the Review Commission

THE QUEST FOR constitutional reform in Kenya is a struggle over the formulation of the norms, structures, and processes to govern the state. It has been difficult to determine the character of the state and how it can accommodate the competing interests of individuals, social groups, regions, ethnic groups, and institutions. It is the interests of Kenyans—class, religious, gender, ethnic, racial, political, and social—that have been at war with each over the reform agenda. The constitutional review process was a display of myopia, political dysfunction, and individual psychosis. Did the various elites that hold the levers of power and social control have the foresight to place the interests of the nation above their own? Or was there an objective matrix that would drive the struggle for reform inevitably toward the public interest? Given the record of the postcolonial political elites, it may have been unwise to leave the process to fate in the naïve belief that those who triumphed would guard the national interest.[1] This basic distrust among civil society drove it to act as the guardian of the nation in the reform agenda.

The consensus within religious organizations, civil society, and opposition political parties was that KANU and the Moi government were opposed to the reformation of the state because they would lose power. The loss of political power in a postcolonial illiberal state often means the economic and political marginalization of the rulers of yesteryear, hence the proclivity to resist reforms. For one-party, or opaque dictatorial states, political democracy can be a death knell to a corrupt and abusive elite. The rationale of dictatorial elites in postcolonial states is to strangle society, a condition that snuffs out any promise of popular participation, perhaps the most essential tool for imposing accountability on the state. But the African state has shown a surprising ability to be impenetrable by the citizenry, a fact that makes its reform a daunting task. Invariably, even new elites who yesterday sang from the hymnbook of reform seemed to quickly fall into the pit of antireform after they ascended to power.

The jockeying over the nature of the Constitution of Kenya Review Commission (CKRC) by stakeholders was a manifestation of these fears and hopes.

Politics and the CKRC

The basic assumption by the main protagonists in the constitutional reform process was that the legal framework for the CKRC would serve the political interests of the groups that would emerge victorious. What many of the players did not seem to appreciate, particularly the Kenya African National Union and the National Development Party (KANU-NDP), was that constitution making is an inherently impure exercise, a process of give-and-take, of compromise, and not a zero-sum game where all the spoils belong to the victors. The KANU government knew that it could not end the popular cries for constitutional review. But it wanted to single-handedly steer the process and impose a charade of reforms that would not jeopardize its power. The opposition politicians sought just enough reforms to permit the defeat of KANU at the polls in a fair political fight for power. The religious organizations were restrained by their suspicion of radical change. Even so, they had become increasingly radical and outspoken against the KANU state because they saw it as uncaring of their flocks. To them, KANU rulers were base and crass materialists. The clergy argued that it sought reforms because repression by KANU was a direct contradiction of its teachings. Inaction would have undermined the legitimacy—and long-term prospects—for established religions among the people.

Perhaps the most complex political actors were drawn from Kenya's budding civil society organizations. The social character of civil society is decidedly middle-class and arises from the professions, academic institutions, and private sector. The social location of civil society actors gave them a class interest that shaped the nature of their engagement with the political process.[2] But the philosophical spectrum within civil society is expansive, with a majority committed to the traditional political democratic model. There are clusters of reformers that are focused on single issues, including agrarian reformers, feminists, women's rights groups, anticorruption advocates, antiglobalization campaigners, human rights organizations, professional associations, pastoralists, minority rights groups, child advocates, activists for persons with disabilities, speech rights agitators, sexual minorities, rule of law reformers, cultural nativists, refugee rights groups, and a host of other specialized cadres. Since the early 1990s, these groups had become increasingly vocal. Some, such as the Kenya Human Rights Commission (KHRC), had established themselves as leaders of the reform movement. As noted by Willy Mutunga, the KHRC was "the mother of the Citizens' Coalition for Constitutional Change (4Cs) and the grandmother of the NCA/NCEC."[3] Although limited by their class interests, civil society actors came to see themselves as the only nonpartisan political players in the reform project with the ability to advocate a truly national agenda.

Most political actors understood the centrality of the CKRC to the reform process. Never before in the history of postcolonial Kenya had nonstate actors been in such a critical position to influence the reconstruction of the state. The intense struggles over the reform agenda focused on the construction of the CKRC. At last, the contest had moved from the streets to the boardrooms. After the failure of Safari Park, the KANU-NDP alliance decided to hijack the reform agenda, while the faiths-led Ufungamano Initiative formed the People's Commission of Kenya (PCK), based on the framework of the 1998 Constitution of Kenya Review Act. Even though the Ufungamano leaders, most notably Oki Ooko Ombaka and Mutava Musyimi, engaged in brinkmanship with KANU, they hoped that the work of the PCK would force the government to agree to a single national process, a position echoed by James Orengo, an opposition MP allied with Ufungamano.[4] The daily attacks on the PCK by KANU-NDP officials betrayed their fear of the Ufungamano Initiative. Musalia Mudavadi, a senior minister, asserted that the PCK was illegal.[5] Raila Odinga and other pro-KANU leaders continually attacked the PCK to discredit it.[6] But the attacks only served to enhance the legitimacy of the PCK.

The Birth of the CKRC

Yash Pal Ghai, the constitutional law expert who wrote the constitutions of several countries, surprised Kenyans when he accepted Moi's appointment to chair the CKRC. Moi, the self-confessed "professor of politics," had deceived and manipulated many a distinguished Kenyan or institution, only to dump them.[7] In November 2000, aware that his appointment might end in heartbreak, Ghai refused to take the oath of office along with the fifteen other commissioners until he had formed an inclusive process with the PCK.[8] Ghai's move was a masterstroke that, if successful, could have accomplished what the opposition, civil society, religious organizations, and government had not—agreement on an inclusive, unitary review process. But it also put pressure on the Ufungamano Initiative to meet him halfway to resolve the impasse. Ufungamano agreed to support a joint process on the condition that the legislative framework of the CKRC was altered to reflect the consensus reached at Safari Park.[9]

Despite positive indications by Attorney General Amos Wako and President Moi that the KANU-NDP side welcomed a merger of the CKRC and the PCK, the government started a drumbeat of attacks on Ufungamano and its motives.[10] Senior government officials, including Julius Sunkuli, the minister for internal security, saw in the merger a ploy to diminish Moi's role.[11] Odinga, the chair of the Parliamentary Select Committee on Constitutional Review (PSC) and the architect of the CKRC, publicly urged Ghai to ignore Ufungamano and impose his terms on them.[12] As 2001 dawned, Moi asked Ghai to stop negotiations with Ufungamano because they did not represent anyone and nobody had given them a mandate to participate in the law review process.[13] In spite of all that, the merger negotiations moved along. But other differences soon emerged within Ufungamano itself and between Ghai and the KANU government. Ghai lived between the hammer of his friends and the anvil of his enemies. Pressed from within and confronted by a restless Ufungamano, he worked hard to produce a merger.

The tensions within Ufungamano reflected the conflicting visions between sections of the civil society, particularly the skeptical National Convention Executive Council (NCEC), which had no faith in Moi-related initiatives. It believed that a merger would doom any genuine reform agenda. Even though the NCEC thought well of Ghai, it could not separate him from Wako, Moi, and Odinga—the triumvirate that had appointed him chair of the CKRC. The NCEC believed that Ghai would end up as a Moi dupe. But the religious organizations and the more conservative factions of civil society—middle-class groups that had never been comfortable with the radical NCEC leadership—balked at NCEC's hardball politics.[14] The differences were twofold. The NCEC had pushed for what it called a "people-driven," comprehensive reform agenda, with Moi and KANU decentered from the process. They cited rigged elections and broken pacts, such as the Inter-Parties Parliamentary Group (IPPG) and Safari Park compromises, as ample proof that Moi could not be trusted to create a process to return sovereignty to the people.[15] Kiraitu Murungi, the opposition shadow attorney general, and Mukhisa Kituyi, another leading opposition MP, said that "the lesson we have learnt from Moi and his agent [Wako] and any agreement done with them is not worth the ink and the paper it is written on."[16] In spite of these misgivings, Odour Ongw'en, the chair of the National Council of NGOs, the official umbrella of the civil society, sharply attacked the NCEC, charging that its opposition to the merger was in bad faith, unconsultative, and undemocratic.[17] Many in civil society saw Ongw'en, a fellow Luo, as a front for Odinga.

The NCEC, with the support of several opposition MPs, intensified its objections to the merger. It accused the Ufungamano leadership of striking deals with the CKRC without adequate consultations.[18] In mid-February 2001, Ghai took the oath of office as chair of the CKRC, apparently satisfied that only technical questions remained to be ironed out for the merger. Ghai's confirmation took Ufungamano by surprise and increased pressure on dissenters to back the merger. According to NCEC spokesman Kivutha Kibwana, a Kenyan constitutional law professor, Ghai's swearing in "makes it difficult for him to act as a mediator and that he has placed himself in a position where KANU and NDP would be dictating things to him."[19] Leading civil society stakeholders, including the NCEC, 4Cs, Release Political Prisoners (RPP), and Muungano wa Mageuzi (Coalition for Change), which was headed by James Orengo, an MP, opposed the merger and called for the public disclosure of the agreements between Ufungamano and PCK, on the one hand, and the CKRC and Odinga's PSC, on the other.[20] Suspicion, distrust, and divergent political and personal agendas had once again come to haunt the search for a national consensus on reform. But for the first time, Kenyans were close to some agreement on a broadly acceptable review process.

The key questions among the negotiators centered on the powers of the CKRC, its independence from the executive and its relationship to the PSC, the number of commissioners and the manner of their appointment, a national referendum on the constitution, the scope of the review process, the mandate and composition of the national constitutional conference, and the legal status of the CKRC in the constitution.[21] Intense pressure mounted on all players because Kenyans expected the 2002 elections to be held under a new constitution, barely a year away.[22] In February 2001, a draft bill to revise the Constitution of Kenya Review Act was unveiled, marking a major step toward the reconciliation of the two competing processes.[23] Musyimi cautioned that the draft bill was not equivalent to a merger and that many questions remained unsolved.[24] In the draft, the number of commissioners was increased from fifteen to twenty-seven, with at least six women; of the twelve additional commissioners, ten were drawn from Ufungamano after consultations with Ghai, and the other two selected by the PSC would be appointed by Moi; the process would last two years; the PSC would supervise the process under Odinga; and each province would have at least two but not more than four commissioners. The bill did not entrench the review in the constitution to protect it from executive interference. In order to put pressure on the state and buy more time to bring the NCEC "dissidents" along, Musyimi and Ufungamano boycotted the public ceremony at which Wako, the attorney general, presented the draft bill to merge the Ufungamano process with the government-led effort.[25]

The NCEC leadership denounced Wako for making the draft bill public before the conclusion of merger discussions.[26] Gibson Kamau Kuria, then chair of the Law Society of Kenya and a constitutional law expert involved in the negotiations for Ufungamano, expressed shock at Wako's draft bill announcement. Kibwana complained that "it is clear the Attorney General and the government want to put pressure on Ufungamano so that it agrees to half-baked propositions."[27] He questioned Ghai's qualifications to chair the CKRC and argued that the merger would not be done until civil society was given control over civic education to prepare Kenyans for comprehensive constitutional reforms. He wanted the number of commissioners raised to thirty and appointed openly without being left solely to Odinga's PSC.[28] Odinga called the NCEC "hardliners" and "pseudo intellectuals seeking to malign the name, reputation and image of Prof. Ghai," and gave Ufungamano a four-day ultimatum to accept the merger or he would terminate the talks.[29] On the eve of the crucial Ufungamano vote on the merger, newspapers ran a blitz of articles and editorials supporting the joint review process and predicting Armageddon if it was rejected.[30] The middle class, business interests, and most stakeholders favored a merger of the two processes.

On March 21, 2001, Ufungamano voted to approve the merger in a session remembered for incivility. Amid bitter wrangling—spiced by boos and heckling from the antimerger groups—the meeting almost collapsed as Musyimi struggled to control it and keep the public address system from being sabotaged and voters menaced. Outraged, Mwai Kibaki, the leader of the Democratic Party (DP), argued that "there is no one in Kenya who wants the review to be scuttled or delayed."[31] He said that "we cannot go back to a parallel process and those who think so are day dreaming."[32] But even after the favorable vote by Ufungamano, government officials, including President Moi, continued to attack Ufungamano. Moi described those in Ufungamano as "unknown" and "outsiders and traitors" who had no mandate to review the constitution.[33] When civil society groups attacked Moi back, Odinga, a cabinet minister and KANU secretary-general, defended him, arguing that "President Moi had every right to express his feelings about the quality of the composition of the Ufungamano team and dispelled claims that the constitutional review process was headed for stalemate."[34] Moi did not trust Ghai and suspected him of secret sympathies with Ufungamano. In April 2001, Moi's attempt to undermine Ghai was exposed when he secretly hosted CKRC commissioners loyal to KANU at State House.[35] The meeting was intended to divide the CKRC and possibly sack Ghai. For skeptics, it proved that Moi had been opposed to the merger all along and did not intend to allow a successful constitutional review process.[36]

The political defeat of the radical Ufungamano stakeholders would haunt the review process throughout. One major issue was the rejection by KANU hardliners of the proposal to entrench the review process in the constitution to protect it from its opponents. The merger had called for the passage of two bills—one to amend the Constitution of Kenya Review Act, and the other to amend the constitution to entrench the review process. KANU-NDP legislators, including Odinga, felt that giving Ufungamano the right to select the twelve additional commissioners would surrender control of the CKRC to Ufungamano, since some of the fifteen original appointees were suspected of being loyal to the faiths-led lobby. KANU wanted to reduce the number of commissioners Ufungamano could recommend and retain the right to vet them. But Odinga split with his KANU colleagues on the question of entrenching the review process in the constitution. Isaac Ruto, a hawkish KANU minister, called entrenchment a mistake because it would turn Parliament into a rubber stamp for an uncontrollable CKRC.[37] But Odinga argued for entrenchment as the only way to protect the review process from its detractors.[38] This chasm between Odinga and KANU is evidence that Odinga did not trust Moi on the question of constitutional review. Odinga wanted a new constitution to cater to his political ambitions, whereas Moi acquiesced to the process to deflect public pressure. Moi refused to protect the process in the constitution so that he could jettison the entire project at the appropriate moment. Despite their differences, Moi and Odinga needed each other: the former to divide and defeat the opposition, the latter to advance his personal political fortunes.

Jockeying for influence became intense before the passage of the legal framework for constitutional review. Odinga increasingly became Ghai's protector and defender against KANU hawks, including Moi. He opposed attempts to reduce Ghai's powers as chair of the CKRC, arguing that it would "emasculate" and make him "a lame duck chairman."[39] Ghai was only good to Odinga if he remained strong enough to deliver a constitution, sufficiently independent from Moi to resist the president's hidden agenda to scuttle the process, and distant enough from Ufungamano, the opposition, and civil society to resist being captured by them to Odinga's detriment. Control of the review process became, for many of the key players, a zero-sum game. Virtually all saw it as the battlefield on which the war for state power would either be won or lost, and no one wanted to come out the loser. The struggle over the merger involved ideological tensions that have defined the Kenyan postcolonial state since independence. They ranged from the antidemocratic, ultraconservative expressions of political thought and practice to the radical, progressivist, and redistributive politics of transformation.

Four political tendencies were manifested in the struggles over constitutional reform. The first was the centralizing of an undemocratic strand, which Kenyatta personified but was now embodied in Moi and KANU. That is the tendency of the fraction of the elite that has historically held power in Kenya, including the Kibaki regime. In power, this particular elite has been opaque, despotic, and resistant to democratic transformation.

The second is the syndrome of the government-in-waiting, represented at independence by Kenya African Democratic Union (KADU) but found later in the political opposition. As with KADU, the postcolonial opposition, except for Odinga's Kenya People's Union (KPU), has generally been unprincipled and subject to corruption by the ruling bloc. Its interest in reform is not centered on the democratization of the state, but rather on those minimum changes to make its ascendancy to power possible.

The third tendency is the "radical" and progressive option, which Oginga Odinga personified but which the NCEC and the more activist civil society organizations had revived. Except for the ill-fated attempt by the Social Democratic Party (SDP), no political party since the KPU had been successful in articulating this tendency.[40] Safina, the opposition party headed by Paul Muite, had the potential to articulate a more radical vision but failed to attract a large following. Raila Odinga's NDP, which could have captured KPU's luster, instead became an ethnic Luo party and nothing more than a vehicle for Odinga's personal ambition. Its merger with KANU killed any potential for a reformist outlook.

The fourth, and last, tendency is the cautious middle, a worldview expressed by religious organizations, which has historically backed either the first or the second tendency, depending on personal, institutional, and external factors. By ideological orientation, the last tendency is generally pro-establishment, hence its distrust and distance from the more vocal fractions of civil society or even the political opposition. This middle, from whence most of Kenya's elites are drawn, has vast interests in land, property, the professions, and the marketplace. This middle is ethnically, racially, regionally, and religiously diverse, a fact that makes it formidable.

These political tendencies have recycled themselves throughout the history of the struggle for reform in Kenya. The most pernicious of them rear their ugly heads at every critical turn. But nonstate actors, who should have been wary of history repeating itself, instead ceded whatever leverage they had to the government-driven PSC process. Ufungamano lost its ability to seriously influence the nature of the merger once it had voted to approve the joint process before the completion of negotiations. From that moment forward, the terrain for the contest over the nature of the review process shifted to Parliament, a development that surrendered control over negotiations to the opposition political parties. Religious organizations and the civil society had extracted concessions from the state, only to cede them to the opposition parties and Parliament. On May 8, 2001, after further negotiations between the KANU-NDP alliance and the major opposition parties, Parliament passed the merger bill.[41] However, Muite, Orengo, Njeru Kathangu, and Shem Ochuodho—the MPs allied to the NCEC—opposed the bill. Moi quickly assented to the bill, expanding the CKRC and giving it the mandate to start the review process.[42] But the review process was not entrenched in the constitution, making it vulnerable to the whims of the executive. In June 2001, twelve additional commissioners—ten nominated by Ufungamano and two selected by the PSC—were sworn in, bringing the total to twenty-seven, but excluding the country's attorney general and the secretary of the CKRC, its ex-officio members. Finally, the reconstituted CKRC took charge of the constitutional review process.

The Legal Framework of the CKRC

Most Kenyans regarded the merger bill and President Moi's assent to it as an important milestone in the reform of the country. For the first time in Kenya's history, ordinary citizens would have some say in the writing of the country's constitution. Even though there was dissent, particularly from sections of civil society and the political opposition, many citizens looked forward to the work of the CKRC. If politics is the art of compromise—and not a zero-sum game—then the CKRC could be judged a qualified success. Religious organizations, civil society, and opposition political parties had prevailed on the KANU state to address some of their concerns. The CKRC was a solid stepping-stone for the reform of the state. But some questions remained unanswered. Was the CKRC viable as a legal institution? Was it conceptually and structurally designed as an impartial conduit for the wishes of Kenyans in their basic law? Or was it a hoax, a top-down straightjacket that would be used by a section of the elite to impose its will on Kenyans? Would the Moi-KANU regime use it to hoodwink Kenyans into believing that it had carried out comprehensive reforms, thus reducing the clamor for fundamental democratic reforms? How easy would it to be to manipulate the CKRC for personal and ethnic agendas?

One of the critical weaknesses of the CKRC was its vulnerability to the executive and the National Assembly because of the role of the PSC. The refusal by the Moi regime to entrench the CKRC in the constitution was a telling admission by the state. The government had left itself, through the KANU-dominated Parliament, the option of either shutting down the process or tampering with it if political circumstances warranted. The regime had sent a clear message to the country—it was not committed to an open-ended, people-driven process over which it had no control. The failure to protect the process from interference was a serious blow because the Constitution of Kenya Review Act was meant to "facilitate the comprehensive review of the constitution of Kenya."[43] But it was classic Moi: when cornered, appear to give in but retain the option to alter the rules of the game when in imminent danger. The regime did not envisage a constitutional review process that would write it out of power. That loophole would come back to haunt the review process.

The manner of appointment of the chair of the CKRC, its commissioners, and the secretary gave the state huge leverage over the process. The law gave the president the right to appoint the chair of the CKRC.[44] He formally appointed all the twenty-seven commissioners, including the ten nominated by Ufungamano, after negotiations with the PSC.[45] Only former judges of the High Court and the Court of Appeal, those individuals qualified for such an appointment, or those who had been engaged in the teaching of law in a "recognized university in Kenya for at least 15 years" could be appointed chair.[46] In contrast, the qualifications to be commissioner were less rigorous. Eleven commissioners had to have "knowledge of and at least five years' experience in matters relating to law," whereas sixteen had to have "knowledge of and experience in public affairs."[47] In a nod to affirmative action and ethnic and regional balancing, at least two but not more than four of the commissioners had to originate from each province, and at least six had to be women.[48] The president was mandated to appoint the secretary of the CKRC, the body's chief executive.[49] Although the commissioners did not enjoy security of tenure, their terms of service, including their ability to discharge their duties, seemed adequate. The executive could not summarily dismiss the commissioners or the secretary, although they could be terminated for a breach of the code of conduct, upon conviction for an offense and imprisonment for more than six months without the option of a fine, if they were adjudged bankrupt, or for the failure to attend three consecutive meetings of the CKRC without a reasonable excuse.[50] In addition, death, physical or mental infirmity, or a voluntary resignation could create a vacancy in the office of a commissioner or secretary.[51] Any commissioner, including the chair or the secretary, could be removed from office by a two-thirds majority of the CKRC for a breach of the review law.[52] Any commissioner or group of commissioners could initiate an action for the removal of one of their own or the secretary. Even so, the terms and conditions of service for the CKRC were very generous and far from onerous. These relatively secure terms made the KANU government eager to pack the CKRC with commissioners loyal to it.

The CKRC was run by a chairperson and three vice chairpersons, appointed from among the commissioners.[53] The chairperson supervised and directed the work of the commission, served as spokesperson, and presided over all its meetings.[54] But the law mandated that decisions of the commission, or of any of its substructures, be arrived at by consensus or by a simple majority of the members present and voting in the absence of consensus.[55] The decisionmaking formula neutralized the seemingly substantial powers of the chair and could turn him or her into a hostage for a bloc of a simple majority of the commissioners. The formulaic decisionmaking process appears deceptively democratic but was designed to make sure that commissioners loyal to KANU would control the chair and the agenda of the CKRC. The other critical office was that of secretary, the chief officer responsible for routine activities, the coordination of the work of the CKRC, the recording of its proceedings, and the custodian of its records and documents.[56] The president appointed the secretary from two persons nominated by the National Assembly. The CKRC had no formal role in the appointment of its secretary. The CKRC's institutional "disunity" as a design model gave external actors, such as KANU, a loophole for manipulation.

The powers of the CKRC were broad and wide-ranging. The commission was mandated to conduct and facilitate civic education to stimulate public discourse on constitutional matters, to collect and collate the views of the Kenyans on proposals to alter the constitution and on that basis produce a draft constitution, to carry out research on comparative constitutionalism, and to make recommendations on various normative and structural questions relating to the state. The CKRC had a mandate to suggest to Kenyans both the framework and the content of a new constitution.[57] It could literally suggest the total reformation of the Kenyan state. It was empowered to visit the entire country and to freely solicit and receive the views of Kenyans, and it had the power to subpoena public officials and documents.[58] The commission had advisory subcommittees, including the Steering Committee, Working Committees, and Panels through which it exercised its functions and duties.[59] The CKRC exercised its powers with the oversight of the PSC, the parliamentary committee that was the liaison between the commission and the National Assembly.[60] In reality, the PSC, particularly its chair, held enormous sway over the CKRC because it could propose amendments to the review law to change the terms of service of the commissioners or trim the powers of the commission. The commission was funded by the state but could accept funds from other sources.[61] The fate of the CKRC, including its lifespan, funding, and access to the executive, especially the president, would depend on who was the chair of the PSC.

The CKRC was given two years to complete its work, although its life could be extended upon request or on the motion of the National Assembly.[62] It was mandated to carry out a series of activities culminating in the submission of a draft constitution to the National Assembly. The most important of these were the visits of the CKRC to every parliamentary constituency to receive the views of Kenyans; the compilation of the reports from each parliamentary constituency; the preparation and publication of a draft constitution based on the views of the people; the convening of the national constitutional conference for the debate, amendment, and adoption of the draft constitution; the organization of a national referendum on contentious questions, if any, that the National Constitutional Conference (NCC) would be unable to resolve; the writing of a final draft constitution based on the bill adopted by the NCC and the decisions of the people at the national referendum; and the submission of the final draft constitution to the attorney general for presentation to the National Assembly.[63] The CKRC would dissolve once the National Assembly had enacted the draft constitution and the terms of office of the commissioners would expire, but the secretary and a skeleton staff would remain in office for three months to wind down the commission's affairs.[64]

The law setting up the CKRC was the quintessential political compromise, in which the KANU state retained control over the constitutional reform process while at the same time appearing to accommodate a "people-driven" review process. The norms and structures adopted reflected the big picture and minutiae of a decade's worth of intense, and oftentimes deadly, contest over the reform of the state. In the end, the state had successfully fended off attempts to create an independent, constitutionally protected review process. But it had left loopholes through which it could exit from the process.

The Cocktail of Ghai, the CKRC, and the State

The appointment by the Moi regime of Yash Ghai to chair the CKRC appeared to be a stroke of genius because it gave the review process instant credibility at home and abroad. It was poetic that Ghai, a Kenyan of Asian descent, would chaperone the review process because he was godson to Jomo Kenyatta, the country's founding president. Ghai had distinguished himself as one of Africa's—and the world's—leading legal minds. A professor of law at the University of Hong Kong, Ghai had taught at leading universities, including Yale, Dar es Salaam, Harvard, and Warwick. He had written several acclaimed works, including one on Kenya that is regarded as a classic.[65] More importantly, he had been involved in constitution making in a number of countries around the world. With his reputation for academic excellence and an enviable human rights profile—and without a history of petty political partisanship in Kenya—he was the perfect candidate to head the review process. But the courtship was not easy; Amos Wako, the attorney general, had to travel to the University of Wisconsin–Madison, where Ghai was a visiting scholar, to plead with him to accept the appointment. For the Moi regime, Ghai would lend the process his enormous prestige, making it virtually unassailable as another Moi-KANU sham. But Ghai seemed to have accepted the appointment, well aware from the start that the Moi government intended to use him for its own political purposes. What Moi did not anticipate, however, was Ghai's political acumen and determination to give Kenya, the country of his birth, a modern democratic constitution. For Ghai, such an accomplishment would have been the most fitting epilogue to a distinguished career.

But almost immediately upon his appointment, Ghai discovered that there was little integrity in Kenyan politics. Political actors from both the left and right often acted out of narrow or partisan interests. Ghai realized that the political elites had virtually no concept of or commitment to any national interests.[66] Public discourse was coarse and vitriolic. Schemes, vendettas, pettiness, and crass greed dominated the lives of many key actors. Above all, the KANU elite was determined to do whatever it took to manipulate the constitutional review process for its narrow advantages. Moi, the long-term autocrat, was the master tactician and puppeteer, the grand old man around whom the pro-establishment figures genuflected and in whose court devious schemes were hatched. But the opposition leadership, with which Ghai sometimes openly sympathized, could also show a remarkable political and moral bankruptcy. Civil society, Ghai's natural ally, was also beset with its own pathologies, and its most progressive wing was skeptical of his ability to navigate Moi's labyrinthine world. To complicate matters, the increasingly vocal religious organizations were not always driven by the public good. Kenya's political terrain was thus treacherous and complex for an academic who had not spent substantial time there in the preceding several decades. As time would prove, it was perhaps the most trying assignment that Ghai had ever undertaken.

To give himself a chance at success, Ghai had to carefully work through—and often balance—the conflicting agendas of the various stakeholders. The negotiations over the review law, the selection of CKRC commissioners, struggles within the CKRC, Moi's machinations, and the Ufungamano–civil society interaction posed real challenges. Raila Odinga created further complications for Ghai. A clever political tactician, Odinga had inherited his father's mantle among the Luo and, unlike almost any other major politician in Kenya, almost exclusively commanded the passions of his populous community. Since the violent Kenyatta-Odinga divorce in 1966, the Luo as a community had become increasingly alienated from the state. With the assassinations of two luminary Luo sons, Tom Mboya under Kenyatta and Robert Ouko under Moi, and the long detentions of Oginga Odinga and his son Raila, the Luo community had developed a victim's psychology. As such, the community hungered for a political messiah to deliver it from the claws of an oppressive state. Raila Odinga, the incumbent messiah, had led the Luo back into Moi's KANU, for which he was rewarded with a cabinet post and the chairmanship of the PSC. He and many in the Luo community saw the review process as an avenue to ascend to the pinnacle of state power. Odinga's interest in Ghai was purely utilitarian, whereas Moi's was deceptive because he did not intend to complete the democratic overhaul of the constitution. But Ghai deftly navigated the divergent Odinga and Moi agendas to advance the review process.

Ghai had little control over the composition of the CKRC. Even though he had refused to take the oath of office until the government's Odinga-driven process had agreed to a merger with the Ufungamano effort, he did not exert any meaningful influence on the number and the actual choice of commissioners. Only twelve commissioners were added to the existing fifteen, and two of them were PSC choices. The final list of commissioners was a hodgepodge, although it was diverse in terms of gender, religion, region, race, ethnicity, and profession. Except for Ghai, Oki Ooko Ombaka, Wanjiku Kabira, Githu Muigai, Isaac Lenaola, P. L. O. Lumumba, Hastings Okoth Ogendo, and Mutakha Kangu, it was difficult to justify why more accomplished individuals were left out.[67] Although many of those selected had legal and other professional backgrounds, it was difficult to see how they could meaningfully contribute to the work of the CKRC. Many had mediocre and unremarkable careers and were certainly not known as thinkers, students of government, constitutional experts, or reform advocates. The CKRC was supposed to be the "thinking" organ of the review process, and the absence of many leading intellectuals or reform advocates was stunning. Many reform advocates or scholars were left out, including Nzamba Kitonga, Pheroze Nowrojee, Willy Mutunga, Kivutha Kibwana, Timothy Njoya, Betty Maina, Maina Kiai, Ali Mazrui, Alamin Mazrui, Ngugi wa Thiong'o, Micere Mugo, Shadrack Gutto, Martha Koome, Wachira Maina, Gibson Kamau Kuria, Betty Murungi, Davinder Lamba, Kathurima M'Inoti, Koki Muli, Peter Wanyande, and Karuti Kanyinga.

The CKRC was a political, not a technical, body. Its large size betrayed the political calculations of its authors. Rather than create a nonpartisan technical body, the politicians crafted a loose receptacle that would advocate their interests from within. The fact that most commissioners enjoyed political patronage made the CKRC a ground for the negotiation of partisan political interests. By this formulation, the CKRC was a microcosm of the National Constitutional Conference, the ostensibly representative national body that would hammer out the draft constitution. The NCC, which was supposed to take over constitution making from the CKRC, was run by the latter, although it was theoretically quasi-autonomous. Many of the crises that engulfed the CKRC were a result of its composition. Take, for example, the April 2001 secret visit to State House by a group of commissioners at Moi's invitation.[68] Ghai accused them of seeking to sabotage the review process. He said that "there is a narrow and personal agenda and that the national agenda is not uppermost in their minds."[69] Gibson Kamau Kuria, an NCEC official, charged that the commissioners had compromised the integrity, objectivity, and impartiality of the CKRC.[70] To the public, the commissioners seemed more interested in what they could get out of the CKRC than in what they would contribute to the review process. Several financial scandals gave the impression that the commission was a cash cow. A scheme to purchase luxury top-of-the-line SUVs rocked the commission.[71] There were reports that the bulk of the commission's expenses had gone to allowances and perks for its members. Matters got so bad that some commissioners charged others with corruption. An anxious Odinga ordered Ghai to resolve the problems within the CKRC and get down to work.[72]

Once Ghai agreed to chair the CKRC, he was under pressure to conclude the review process within the allotted two years because he was on leave from the University of Hong Kong. This made him impatient with the internecine conflicts and unnecessary delays caused by the petty squabbling of political actors. He moved quickly to restore sanity to the CKRC. First, he integrated Ufungamano commissioners into the structures of the CKRC when Ombaka and Abida Ali-Aroni, two of the Ufungamano commissioners, were appointed first and second vice chairs, respectively.[73] Then Ghai ordered the commissioners to stop consulting with KANU officials, including cabinet ministers. He warned them to stop reporting to their political godfathers.[74] He vowed to take disciplinary measures against errant commissioners in strict accordance with the laws establishing the CKRC.[75] In August 2001, Arthur Okoth Owiro, the commission's secretary, resigned under a cloud because of the scandals and conflicts within the CKRC. He cited the "rancor and acrimony" between himself and Ghai as the reason for his resignation.[76] P. L. O. Lumumba, a lawyer and flamboyant orator with a penchant for the grandiose, replaced him as secretary. But petty personality differences among the commissioners persisted and coalesced into blocs. Ghai and Okoth Ogendo, a respected constitutional law professor, engaged each other in a protracted struggle for control of the CKRC. The infighting intensified and almost paralyzed the CKRC in July 2002 after the death of Ombaka, who was widely respected as a force of moderation.[77] But Ghai persevered and would not resign until after the conclusion of the National Constitutional Conference in 2004.

The Work of the Review Commission

The first substantive function of the CKRC was to "conduct and facilitate civic education in order to stimulate public discussion and awareness of constitutional issues."[78] This exercise assumed that ordinary Kenyans needed to be educated about constitutional questions in order to participate effectively in the

review process. Since Kenyans had known only an opaque and autocratic government, it was essential that an environment conducive to the free and informed exchange of views be created prior to the solicitation of views. Otherwise, the CKRC would not receive useful information from the majority of
Kenyans, who were poor, uneducated, and excluded from the public square—
particularly women. But civic education for review purposes was an inherently
political exercise that would determine the views of the people, depending on
the level of freedom in which it was carried out as well as the nature of the information and the public documentation available. Thus the content, process,
atmosphere, and choice of providers of civic education were critical questions.
Different stakeholders sought to vindicate their interests through the provision
of civic education to the people.

The Kenyan postcolonial state has been viewed by a majority of the population as predatory, untrustworthy, and oppressive.[79] Its institutions and officials did not enjoy the confidence of the people. The mention of government
to many Kenyans would normally invoke fear, disdain, or even horror. In the
face of such antagonism and suspicion, few state-directed efforts succeeded, a
fact that over the years created a vacuum of governance in the lives of the people. In the place of the state, voluntary nonstate actors, such as NGOs, arose
to address the needs of the people. For example, in 1985, the Kenya Women's
Bureau reported the existence of 18,000 registered women's organizations.[80]
The nonstate landscape is dotted with development organizations, human
rights groups, professional associations, organized labor, women's groups, religious organizations, community-based organizations (CBOs), and other reform and advocacy formations. The growth and influence of the nonstate sector picked up in the late 1980s and exploded in the 1990s. As Mutahi Ngunyi
correctly points out, two historical developments were responsible for this
change. First, donors lost confidence in the increasingly corrupt and opaque
Kenyan state to implement the projects they funded.

> Aid agencies began to look for alternative implementing organizations to re
> place the government. These would be organizations operating closer to the
> people and not bogged down by a rigid bureaucratic system. The Non-
> Governmental Organizations (NGOs) became the natural choice of the donor
> community and some of the grants going to government began to flow to
> them.[81]

The second development is what Ngunyi frames as the imposition of conditions
on Kenya by international financial institutions such as the International Monetary Fund (IMF) and the World Bank. These conditions, imposed on Kenya
with the intent of paring down the bloated state, forced the government to retreat from many ventures, leaving the door open to NGOs.[82] This process was
the beginning of renewed attacks on the sovereignty of the Third World in order
to pave the way for rapid globalization. But the impoverished undemocratic

state, at odds with its people, could not resist these pressures. NGOs and religious organizations, two well-organized nonstate actors, were ready to take advantage of these circumstances. Direct external funding, which previously went almost exclusively to the state, was now funneled through NGOs and the churches. Naturally, as NGOs and religious groups became increasingly powerful, the state heightened its efforts to regulate, register, persecute, and circumscribe NGOs.[83] By 2001, when the CKRC commenced its activities, NGOs and religious groups had long established themselves as the institutions most trusted by the people, especially in the rural areas where the majority of Kenyans lived. Consequently, the participation of NGOs in civic education for the review process was unavoidable if it was to be successful and effective. Ghai and a number of commissioners had long realized that they would need the expertise, reach, and zeal of NGOs to pull off this critical stage of the process. But the KANU state was worried that NGOs would "radicalize" the people against it.

Kalonzo Musyoka, a powerful and hawkish KANU minister, vigorously opposed the provision of civic education by NGOs. He charged that "these NGOs have been spending a lot of money but their programs have not benefited Kenyans" because they "do not understand the priorities of the people."[84] But Odour Ongw'en, the chair of the government-sanctioned National Council of NGOs, defended the participation of civil society groups as legitimate stakeholders in the process. Muite, the influential Kabete MP and a longtime ally of civil society, vehemently disagreed with Musyoka and supported NGOs and religious groups because their wide reach and superior knowledge of the work required their inclusion.[85] Powerful cabinet ministers Nicholas Biwott, Julius Sunkuli, and Henry Kosgey opposed the inclusion of NGOs and churches. They told Ghai that civic education should not be hijacked by outside groups who then impose their views on local people and poison them against the government.[86] State panic reached a fever pitch when President Moi told NGOs to "keep off the review process" because they had no right to lead anyone. He accused NGO officials of being spies and told donors to leave Kenyans alone to decide their own fate.[87]

In spite of the public disagreements, or perhaps because of them, the CKRC intensified its efforts to launch civic education throughout the country. It set up structures at the district and constituency levels and staffed them with local personnel to facilitate the work of the review process. Key among them was the establishment of documentation centers that housed materials on constitutional questions, including the work of the CKRC.[88] Some of the materials were carried by local public libraries. In every parliamentary constituency, the CKRC set up a constituency constitutional forum (CCF) run by local people to "mobilize various sectors of society to participate in the review and in public hearings."[89] District coordinators were appointed to "mobilize people in districts and constituencies, and played a central role in the management of the documentation centers, the coordination of civic education, and the activities of the CCF and in facilitating public participation in the hearings."[90] The CKRC established its own website and posted key materials on it.[91] The website was an important source of information for the few Kenyans with access to the Internet, but was particularly useful to those in the diaspora. In that way, the CKRC set in motion a process of mass mobilization.

In July 2001, the CKRC started visiting people throughout the country to provide information about the review process and the reform agenda. It prepared a national curriculum to guide the providers of civic education.[92] It released two other important documents to prepare the people for the review process.[93] Before the dust settled on the controversy of the participation of NGOs and religious groups in civic education, the CKRC published an extensive and inclusive list of over 200 grassroots and national civic education providers, including NGOs, religious organizations, CBOs, professional groups, state institutions, political parties, student associations, academic institutions, trade unions, and others with an ability to reach wide audiences.[94] By including virtually any organization or group with a modicum of capacity to reach segments of the population, the CKRC had erred on the side of overinclusion and thus defused the spurious charge that favoring NGOs and religious organizations at the expense of state actors would distort the process against the KANU state. The CKRC itself traveled widely throughout the country and addressed groups from virtually all sectors of society. It extensively used electronic and print media and sponsored many workshops and public forums. Ghai even traveled with his vice chair to the United States and the United Kingdom to meet with Kenyans on the review process.[95]

In late 2001, the CKRC began conducting public hearings in Nairobi and the provincial capitals. According to its report, the commission visited every constituency from April to August 2002 in panels of at least three commissioners, and spent at least two days in each. By all accounts, the hearings were open, inclusive, and highly productive. Fears that educated elites would dominate the hearings to the exclusion of others were largely allayed as Kenyans from all walks of life turned out to voice their views. Even so, it is important to note that elites and organized groups submitted the most coherent and thoughtful contributions and memoranda. The CKRC reported that altogether it received 35,015 submissions, "many from organized groups, like political parties, religious communities, professional organizations, trade unions, NGOs, and ethnic communities."[96] The CKRC concluded that "through formal hearings and memoranda, millions of Kenyans, throughout the country and overseas, have spoken to the Commission."[97] It was a critical point for the CKRC since the legitimacy of its draft constitution would hinge on the credibility of the process. But inclusivity is not always a proxy for legitimacy. Much depended on the ideological content of the curriculum developed by the CKRC and the nature of the questions it posed to Kenyans. These variables could predetermine the outcome, although not necessarily nullify its legitimacy.

The work of the CKRC faced challenges from many quarters as political temperatures rose because of the impending 2002 general elections. Would the CKRC complete the review process and produce a new constitution before the elections? Political actors and interest groups started to view the schedule and timetable of the CKRC with anxiety and suspicion. Given the multiple stages of the review process, many expressed doubts that a new constitution could be completed in time for the 2002 elections. Whether by design or happenstance, the failure of the Safari Park compromise and the resultant conflicts, including the merger negotiations, had eaten into valuable time. Nor had the internal wrangles and scandals with the CKRC been of any help. In March 2002, the CKRC expressed doubt that it would complete the review process on time.[98] Many people, including some KANU officials, MPs, and even some religious leaders, charged the commissioners with incompetence for their failure to deliver a new constitution and called for the dissolution of the CKRC.[99] Ghai himself admitted that it was "no longer possible for the Commission to complete its work by October 4, 2002, as stated in the Act" and requested an extension of its life.[100] He wanted a shorter extension, whereas his opponents on the commission sought a longer one, possibly to prolong their terms for pecuniary benefit.[101] Odinga was displeased with calls for the extension and charged that the "review work calls for dedication, commitment, and patriotism which is lacking among the commissioners."[102] But the CKRC was granted more time, and calls to either extend the life of Parliament or postpone the 2002 elections were rejected.[103]

In spite of the extension, the Moi regime orchestrated yet another attempt, this time through the courts, to kill the review process. The KANU state feared that Ghai could still spring a surprise on it by completing the review process in time for the 2002 elections. One of the major targets for constitutional reform was Kenya's judiciary, long a haven of incompetence, mediocrity, and rampant corruption.[104] The public demanded that the new constitution retire and completely reconstitute the entire judiciary. Ghai called the judiciary incompetent and lethargic and said that it had never produced a "landmark decision worth talking about."[105] But Chief Justice Bernard Chunga bitterly counterattacked. Chunga called Ghai's charges "sheer flippancy and caprice to make sweeping statements in vague and general terms that all judges are incompetent, lethargic, and incapable of producing a judgment."[106] President Moi heightened the growing official hostility toward the CKRC when he loudly rejected its invitation to share his views on constitutional reform.[107]

It became apparent that the state was determined to deal the review process a mortal blow. As the CKRC convened to write the draft constitution, Justice Richard Kuloba ordered it to suspend the exercise pending a court challenge.[108] Two pro-establishment attorneys had filed suit against the commission, seeking to prevent it from addressing judicial reforms. Nevertheless, the CKRC produced a draft bill to amend the constitution of Kenya on September 18, 2002, in effect a draft constitution.[109] In another attempt to derail the review, Justice Moijo ole Keiuwa of the Court of Appeal and Justice Joseph Vitalis Juma of the High Court filed suit to stop the CKRC from addressing reforms in the judiciary in the draft constitution.[110] The widely condemned suit was described by Raychelle Omamo, the outspoken chair of the Law Society of Kenya, as "outrageous, despicable, preposterous, and contemptuous of the constitution and people of Kenya."[111] The CKRC's draft constitution proposed substantial reforms in the organization of the state and the distribution of power within it. On its face, the report of the CKRC and its draft constitution eliminated the concentration of power in the executive and removed most of the unbridled coercive authority from the person of the president. It included a comprehensive bill of rights and proposed norms, institutions, and structures that would democratize the state.[112] Though far from perfect, the draft constitution realized the worst fears of President Moi and KANU.

Under the extant Constitution of Kenya, the president could dissolve Parliament at any time and call fresh elections.[113] On October 25, 2002, just as the CKRC was welcoming delegates to the Bomas of Kenya, the historic cultural venue, for the National Constitutional Conference, President Moi abruptly dissolved Parliament, effectively ending the review process before the 2002 elections.[114] Heavily armed policemen took over the conference venue and denied delegates entry to it.[115] Ghai and the CKRC had no choice but to call off the conference since MPs comprised one-third of all delegates. Several days later, President Moi announced, apparently without good legal advice, that he had disbanded the CKRC and that a new commission, "one not headed by a foreigner," an incorrect and racist reference to Ghai, would be created after the elections.[116] But the Review Act did not empower President Moi to disband the CKRC, a legally sound correction that was made by Wako, the attorney general, and Lumumba, the secretary to the CKRC, both its ex-officio members.[117] Lumumba reminded the country that it was "only the parliament that has the last authority to disband the commission by repealing the Act that created it."[118] Moi had shown his true colors—he would not permit the conclusion of a process he could not control, particularly before the 2002 elections.

Notes

1. George B. N. Ayittey, *Africa in Chaos* (New York: St. Martin's Press, 1998).

2. Mutahi Ngunyi, "Comparative Constitution Making in Africa: A Critique of the Kenyan Process from Seven Countries," in Willy Mutunga, *Constitution-Making from the Middle: Civil Society and the Politics of Transition in Kenya, 1992–1997* (Harare: MWENGO, 1999), 258.

3. Willy Mutunga, "So, What Is Non-Partisanship?" in *Eyes on the Prize,* ed. Athena D. Mutua (Nairobi: Kenya Human Rights Commission, 2003), 31, 37.

4. "I Will Personally Lead Demos, Vows Orengo," *East African Standard,* April 11, 2000.

5. "Ufungamano Initiative Illegal," *East African Standard*, November 24, 2000, 9.

6. "Church Criticizes KANU on Reforms," *East African Standard*, May 1, 2000, 1; "Biwott Hits Out at Raila Critics," *East African Standard*, April 17, 2000, 1.

7. Philip Ochieng', "Why Prof. Nyong'o Can't Win the War with Ngilu," *Sunday Nation*, April 2, 2000.

8. "Ghai Declines Oath, Invites Ufungamano," *East African Standard*, November 29, 2000.

9. "Ufungamano Conditions for Joint Constitutional Review," *East African Standard*, November 30, 2000.

10. "Ghai: Moi Backs Reform Merger," *East African Standard*, December 1, 2000; "Ministers Slam Ufungamano," *East African Standard*, December 25, 2000, 3.

11. Ibid.

12. "Ignore Ufungamano, Raila Urges Prof. Ghai," *East African Standard*, December 11, 2000, 1.

13. "Moi Stops Ghai Talks," *Daily Nation*, January 8, 2001.

14. "Ufungamano Split over Merger Plan," *East African Standard*, February 1, 2001.

15. "State Out to Scuttle Reform," *Daily Nation*, February 18, 2001, 2.

16. Ibid.

17. "NCEC Is Chaotic, Says NGO Council," *East African Standard*, November 14, 2000.

18. "MPs Wary of Ghai Deal," *Daily Nation*, February 14, 2001, 9.

19. Ibid.

20. "Ufungamano Radicals Oppose Merger," *People Daily*, February 9, 2001.

21. "Experts Work on Reform Issues," *Daily Nation*, February 10, 2001.

22. "New Constitution Needed by 2002—Ghai," *People Daily*, March 1, 2001; "Attorney General Sees the New Constitution Before 2002," *People Daily*, February 8, 2001.

23. "Caution from Ufungamano as Draft Is Ready," *Daily Nation*, February 22, 2001.

24. Ibid.

25. "Ufungamano Skips Draft Handover Ceremony," *East African Standard*, February 22, 2001.

26. "NCEC Slams Wako over Draft," *East African Standard*, February 23, 2001.

27. Ibid.

28. Ibid.

29. "Raila Gives Faiths-Led Team 4-Day Notice," *Daily Nation*, March 18, 2001, 2.

30. "Hurdles Should Not Derail Ufungamano," *People Daily*, March 18, 2001, editorial; "Time to Pull Down Barrier for Reform," *Daily Nation*, March 21, 2001, editorial; Yash Ghai, "Unite or It Will be Chaos," *Daily Nation*, March 19, 2001.

31. "Yes for Merger: Uproar as Ufungamano Backs Joint Reform Team," *Daily Nation*, March 22, 2001, 1.

32. Ibid.

33. "Ufungamano: Raila Defends President," *Kenya Times*, April 11, 2001; "Prof. Ghai Faces Acid Test as KANU Hardliners Come out in Their True Colors," *East African Standard*, April 16, 2001.

34. "Ufungamano: Raila Defends President," *Kenya Times*, April 11, 2001, 1.

35. "Now Visit to Moi Splits Ghai Team," *Daily Nation*, April 13, 2001; "Ghai: I Feel Let Down," *People Daily*, April 15, 2001.

36. "Plans Afoot to Sack Prof. Ghai by KANU Hardliners," *People Daily*, April 15, 2001.

37. *East African Standard*, April 13, 2001.

38. "Raila and KANU Split over Review," *Daily Nation*, April 12, 2001, 1.

39. "Don't Amend Bill," *East African Standard*, April 19, 2001.

40. The SDP, which was the contested terrain for a more radical expression of politics, attracted populist politicians such as Charity Ngilu, James Orengo, Pheroze Nowrojee, Apollo Njonjo, and Peter Anyang' Nyong'o. It collapsed before its maturity because of leadership squabbles driven by ethnicity, ideological differences, and conflicting personal ambitions. See Philip Ochieng', "Why Prof. Anyang' Nyong'o Can't Win the War with Ngilu."

41. "Review Merger Bill: When Unity of Purpose Prevailed," *Kenya Times*, May 9, 2001; "Moi Assents to the Merger Bill," *East African Standard*, May 17, 2001.

42. *The Constitution of Kenya Review Act*, Chapter 3A, 2001 (hereinafter *Review Act*); "Moi Assents to the Merger Bill," *East African Standard*, May 17, 2001.

43. Preamble, *Review Act*.

44. *Review Act*, Section 9(1).

45. Ibid., Section 6(4)(b).

46. *The Constitution of Kenya Review Act*, No. 13 of 1997.

47. *Review Act*, Section 8(1)(a–b).

48. Ibid., Section 8(1).

49. Ibid., Section 11(1).

50. Ibid., Section 15 (4)(c–f).

51. Ibid., Section 15(4)(a), (b), (g).

52. The Constitution of Kenya Review (General) Regulations, 2001 (hereinafter CKRC Regulations).

53. *Review Act*, Section 9.

54. Ibid., Section 21(4).

55. Ibid., Section 21(6).

56. Ibid., Section 21(7).

57. Ibid., Section 17.

58. Ibid., Section 18.

59. Section 14(1), CKRC Regulations.

60. *Review Act,* Section 10.

61. Ibid., Part V.

62. Ibid., Section 26.

63. Ibid., Sections 26–28.

64. Ibid., Section 33(1).

65. Y. P. Ghai and J. P. W. B. McAuslan, *Public Law and Political Change in Kenya: A Study of the Legal Framework of Government from Colonial Times to the Present* (Nairobi: Oxford University Press, 1970).

66. Author's interviews with Yash Ghai at various times, and in different locations, from 2002 to 2004.

67. The other commissioners were Abida Ali-Aroni, Mohammed Swazuri, Charles Maranga Bagwasi, Salome Wairimu Muigai, Phoebe Asiyo, Alice Yano, Bernard Njoroge Kariuki, Abdirazak Arale Nunow, Zablon Ayonga, Nancy Makhoha Baraza, Kavetsa Adagala, Paul Musili Wambua, Abubakar Zein Abubakar, Riunga Raiji, Idha Salim, Ibrahim Lithome, Keriako Tobiko, K. Mosonik arap Korir, Domiziano Ratanya, Ahmed Isaac Hassan, Adronico Adede (appointed to replace the late Ombaka), Amos Wako (attorney general, ex-officio), P. L. O. Lumumba (secretary, ex-officio). See http://www.kenyaconstitution.org/html/comm02.htm, accessed April 27, 2005; Constitution of Kenya Review Commission, *National Constitutional Conference: Information Handbook for Delegates* (2003): 58.

68. "Ghai: I Feel Let Down," *Daily Nation*, April 14, 2001.

69. Ibid., 2.

70. "Plans Afoot to Sack Prof. Ghai," *People Daily*, April 15, 2001, 2.

71. "Kshs. 121 Million Deal Splits Ghai Team," *Daily Nation*, June 7, 2001; "Owiro Quits Law Team over Clashes with Ghai," *Daily Nation*, August 25, 2001.

72. "Raila to Ghai: End Rows," *Kenya Times*, June 11, 2001, 1.

73. "Ghai's New Team Appoints Ombaka," *Daily Nation*, June 18, 2001, 32.

74. Professor Ghai, interview with author, September 2002, Nairobi, Kenya.

75. Ibid.

76. "Owiro Quits Law Team over Clashes with Ghai," *Daily Nation*, August 25, 2001.

77. John Githongo, "Ooko-Ombaka Is Dead, the Review Goes On," *East African Standard*, July 29, 2002.

78. *Review Act*, Section 17(a).

79. Kivutha Kibwana, ed., *Law and the Administration of Justice in Kenya* (Nairobi: International Commission of Jurists, Kenya Section, 1992); Journal of African Marxists (proxy for anonymous authors), *Independent Kenya* (London: Zed Books, 1982).

80. Maria Nzomo, "Women, Democracy and Development in Africa," in *Democratic Theory and Practice in Africa*, ed. Walter O. Oyugi, Afrifa K. Gitonga, Atieno Adhiambo, and Michael Chege (Nairobi: East African Educational Publishers, 1988).

81. Mutahi Ngunyi, "Civil Society and the Challenge of Multiple Transitions in Kenya," in *Civil Society and Democratic Development in Africa: Perspectives from Eastern and Southern Africa*, ed. Julius Nyang'oro (Harare: MWENGO, 1999), 117, 118.

82. Ibid.

83. See *The NGO Coordination Act* (Nairobi: Government Printer, 1992).

84. "Row Rages over Reform Funds," *East African Standard*, July 16, 2001.

85. "Musyoka Answered on Civic Education," *East African Standard*, July 18, 2001.

86. "Big Kanu Men Face Law Team," *Daily Nation*, July 21, 2001.

87. "Moi Takes Hard Line on Review, " *Daily Nation*, July 22, 2001.

88. CKRC Regulations, Section 26, 2001; Constitution of Kenya Review Commission, *The People's Choice: The Report of the Constitution of Kenya Review Commission, Short Version*, 4, September 2002.

89. CKRC Regulations, Section 27, 2001; Constitution of Kenya Review Commission, *The People's Choice: Short Version*, 4.

90. Constitution of Kenya Review Commission, *The People's Choice: Short Version*, 4.

91. CKRC, http://www.kenyaconstitution.org/, accessed April 28, 2005.

92. Constitution of Kenya Review Commission, *Curriculum for Civic Education* (2002), http://www.kenyaconstitution.org/docs/04d001.htm, accessed April 28, 2005.

93. Constitution of Kenya Review Commission, *Reviewing the Constitution* (2001); Constitution of Kenya Review Commission, *The Constitutional Review Process in Kenya: Issues and Questions for Public Hearing*, 2001; "Issues and Questions for Public Hearings," *Sunday Nation*, November 25, 2001, Special Section, 1–8.

94. CKRC, http://www.kenyaconstitution.org/html/04a.htm, accessed April 28, 2005.

95. Constitution of Kenya Review Commission, *The People's Choice: Short Version*, 3–4.

96. Ibid., 4.

97. Ibid.

98. "Constitution Still a Long Way from Completion," *East African Standard*, March 31, 2002.

99. "Delay Puts CKRC and Parliament on the Spot," *East African Standard*, March 29, 2002.

100. "Ghai Plea Welcomed, Extension of Parliament Opposed," *Daily Nation*, March 29, 2002, 2.

101. Kivutha Kibwana, "It Is Ghai Who Is on the Right Track," *East African Standard*, April 25, 2002, 6.

102. "Ghai Team Members Accused of Stalling," *Daily Nation*, April 8, 2002.

103. "Review Commission to Wind up on Enactment of New Constitution—Bill," *Daily Nation*, August 7, 2002.

104. Republic of Kenya, *Report of the Administration of Justice: Summary of Recommendations*, 1998 (known as the Kwach Report for Justice Kwach, who chaired the committee); Drew S. Days, *Justice Enjoined: The State of the Judiciary in Kenya* (New York: Robert F. Kennedy Memorial Center for Human Rights, 1992). See also Paul Mwangi, *The Black Bar: Corruption and Political Intrigue Within Kenya's Legal Fraternity* (Nairobi: Oakland Media Services, 2001).

105. "Ghai Is Right About the Judiciary," *Sunday Nation*, July 21, 2002, editorial.

106. "High Court Judge Quizzed by Graft Police Squad," *Daily Nation,* January 20, 2003.

107. "Moi Declines to Meet Ghai," *Daily Nation*, August 25, 2002.

108. "Two Lawyers Threaten to Sue Ghai over 'Contempt,'" *Daily Nation*, September 6, 2002.

109. Constitution of Kenya Review Commission, *Draft Bill to Amend the Constitution*, September 18, 2002 (hereinafter *2002 Draft Constitution*).

110. "Case Against Ghai Splits the Bench," *Sunday Nation*, October 14, 2002.

111. "Uproar over Judges' Bid to Stop Ghai," *Daily Nation*, September 26, 2002.

112. Constitution of Kenya Review Commission, *The Main Report of the Constitution of Kenya Review Commission*, September 18, 2002; *2002 Draft Constitution*.

113. Section 59, *Constitution of Kenya* (1998), 1992.

114. "Can Kibaki or Uhuru Give Kenya a New Constitution After the Polls?" *Daily Nation*, November 11, 2002.

115. "Police Seal Law Review Venue," *Daily Nation*, October 28, 2002.

116. "Moi Moves to Disband Ghai Team," *Daily Nation*, October 28, 2002.

117. "Ghai's Commission Is Still Intact," *East African Standard*, October 30, 2002.

118. "Police Seal Law Review Venue," *Daily Nation*.

8

The National Constitutional
Conference as Process

TO BE SURE, Kenya did not invent the concept of the National Constitutional Conference (NCC), a device that has been used by a number of African countries to write a new contract between the state and society. Unlike several African dictatorships that had succumbed to popular pressure as reformist waves swept the continent, the Kenya African National Union (KANU) regime had managed to avoid a rout by pro-democracy advocates. President Moi had pushed back against the reformist surge, which had coalesced in 1991 with the formation of the Forum for the Restoration of Democracy (FORD). Through a series of heavy-handed tactics and self-destruction on the part of FORD, the Kenyan state had escaped the fate of its ilk in Mali, Congo, Zambia, and Benin, where autocrats had been ousted in a fever of regime change. Instead, Moi used his enormous constitutional powers and naked brutality to defeat a divided opposition. Perhaps his saving grace was the speed with which in 1991 he repealed the constitutional prohibition on multipartyism. By agreeing to open competitive politics, Moi had defused a long and possibly fatal standoff with a rejuvenated opposition. But through a swift decision, he had outmaneuvered an immature opposition that mistakenly believed that it could beat him at the polls, absent fundamental legal and constitutional reforms. That is how Kenya lost an opportunity for a national conference, despite calls for such a forum.[1]

In his matrix for political transitions in Africa, Paul Tiyambe Zeleza classified the Kenyan case among "countries where opposition parties were legalized and multiparty elections authorized through amendments to the existing constitutions by the incumbent regime."[2] In a description that fits Kenya, he argued that such a "pattern was followed mainly in one-party states where the opposition forces were too weak or fragmented to force national regime capitulation and the regime itself enjoyed considerable repressive and hegemonic capacities."[3] That is why the second path, that of the national conference, which "brought together members of the political class and elites of civil society to forge a new political and constitutional order,"[4] was only possible where it was "held early before incumbent regimes had learnt how to manipulate them, and where the opposition was strong and united and the regime weakened and fractionalized."[5] None of these factors were present in Kenya.[6] Even in 1997, when civil society led the charge for a national convention, it was the opposition political class that blinked and acquiesced to the minimum reforms proposed by Moi through the Inter-Parties Parliamentary Group, which he never fully implemented.[7] As a result, Kenya's political transition was not accompanied by any substantive legal or constitutional reforms, save for the minimal legal changes effected to remove formal barriers to political pluralism.

The institution of the national constitutional conference in Kenya had virtually nothing in common with the regime-changing forums witnessed in other autocratic states in Africa. Even though thousands of lives had been lost over a decade to state repression, Kenya's national constitutional conference was an inconclusive failure. Perhaps a constitution is best made during a historical moment when one order dies and another is born, preferably through violence, conflict, or a deeply embedded social dysfunction. Such a moment, known as a *constitutional moment*, is a rarity in a nation's history. Constitutional moments are forced on states by circumstances and cannot just be wished on a country by an elite. Besides, there must be a national consensus among the political class and the large majority of the citizenry that a new constitutional order is overdue or that the extant one is obsolete. Otherwise, the necessary national investment for a new constitutional dispensation may not be possible.

Perhaps the constitutional moment had passed by the time Kenya convened the National Constitutional Conference in 2003. If that is the case, then there have been three constitutional moments in recent Kenyan history: late 1991 and 1992, before that year's general elections; 1996 to 1997, just before the 1997 elections; and 1998 to 2002, before the general elections that year. These periods coincide with feverish demands for a new constitutional order, which many Kenyans saw as the vehicle for voting the Moi-KANU state out of office, changing the relationship between the people and the state, and making a political and legal break with the past. The national elections cycle provided constitutional moments because they were perceived as crucibles of regime change. A National Constitutional Conference in either one of the three periods—before any of the general elections—could conceivably have borne fruit. The constitutional moment may have passed in 2002 once the KANU party-state—the demon that bestrode society—lost power. That change may have created a constitution-making vacuum in which powerful pro-reform stakeholders did not see any further need for a new democratic constitution.

The groups that lost the fervor for a new constitution after the 2002 elections were neither duplicitous nor treacherous. Conversely, altruism cannot be the simple attribution of those groups that still pushed for a new constitution at the National Constitutional Conference. Both groups—particularly the political parties—took their respective positions based on their political location. Groups that had taken over the state saw no urgency for change, whereas groups that were excluded from the center of power sought a new constitution that they believed would be an ally in their drive for power. Even though there has been a liberal democratic consensus among Kenyan elites, different political parties, particularly those in power, have shown a disdain for the fundamental democratization of the state. They are driven by the fear of losing the political advantages that the concentration of power in the executive gives the incumbent government. This tendency of Kenyan political parties to withdraw from the reformation of the state is both a natural response to the assumption of power and a manifestation of the political bankruptcy of the ruling elites, which have had trouble envisioning national interests broader than their own political survival.

Had the national constitutional conference been conducted during any of the periods of the constitutional moment, there would have been a better opportunity for success. Allowing those moments to lapse, and then attempting to reform the constitution under a "democratic" government, rendered the national constitutional conference a forum for elite bickering instead of a solemn occasion to remake the state. Thus any new constitution written under an incumbent government—one not burdened by the deep-seated illegitimacy of the Moi-KANU state—would be unlikely to radically depart from the previous constitutional dispensation. That partially explains why the Kibaki government rejected the Bomas constitution produced in March 2004. In that sense, the National Constitutional Conference in Kenya, unlike its counterparts elsewhere in Africa, was a misnomer. National conferences elsewhere on the continent were spontaneous, unscripted revolutionary situations through which ancien regimes were written out. In contrast, the Kenyan conference was a staid affair calculated and scripted by the departing KANU regime. The democratic elections of 2002, in which the united opposition routed KANU, were instead viewed as the moment of transformation. Ironically, the elections diminished the importance of the national conference.

NARC and Process Paralysis

The political character of the National Rainbow Coalition (NARC), the new ruling party that ousted KANU, wreaked havoc with the reform agenda, particularly the pursuit of a new constitution. But only the history of NARC can explain its stubborn resistance to reform. The 1992 and 1997 general elections were bitter lessons to Kenya's chronically fragmented opposition. In both elections, the opposition presidential candidates split the vote, allowing Moi to be returned as head of state, even though their combined vote totals were higher than Moi's. In 1992, Moi faced three major opposition candidates, FORD-Kenya's Oginga Odinga, Kenneth Matiba's FORD-Asili, and Mwai Kibaki's

Democratic Party, whom he defeated with a bare plurality of the vote.[8] In 1997, the opposition again self-destructed by fielding four major opposition candidates against President Moi: Kibaki of the Democratic Party (DP), Michael Wamalwa of FORD-Kenya, Charity Ngilu of the Social Democratic Party (SDP), and Raila Odinga of the National Development Party (NDP). All but KANU were narrow ethnic political parties. Not surprisingly, Moi's take of the vote was higher this time, although still a plurality of the total.[9] An intransigent KANU regime had refused to reform the state to permit free and fair elections, and a fragmented opposition had once again failed to insist on complete reforms before the elections. Joel Barkan correctly notes these pathologies.

> Moi prevailed in Kenya's first two multiparty elections, held in 1992 and 1997, but with only a plurality of the vote. KANU won a narrow majority of seats in the National Assembly but not a majority of the votes cast. Both elections were characterized by unprecedented levels of communal violence and foul play. Neither could be described as free and fair, despite the presence of domestic and international observers. The main reason for the opposition's defeat, however, was failure to unite behind a single slate of candidates. In both elections, the opposition split its vote among three major ethno-regional parties and several smaller ones.[10]

It was evident that the opposition electoral defeats would never end unless the major opposition parties tamed rabid ethnicity and the gargantuan egos of their leaders. This conclusion was not a revelation to the opposition; one conclave after another had made the same determination. Civil society actors had repeatedly raised it and tirelessly worked to make opposition unity a reality, but to no avail. In 2002, opposition parties and leaders of the most vocal civil society organizations came together and formed the National Alliance for Change (NAC), a coalition that would finally create unity among the disparate opposition.[11] NAC brought together the most credible opposition political actors and the leading civil society barons in a masterstroke similar to the Citizens' Coalition for Constitutional Change and the National Convention Executive Council (NCEC), the organ that almost ended the Moi regime in 1997 before it was sidelined by the Moi-driven IPPG reforms.[12]

NAC brought together Kibaki; Wamalwa; Ngilu of the National Party of Kenya (NPK), the party she had formed after leaving SDP; Willy Mutunga of the Kenya Human Rights Commission (KHRC); Kivutha Kibwana of the NCEC; and a number of smaller political parties, including the Social Party for Advancement and Reforms Kenya (SPARK) of Shem Ochuodho, a rising opposition political star.[13] They all signed a memorandum of understanding on a framework for reform, including opposition unity, a single opposition presidential candidate, economic reconstruction, democratization, and the need for a people-driven constitutional review process.[14] Mutunga, who had been the spirit behind the civil society reform agenda of the past decade, was chosen chairperson of the NAC. But the NAC immediately faced the bane of Kenyan politics—which among the senior leaders within NAC would be the single opposition presidential candidate? All three key politicians—Kibaki, Wamalwa, and Ngilu—had been bitter rivals in the 1997 elections. Could they put aside their personal ambitions and unite? The merger between KANU and NDP had heightened the pressure on NAC.[15] As the choice for a single opposition flag bearer threatened to derail NAC, suggestions were floated to front an outsider, a nonpolitician, as a compromise. Those frequently mentioned were Mutunga, Kibwana, and Mutava Musyimi, the charismatic secretary-general of the National Council of Churches of Kenya.[16]

NAC soon converted into the National Alliance Party of Kenya (NAK), an opposition coalition party with DP, NPK, and FORD-Kenya at its core, as well as a constellation of other minor parties. But once NAC became NAK, a political party, civil society organizations pulled out and Mutunga stepped down from the chair, declining to lead an overt political party, a position that could have compromised his role as the executive director of the KHRC and the undisputed doyen of civil society.[17] NAK represented the first credible effort by leading opposition figures to form a united front against KANU since the split of the original FORD in 1992. The formation of NAK opened the first real possibility that KANU could be ousted in the 2002 elections. Since President Moi was barred by the constitution from running for another term, KANU had to choose his successor, a decision that set off an acrimonious power struggle among its senior leadership.[18] Among those with presidential ambitions within KANU were George Saitoti, the long-serving vice president; Raila Odinga, the former oppositionist turned KANU secretary-general; Musalia Mudavadi, a powerful minister; and Kalonzo Musyoka, another Moi protégé. But Moi, in an uncharacteristically shoddy fashion, openly dismissed them as unworthy and instead anointed Uhuru Kenyatta, a political novice but scion of Jomo Kenyatta, his handpicked successor. Under the tutelage of Odinga, the spited aspirants formed the renegade Rainbow Alliance, a rebel KANU group, with the intention of forcing Moi to abandon Kenyatta and settle on one of their number for the presidency. But Moi forcibly imposed Kenyatta on them. Then he corralled Mudavadi into abandoning the Rainbow Alliance and backing Kenyatta. With the exception of Mudavadi, whom Moi later appointed as vice president after sacking Saitoti, Odinga led the other rebels out of KANU, where they formed the Liberal Democratic Party (LDP), an opposition political party.[19]

The formation of LDP jeopardized the ouster of KANU because it could have splintered the vote, possibly giving Kenyatta a narrow victory. To complicate matters, Simeon Nyachae, the senior politician and long-serving KANU apparatchik, left the reeling ruling party and formed FORD-People. FORD-People later allied itself with Safina and the Social Democratic Party to form the Kenya People's Coalition (KPC). Three-way negotiations among

NAK, LDP, and KPC sought to form a superopposition alliance to face Kenyatta and KANU at the polls.[20] NAK, LDP, and KPC included within them virtually all the surviving and able-bodied leaders that had formed the original FORD, in addition to new, high-profile KANU defectors. Odinga and his NDP had come full circle. He had abandoned the opposition in 1998 to "cooperate" with and later merge with KANU. Moi made him cabinet minister and KANU secretary-general before he decamped to rejoin the opposition ranks in 2002 in the LDP. It was unlikely that such a motley collection of individuals, many driven by personal ambition and united only by desire to take power from Moi, could find a deeper common cause. There was no doubt that to a person they wanted Moi's protégé defeated, but beyond that narrow interest and the preservation of their political careers, they did not have a unifying ideology or encompassing philosophy.

Kenyan political parties are not driven by ideology but by personalities, particularly of their leaders. Since the death of the Kenya People's Union (KPU) in 1969 when it was banned by the government, there had been little ideologically to distinguish parties. Kenyan political parties, with the exception of KPU and to some extent SDP, have been to the right or the center-right of the political spectrum. Even reformist parties, such as the original FORD, hewed to a cautious liberal democratic model, endorsed open market reforms, and shied away from agrarian, radical center-left, or leftist politics. There was little to distinguish opposition parties even from KANU, itself a kleptocratic party, except its resistance to political and legal reforms to remove formal impediments to liberal democracy. Nevertheless, one could identify some minor differences in the ideological fingerprints of the three main opposition groups. NAK was the only relatively progressive party among the three. Among its senior ranks were reform-minded lawyers, politicians, and academics who had fought to reform the dictatorial state. They included Kiraitu Murungi, Mukhisa Kituyi, Martha Karua, Peter Anyang' Nyong'o, Charity Ngilu, Michael Wamalwa, Kivutha Kibwana, Shem Ochuodho, Maria Nzomo, and Wangari Maathai. Kibaki, the most senior politician in NAK, was a politically cautious former economics professor and Kenyan vice president who until 2002 had enjoyed an incorruptible reputation.[21]

The LDP, a haven for KANU rebels jilted by Moi, had virtually no reformers except for Odinga, with his mixed history. Frequently detained by Moi for long periods, Odinga had tarnished himself when he worked with Moi after the 1997 elections to sabotage the opposition reform agenda.[22] Even though the opposition welcomed him back as a prodigal son, there were no illusions that had Moi anointed him or one of his allies, and not Kenyatta, as the heir apparent, Odinga would have left KANU. Nyachae, the FORD-People leader and head of the KPC, had a reputation for administrative efficiency and honesty, but he had served Moi as secretary to the cabinet and senior cabinet minister and was therefore implicated in the abuses of the regime. But some of his partners in the KPC, such as Muite of Safina, and James Orengo and

Pheroze Nowrojee of the SDP, had stellar reputations as reformers and champions of basic rights. Even so, the KPC was seen as a front for Nyachae's presidential ambitions and was not taken seriously, in part because of his heritage in the relatively small Kisii ethnic group. The KHRC called on Nyachae and the KPC either to join NAK or quit, and later acknowledged his right to exit from the negotiations when he chose to do so.[23] Nyachae claimed that he quit because LDP and NAK struck a deal behind his back, settling on Kibaki as the opposition presidential candidate.[24] That left NAK and LDP, the two most popular opposition groups, to negotiate a merger.

The merger negotiations between NAK and LPD were influenced by the fever sweeping the land. Odinga and the rebel Rainbow Alliance had achieved folk hero status because of their open defiance of Moi. Never before had President Moi been so openly and boldly defied within KANU. The challenge by the KANU rebels sent throngs of massive crowds into delirium at the alliance's rallies around the country.[25] Even Kalonzo Musyoka, widely regarded as Moi's most obedient pupil, openly challenged his master and refused to be cowed.[26] Such nose thumping at the once invincible dictator was music to frenzied crowds that embraced the Rainbow Alliance, seduced the media, and captivated the nation. The public euphoria obscured the fact that even though Odinga and his fellows were defiant, they were still KANU officials. Even more significantly, the alliance's—and later LDP's—popularity depressed the public excitement over NAK. In contrast to NAK, which was led by the aged Kibaki, the LDP and its duo of the younger Odinga and Musyoka emitted energy, confidence, and popular engagement with the masses. An air of invincibility and inevitability started to coalesce around the LDP. Overnight, the KANU rebels had stolen the thunder of NAK and seemed poised to lead the opposition against Moi. Even so, the LDP did not have the numbers to go it alone. The Kenyan electoral map is deeply split along ethnic lines, and LDP's numbers did not add up. NAK, which was backed by leaders from the Kikuyu, Kamba, and Luhya, three of the five largest ethnic groups, still held an edge over LDP, whose only solid support was among the Luo. But NAK knew that it needed to capitalize on LDP's momentum and pad its numbers. It was these realities that on October 22, 2002, drove NAK and LDP to sign the infamous Memorandum of Understanding (MOU) and form the National Rainbow Coalition in a memorable ceremony at the Hilton Hotel in Nairobi.[27] As explained by Joel Barkan, realpolitik drove the calculations behind the coalition.

> NAK could only win with just over half the national vote if its constituent parties delivered all of their potential supporters. But betting the elections on such tight margins was too risky. The party found additional allies in another coalition: the Liberal Democratic Party (LDP). The LDP was formed ten weeks before the elections by three disaffected members of KANU, the most prominent of whom was Raila Odinga, the acknowledged leader of the Luo people. On October 22, 2002, NAK and LDP signed a memorandum of understanding,

thus creating NARC. The memorandum's key provisions were that Odinga would be appointed to the new post of prime minister and that cabinet posts would be divided "equally" between NAK and LDP. Once NARC was formed, the outcome of the election was never in doubt.[28]

But no sooner had Kibaki been elected president than NAK reneged on some, though not all, of the main stipulations of the MOU. Under the MOU, Kibaki would be president and FORD-Kenya's Wamalwa vice president. The tacit agreement was that, once a new constitution was enacted, Odinga would be named to the new post of prime minister and Charity Ngilu, George Saitoti, and Kalonzo Musyoka, among several others, would most likely be considered for the posts of deputy vice president and the two deputy prime ministers.[29] Even though Odinga and the LDP received choice appointments to the cabinet, they remained disgruntled. The MOU was not a principled document because those who signed it shared little else except their thirst for power. As put by Barkan, "the new party [NARC] was—and remains—a coalition of convenience, united more by what it opposed than by what it actually stands for."[30] In other words, although NARC was rhetorically committed to reforms for electoral purposes, its slogans and policy papers were little more than window dressing, not a coherent, internalized political ideology. The coalition rapidly deteriorated once Kibaki suffered a stroke in early 2003 from injuries he received in a car accident shortly before the elections.[31] His poor health and hands-off leadership style left a power vacuum that his closest aides, most drawn from the Kikuyu, Meru, and Embu communities, exploited to marginalize Odinga and the LDP.

Odinga had expected to be fully consulted on most government matters, particularly senior appointments to the cabinet and other key positions pursuant to the MOU. He remarked, "I do not know what happened between December 27 [Election Day in 2002] and January 3, 2003 [the day Kibaki appointed his cabinet]."[32] Within that one week, a new year had dawned, both literally and metaphorically. The hard reality was that it was Kibaki, not Odinga, who had been elected president under a constitution that concentrated power in the head of state. But Odinga and the LDP leadership believed that they had been used by NAK to capture state power and then dumped.[33] Even so, NAK's refusal to fulfill many of the promises of the MOU, which had no legal force, reflected the reality of power under an autocratic constitution. There is little doubt that Odinga would have acted similarly had he inherited such enormous constitutional powers.

Barkan correctly argues that NARC suffered from a common weakness that afflicts political parties across Africa. This fundamental flaw is the lack of a coherent ideology, a set of values that define the party and that for which it stands.[34] NARC was a bastardization of the notion of a political party. It was a coalition of parties with no party structures, except for a mock secretariat and the Summit, ostensibly the executive committee composed of the top barons drawn from NAK and LDP. The Summit, which Kibaki refused to attend, rarely met and was a dysfunctional battleground for the MOU when it did. Eventually, the Summit became defunct even after it was expanded to admit more of Kibaki and Odinga's proxies in the hopes of sorting out the fledgling coalition.[35] Once touted as the top organ of the party that had ousted KANU, the Summit quickly vanished from Kenya's political lexicon. Its death was the beginning of the end for NARC. The lack of commitment to NARC was evident in the retention of its respective constituent parties. Thus DP, FORD-Kenya, LDP, NPK, NAK, and other coalition parties were never dissolved and continued to operate solo. In that way the various ethnic barons who formed NARC were able to keep alive their communal strongholds and patronage networks. NARC itself was not internally transformed into a single membership party.

NARC's failure to agree on a power-sharing agreement between NAK and LDP split the government into many factions. NARC's constituent parties—all of which had an ethnic core—became the actual players in the country's politics. The DP, Kibaki's party, whose base was among the Kikuyu, Meru, and Embu—dubbed by the press the Mount Kenya Mafia—controlled the state and was the nerve center of power. It had a loose working relationship with FORD-Kenya, the mainly Luhya NAK constituent party that was led by Vice President Michael Wamalwa but was taken over by Musikari Kombo upon Wamalwa's death in 2003. The other major NAK player was Charity Ngilu, the NPK founder and registered chair of NARC.[36] At times she had a stormy relationship with DP after it became part of NAK and flirted with Odinga's LDP, but her struggle for supremacy in Ukambani against Musyoka, an LDP stalwart, precluded her from joining LDP. It was inconceivable that Musyoka and Ngilu, bitter rivals for the leadership of the populous Kamba community, would coexist in LDP. Even though they were in the same cabinet, these factions attacked each other often and bitterly, sometimes publicly contradicting stated government policies. The Kibaki government appeared like a political madhouse with no one in charge. But even as the NARC coalition failed and the government appeared chaotic, Kibaki remained aloof, apparently unperturbed by the din around him. Barkan has written that Kibaki's "laid-back" style resulted in confusion and conflict within NARC and the government.[37]

The result was a government unable to speak with one voice on the most important political questions. No other issue was more divisive within the government than the constitutional review process. When the National Constitutional Conference commenced in April 2003, the ruling NARC party did not have a coherent strategy to lead the process. On virtually every important question at the conference, the two NARC factions took opposing positions. Odinga and the LDP saw the conference as the forum through which the MOU would be fulfilled. This faction would push for a constitution with offices beneficial to them. The NAK faction in control of the state was determined to block a constitutional order that would grant LDP's wishes and emasculate the executive. The national conference became a battleground for power between NAK and LDP. With an eye to succession politics, both factions assumed that whichever group managed to get the conference to adopt its positions would control the post-Moi state. It is my opinion that Odinga outmaneuvered the NAK faction at Bomas.

> Odinga, a cunning political animal, has run circles around the Kibaki government, in which he remains a powerful minister. At the constitutional conference, he outmaneuvered President Kibaki's chief aide, Justice Minister Kiraitu Murungi, and prevailed upon the conference to adopt an unelected powerful premiership with an elected but ceremonial president.[38]

Odinga's victory at the national conference was political but unreal. It is virtually impossible to birth a new constitution without the leadership or acquiescence of a legitimate incumbent government, unless the rare opportune moment presents itself in the history of a nation. Such a moment usually comes when there is a chance of a radical break with the past, such as after a conflict or following a long and difficult era. For Kenya, it seemed such a moment was at hand, although divisions within NARC foiled the moment. The NAK wing of NARC, not the LDP, was the government in power. NARC, elected overwhelmingly on the promise of a new constitution, turned out to be the main obstruction to a long-held national aspiration. Political elites within NARC assiduously courted groups within KANU, the main opposition political party, to manipulate the national conference to their advantage. Different KANU factions happily obliged, themselves not keen on a new constitutional framework that might adversely affect the interests they had acquired over four decades of misrule. Ironically, NARC, which had bitterly attacked Moi and KANU when the government undermined and torpedoed the National Constitutional Conference in late 2002, became the major obstacle to a new democratic constitution.

The Struggles over the CKRC and the PSC

NARC's triumph in the 2002 elections created hope that the long-elusive democratic constitution would soon be completed. During the election campaign, NARC had mobilized public support on the delivery of a new constitution, among other key campaign issues. Different NARC leaders had even promised that a new constitution would be in place within 100 days of their assumption of power.[39] It was none other than Mwai Kibaki, NARC's presidential candidate, who, on December 26, 2002, the eve of the election, reiterated the 100-day promise for a new constitution in a widely read article in the country's leading newspaper.[40] No sooner had the dust settled than new and old struggles over the review process emerged. Much of the wrangling centered on the composition and the roles of the Constitution of Kenya Review Commission (CKRC), the Parliamentary Select Committee on Constitutional Review (PSC), and the National Constitutional Conference. Once again, different stakeholders scrambled to protect their turf, screen out opponents, and vindicate their interests. These struggles—petty, class, gender, sectarian, political, ethnic, and ideological—dogged the conference throughout and resulted in the stillbirth of a new democratic constitution.

Problems within the CKRC were the first signs that the national conference might turn out to be a hotly contested battleground. Whereas under the ancien regime the National Assembly's PSC had played a central role in the constitutional review process, the NARC government sought to take charge of the process through the new Ministry of Justice and Constitutional Affairs.[41] Kiraitu Murungi, formerly the opposition shadow attorney general, was appointed to the new powerful portfolio. Henceforth, Murungi would take the lead on the review process, a position he solidified by his oversight over the CKRC and the marginalization of the PSC. The executive, through Murungi, sought to steer the review process. The KHRC called for the disbanding of the bloated CKRC and its reconstitution with seven competent appointees, as opposed to the twenty-seven, whose exorbitant salaries and perks were a drain on public resources.[42] The KHRC was later supported by other organizations, including the influential Ufungamano Initiative, which remained an influential voice in the constitution-making debates.[43] Relations between commissioners at the CKRC sharply deteriorated, with a threat to oust Yash Ghai from the chair.[44] It was dispiriting that the machinations against Ghai, which had started when Moi was in power, and before the 2002 elections, continued unabated under the Kibaki regime. Now, commissioners were upset with Ghai because he wanted their salaries and perks stopped during lulls in the review process. They also accused him of working with the KHRC, the Institute for Economic Affairs, and other "outsiders"—the so-called Palacina Group, named for the Nairobi hotel where it met—to write the constitution to the exclusion of the CKRC.[45] The group had in fact invited the entire CKRC to its meetings, but only Ghai had bothered to show up.[46] Murungi stepped in and brokered a truce between Ghai and the commissioners. He announced that their payments would continue and ruled out disbanding them or trimming their numbers.[47]

But the truce within the CKRC was more apparent than real. A climate of suspicion and jealousy pervaded the entire organization. P. L. O. Lumumba, the silver-tongued secretary of the CKRC, played the role of the neutral bureaucrat. Caught between Ghai, the commissioners, and ethnic interests, Lumumba retained a level head. Meanwhile, the NARC government, in the person of Murungi, started to decenter Ghai from the review process. Attempts by Ghai to meet President Kibaki in early 2003 were thwarted by Murungi and other senior aides, partly because of Kibaki's poor health but also due to a cooling of interest by NAK in a new constitution. Ghai had assumed that NARC would quickly deliver a new constitution, but it soon became apparent that those close to NAK viewed the constitutional review process with some alarm. A clique of NAK politicians drawn from the Kikuyu, Meru, Embu, and related peoples and led by Murungi and Chris Murungaru, the internal security minister, threw a cordon around Kibaki and took a dim view of the national conference. The LDP clique, on the other hand, coalesced around Odinga and drew mostly from senior Luo politicians, although it also included several non-Luos who felt slighted by the Murungi group. Caught between the two factions, Ghai and the CKRC were drawn into the quagmire of Kenyan political intrigues. It was now clear: the new constitution had two key protagonists—Odinga and Kibaki.

A heated battle was waged over the composition of the PSC, the parliamentary committee that would work with the government and the CKRC in the review process. Odinga, the public face of the official constitutional review efforts until the 2002 elections, desperately sought to continue as the chair of the PSC, a position from which he believed he could neutralize the influence of the Murungi clique and prevail upon the national conference to adopt a constitution favorable to his political plans. Murungi, the Kibaki proxy, pointedly told Odinga, his cabinet colleague, to "stick to matters pertaining to roads and public works [Odinga's portfolio] because matters of the law are under my docket for me to address."[48] NAK, which was determined to stop Odinga's candidacy for the chair of the PSC, instead lobbied KANU and FORD-People, the two significant opposition parties, to support Muite of Safina over Odinga for the PSC chairmanship. With the LDP isolated, Muite defeated Odinga by a vote of eighteen to nine.[49] KANU ganged up against Odinga, whom it blamed for its election defeat the previous year.

The Composition of the National Constitutional Conference

The National Constitutional Conference, a conclave of both elected and appointed delegates drawn from the key sectors of Kenyan society, was conceived as the penultimate step in the review of the constitution. The creators of the NCC, widely depicted as a representative forum, argued that it would, together with the collection and collation of the views of the people by the CKRC, make the process broadly participatory and legitimize it as "people-driven." The proponents of the NCC contrasted it to the London Lancaster House process, held far away from Kenya and without the active participation of ordinary Kenyans. To them, Bomas (named for the venue of the NCC), unlike Lancaster, was inclusive and participatory. The NCC would convene for "discussion, debate, amendment and adoption" of the draft constitution prepared by the CKRC and Ghai, and could reject it and instead introduce other provisions.[50] The conference was presented as an open-ended forum in which its delegates, the so-called people's representatives, would be unfettered by the predetermined draft constitution and views of the CKRC.

The architecture of the constitutional review process was a product of difficult negotiations conducted under the Moi regime. The regime had never supported the process and only gave in when pushed to the edge of the abyss. Moi's intentions became clear on October 25, 2002, when he abruptly dissolved Parliament, prematurely ending the NCC as it was about to start.[51] Moi had jointly crafted the review mechanism with Odinga, but now torpedoed it once Odinga had decamped from KANU and joined NARC. Even though the structures of the review process—the NCC, CKRC, and PSC—favored KANU, President Moi was not comfortable enough to permit the conclusion of the process. An institution born through manipulation and hampered by elites afraid of fundamental change was unlikely to write the constitution desired by the majority of Kenya's impoverished masses. This critique, which was lodged at the NCC by some vocal sections of civil society, could have been dismissed as sour grapes, except that it was vindicated by history. Instead, opponents of the NCC argued that the process be reconceived since a new democratic regime had been elected in a free and fair vote.

The composition of the NCC was a critical factor in the outcome of the review process. Negotiations over the number and composition of delegates to the conference had been tense and emotional. Civil society actors and the Ufungamano Initiative, wary of the government's determination to pack the NCC with its loyalists, sought a transparent process for picking delegates to ensure the broadest representation.[52] Negotiations over representation had settled on a quota system in which key stakeholders were allocated slots and required to determine their choices. According to this matrix, the national conference was to be composed of all 29 CKRC commissioners as ex-officio members (27 plus the secretary and the attorney general), without the right to vote; all 223 members of the National Assembly (222 MPs plus the Speaker); 41 representatives from registered political parties, but not MPs; 126 delegates from civil society, professional associations, religious groups, and other interest groups; and 210 district delegates.[53] The total count of delegates was 629—with two-thirds divided equally between elected MPs and district delegates and the final third reserved for representatives of political parties (but not MPs), NGOs, women's groups, trade unions, professional associations, and special interest groups, such as the judiciary, industrialists, the media, persons with disabilities, and others.

A critical analysis of the matrix reveals some fundamental flaws in the logic and design of the list of delegates. First, there was no uniform method for determining delegates from the various sectors. One-third of the delegates— MPs—were predetermined by virtue of their membership in the National Assembly, as were the members of the CKRC. The MPs, a dominant group at the

conference, were divided along party, ethnic, and other cleavages. But they also
exercised sway over many other categories of delegates because of their political seniority and high social status. Most were wealthy individuals because the
cost of mounting a successful electoral campaign requires a formidable war
chest. Thus virtually all the MPs were members of an exclusive elite with
strong ties to the previous regime and business interests. This elite constituted
a minuscule percentage of Kenyan society, but gave itself one-third of all seats
at the NCC, a numerical strength that vastly outstripped its numbers in the general population. The counterargument was that MPs were entitled to such representation because they were the elected proxies of the people. The bottom
line, however, is that it was the MPs who wrote the review law and therefore
granted themselves a disproportionate share of the public square at the National
Constitutional Conference.

Perhaps the most controversial delegates were those drawn from the districts. The law required that each district elect, through its respective county
council, three delegates, at least one of whom had to be a woman.[54] The one-
third affirmative action principle for women was admirable; otherwise men
would have completely dominated the district lists. Most county councils were
cesspools of fascist ideologies, corruption, political cronyism, and KANU
domination. Some critics argued that most councilors were not competent in
questions of constitutional review and political governance to pick able delegates.[55] MPs exercised immense control over local authorities where prominent businessmen and government officials were interwoven by a tapestry of
property interests in a corrupt system of favors and kickbacks.[56] This system
prevented the emergence of independent and corruption-free advocates from
the grassroots, which was the ostensible logic of allocating one-third of all the
seats in the NCC to district delegates. Dubbed *wanjiku*, the Kenyan female
name and euphemism for the commoner, the district delegate was more likely
to be a local notable, businessperson, or politician rather than the average
Kenyan. Perhaps an open election, with a built-in one-third principle to ensure
the representation of women, could have yielded a more legitimate list. A leading daily warned against the politicization of the selection of delegates to
avoid the domination of the NCC by "short-sighted political interests."[57]

Critics argued that the verdict of the people in the 2002 elections called
for revisiting the review process. Although many found no major problems
with the first phases of the review process—particularly the collection and collation of the people's views by the CKRC—they argued that the NCC ought
to be reconceptualized. The selection of delegates drew the most ire. Several
options had been debated in the public domain. Some argued that the list of
delegates be reconstituted afresh following regime change in 2002 to reflect
the new political dispensation. Why allow Moi-era delegates, particularly
those from the districts, to write a constitution in the NARC era, a dispensation that had rejected the autocratic order of the past? Others argued that the

principle of equal representation had been abrogated by the decision to allocate three delegates per district, even though some districts were vastly more populous than others. Nairobi, with a population of 2,148,254, was, like Moyale with its 53,479 residents, given only three delegates, the same number allocated to all districts no matter their population size.[58] Under Moi, dozens of so-called political districts had been created, many in underpopulated KANU strongholds, to reward political cronies. Mirugi Kariuki and Koigi wa Wamwere, both MPs and NAK delegates, questioned the legality of the NCC and sought to stop it on account of the inclusion of delegates from "illegal" and "political" districts.[59] Their ill-fated attacks on the NCC were seen as a plot on the part of NAK to derail the conference.

Many district delegates displayed a palpable hostility toward NAK and its sympathizers at the conference, aligning themselves with KANU and the LDP against NAK. The conference took on an ethnic tone with accusations that the "Mount Kenya Mafia," a euphemism for NAK leaders (many belonging to DP) from central Kenya led by Murungi, were out to torpedo the forum.[60] Most delegates from religious organizations, civil society, and other interest groups became divided along this political and ethnic cleavage, with KANU and LDP on the one hand and NAK on the other. The paralysis was partially a result of the composition of the NCC, a problem that could have been cured by an open election to create a constituent assembly. It was noticeable that many reform advocates and human rights activists who had long fought for a new constitutional order were not part of the NCC, having been left out or declined inclusion in what they saw as a flawed process. They included Timothy Njoya, James Orengo, Pheroze Nowrojee, Davinder Lamba, Gibson Kamau Kuria, Kepta Ombati, Koki Muli, Betty Murungi, Joe Donde, Rumba Kinuthia, Jane Michuki, Tirop Kitur, Betty Maina, Nzamba Kitonga, John Munuve, Maina Kiai, Njeru Kathangu, and many others. Some of them, such as Lamba, Muli, and Njoya, were granted observer status at the conference, a sleeper position from which they could lobby on the grounds of the forum but not officially participate in the conference.[61] Many leaders of the constitutional reform movement had been shut out of the National Constitutional Conference, arguably the most important phase of the process. Their places were taken by former regime elements, some of whom had bitterly opposed reforms.

The Institution of the National Constitutional Conference

The political landscape dramatically changed in December 2002 following the ouster of KANU. Key sectors had to recalculate what constitutional review meant for them and how they would influence it. Kenyans had always been ruled by KANU, and for that reason the NARC regime was a great unknown. Would President Kibaki and the small band of reformers transform politics?

What would the state do about grand corruption, past atrocities, and other illegal acts of the previous regime? Did the new rulers plan to prosecute and hold accountable the worst offenders of the ancien regime, or would it be business as usual? Which institutions would be reformed? Key actors seemed convinced that the new constitution would signify what the NARC state planned for the country. They jostled to protect their interests in the review process at the national conference. These maneuvers led me, the chair of the KHRC, to warn of "serious attempts by some organizations, the elite, and politicians to manipulate and hijack the Constitutional Conference and enter into selfish agreements."[62] On April 28, 2003, the National Constitutional Conference formally opened at the Bomas of Kenya amid fanfare and the glare of the media.

President Kibaki invoked the nobility of the task of writing a constitution when he spoke at the conference on April 30, 2003. Belying the deep divisions between the delegates, President Kibaki called the conference a "gathering of the whole nation" and likened it to a "constituent assembly" that must be guided by the "national interest."[63] He decried the "corruption and tyranny that many brave and patriotic Kenyans" fought against to bring about reform.[64] He paid a "special tribute to civil society organizations, which played a leading role to bring us to this stage, in our review process."[65] He acknowledged the inspiration of the Ufungamano Initiative and called upon all the organs of the review process, including Parliament, to be guided by the values of "democracy, transparency, accountability, integrity and people's participation, rights and freedoms."[66] He commended the CKRC for a "good job" in collecting the people's views and for its "draft constitution that shows great respect for the people."[67] He pledged that his government would support the review process. In an allusion to the divisions at the NCC, he reached out to the delegates and appealed for the best in them.

> The conference is a gathering of the whole nation. It should strengthen national unity. The delegates must discharge their duties responsibly. You must be mindful of the national interest. As individuals, we are bound to have our own personal interest. But, as Kenyans, we are enjoined to promote the national good, the integrity of the state, and the rights and the welfare of the people. Our own narrow interests must be subordinated to the greater good.[68]

Kibaki's speech was presidential and inspired, but it seemed to have fallen on deaf ears as delegates went for each other's jugulars as soon as he walked out the door. Although the CKRC was charged with the responsibility of convening the national conference to the draft constitution, its leadership was greatly compromised by contending political factions and players.[69] It was not clear what role, if any, Yash Ghai, the chair of the CKRC as well as the NCC, would permit Muite, the chair of the PSC, and Murungi, the minister for constitutional affairs. The PSC, the parliamentary review oversight body, was not given any specific function or powers over the national conference, although by law it was the puppeteer of the CKRC.[70] Murungi sought to exert himself as Kibaki's proxy, although he, too, had no specific mandate over the conference. Even though a certain degree of collaboration with the Parliament and the executive through Muite and Murungi, respectively, was necessary, it was Ghai who as chair of the NCC had the clear-cut, if not sole, responsibility to chair and lead the national conference. Murungi and Muite were in the NAK camp, whereas Odinga led a newly resurgent LDP-KANU faction at Bomas. Odinga and KANU had informally come together again at Bomas to oppose NAK. For Ghai, it was slippery political ground because he had long worked with Odinga when the latter was chair of the PSC and had protected him from Moi's machinations. Yet Ghai had to work with the NAK side, which controlled the state, if he had any hopes of successfully completing the review process. Visible bias on either side could doom Ghai. The government could withdraw its support for him, whereas Odinga could mobilize and agitate the delegates against him.

It was on these tenterhooks that Ghai gaveled the national conference to order. Ghai, Lumumba, and the CKRC's commissioners drafted the key conference documents, including the regulations governing it. As an institution, the CKRC would administratively run the conference, keep its records, and process any documents issuing out of it. The commissioners assigned themselves leading roles at the NCC, including chairing sessions and taking the delegates through the draft constitution. Some critics felt that the CKRC should not have been granted such a leading role since the conference would be deliberating on the draft constitution it had written, and it might be too defensive or biased against external views. Ghai was cornered from every quarter by powerful interests: NAK, LDP, district delegates, KANU, CKRC, PSC, and the government. Add to these forces civil society and the Ufungamano Initiative, to which Ghai retained deep links. Although the latter two had been edged out of the center of the review process by the design and composition of the NCC, Ghai counted himself one of them. But he had to balance all these interests by listening to everyone while keeping his own counsel. His task was nothing short of Herculean. He had to project the image of a firm and decisive leader, someone who could play fair, stick to basic moral principles, and objectively judge all entreaties from the protagonists. Otherwise, the constitution-making project would degenerate into a corrupted and petty affair.

The first test for Ghai came with the selection of the Steering Committee, the executive organ of the conference, the body responsible for making and approving the work plan, procedures, and rules of the NCC.[71] In the end, the Steering Committee effectively turned Ghai into a titular head of the forum. The initial CKRC regulations provided for a Steering Committee of a core of twenty-seven delegates, and all CKRC commissioners as ex-officio members, but the National Constitutional Conference expanded the core number to fifty-seven, which brought the total number to eighty-nine.[72] The Steering Committee comprised 14 percent of the NCC and included the leading protagonists from the opposing camps. It was large enough to be considered a conference within a conference. Its composition exacerbated the sharp ethnic divisions, political conflicts, and personal ambitions at the NCC. It was dominated by former regime elements such as KANU's Bonaya Godana, who was elected to one of three vice chair positions. The Steering Committee included only a handful of prominent reform advocates.[73] Those vice chairs of the Steering Committee were also vice chairs at the conference. This organizational structure was frustrating and often led to paralysis and obstruction at the committee and the conference.

CKRC regulations governed NCC proceedings. The regulations followed a parliamentary script for debate and decorum. They were designed to maximize open debate that was carried out in sessions organized by the chapters in the CKRC draft constitution. Delegates were given a limited time to express their views, after which debate was closed on that chapter of the draft constitution. A few delegates made useful contributions in these open-ended sessions, but the majority seemed baffled by the complexity of the subjects.[74] The debates were not concluded with any process, such as a vote, for reaching decisions on the key questions. That is why the conference report of the rapporteur-general was incorrect to assert that broad areas of agreement had emerged.[75] This failure to resolve major areas of concern early opened room for sabotage later. In effect, Bomas I, or the first phase of the conference, which would end up convening in three phases, was redundant because it was simply a collection of the views of delegates, a task identical to that which the CKRC had performed throughout the country during the first phase of the review process.

After Bomas I, attention at the national conference shifted to the technical working groups (TWGs) corresponding to each of the chapters of the CKRC draft constitution.[76] When Bomas II, or the second phase of the conference, convened in September 2003, the TWGs, themselves composed of roughly the same number of delegates, took up consideration of the various chapters of the draft. Their task was to debate matters pertinent to their chapters and make decisions to be reported to the plenary of the national conference for adoption and inclusion into the final draft constitution. The working groups were a crucial stage in the decisionmaking process because it was within them that critical decisions would be made and reported to the plenary. The working groups became battlegrounds for the competing factions, again reproducing the animosities and pathologies of the CKRC, the Steering Committee, the PSC, and the NCC itself. Temperatures rose substantially when Crispin Mbai, the Luo chair of the Devolution Working Group, one of the hotly contested issues, was murdered gangland-style at his home.[77] Rumors linked NAK to the murder, which Odinga, a close friend, described as an assassination.[78] The death heightened factional fighting at the conference as key decisions were being made. "Indeed, the second phase of the Bomas talks has been the most explosive since the whole process began. The progress in the deliberations has been painstakingly slow, and all because of the immense tension, fuelled by divisions and a simmering power struggle in the ruling National Rainbow Coalition."[79]

When Bomas II ended in late September 2003, the two NARC factions indicated willingness for mutual accommodation on the contentious issue of a prime minister. Murungi indicated that the government was not opposed to the office, giving hope that the one issue that had paralyzed Bomas might be resolved. But the truce was a fig leaf. The crisis did not abate, and in January 2004 when Bomas III, the third and terminal phase of the conference, opened, the daggers were drawn. In March 2004, the final phase of the conference ended in infamy when the LDP-KANU majority adopted the final draft constitution after Vice President Moody Awori and Murungi led a government walkout at the conference because they failed to prevail on the most contentious issues, particularly on the structure of the executive and devolution.[80] The final draft constitution, which provided for a powerful prime minister and relatively weak president, was the document that Odinga had long advocated for but one that NAK had vehemently opposed.[81] Although the National Constitutional Conference ended with the adoption of a draft constitution, the exercise was a failure because the government and a substantial portion of the population opposed the document. It was an empty victory for the LDP-KANU alliance, although it is arguable whether the NCC as a whole had been an exercise in futility, or even a harmful process, once it is viewed in the fullness of history. What is clear is that the conceptual and structural weaknesses of the NCC had been exploited by political elites to deny the country an opportunity to reform the predatory state.[82]

Notes

1. Makau wa Mutua, "A Call for a National Dialogue," *Nairobi Law Monthly* 36 (September 1991): 25.

2. Paul Tiyambe Zeleza, "Introduction: The Struggle for Human Rights in Africa," in *Human Rights, the Rule of Law, and Development in Africa*, ed. Paul Tiyambe Zeleza and Philip J. McConnaughay (Philadelphia: University of Pennsylvania Press, 2004), 1, 3.

3. Ibid.

4. Ibid.

5. Ibid.

6. International Human Rights Law Group, *Failing the Pluralist Challenge: Human Rights and Democratization in Kenya's December 1992 Multi-Party Elections*, Washington, DC, November 1992.

7. Willy Mutunga, *Constitution-Making from the Middle: Civil Society and Transition Politics in Kenya, 1992–1997* (Harare: MWENGO, 1999).

8. National Election Monitoring Unit, *The Multi-Party General Elections in Kenya, 29 December 1992* (Nairobi: NEMU, 1993), 1003; Frank Holmquist and Michael Ford,

"Kenya: State and Civil Society the First Year After the Election," *Africa Today* 41 (1994): 5, 19.

9. Institute for Education in Democracy, Catholic Justice and Peace Commission, and National Council of the Churches of Kenya, *Report on the 1997 General Elections in Kenya, 29–30 December 1997* (Nairobi: Institute for Education in Democracy, 1998).

10. Joel D. Barkan, "Kenya After Moi," *Foreign Affairs* 83 (2004): 90.

11. "Opposition Leaders Sign Unity Accord," *Daily Nation*, February 13, 2002.

12. Mutunga, *Constitution-Making from the Middle*.

13. "Opposition Leaders Sign Unity Accord," *Daily Nation*.

14. Ibid.

15. "Can Big Three Agree on 'Outsider' Candidate?" *Daily Nation*, April 18, 2002.

16. Ibid.; "How to Settle on One Presidential Hopeful—Dr. Mutunga," *Daily Nation*, April 30, 2002.

17. Willy Mutunga, "So, What Really Is Non-Partisanship?" in *Eyes on the Prize*, ed. Athena D. Mutua (Nairobi: Kenya Human Rights Commission, 2003), 31, 33; email response from Willy Mutunga to Makau Mutua, May 4, 2005.

18. The constitution was amended in 1992 to limit the office of the president to two five-year terms. Section 9(1) and (2), *Constitution of the Republic of Kenya* (1992), 1998.

19. "Beth Mugo Heckled at Funds Rally," *Daily Nation*, October 27, 2002.

20. "Nyachae, Saitoti in 'Tricky Position,'" *East African Standard*, October 21, 2002.

21. Makau Mutua and Willy Mutunga, "Why and How to Bring About Regime Change in Kenya," in *Eyes on the Prize*, ed. Athena D. Mutua (Nairobi: Kenya Human Rights Commission, 2003).

22. Kiraitu Murungi, *In the Mud of Politics* (Nairobi: Acacia Stantex Publishers, 2000), 80.

23. Kenya Human Rights Commission, "The Opposition Unity Talks: Kenyans Need Fundamental Regime Change, Not Just New Faces," October 20, 2002; *East African Standard*, October 21, 2002.

24. "How Rainbow Coalition Picked Kibaki and Kept Nyachae in the Dark," *Daily Nation*, October 28, 2002.

25. "Moi Now Sacks Assistant Minister Khaniri," *Daily Nation*, September 23, 2002.

26. "Members of the Rainbow Alliance Fighting a Lost Cause," *Daily Nation*, September 10, 2002.

27. "The Broken MOU Dealt the First Blow to NARC," *East African Standard*, December 31, 2006.

28. Joel D. Barkan, "Kenya After Moi," 91–92.

29. "How Rainbow Coalition Picked Kibaki and Kept Nyachae in the Dark," *Daily Nation*.

30. Joel D. Barkan, "Kenya After Moi," 92.

31. Ibid.

32. Interview with Raila Odinga by Makau Mutua and Willy Mutunga, May 2003, Bomas of Kenya, Nairobi, Kenya.

33. Ibid.

34. Barkan, "Kenya After Moi," 92.

35. "NARC Summit Is Dead, Declares Kalonzo," *Daily Nation*, November 11, 2003.

36. "NARC Enrollment Moves to Kambaland," *Daily Nation*, February 24, 2004.

37. Barkan, "Kenya After Moi."

38. Makau Mutua, "The End of Reforms in Kenya," *Boston Globe*, August 14, 2004.

39. "The Way Ahead for NARC," *Daily Nation*, November 27, 2002, editorial; "New Laws Ready by June," *Daily Nation*, January 9, 2003; "Kamotho: Constitution in 100 Days," *East African Standard*, October 29, 2002.

40. "How Kenyans Can Get Back on Track," *Daily Nation*, December 27, 2002.

41. "Kibaki's New Look Cabinet Structure," *East African Standard*, January 16, 2003, 1.

42. Kenya Human Rights Commission, "The Agenda for President Kibaki," *Daily Nation*, January 9, 2003, press release.

43. "Call to Drop CKRC Commissioners—Ufungamano," *East African Standard*, April 4, 2003.

44. "New Bid to Oust Ghai from CKRC," *East African Standard*, January 15, 2003.

45. Ibid.

46. "Reasons for Tension in the Law Review Team," *East African Standard*, January 18, 2003, Ghai interview with Njonjo Kihuria; "If Ghai Takes Flak, Why Not Credit?" *East African Standard*, January 16, 2003, editorial.

47. "Commissioners Meet Murungi over Ghai Stalemate," *East African Standard*, January 16, 2003.

48. "Keep Off My Docket, Murungi Tells Raila," *East African Standard*, February 5, 2003.

49. "Constitution Review Back on Course," *Daily Nation*, March 20, 2003.

50. *The Constitution of Kenya Review Act*, Section 27(1)(b), Chapter 3A, 2001 (hereinafter *Review Act*).

51. "Parliament Is Dissolved: Constitutional Process in Disarray," *East African Standard*, October 26, 2002.

52. "Fears KANU May Manipulate New Constitution," *Daily Nation*, January 22, 2002.

53. *Review Act,* Section 27(2); see also Constitution of Kenya Review Commission, *National Constitutional Conference: Information Handbook for Delegates* (2003): 2.

54. Ibid., Section 27(c).

55. "Fundamental Issues That the Law Review Team Must Address," *Daily Nation*, March 26, 2003, letters.

56. Jennifer A. Widner, *The Rise of a Party-State in Kenya: From Harambee to Nyayo!* (Berkeley: University of California Press, 1992).

57. "Critical Time for Law Review," *Daily Nation*, September 18, 2002.

58. Institute for Economic Affairs, *The Little Fact Book: The Socio-Economic and Political Profiles of Kenya's Districts* (Nairobi: Institute for Economic Affairs, 2002), 54, 80.

59. "New Power Struggle in Bid to Halt Review," *Daily Nation*, May 8, 2003.

60. Ibid.

61. Constitution of Kenya Review Commission, Constitution of Kenya Review (National Constitutional Conference) (Procedure) Regulations, Section 8, 2003 (hereinafter National Conference Regulations).

62. *Kenya Times*, April 23, 2003, at 1.

63. "Speech by His Excellency President Mwai Kibaki, During the Opening of the National Constitutional Conference at Bomas of Kenya on 30 April, 2003," available

at http://www.kenyaconstitution.org/docs/12d006.htm, accessed May 11, 2005 (hereinafter Kibaki Speech).

64. Ibid.

65. Ibid.

66. Ibid.

67. Ibid.

68. Ibid.

69. *Review Act,* Section 27(1)(b).

70. Ibid., Section 10.

71. National Conference Regulations, Section 46.

72. Constitution of Kenya Review Commission, *The Report of the Rapporteur-General to the National Constitutional Conference on the General Debate Held Between April 28, 2003, and June 6, 2003, at the Bomas of Kenya,* July 17, 2003 (hereinafter *Report of Bomas I*).

73. Ibid., 107.

74. Makau Mutua, "The Bomas Constitutional Talks Were One Big Farce," *Sunday Nation*, October 5, 2003.

75. *Report of Bomas I,* 16.

76. National Conference Regulations, Section 20, 49.

77. "Guard Held as Police Probe Killing," *Daily Nation*, September 16, 2003.

78. "Police Seek Matatu in Hunt for Mbai's Killers," *Daily Nation*, September 17, 2003.

79. "Enhance Bomas Consensus," *Daily Nation*, September 28, 2003, editorial.

80. "VP Leads Bomas Walkout," *Daily Nation*, March 16, 2003.

81. National Constitutional Conference, *The Draft Constitution of Kenya—2004,* Chapters 12 and 14, March 2004.

82. Makau Mutua, "After Bomas, Kibaki Must Take Lead," *Daily Nation*, April 7, 2004.

9

Matters of Convergence

THE SCRIPT OF the National Constitutional Conference might as well have been rehearsed before the forum opened. It was a battleground for the contest of state power between individuals, groups, and factions. It was also a theater of conflict between those with competing visions for Kenya. A complex stew of motives drove every participant. But the leaderships of the key interest groups at Bomas already knew what they wanted out of it before it started. That is what the struggle of the 1990s had been about—the character and identity of the state. But advocacy civil society organizations, the single most important actors in the struggle for constitutional reform, had the clearest and the most steadfast vision of a democratic constitution. Over the years, they had forged a national consciousness on such a document. The general areas of convergence were known because of that struggle: the democratization of the executive, the reform of the judiciary, a full bill of rights, affirmative action for women and marginal groups, devolution, and economic and land reforms. The Constitution of Kenya Review Commission (CKRC) confirmed this consensus after it collected the views of Kenyans.[1]

Civil Society and the
National Constitutional Conference

Advocacy civil society organizations have often led the reform agenda since the late 1980s.[2] Although opposition political parties played key roles in galvanizing opposition to the KANU state, it was civil society groups that initiated and led the struggle against tyranny. Nongovernmental organizations (NGOs) have for long been the most consistent and organized sector of society. In the late 1970s and 1980s, when open political opposition was not permitted, student leaders at the University of Nairobi drove advocacy against government policies. Trade unions and women's organizations, such as Maendeleo Ya Wanawake, had long been co-opted by the KANU state, eliminating their voices as dissenters. The private media, although lively, had been heavily self-censored until the 1990s. Even so, it operated under a climate of fear and persecution by the state. Government-owned electronic media continued to enjoy a virtual monopoly until the mid-1990s. Under these circumstances, student activism was for long the only avenue to challenge KANU's monopoly over political space. It is little surprise that former student activists and academics from the University of Nairobi formed the civil society organizations that arose in the early 1990s.[3] As political space contracted, only university students and a tiny fraction of the faculty dared to openly challenge the KANU state. This coalition of students and faculty was smashed through expulsions, detentions, and dismissals, but later reassembled as the nerve center of civil society.

In contrast to civil society groups, opposition political parties were largely opportunistic and often unprincipled advocates for reform. Because they are governments-in-waiting, political parties often adopted myopic tactics and strategies. In the case of Kenya, the ideological vacuum in which most political parties operated made them havens of the worst of human proclivities. As such, they became magnets and receptacles for conservative and even fascist ideologues driven by ethnicity, personal power, and demagoguery. Although civil society was not completely free of these pathologies, its general raison d'être was the public good. The struggle to capture political power, the major objective of political parties, substantially narrows their vision, particularly in the context of the African postcolonial state. That is why NGOs, which only seek to influence power, not capture it, have a natural tension with political parties. In the Kenyan context, these differences were repeatedly manifested in the approach and strategies adopted by these erstwhile allies in 1992 and 1997, both election years. In each case, political parties abandoned the reform agenda in the hopes of winning elections. In both instances, they returned to work with the civil society once they lost.

No other sector of society has raised the banner for constitutional reform higher than civil society. Through their advocacy, NGOs have mobilized broad public support for constitutional reform and kept the KANU state on the defensive. Since the early 1990s, the high moral ground unquestionably belonged to NGOs, a coterie of urban-based, elitist organizations that articulated popular demands. Even though they lacked a popular base, NGOs tapped into popular sentiments against a repressive, impoverishing state. Although political parties had potentially deeper and more extensive reach among the masses, they had failed to lead the reform agenda. The opposition parties had become largely reactive and oftentimes blocked the more radical initiatives of civil society. But President Mwai Kibaki recognized the leadership of civil society in the review process when he officially opened the National Constitutional Conference (NCC) in April 2003. He paid "special tribute" to civil society, which had "played a leading role" and whose "vigilance and research were essential."[4]

However, the role of civil society at the national conference was marginal and muted. The sector that had done the most to bring about the constitutional review process was virtually shut out. Instead, groups and individuals, most of whom either had been ambivalent to the reform agenda or had openly opposed it, including the persecution of civil society and reformists, took center stage at the NCC. This marginalization of civil society at the critical state of the review was a built-in contradiction in the structure of all the organs of review, including the CKRC and the NCC. The composition of the Steering Committee of the NCC, and in particular its leadership, sealed the fate of reformers. No prominent civil society reformer was elected to its leadership, and only several made it onto the committee. Leading civil society actors were shouted at, humiliated, or rejected on the floor of the conference during elections for the committee, as well as in subsequent sessions of the plenary.[5] As put by a columnist, "some of the most illustrious names in the fight for a new constitution, including Prof. Kivutha Kibwana, Archbishop David Gitari, and Dr. Willy Mutunga, found that they could hardly get a word in edgewise."[6] It was impossible to forget the humiliation of the trio "at the hands of a surging, hissing mob of delegates."[7] Except for Kibwana and Wangari Maathai, there were no other individuals with a nationally distinguished civil society record among the conveners of the thirteen technical working groups at the conference.

Nevertheless, civil society actors did not abandon the national conference in spite of their alienation. Many took advantage of the observer status offered by the CKRC to attend the proceedings of the NCC and lobby delegates. To its credit, the CKRC allowed information desks within the grounds of Bomas where NGOs with observer status could display their materials and canvass the support of delegates. Local and international media, including live television, extensively covered the conference, allowing the nation to closely follow the plenary sessions. Civil society denizens used the press to great effect, giving running commentary to various media houses, spinning the day's deliberations, and pushing the agenda of reform. The most effective NGOs, however, were those with serious reform programs, professional bureaucracies, and a long history of advocacy in constitutional reform. Particularly well organized was an umbrella coalition of NGOs formed by the Kenya Human Rights Commission, the Federation of Women Lawyers (FIDA), the Institute for Education in Democracy (IED), and the League of Kenya Women Voters to promote women's rights in the draft constitution. Athena Mutua has written an authoritative analysis of the role that women played in engendering the constitutional review process.[8] The receptivity of the national conference to some of the groundbreaking women's rights proposals was attributable to the yeoman work in education and advocacy done by the coalition among delegates.

To be sure, civil society in Kenya was not a monolith, as evidenced by Bomas. Apart from the chasms between various groups' mandates and jealousy between NGOs, Kenya's civil society is highly stratified by class and ideology. There are two broad classifications of NGOs. The first, and probably the most vocal, is composed of elite, urban-based, foreign-funded NGOs that have virtually no social base at the grassroots. They include most human rights and other reform advocacy groups. The other category includes low-budget community-based organizations that are part of the communities where they work and are embedded among marginalized groups in the country. These grassroots organizations have no access to media houses or the boardrooms of the country's elites. Although they can be extremely effective, particularly in their communities, they do not enjoy a national profile and are usually invisible in public discourse. True to their predicaments, these groups were absent from Bomas, leaving the field to the elite-based, donor-supported NGOs, which generally pushed for a reformist constitution. Many, however, were trapped in the ethnic, personal, political, and class squabbles that wracked the national conference. It was mostly on politically charged issues pitting NAK against LDP and KANU that these fissures emerged.

The civil society–led constitutional reform struggles of the 1990s clarified and crystallized the broad parameters of a democratic constitution in Kenya. Broadly defined, the cluster of values for which civil society fought was expressed by the notion of constitutionalism. The most important value was popular sovereignty as the basis of an openly elected and accountable government whose power is limited by the rule of law and an independent judiciary. In Kenya's case, the struggle has been to tame a despotic executive that held the judiciary captive and presided over a corrupt state system. The democratization of the state and the construction of strong, independent, and accountable institutions have been at the core of that struggle. The centrality of individual rights, defined as freedom from the state, has been an article of faith in that struggle. Unfortunately, opposition political parties have not always understood the importance of these basic principles in the reformation of the state. Worse still, their short-term interests and political myopia overcame any larger vision they had for the country.

These contrasting identities of the Kenyan polity found ample expression at Bomas. Civil society actors played their traditional role as the torchbearers of human rights values and the national interest. Political parties and district delegates generally maneuvered along narrow corridors, animated by the personal agendas of party barons, ethnic chauvinists, and self-seekers. But not even they could wish away, or ignore, the national consciousness on the fundamental norms that a democratic constitution required. The advocacy work of NGOs had instilled in the general public an appreciation for a democratic constitutional order. That is why it was not difficult for most of the delegates to appreciate the broad contours of a democratic constitution. As a consequence, there was a surprising convergence by most delegates on the important principles essential for the redemption of the state from the culture of dictatorship.

However, political parties and key personalities that harbored personal ambitions were concerned that the inclusion of certain norms and structures in a new constitution would negatively affect them. The only areas of convergence were those that either did not threaten entrenched interests or had achieved a national consensus. In contrast, the areas of divergence revolved around structures and norms that could radically alter the balance of power between the competing political elites in the National Alliance Party of Kenya (NAK), the Liberal Democratic Party (LDP), and the Kenya African National Union (KANU).

The Bill of Rights

In Kenya's quest for reformation of the state, the liberal constitution was viewed as the best vehicle for protecting individual rights.[9] Political democracy built on the protections of the liberal constitution was seen as the best guarantee for the enjoyment of human rights.[10] Liberal theory is premised on the liberty and rights of the individual on whose consent the legitimacy of the state is founded. The human rights regime, which is now presumed to be an integral basis for democratic constitutions, is rooted in liberal theory. Thus, for example, Article 21 of the Universal Declaration of Human Rights (UDHR) provides that the "will of the people shall be the basis of the authority of government," whereas Article 25 of the International Covenant on Civil and Political Rights (ICCPR) states that only "genuine periodic elections" can guarantee the "free expression of the will of the electors."[11] For most of the 1990s, civil society was concerned with the formulation of norms and a state typology that would limit the reach of state power. Within it, the view that human rights act as a guarantor against state despotism had coalesced into a vision for the struggle against autocracy.

The skepticism by Kenya's civil society of state power was contained in a genus of constitutional system known as constitutionalism. Political debates within Kenya had, over the decade of the 1990s, zeroed in on the essential features of this genre of government. There was broad agreement within civil society, and to a large extent the opposition, that popular sovereignty as a principle was the floor and therefore incontestable. Once boiled down, the essential features of the system sought by reform advocates in Kenya were accountability of the state through a series of techniques, institutions, processes, and mechanisms, the most important of which was periodic, regular, and genuinely competitive elections; a tangible scheme of checks and balances, with real and effective separation of powers; an independent judiciary to safeguard the rule of law; and a guarantee of individual rights, enshrined in a bill of rights.[12] These features, which were first developed in Western Europe and the United States, have become increasingly common in African, Asian, and Latin American countries.[13] By the time the National Constitutional Conference opened in 2003, there was consensus among broad sectors of Kenyan society, and even begrudging acknowledgment within KANU, that the new constitution had to embody these basic norms. The only questions were, first, whether the formulaic liberal constitution would tame the Kenyan state, and second, whether the fractionalized elites at Bomas would come to agreement.

The 2002 CKRC Draft Constitution, also called the "Ghai Draft" after the chair of the NCC, Yash Ghai, provided the basic framework for debate at Bomas.[14] That draft, although hastily drawn up, was a largely progressive document that captured the essence of a liberal constitution.[15] It was widely hailed by the opposition as representative of the people's views, even as Julius Sunkuli, a powerful KANU minister, vilified it as an inoperable and impractical document that could "only be applied in utopia."[16] Hyperbole aside, the document was a quilt of modernist philosophy embroidered with vestiges of illiberalism and pre-Enlightenment religious clawbacks. Its bill of rights was vast and comprehensive, an array of protections and freedoms that captured the contradictions of the rights language. Without a doubt, the Ghai Draft took a cue from the 1996 South African constitution, arguably the most progressive basic law in the world.[17] In addition to the traditional staples of civil and political rights, long the cornerstone of the liberal constitution, its inclusion of many social, economic, and cultural rights seemed to have been inspired by the South African experience. Both protected an almost identical set of these rights, including rights to the environment, property, housing, water, social security, education, language, culture, food, labor relations, and the freedom of trade, occupation, and profession.[18] In fact, the bills of rights in both documents borrowed heavily from the UDHR, the ICCPR, and the International Covenant on Economic, Social and Cultural Rights (ICESCR), the trio of texts known as the International Bill of Rights.[19]

South Africa's constitution had come about after centuries of one of the most abominable racist systems and decades of concerted domestic and international struggles against apartheid. The depth and striking nature of its provisions resulted from deep historical trauma and the rejection of the racist political order both internally and externally. In contrast, Kenya's cleavages had not been nearly as sharp. The Ghai Draft saw "the Bill of Rights as the foundation stone of Kenya's democratic state."[20] Except with respect to women, the bill generally prohibited limitations on the rights therein in the generic language common to democratic constitutions and without derogation from the "core or the essential content of the right."[21] It provided everyone with the right to life and abolished the death penalty.[22] In its equal protection clause, the draft provided that the state "shall not unfairly discriminate" on the basis of race, sex, pregnancy, marital status, ethnic or social origin, color, age, disability, religion, conscience, belief, language, or birth.[23] But unlike its South African counterpart, it pointedly left out sexual orientation, a reflection of Kenya's deeply homophobic culture.[24]

The bill of rights permitted the passage of legislation and other measures "designed to benefit individuals or groups who are disadvantaged, whether or not as a result of past discrimination."[25] Human rights law authorizes this nod to affirmative action to alleviate the historical legacy of discrimination, exclusion, or marginalization.[26] However, the Ghai bill of rights authorized discrimination against women on the basis of religion. It provided, in a departure from its human rights foundation, that equality in the bill of rights "shall be qualified to the extent strictly necessary for the application of Islamic law to persons who profess the Muslim faith in relation to personal status, marriage, divorce, and inheritance."[27] It is well-known that the application of sharia, or Islamic law, in the specific areas that fall under family law abrogates the rights of women and subjects them to the oppressive and abusive patriarchy.[28] Provisions such as this one were a reflection of tensions within the CKRC to reconcile religion, women's rights, and the popular desire for a largely liberatory document. But the CKRC succumbed to the antiwomen sentiment embedded in aspects of sharia.

The draft bill of rights broadly reflected the recommendations of citizens across the country.[29] In that sense, popular sentiments on a constitutional order were largely progressive. However, delegates at the National Constitutional Conference proved to be less democratic and progressive than the population at large. The elites at Bomas, particularly members of Parliament and district delegates, sharply curtailed the bill of rights in important areas, limiting its reach and a number of critical protections. Predictably, the contraction applied to matters relating to the family and women's rights. In the final 2004 Bomas Draft Constitution various groups incurred key losses. Although the 2004 Draft Constitution provided for the right to life, it removed the abolition of capital punishment contained in the Ghai Draft. Most delegates were unimpressed by the argument that international legal trends—jurisprudentially and practically—leaned sharply toward the elimination of the death penalty. In a blow to women's rights and under pressure from religious and political groups across the spectrum, the delegates added the provision that the "life of a person begins at conception."[30] For the avoidance of doubt, it also provided that "abortion shall not be permissible unless, in the opinion of a registered medical practitioner, the life of the mother is in danger."[31] For all practical purposes, this clause prohibited all abortions, even where conception occurs through incest or rape. The coalition of NGOs working on gender questions in the constitution lamented this "real loss for the Coalition."[32]

The bill of rights in the 2004 Draft Constitution is not simply a manifesto for the protection of individual rights. To be sure, it grants fundamental rights to individuals on the assumption that the rights of all—whether individuals or groups—can be protected through a regime of equal protection and antidiscrimination. That is the same logic that directs the international regime for the protection of groups and minorities. But the 2004 Draft Constitution goes further. In the bill of rights it seeks to specifically protect marginalized groups and communities, by which it means pastoralist, nomadic, and other impoverished groups. It includes communities such as the Somali, Maasai, Turkana, Borana, and Rendille, among others, and would be applicable to marginal groups elsewhere. It directed the state to adopt affirmative action and other measures to ensure that such groups and communities enjoy the freedoms and rights in the bill of rights.[33] Other classes of people that are treated as groups include women, the elderly, youth, children, and persons with disabilities.[34] These provisions imply a group-based perspective on rights in which the rationale for addressing the disadvantage is group membership. The intrinsic assumption is that the occasion for exclusion, discrimination, or marginalization was group membership. The scheme of rights in the rest of the bill of rights was traditional and individualistic.

Large sections of the 2004 Draft Constitution were quite forward-looking. That can be explained partly by the veneer of liberalism and legality—even though honored by the state more in breach than in observance—that had defined the Kenyan legal system for decades. In addition, where the bill of rights directly threatened the political power held by elites, such as the patriarchy and organized religion, the rights of women were curtailed or compromised. KANU, which was now the minority party, supported many of the protections, whereas NARC could not oppose them because it was elected on the promise of reform. In any case, these basic rights would not weaken either party or cause a shift in political power. As such, the cost of opposing them would not have been worth the political price. That is why there was a relatively broad consensus on many political and civil rights.[35]

Women in the 2004 Draft Constitution

Women's rights were the one issue on which the constitutional conference made substantial progress. In a handbook for parliamentarians, the NGO gender coalition stated that the "Draft Constitution is progressive on women's issues" and warned that those "gains are causing concern amongst conservative circles in the country."[36] In a pamphlet entitled "Gathering Storm,"[37] a grouping of major Christian churches calling itself the Kenya Church opposed some of the proposals on women in the draft constitution, including affirmative action.[38] The NGO women's coalition adopted a number of strategies to elevate the discourse on women and fight to retain the gains in the Ghai Draft. It carried out education and mobilization campaigns in key constituencies, particularly among women delegates and parliamentarians and in the media. The coalition produced *Yawezekana: Bomas Agender*, a weekly publication for distribution at Bomas. *Yawezekana* became the most popular publication at Bomas. It published highly accessible documents expounding the law and advocating particular positions, and it produced booklets with analysis and draft language on every provision with a gender dimension in the Ghai Draft. As Bomas drew to a close in early 2004, the coalition published *Model Proposals*, its own draft constitution focused on the rights of women.[39] The coalition was the most organized player at Bomas, although its key leaders were observers, not delegates.[40]

Kenyan society is controlled by a deeply religious and socially conservative patriarchy. Women are largely invisible in public life and have been marginalized by both the institutions of tradition and the exclusionary practices of the postcolonial state. Their lot is defined by hard labor in the fields and in the home, rampant violence, rape, and other forms of exploitation and abuse. Although women till the land, they rarely own or control it and exist in a system of economic vassalage to men. The memoir of Wangari Maathai, the 2004 Nobel Peace laureate, is one woman's irrevocable testament to the cancerous nature of Kenya's deeply patriarchal culture.[41] Even though women make up half the country's population, their underrepresentation in the public square is obscene. Kenyans know these cruel statistics because they are part of the lived experience. Yet little has been done by the state and civil society to transform the lot of women. Traditional national women's organizations, such as Maendeleo ya Wanawake, lacked a feminist foundation and were part of the system of marginalization. More recently, however, advocacy women's rights organizations, led by FIDA, emerged to challenge the status quo and seek normative and institutional changes in the character of the state and society. That is why FIDA, KHRC, IED, and the League of Kenya Women Voters saw constitution making as the golden opportunity to transform gender relations in Kenya. They saw gender mainstreaming within the new democratic constitution as the sword that would slay the dragon of the patriarchy in Kenya. The coalition therefore targeted a number of key questions in the draft constitution, including the bill of rights, representation, reproductive rights, and economic empowerment. They adopted antidiscrimination and equality norms as the operational principles for gender mainstreaming. Language was the essential tool for creating a constitution that guaranteed both gender equality and equity.[42]

Although the Ghai Draft was driven by human rights values, it did not state explicitly, as a matter of national urgency, the centrality of the principle of equality in the transformation of the state.[43] Even so, with the exception of the limitation on equality for Muslim women in the bill of rights, its failure to provide for an independent gender commission, and several other important shortcomings, the coalition lauded the Ghai Draft for its advanced thinking on women.[44] The draft, which prohibited discrimination against women, was built on conceptual and substantive notions of equality.[45] In a move beneficial to women, the draft created a mixed member proportional representation system (MMPR), a hybrid of the first-past-the-post system (FPTP) and the proportional representation system (PR).[46] In its representation clauses, the draft required that every political party ensure that at least one-third of its candidates for direct elections and 50 percent of those for proportional representation were women.[47] Political parties, which would be funded by the state, were required to be democratic and promote women's participation.[48] Furthermore, half of the party's allocated funding would be proportionate to the number of women the party fielded in Parliament.[49] In a proposed second chamber, or upper house of Parliament, the draft provided that 30 of the 100 seats would be reserved for women.[50] The new proposals permitted independent candidates, a rule that favored women because they would not have to compete for nomination under parties dominated by men and socialized misogyny.[51] The draft provided the one-third principle for women in most elective and appointed positions.

The Ghai Draft sought to correct multiple forms of discrimination against women that had been legal under the extant constitution. The draft gave women equal rights to pass citizenship to their offspring and provided wives and husbands of Kenyans an equal right to acquire citizenship.[52] It guaranteed land and property rights for women, including the rights to inherit and control property.[53] It recognized and protected matrimonial property even after the termination of marriage.[54] In a related question, the draft required all customary laws to conform to the bill of rights and constitutional principles.[55] Although the coalition supported the inclusion of Kadhi courts, which apply Islamic law and enjoy a special status in the Kenyan legal system, or sharia courts in the draft, it proposed that they be subjected to social justice norms and equality in fact in family law disputes.[56] Elsewhere, it guaranteed women the right to maternity leave and other protections because of their gender.[57] Finally, the draft provided for the inclusion of a gender commissioner within the Commission on Human Rights and Administrative Justice, a rather cumbersome human rights watchdog.[58] In spite of these advances, the coalition heavily critiqued the draft, exposing serious omissions and misconceptions of the politics and law relating to the complex question of gender, and proposed far-reaching revisions of language on virtually every provision with a gender implication.[59]

The 2004 Draft Constitution was deeply influenced by the work of the coalition and corrected a number of key provisions, although it severely retrogressed in others. For women, the final draft was a mixed bag, a less than coherent quilt of feminism, intolerance, patriarchy, gender equity, equality, and misogyny stitched together in an undulating pattern. Even so, it was a great advance over the previous constitution, which never considered gender and treated women and girls as the invisible but natural chattel of men. The 2004 final Draft Constitution took back some of the gains of the Ghai Draft while adding welcome provisions. Although it failed to provide for equality between men and women as a national principle or goal, the 2004 Draft Constitution, in an improvement over the Ghai Draft, situated the one-third principle at the center of national policy by requiring that no more than two-thirds of the members of elective or appointed bodies belong to the same gender.[60] It, however, did not make affirmative action a national goal.

But the 2004 Draft Constitution, unlike the Ghai Draft, prohibited virtually all abortions and provided that life began at conception.[61] Although in the gender clause of the bill of rights, the draft constitution provided that "women and men have an equal right to inherit, have access to and *manage* property," it did not grant them the power to *control* it.[62] Significantly, it did not engender the chapter on land, a critical occasion for discrimination against women and girls, who often are denied ownership of land on account of their gender. The draft constitution retained the odious limitation of equality in the bill of rights on the application of Islamic family law.[63] It included the institution of Kadhi courts but did not subject it to equal protection norms or the bill of rights.[64] It protected the one-third principle for all elective and appointive positions, but rejected the MMPR system in favor of a system in which each district would be required to elect a woman in addition to the other gender-open constituency seats in the district.[65] The electoral and representation clauses, particularly the engendering of political parties in the draft constitution, were hailed as "profound gains for the Coalition, in terms of content and alternative language."[66] Whereas the Ghai Draft had ghettoized women's rights in the Commission on Human Rights and Administrative Justice under the guise of an innocuous gender commissioner, the final draft constitution provided for a separate and independent Gender Commission.[67] To the coalition, the Gender Commission was "an important gain because it provides an institutional framework for monitoring and ensuring gender mainstreaming in Kenya."[68]

The Normative Identity of the State

Kenyans have long viewed the state as a predator. The CKRC documented this strong antagonism between the state and the people.[69] These views were confirmed by the government report by the Task Force on the Establishment of a Truth, Justice, and Reconciliation Commission.[70] Although the people may not have known the precise norms and structures the new democratic constitution should include, they had a grasp of the general principles and values that should direct the constitution-making effort. At the center of the nation, the people placed their own sovereignty as the basis of the state.[71] But they also recognized that Kenya was not a monolithic state but a collection of many different nationalities and races with their own unique attributes, histories, fears, and hopes. Even so, they wanted a unitary state forged out of this motley amalgam of peoples. As such, they sought unity in their diversity and equal value for all communities. It was an obvious attempt by Kenyans across the board to accept the forced creation of the state by Britain as a fait accompli but also to make it a nurturing political society for all, despite its conceptual incoherence and perverse historical legacy. Although different Kenyan communities had not voluntarily made Kenya their bed, their conclusion—which precluded a divorce from the state—was an affirmation to lie in it.

The new Kenya would be constructed from an appeal to the Enlightenment project. At the center of reform would be a democratic order, good governance, and the rule of law, the broad concepts of the good society that the postcolonial state had been unable to embed. Human rights, and the core principles of equal protection and antidiscrimination for individuals and groups, would become the creed of the new state. Equality and equity for all, including between men and women, would animate the new constitution. Yet the Ghai Draft and most delegates at the national conference did not include protection of women in the equality principle. In a masterstroke, however, Ghai appears to have avoided flagging the controversial principle in the preamble and the first three chapters, and instead opted for the inclusion of substantive provisions in the body of his draft, as well as that of the 2004 Draft Constitution. Perhaps bringing in the principles of gender equality and equity under the radar saved a bruising battle with conservative forces, including the church and the mosque, and removed one more possible nexus for paralysis and gridlock. But the invisibility of the explicit principle of equality, particularly on gender, spoke of a deep-seated illiberalism and patriarchy, both serious threats to a meaningful reform of the state.

The constitutional project was driven by other, equally important values and principles, many of them germane to democracy. There was recognition that political democracy would mean little without economic freedom from daily privation and Kenya's grinding poverty. The inclusion of a number of important economic, social, and cultural rights in the draft constitution sought to address this question, although it did not envisage any programs for land and agrarian reform, which were necessary to address the problems of landlessness, land redistribution, and equity in landownership. Neither the Ghai Draft nor the 2004 Draft Constitution addressed the endemic problem of landgrabbing, in which prominent individuals and corporations had illegally and corruptly acquired vast tracts at the expense of entire communities.[72] Nor did they interrogate the viability of free market practices and their effect on democratization. On the restructuring of the economy, both drafts assumed that the containment of state despotism would be sufficient to spur economic growth. There was a naïve assumption that the rewriting of the internal polity would suffice to bring about economic renaissance.

The 2004 Draft Constitution paid heed to the broader principle of democratization and sought to create institutions of transparency, accountability, and popular participation. Of critical importance here was the draft's understanding of the central role that political parties play in a democracy. It cast parties as the vehicles through which popular will and the consent of the governed would be freely expressed, although it expanded political space by permitting the contest for power by independent candidates.[73] That tempers the monopoly that parties may exercise over electoral politics and permits the rise of independent thinkers, nonconformists, and even radically progressive candidates. The creation of an official fund for political parties was a critical building block that could force the maturation of Kenya's ideologically bankrupt and vacuous political parties. The pegging of public funding for political parties to internal democracy, transparency, and inclusiveness, particularly with respect to women, was an enormous step forward.[74] These measures were meant to professionalize Kenyan political parties and free them from the syndrome of the Big Man who funds and "owns" the party.

Importantly, the 2004 Draft Constitution embodied the principle of the separation of powers and gave each of the three branches the powers to resist control and penetration by the others. The executive still remained the first among equals, although its proclivity for despotism was sharply curtailed through checks and balances within and by both the judiciary and the legislature. The creation of independent constitutional commissions was meant to check the abuse of power.[75] The structure of the executive itself—embodied in a directly elected, largely ceremonial president and a powerful prime minister—was inherently conflictual: it vanquished the despot but created a hydra.[76] Given Kenya's deep ethnic divisions and egomaniacal elites, such an executive could be a recipe for a national catastrophe if the two heads of the hydra were to engage in a zero-sum game. The design of the executive, which was deeply influenced by the power struggle between NAK and LDP, did nothing but seduce the two offices into a fatal duel. But the principle of the decentralization of power from the center and its devolution to other branches, including to regional and local authorities, was a laudable effort, even though it was highly problematic.

The legislature was granted broad autonomy in the 2004 Draft Constitution to give it teeth to check executive despotism and exercise its authority as the independent voice and eye of the electorate. It provided for a bicameral legislature with a Senate, or an upper house, and a National Assembly, or a lower house, which together were known as Parliament.[77] The Senate, subordinate to the National Assembly in most matters, was meant to protect the interests of the devolved regional authorities, ethnic groups, and marginalized communities. A virtual replica of the structure of the state under the independence Majimbo or Lancaster Constitution, the provision for the Senate was a reemergence of the earlier schism between KANU and KADU over whether Kenya would be a unitary or quasi-federal state. This conflict, which was ostensibly over the devolution and decentralization of power, turned out to be one of the proposals that would torpedo the 2004 Draft Constitution. This arrangement vested enormous powers in the Parliament and substantially curtailed the draconian authority enjoyed by the imperial presidency in the previous constitution. The unchecked presidential power to appoint senior officials, including ministers, was removed, and Parliament was vested with the power to impeach or remove the president. The effect of these provisions was to enhance and strengthen the oversight function of Parliament.

Despotism in Kenya has been greatly aided by the powers of the executive relative to a judiciary that has only been nominally independent. A key concern of both the Ghai Draft and the 2004 Draft Constitution was the creation of a credibly independent, incorruptible, and competent judiciary as the cornerstone of a democratic state. The key proposals sought to create a system that would end the politicization—executive interference, corruption, and incompetence—of the judiciary. To cure these problems, the 2004 Draft Constitution provided for a formally transparent and corruption-free system for the appointment and dismissal of judges. The prosecutorial powers of the state were removed from the attorney general and vested in an independent office of the director of prosecutions. In addition, a strong Judicial Service Commission to foster accountability and the transparent administration of justice and the courts, including the review and discipline of the judiciary and the magistracy, was established.[78] Defusing a potentially paralyzing question, the 2004 Draft Constitution provided for Kadhi courts as subordinate tribunals with limited jurisdiction over family matters. Overall, the chapter on the courts was a valiant attempt to address the endemic malaise of the Kenyan judiciary.

In sum, there was convergence in many critical areas at Bomas. Most portions of the 2004 Draft Constitution attracted a broad consensus, even though there remained many disagreements. It was heartening that on most questions there was agreement on the basic principles, although not necessarily in their translation into provisions and structures. In the end, social conservatives and traditional religionists clawed back women's rights, and the abolition of the death penalty was rejected. But a gender commission was created and an across-the-board one-third principle adopted. The resultant document was a centrist liberal constitution laced with elements of illiberalism and patriarchy. Even though as a legal document it was untidy, shoddily drafted, and unnecessarily detailed, it was a marked vast improvement over the previous constitution.

Notes

1. Constitution of Kenya Review Commission, *The Main Report of the Constitution of Kenya Review Commission,* September 18, 2002.

2. Willy Mutunga, *Constitution-Making from the Middle: Civil Society and Transition Politics in Kenya, 1992–1997* (Harare: MWENGO, 1999).

3. For example, Makau Mutua and Willy Mutunga, two of the founders of the Kenya Human Rights Commission, Kenya's leading human rights NGO, were hounded out of the University of Nairobi by the state.

4. Constitution of Kenya Review Commission, "Speech by His Excellency President Mwai Kibaki, During the Opening of the National Constitutional Conference at Bomas of Kenya on April 30, 2003," http://www.kenyaconstitution.org/docs/12d006.htm, accessed May 12, 2005.

5. John K. Njiraini, "Is Kenya Polarized Along Ethnic Lines?" *Daily Nation*, January 30, 2004.

6. Macharia Gaitho, "Wanjiku: Was Moi Right After All?" *Daily Nation*, May 27, 2003.

7. Makau Mutua, "The Bomas Constitutional Talks Were One Big Farce," *Daily Nation*, October 5, 2003.

8. For a comprehensive analysis of the role of women in the constitution-making process, see Athena Mutua, "Gender Equality and Women's Solidarity Across Religious, Ethnic, and Class Difference in the Kenya Constitutional Review Process," *William and Mary Journal of Women and Law* 1, no. 13 (2006). Federacion International d'abogadas or Federation of Women Lawyers (FIDA), Institute for Education in Democracy (IED), KHRC, and League of Kenya Women Voters (LKWV), *Safeguarding Women's Gains Under the Draft Constitution: Parliamentary Handbook,* 2003 (hereinafter *Safeguarding Women's Gains—Handbook*).

9. See, generally, Vicki Jackson and Mark Tushnet, *Comparative Constitutional Law* (New York: Foundation Press, 1999).

10. Henry J. Steiner, "Political Participation as a Human Right," *Harvard Human Rights Yearbook* 77, no. 1 (1988).

11. Universal Declaration of Human Rights, General Assembly Res. 217A, U.N. Doc. A/810, 71 (1948); International Covenant on Civil and Political Rights, opened for signature December 19, 1966, 999 U.N.T.S. 171, entered into force March 23, 1976.

12. See, generally, P. L. Agweli Onalo, *Constitution-Making in Kenya: An African Appraisal* (Nairobi: TransAfrica Press, 2003).

13. Samuel P. Huntington, *The Third Wave: Democratization in the Late Twentieth Century,* 6th ed. (Norman: University of Oklahoma Press, 1990).

14. Constitution of Kenya Review Commission, *The Draft Bill to Amend the Constitution,* 2003 (hereinafter *Ghai Draft*).

15. "Threat of Split over the Ghai Proposals After Poll Victory," *Daily Nation*, February 2, 2003.

16. Njeri Rugene, "Ghai Team's Draft Wins Praise," *Sunday Nation*, September 22, 2002.

17. *Constitution of the Republic of South Africa*, entered into force December 10, 1996 (hereinafter *Constitution of South Africa*).

18. *Constitution of South Africa,* Chapter 2; *Ghai Draft,* Chapter 5.

19. International Covenant on Economic, Social and Cultural Rights, General Assembly Res. 2200 (XXI), U.N. GAOR, 21st Sess., Supp. No. 16, 49, U.N. Doc. A/6316 (1966) (entered into force January 3, 1976).

20. *Ghai Draft,* Article 29(1).

21. Ibid., Article 29(2).

22. Ibid., Article 32.

23. Ibid., Articles 33, 34(1).

24. *Constitution of South Africa,* Section 9(3).

25. *Ghai Draft,* Article 34(3).

26. See, for example, Article 4, Convention on the Elimination of All Forms of Discrimination Against Women, General Assembly Res. 34/180, 34 U.N. GAOR Supp. (No. 46) 194, U.N. Doc. A/34/830, 1979.

27. *Ghai Draft,* Article 31(4).

28. Abdullahi A. An-Na'im, "The Rights of Women and International Law in the Muslim Context," *Whittier Law Review* 491, no. 9 (1987); Abdullahi An-Na'im, "Human Rights in the Muslim World: Socio-Political Conditions and Scriptural Imperative," *Harvard Human Rights Journal* 13, no. 3 (1990).

29. Constitution of Kenya Review Commission, *The People's Choice: The Report of the Constitution of Kenya Review Commission—Short Version, 2002* (hereinafter *People's Choice—Short Version*).

30. *The Draft Constitution of Kenya,* March 2004, Article 34(2) (hereinafter *2004 Draft Constitution*).

31. Ibid., Article 34(3).

32. FIDA, IED, KHRC, and League of Kenya Women Voters, *Audit Report: The National Constitutional Conference* (Nairobi: Kenya Human Rights Commission, 2004), 21 (hereinafter *Bomas Audit*).

33. *2004 Draft Constitution,* Article 43.

34. Ibid., Articles 37, 38, 39, 40, and 42.

35. Constitution of Kenya Review Commission, *The Report of the Rapporteur-General to the National Constitutional Conference on the General Debate Held Between April 28 and June 6, 2003 at the Bomas of Kenya,* July 2003 (hereinafter *Bomas I Report*).

36. *Safeguarding Women's Gains—Handbook,* 1.

37. Kenya Church, *A Gathering Storm: Critical Concerns on the Draft Constitution* (Nairobi: Kenya Church, 2003).

38. *Safeguarding Women's Gains—Handbook,* 1.

39. FIDA, IED, KHRC, and League of Kenya Women Voters, *Model Proposals: Safeguarding the Gains of Women in the Draft Constitution,* January 28, 2004 (hereinafter *Model Proposals*).

40. The key leaders of the coalition were Jane Kiragu, the executive director of FIDA; Koki Muli, the executive director of IED; Athena Mutua, an associate professor of law at Buffalo Law School in the United States and a consultant to the KHRC; Jacinta Muteshi, a board member of the KHRC; and Cecilia Kimemia (later replaced by Grace Okello), the executive director of the League of Kenya Women Voters. But the coalition was the brainchild of Willy Mutunga, the executive director of the KHRC, Jacinta Muteshi, and Athena Mutua. The coalition was born when Mutua and Muteshi approached Kiragu and FIDA on behalf of the KHRC and asked FIDA to be its host. The idea of the coalition was hatched in late 2002 at the Palacina Hotel, where the KHRC and the Institute for Economic Affairs (IEA) led weekly meetings, in which Yash Ghai participated and to which other CKRC commissioners were invited, to discuss the Ghai Draft in preparation for the National Constitutional Conference. Mutua, Muteshi, and Muli led the gender group at the Palacina Hotel meetings. Malicious and insecure commissioners attacked the Palacina Hotel meetings and implausibly argued that the KHRC was out to replace them. See "Threat of Split over Ghai Proposals After Poll Victory," *Sunday Nation,* February 2, 2003.

41. Wangari Maathai, *Unbowed: A Memoir* (New York: Alfred A. Knopf, 2006); FIDA-Kenya, *Step-by-Step: Backwards or Forwards?* Annual Report, 2003.

42. FIDA, IED, KHRC, League of Kenya Women Voters, *Safeguarding Women's Gains Under the Draft Constitution—Training Manual,* 2003, 16 (hereinafter *Safeguarding Women's Gains—Training Manual*).

43. *Ghai Draft,* Chapter 3.

44. *Safeguarding Women's Rights—Training Manual,* 1.

45. *Ghai Draft,* Articles 33, 34, and 35.

46. Koki Muli, "Mixed Member Proportional Representation," in *Safeguarding Women's Rights—Training Manual,* 57.

47. *Ghai Draft,* Article 77(2).

48. Ibid., Article 90.

49. Ibid., Article 95(3).

50. Ibid., Article 106(b).

51. Ibid., Article 50(3)(b).

52. Ibid., Articles 19(1), 20.

53. Ibid., Article 35(3).

54. Ibid., Article 235(4)(v).

55. Ibid., Articles 35(4), 63A.

56. Athena D. Mutua (in consultation with Jacinta Muteshi and Koki Muli), "Gender in the Draft Constitution: Suggested Alternative Language," in *Safeguarding Women's Rights—Training Manual*, 87–88.

57. *Ghai Draft,* Article 35(5).

58. Ibid., Article 288(1)(d).

59. See, generally, *Safeguarding Women's Rights—Training Manual.*

60. *2004 Draft Constitution,* Article 12(2)(j).

61. Ibid., Article 34.

62. Ibid., Article 37(2).

63. Ibid., Article 33(4).

64. Ibid., Articles 198 and 199.

65. Ibid., Article 123(2).

66. *Bomas Audit*, 31.

67. *2004 Draft Constitution,* Article 300.

68. *Bomas Audit*, 55.

69. Constitution of Kenya Review Commission, *Report of the Constitution of Kenya Review Commission,* September 18, 2002.

70. Republic of Kenya, *Report of the Task Force on the Establishment of a Truth, Justice, and Reconciliation Commission* (Nairobi: Government Printer, 2003).

71. Ibid., 22.

72. Republic of Kenya, *Republic of the Commission of Inquiry into Illegal/Irregular Allocation of Public Land* (Nairobi: Republic of Kenya, 2004).

73. *2004 Draft Constitution,* Article 105.

74. Ibid., Articles 111–119.

75. Ibid., Chapter 18.

76. Ibid., Chapter 12.

77. Ibid., Article 120.

78. Ibid., Chapter 13.

10

Things Fall Apart

THE OLD ADAGE that power corrupts and absolute power corrupts absolutely was a fitting metaphor for what had ailed Kenya since Mwai Kibaki was elected president in December 2002. Although he did not, nor could he, enjoy the untrammeled power held by former president Daniel arap Moi, President Kibaki was entranced by the enormous power granted the executive by the extant constitution. But Kenyans in the post-2002 period were simply not impressed or cowed by state despotism. The ignominious fall of Moi and the Kenya African National Union (KANU) in 2002 ended an era and buried with it the "father of the nation" syndrome. The mystical hold of state power centered on the maximum leader seems to have vanished with Moi, one of the longest-surviving Cold War autocrats. In the only election to break KANU's back, Kenyans seemed to have achieved a measure of liberation from the claws of the postcolonial state. Across the board, Kenyans seemed to expect an accountable, democratic, and transparent leadership. Yet the National Rainbow Coalition (NARC), the coalition party elected on these principles, was trapped between granting the wishes of the people and retaining the imperial presidencies of Moi and Kenyatta. But NARC collapsed even before it cohered because of competing ambitions and interests between its factions and leaders.

Unbridled Ambitions

The fencing within NARC started before the elections results were officially certified. Two diametrically opposed camps emerged—the National Alliance Party of Kenya (NAK) and the Liberal Democratic Party (LDP). In reality, the LDP was a vehicle that Raila Odinga took over to bargain for power with NAK, the Kibaki-led coalition of opposition parties that had opposed Moi since 1992. With him, Odinga brought high-priced KANU mandarins, among them George Saitoti, a former vice president, and Kalonzo Musyoka, formerly a trusted Moi protégé with presidential ambitions. But the trio of Odinga, Saitoti, and Musyoka had nothing in common except their estrangement from Moi, their former patron. In the fractured world of Kenyan politics, they had been brought together under Moi's shadow by personal ambition. Odinga was Luo, Saitoti a Kikuyu who had always conveniently masqueraded as a Maasai, and Musyoka the Kamba politician. Other, less important figures in the LDP were Joseph Kamotho, an unpopular Kikuyu long viewed as a Moi puppet and onetime KANU secretary-general; Moody Awori, an elderly Luhya KANU fixture; and the boorish Fred Gumo, another Luhya with a reputation for violence.[1] But the backbone of LDP was the defunct National Development Party (NDP), which became a Luo party after Odinga took it over following his failure to capture the leadership of FORD-Kenya. NAK, however, had Kibaki's Democratic Party (DP), Michael Kijana Wamalwa's FORD-Kenya, and Charity Ngilu's National Party of Kenya (NPK) as its core parties. Soon NAK was seen as a front for Kibaki, the Kikuyu, and related communities, whereas LDP was cast as the Odinga-Luo party.

This calculus produced two main protagonists: Kibaki and Odinga, both backed by a coterie of intriguers and strategists. Both NARC factions would make a play for KANU and FORD-People, Simeon Nyachae's Kisii party, with varying degrees of success. The NARC faction that would capture the bulk of sympathizers among the delegates at the National Constitutional Conference would have its version of the draft constitution passed. This sharply ethnic schism was complicated by other factors, including individuals and groups that supported either of the camps for complex reasons. Certain key politicians who fell between the cracks might have chosen either camp in the belief that their values and interests would be better served there. For instance, some backed the NAK camp because they saw the biggest potential for reform in it, given the long history of reformist politics by some of its leaders. Others threw their weight behind Odinga and the LDP because they were wary of what they saw as NAK's crafty Mount Kenya Mafia, a term used by the press to describe the powerful Kikuyu, Meru, and Embu courtiers around Kibaki, drawn mostly from DP.[2] Yet, most in KANU connived with Odinga because they wanted to exacerbate the differences within NARC. Christian religious organizations bargained by trading away political sympathies for conservative agendas. Muslims became the proverbial reluctant bride by playing only to those suitors who supported Kadhi courts, minorities or marginalized communities, and a more restrictive construction of women's rights. Many in civil society attempted to stay neutral and focus on the issues, but even they were caught up in the NAK/LDP fight. But there were some who fit nowhere or saw nothing to like in either camp. The national conference became a cesspool of intrigue, tribalism, sectarianism, and narrow politics that muddied everyone who came close to it. Simply put, it was a national spectacle.

The NARC factions geared for battle soon after the elections, when it became obvious that President Kibaki and his NAK allies were not anxious to deliver a new constitution. One major daily accused the government of showing diminished interest in the review process.[3] Odinga's impatience that the review process be restarted immediately was obvious: he took every public forum to drive home the point.[4] Sospeter Ojaamong, an LDP legislator, accused Kibaki's senior aides of reneging on the promise to create a prime ministerial post in the new constitution. He charged that the "group around the President wants to enjoy the powers of an executive for a long time."[5] In March 2003, the battle lines were starkly drawn when NAK co-opted KANU to elect Paul Muite chair of the Parliamentary Select Committee on Constitutional Review (PSC). It was not lost on anyone that Muite, leader of the opposition Safina party, handily beat Odinga, a leading light in the NARC ruling party. Muite, a bitter opponent of Odinga, was an asset in NAK's arsenal. It was known among key players that Muite was one of the few politicians Odinga begrudgingly respected and even feared. Since he would not be anxious to create a strong prime minister's post from which Odinga would benefit, Muite was NAK's perfect foil as the chair of the powerful PSC. With the election of Muite, NAK had sent two powerful messages to Odinga and the rival LDP: first, that the premiership would be difficult, if not impossible, to create, and second, that NAK thought little of the pre-election Memorandum of Understanding (MOU), the aborted power-sharing pact between the two NARC rivals. NAK's foot-dragging was an open secret, even as it continuously paid lip service to a new democratic constitution.

> The Kibaki regime came to office promising to deliver a new constitution within 30 days; then it was six months. Today [2005] the process, let alone the completion date, is unclear. The quest for a new constitution has been under way for roughly 15 years. From the perspective of the opposition, the current constitution is a problem because of the broad powers it lodges in the presidency. But from the point of view of State House politicians past and present, those powers look very good indeed. This helps explain the foot dragging on constitutional reform by both Moi and Kibaki.[6]

Although it is tempting to place the stalemate on constitutional reform at the feet of individual politicians, it bears reminding that the reformist element within NARC was tiny, a fact belied by the progressive rhetoric in its campaign platforms and the populist tenor it adopted against KANU. Some key members of NARC, such as Peter Anyang' Nyong'o, Kiraitu Murungi, Martha Karua, Mukhisa Kituyi, Kivutha Kibwana, Koigi wa Wamwere, Mirugi Kariuki, Wangari Maathai, and Charity Ngilu, had solid reform credentials. But these politicians, most of whom had been forged by civil society, were a small group compared to the bulk of the NARC leadership. When reference was made to NARC's reformist bent, it was usually to this tiny minority. But sooner than later, most in this group would be seduced by power, ethnicity, and self-interest to abandon the struggle to reform the Kenyan state. Particularly deflating was this group's inability and reluctance to prevail upon the more conservative elements in NARC to broker a new constitution. Murungi, the poker-faced leader of the group and Kibaki's point man in the review process, became one of the major obstructionists to reform and the quest for a new constitution himself. The amiable Chris Murungaru, the powerful internal security minister and a Kibaki confidant, joined him in the subterfuge as co-conspirator. Arguably, NARC could not be a force for reform.

> The coalition [National Rainbow Coalition], known by its acronym, NARC, constituted a marriage of convenience. It was not a love match. The coalition included a minority of serious and committed reform politicians and leaders of civil society who thought they had more power than they really had; the majority had no reform records, and some were implicated in prior scandals. Several, like Kibaki, were ministers or assistant ministers in earlier cabinets. The transition to Kibaki was not a radical break with the past, even though the electoral majority demanded change and not politics as usual.[7]

There is evidence that, the clash of personal ambitions aside, there was a flicker of hope at the very beginning of the NARC regime. In the first six months, some NARC leaders, particularly Murungi, seemed genuinely interested in reforming the state. Although that attitude was at odds with his ambivalence over the constitutional reform process, it showed that a window of opportunity was still open. As Frank Holmquist notes, "reform regimes often leave their strongest mark in the early weeks and months of their rule."[8] But as is well-known, Kibaki took power hobbled by a terrible pre-election accident that almost killed him, followed by at least one serious stroke in January 2003. Although it is unclear whether his regime would have taken a more reformist course had he been healthy, the fact is that precious time was lost at the outset.

Some initial steps were hopeful, showing a willingness to take on the old order: Kibaki's appointment of John Githongo, the anticorruption czar; the implementation of free universal primary education; the government's appointment of the Task Force on the Establishment of a Truth, Justice, and Reconciliation Commission; a partial purge of the judiciary; and the creation of the Judicial Commission of Inquiry into the Goldenberg Affair to probe the looting of millions of dollars from the public treasury by the Moi regime. But as the stalemate over constitutional review deepened and both factions of NARC cut deals with KANU and other antireform elements, any efforts to carry out reforms were visibly abandoned. To make matters worse, the legislature became part of the problem. Parliament, which voted itself hefty raises completely out of tune with a poor economy, became a forum for members' self-interest and bickering between the NARC factions, with a gleeful KANU stoking the fires.[9] Holmquist has summarized this descent into greed and antireform by virtually the entire political class.

> The most debilitating [move under NARC] was the informal capture of State House—the politicians, civil servants, and advisers enjoying special access to the president—by the Kikuyu, Kibaki's ethnic group, with allied ethnicities, the Embu and Meru. This provoked serious and lasting distrust within the regime coalition. In their first legislative act, members of Parliament (MPs), led by NARC, voted themselves hefty pay raises to the point that MPs, along with cabinet ministers, now hold some of the best remunerated positions in Kenya. This move by the representatives of a population beset by spreading poverty hardly struck a note of austerity or serious reform purpose. *It may have been in keeping, however, with the character of Kenya's political class, which has fared quite well under Kibaki.*[10] [emphasis added]

Matters of Divergence

The national constitutional conference should have been a noble national exercise for Kenyans to embark on the reform of the state. Public commentary suggested that most Kenyans hoped the forum would be a success. To be sure, the conference was sharply divided over many social, cultural, normative, and structural questions. Many of these deep disagreements reflected the diversity of public opinion, the strength of different stakeholders, and the stubbornness of tradition. Socially and culturally, most of the delegates at the conference could be described as conservative. In this respect, only a vocal minority, drawn largely from civil society and the professions, held progressive views. Surprisingly, women's rights found broad support among the delegates, even though most limited their support to political participation rights. This phenomenon was attributable to the work of the NGOs, the support of delegates from civil society, and the large number of women delegates from the districts. But the prominence of the religious sector at the conference precluded the adoption of socially and culturally progressive measures on reproductive rights, the death penalty, sexual orientation, and equality rights that might eradicate the patriarchy and its control of the family, land, and other economic resources. The religious sector, which had led the reform effort in Ufungamano, saw Bomas as not only a forum for the containment of state despotism but also an opportunity for the entrenchment of certain basic moral and religious values. Thus, it opposed proposals that would have opened the door to what it deemed sinful, immoral, and permissive practices. On these matters, it had ready allies in most of the delegates. But none of these questions were so contested as to threaten the conference. Instead, the conference deadlocked on three critical disagreements: Kadhi courts, devolution, and the structure of the executive.

Kadhi Courts

Kenya is tightly gripped by Christianity and Islam, the two dominant Abrahamic faiths. As was expected, they fought over the role of religion in the state. In most modern secular societies, the state is separate from religion. Christians, who hold a commanding position in Kenya, favored a formal secular state—without a de jure state religion and with the equal treatment of all religions in law. That would ensure the continued domination of the state by Christians since the secular tradition is the liberal, Eurocentric philosophical and practical balance between church and state. The political history of ideas demonstrates that *secularism is a Christian tradition*. Even though Kenya has formally been a secular state, it is for all practices a Christian state because it has been governed, dominated, and developed primarily by Christian politicians, institutions, and norms. As much as 78 percent of the population is thought to be Christian, whereas at least 10 percent, and possibly higher, is Muslim.[11] Kenyan Muslims, too, generally supported the separation of religion and state but wanted the explicit protection of Kadhi courts in the constitution. They cited historical, religious, and pragmatic reasons for the inclusion of Kadhi courts in the constitution. They argued that such tribunals would not give Muslims any special privileges or detract from the rights of other religions.

> Kadhis are not religious leaders; they are legal officers who are versed in Muslim personal law. They do not issue religious fatwas or edicts but adjudicate on the day-to-day family law disputes between Muslims. They provide an informal and specialized way in which family disputes can be settled, saving time and money as well as dispensing justice in an efficient and expeditious way.[12]

But the dominant churches were determined to reject the explicit recognition of Kadhi courts in the constitution. In April 2003, Muslims quit the Ufungamano Initiative, the powerful faiths-led lobby that had fought the Moi regime for a democratic constitution. Both the Supreme Council of Kenya Muslims (SUPKEM) and the Muslim Consultative Council, the two key Islamic groups, left Ufungamano because it had refused to support the inclusion of Kadhi courts in the constitution.[13] Archbishop John Njue, a leading Catholic cleric, opposed the Islamic courts, saying, "We want to see a constitution that treats all Kenyans and religions equally."[14] The Reverend Mutava Musyimi, the Ufungamano boss, added that the "Kadhi courts should exist in their rightful place—normal laws."[15] Kivutha Kibwana, a NARC legislator, argued that Kadhi courts in the constitution would be seen as "introducing Sharia."[16] Ufungamano vigorously argued that protecting Kadhi courts in the country's constitution would be tantamount to elevating them above all the other religions. The only acceptable solution was to provide for such tribunals in an act of Parliament. But Muslims rejected this option since a Christian-dominated legislature could easily repeal such a law in the future.

At the national conference, Muslims lobbied hard and made unlikely alliances while exploiting the factional fighting within NARC. Perhaps their most surprising ally was the NGO women's coalition, which ironically supported Kadhi courts out of its solidarity with Muslim women. The coalition sought the retention of Kadhi courts as they existed in the constitution. Although the coalition had opposed the restriction of the equality rights of women under Muslim family law, it nevertheless fought for the Kadhi courts in a tactical alliance with Muslims to advance its broad agenda on women's rights. It sought their support for affirmative action, reproductive rights, the gender commission, political participation rights, and other equal protection and antidiscrimination measures. In expansive and detailed language, the coalition advocated a professionalized and streamlined Kadhi system as subordinate tribunals within the regular judiciary.[17] The language permitted Kadhi courts "consistent with the ends of social justice" in family law matters.[18] However, the coalition did not admit to its tactical thinking when it explained its support for the tribunals.

> The *Model Proposals* took the view that these courts should be retained as they currently exist in the 1963 constitution, where they have jurisdiction only over personal matters. The Coalition took this view because the enhancement of the jurisdiction of these may constitute a creation of a parallel judicial system. However, their retention in the constitution is crucial as they successfully protect women and children in the contentious matters of inheritance, property, and marriage. They address the historical marginalization of women. It was, therefore, contradictory to support Affirmative Action and oppose Kadhi Courts.[19]

Perhaps to avoid controversy with its allies, the coalition did not focus on the gender problems when Kadhi courts apply sharia. A private law that is applicable in family matters, sharia has traditionally oppressed women, whom it treats as inferior and subject to men.[20] At the very least, serious reform is necessary to bring the law into conformity with human rights standards and the equal protection demands of the bill of rights in a liberal constitution. Support for Kadhi courts therefore need not bargain away basic rights for Muslim women, even though most support them. As noted by Makau Mutua, the failure to entrench Kadhi courts in the constitution would be interpreted by Muslims as an act of exclusion and could radicalize them.[21] The key was to protect them but impose strict requirements for compliance with equal protection norms. That would spur them to develop a jurisprudence of equity and antidiscrimination.

In the end, however, the Muslims triumphed at Bomas. At the technical committee on the judiciary, the critical decision was made to protect Kadhi courts in the constitution. Attempts by Christians to deny the proposal were strongly defeated after a vigorous debate within the committee.[22] The final 2004 Draft Constitution protected the Muslim courts in a major defeat for the Kenyan Church. In addition to the women's coalition, Muslims had secured the support of Raila Odinga and the LDP, KANU, and civil society. On this, the NAK faction, which enjoyed the sympathies of the church, was woefully isolated at the conference. But Odinga and the LDP expected the Muslims to return the favor when questions critical to the LDP came up for a final vote on the floor of the conference. The vote on Kadhi courts indicated a coalescence of alliances at the conference. Two major blocs had solidified. The dominant bloc commanded the majority of delegates, was aligned with the LDP, and included KANU, Muslims, many women delegates, and a portion of civil society. On the other hand, the church and a segment of civil society supported the NAK faction, perceived as the "government" bloc. In ethnic terms, the NAK faction was primarily drawn from central Kenya, whereas the LDP pulled its support from most parts of the country, including the pastoralist and marginalized communities. This sharp chasm was the downfall of Bomas.

Devolution

The other important cleavage on which the fate of the 2004 Draft Constitution hung was devolution. One of the basic flaws of the postcolonial African state— and Kenya has been no exception—was the concentration of power in the central government and the alienation of the people from it. Alienation exacerbates the problem of nation building where competing ethnic loyalties and precolonial identities are stoked by elites to retard the development of a national consciousness. At the same time, the new state forged out of disparate groups must respect various identities but simultaneously exercise enough power and control to govern, create a national psyche, and advance liberty. Thus a delicate balance must be achieved between competing loyalties and control over political spaces. The trick is to permit a high degree of self-governance at the local level without weakening the central state. Several African states have adopted a federal system of government as an antidote to subnationalism, whereas others have opted for less autonomous structures of devolution. Kenya faced this dilemma on the eve of independence and accepted in the Lancaster or Independence Constitution a quasi-federal system of regional governments. But Kenyatta quickly smashed it and brought the entire country within the total control of the central government, and more specifically under his personal rule. Ironically, Moi, his successor, perfected the institutions of central control even though he had led Kenya African Democratic Union (KADU), the party whose central platform at Lancaster was the quasi-federalist Majimbo Constitution.

Structures of government are usually the most contested sections of any constitution-making process because they are about the distribution of power and control of resources. These contests are sharper in embryonic states or societies emerging out of a traumatic period. What's more, the diversity of the society and the numerical strengths or weaknesses of various groups, including their location relative to national resources, could make the choice a matter of life or death. Elites exacerbate these cleavages because they use their ethnic bases as props for political power in order to bargain for their share of the spoils. As such, political elites deliberately conflate their interests with those of their ethnic bases through demagoguery and the worn appeal to "my people." Except for lip service, most African postcolonial elites rarely act for the benefit of the ethnic base but rather use it to corral for themselves "their" share of the "national cake." In Kenya, elites have perfected this cynical manipulation of ethnic emotions and identities to the detriment of the larger nation. That is the conceptual context in which deliberations on devolution were conducted at Bomas.

The Constitution of Kenya Review Act gave the commission it created a wide mandate to imagine a system of government that would devolve power vertically and horizontally.[23] As put by the Constitution of Kenya Review Commission (CKRC), its task was to examine and make recommendations on the "structures and systems of government, including the federal and unitary systems; the place of local government in the constitutional organization of the Republic; and the extent of devolution of power to local authorities."[24] Devolution means the practical delegation and transfer of authority to subnational entities so that they can effectively participate in decisionmaking on specific matters. It does not necessarily entail federalism, although it is the intrinsic purpose of a federal state. It is a political device meant to accommodate a limited form of internal self-determination for groups or regions within a state. Devolution therefore seeks to ensure that the political center cannot exercise suffocating control over the periphery. Although devolution does not necessarily democratize the state, it nevertheless curbs the despotic powers of the center over the regions. Devolution enlarges the number of citizens who can participate in governance, accommodates the interests and identities of different groups, and fosters the affinity of the people to the state. But it has its limitations and need not guarantee democracy.

> However, devolution may not necessarily translate into greater democracy because, in a number of instances, it may serve only to put power in the hands of the local autocracy. This is why it is necessary, while considering the options, to keep in mind the need to ensure that the subjects of devolution are sufficiently motivated and organized to participate vigorously in managing local affairs and that appropriate mechanisms are in place to underpin democratic values.[25]

Devolution can take place in an autocratic state in which local authorities wield the instruments and mechanisms of repression. That is what happens when autonomy regimes for minorities are not subjected to higher ideals. Even though their purpose is to ensure the protection of groups, safeguard their survival, and enrich the larger body politic, they must be viewed with caution. Respect for difference, contact with otherness, and openness are central themes in the human rights corpus and must inform any autonomy regime or unit of devolution. Such systems cannot be permitted to erect barriers against outsiders or seal off all exits to forcibly deny their members the opportunity to opt out. Nor should they establish systems of tyranny against smaller minorities within them. Significantly, devolved units cannot be achieved at the expense of a subcategory of the group. Women, for example, cannot be subjected to abusive practices under the veil of devolution. Illiberal, autocratic, and exclusivist practices would frustrate goals of devolution. To pay off, devolved units must be placed under equal protection and antidiscrimination norms that bind the larger society.

Kenya's history and demography are ideal for devolution. Even though it has not been wracked by the bloodletting common to many African states, Kenya has a heightened ethnic consciousness. Kenyan Somalis have at times entertained separatist ambitions. Most in the poor northern regions of the country are so marginalized that their formal identity as Kenyan citizens is virtually meaningless. Uneven development among regions and ethnic groups has given rise to animosities. Ethnic demagoguery by the political class and the instigation of "ethnic" clashes, particularly by the KANU regime to eliminate the opposition, deepened ethnic tensions and fractured a fragile trust between different groups. In spite of that, no group has really wanted to exit the state, although some have advocated a Majimbo system of autonomous ethnic homelands, but within the state.[26] In a society with scarce resources, where the state is the basic conveyer of wealth and status, devolution assumes a survivalist dimension. For this reason, it is not clear whether devolution would empower the people at the bottom of the pyramid or simply create local feeding troughs for a few elites in rural and remote areas of the country. Elites from larger groups deploy a generic rights language, whereas those from smaller ones use ethnic identity and culture to create exclusive enclaves.

> Elites from the dominant tribes receive most-favored treatment while the elites from other tribes are subjected to various forms of oppression, exclusion, and discrimination. The excluded elite devises various strategies for capturing state power, seducing it, or reducing its impact upon them. Majimbo could be such a strategy. It is an instrument for the elite to win, retain or access political power and resources.[27]

The CKRC found that Kenyans were virtually unanimous in their support for devolution, but the devil was in the details. There was agreement that the people were alienated from the government and that too much power was concentrated at the center. Many Kenyans felt that they were not citizens but subjects, without a voice.[28] They singled out the provincial administration, long the instrument of repression of the regions by the central government, for elimination. Chiefs and local administrators were instruments of oppression and neglect. Most citizens recommended several tiers of devolution with elected representatives to control and regulate land and other resources. There was consensus that functions between the central and local authorities ought to be clearly delineated and observed so that communities could help in the administration of their own affairs, including development, planning, policy formulation, and budgetary allocation.[29] But they also wanted competent, democratic, and transparent local authorities run by elected persons of integrity. The CKRC found that the government was not only reviled but that it bordered on total illegitimacy in the eyes of the people. It was a revealing indictment of one-party rule, patrimony, and executive dictatorship writ large.

> At present, they [the people] feel disempowered and alienated from the government. They feel that decisions about their lives are being made in places remote from themselves and without consultation with them. They consider that they are discriminated against and that they have been unjustly deprived of their resources. There is a widespread wish for people to take charge of their own lives. They want to use community institutions for land management and other local affairs; they want power closer to where they live and to participate in public affairs.[30]

It was noteworthy that populations in marginalized areas or regions characterized by ethnic tensions favored a federal system as opposed to devolution within a unitary state. The Coast, Rift Valley, and Northeastern provinces proposed a federal or Majimbo system, whereas Western, Central, Eastern, Nyanza, and Nairobi provinces favored simple devolution.[31] Except for the Western Province, whose leaders had supported Majimbo in the Lancaster constitutional conference, the other provinces remained true to history. Provinces with large "foreign" or "settler" populations, that is, migrants with ancestral roots in other regions, such as the Rift Valley and the Coast, favored the more drastic federal system that would give them control over the "settler" groups. In the case of the Coast, the "settler" groups were Kikuyu and Kamba, whereas in the Rift Valley they were Kikuyu, Luo, and Luhya. In the so-called ethnic clashes of the 1990s, the Kalenjin in the Rift Valley ostensibly attacked the "settler" groups, and the Kikuyu and Kamba were supposedly persecuted by coastal ethnic groups at the instigation of the state in the Coast Province. Even though the Kalenjin and Maasai numerically dominate the Rift Valley, they have lost ground to the Kikuyu and other migrant groups. Northeastern Province, which is Somali-dominated and has been severely marginalized, is ruled from Nairobi by an officer corps largely drawn from other groups. For that reason, it seeks a federal structure. Unlike minorities or marginalized communities, dominant groups do not generally favor federalism. That is why Nairobi, Eastern, Western, and Nyanza provinces, which are dominated by the largest ethnic groups in the country, favored simple devolution. Kiraitu Murungi captured clearly some of these crosscurrents.

The Majimbo appeal lies in the failure of the centralized postcolonial state and its unfair and irrational resource distribution mechanisms. The postcolonial state like its colonial predecessor is based on the principles of concentration and centralization of power. Its dominant ideology is that of cronyism and client. This has resulted in the marginalization of the majority of the people. The people are not seeking Majimbo per se. What they are seeking are structures of government which will guarantee them participation in political power, and a rational, equitable distribution of national resources. They all want a piece of the pie.[32]

It is clear from the reports of the CKRC that the people did not have a developed understanding of the structures and mechanisms for creating a workable system for the devolution of power. As it noted, there was "no doubt that—consistent with the goals of the review and people's views—there has to be a transfer of very substantial powers and functions to local levels."[33] The CKRC added that it "is also very clear to us that the transfer has to be to bodies which are democratic and participatory" because the "people will not be content with mere administrative decentralization (deconcentration)."[34] But it was left to the CKRC to study various models of devolution and craft proposals that would capture the wishes of the people but at the same create a practical system of government. In addition to the upper house, which would act as the guarantor of devolution, and the various local authorities to ensure that central government would not overwhelm them, the CKRC proposed in the Ghai Draft four tiers of devolution—at the village, location, district, and provincial levels.[35] Elections were required for all four levels except at the village level, where the government could be chosen through elections or constituted by village elders. The focus of devolution, however, was the district, which was the principal unit of devolution.[36] The provincial government would be a shell of its former self, virtually stripped of all powers and relegated to the role of supporting the district government.[37]

Devolution is about localizing governance and regulating, controlling, and owning resources, particularly land. In addition to creating institutions for political participation, the Ghai Draft provided that districts would be "entitled to a substantial share of the national revenue of a fixed percentage to the communities in whose areas the resources are generated."[38] But to avoid the further marginalization of poor devolved units, the draft provided that "revenue from the national resources shall be shared equitably between the Districts and National Government."[39] District governments were vested with substantial powers in the control, regulation, and allocation of resources, as well as the provision of critical services in education, the health sector, water, roads, land, trade, culture, information, labor, local taxes, agriculture, and the probation and welfare of convicts.[40] This new constitutional scheme would effectively end the tyranny of the central government over local communities. The central government was granted jurisdiction over defense, foreign affairs, citizenship, law enforcement, the judiciary, national elections, the treasury, and other over-arching national matters.[41] Devolution would free the central government to concentrate on the weighty obligations of national statehood, instead of dissipating its scarce energies overseeing provincial structures of oppression. Importantly, devolution would free local politics from the patronage and patrimony of the center, a fundamental shift that could allow democracy to flourish and deepen.

The scheme of devolution proposed by the Ghai Draft was met with enormous hostility at the conference, even though it was a radical departure from the existing structure that concentrated power at the center. The principle of devolution was not questioned, but the structures and powers proposed for local authorities were deemed unacceptable. The Ghai Draft's assumption that the extant seventy districts would form the basis of devolved units was rejected.[42] Yash Ghai, the principal author of the devolution chapter, took the negative reaction as a rebuke and was crestfallen.[43] Most delegates wanted to go further and create a more elaborate devolution structure, complete with a new cartography. The consensus seemed to be that a "new structure of devolution should be designed *de novo*."[44] It was agreed that the new structure take into account the following key variables: economic viability, including resources; cultural and linguistic homogeneity, affinity, and historical association; the area's capacity for autonomy; population clusters and distribution; and ecology and geography.[45] Analyzed in the context of Kenyan politics and history, these factors are a code for ethnic autonomy. In other words, most delegates at the conference had decided that power would be devolved to ethnic entities through which each precolonial community would exercise self-governance at the local level. It was a powerful rejection of the postcolonial state as a legitimate political entity. It was also a repudiation of internal colonialism, the system by which a unitary central government is controlled by one group that dominates all the others.

It is not difficult to understand why the government or any group in power would not be enthusiastic about devolution in general and ethnic-based devolution in particular. Simply put, devolution means the loss of power and the ability to rule by fiat, not to mention limitations on powerful barons who govern through patronage, cronyism, and ethnic favoritism. Devolution also raises legitimate concerns about the cost of its administration to the people. Is the particular structure viable economically, or will it impose an unacceptably high tax burden on an already poor and overtaxed populace? Furthermore, an ethnic-based system would substantially curtail the ability of the central government—and dominant groups—to control economic resources and protect the interests of "settler" groups. For instance, the NARC government, which was controlled by the Kikuyu and kindred communities, would have had a diminished capacity to protect the interests of Kikuyu and other migrant groups in the Rift Valley or the Coast province. Importantly, it would have been unable to safeguard the business and commercial interests of the Kikuyu and related business elites outside their ancestral regions. Conversely, ethnically dominated local authorities could disfavor "settler" groups through exclusion, discrimination, and even dispossession. Politically, such structures could also make it difficult for outsider groups to penetrate different parts of the country to canvass for their political parties. At best, Majimbo or ethnic-based devolution could foster ethnic democracy, a contradiction in terms, or lead to the hardening of ethnic consciousness, increase intolerance, and atrophy the development of a national identity, at worst. A return to this type of devolution would bring Kenya full circle to the independence Majimbo Constitution. The DP used this rationale in 2001 to argue against Majimboism.

> Those against Majimbo are not opposed to the devolution of political power and resources to lower levels. What they are afraid of is the very real possibility that Majimbo will disrupt free trade and investment, entrench tribal hatred, and provide a basis for ethnic cleansing. Some people still bear the painful psychological and economic scars of ethnic clashes from Molo, Olenguruone, Man Narok, Likoni and Enoosupukia from which Majimbo proponents killed, maimed, and expelled politically incorrect "foreigners."[46]

These complex political and historical variables explain why devolution was such a hotly contested issue at Bomas. Its technical committee was a matter of great interest and debate at the forum and in the country at large. Delegates jostled fiercely to be assigned to it. Its leadership was highly sought because its chair would play a very important role in shaping the future of the country. But it was no surprise when Crispin Mbai, an academic and Odinga confidant, was elected its chair. Odinga's LDP had clearly outmaneuvered NAK at the conference. It was a great shock to the country, however, when Mbai was murdered just as the committee was making important decisions. Both Odinga and Ghai termed the killing an assassination, language that implied a government hand in the murder.[47] Accusations of death threats against other delegates close to Mbai fueled anger and fear at the conference.[48] Odinga himself said that individuals who were afraid of Mbai's role in the critical committee had killed him.[49] Suspicions ran so high that Odinga and Martha Karua, a Kikuyu and the water minister, almost came to blows.[50] Adhu Awiti, an LDP legislator and another Odinga ally, replaced Mbai as head of the devolution committee. The murder raised the stakes higher and galvanized the majority of delegates behind the LDP-KANU alliance. NAK and the government were increasingly isolated.

Under these circumstances, the NAK faction tried without success to lobby against a conference determined to adopt a Majimbo constitution. The government publicly disowned an unsigned document attributed to it and circulated at Bomas criticizing the Ghai Draft's devolution.[51] NAK instead favored a slight modification of the existing structures with the county, a unit similar to a district, as the focal point of devolution. The constituency would be the finite level of devolution. In 2001, the Democratic Party, the core party in NAK, had presented this outline of devolution at a CKRC public forum.[52] But these structures, although self-governing, would not enjoy any substantial autonomy from the center. The NGO women's coalition took a similar position, but offered more coherent proposals.[53] At any rate, NAK and the government were unable to put before the conference or argue for a coherent alternative to the Majimbo system favored by most delegates. Instead, critics of the proposed system attacked it as too costly and inoperable.[54] It was no surprise when in March 2004 the conference rubber-stamped the recommendations of the devolution committee and adopted a scheme that went beyond the proposals of the Ghai Draft. The 2004 Draft Constitution returned to the Majimbo structures that would have sharpened further the ethnic dimensions of the envisaged state. In it, Kenya was carved up into ethnic enclaves to the purest extent possible. Virtually every ethnic group was given its own government. Regions were composed of either members of the same community or related communities. The 2004 Draft Constitution imposed a total of eighteen provincial bureaucracies and seventeen district governments on the country.[55] The district remained the focus of devolution, with location the lowest tier.[56] All local governments had legislative and executive branches. A premier ran provincial governments, whereas districts were presided over by a governor, both of whom would be elected, the former by a college of electors and the latter directly by the voters.[57] The location administrator was also an elective office.[58]

Unlike the Ghai Draft, the 2004 Draft Constitution placed emphasis on the tax powers of districts, which were substantial and covered a wide array of services, including most businesses.[59] The jurisdiction of district governments was enlarged and more clearly spelled out in the Draft Constitution. The enormous devolution of power to the districts left the central government with only the most overarching responsibilities, such as defense, energy policy, public works, aviation, the judiciary, and other national functions.[60] The scheme contemplated by the draft constitution made the district a real center of power and virtually removed the central government from the lives of communities. It created autonomous political societies but obligated the center to share national revenues equitably among them.[61] But there was no obligation on the central government to bail out a local government that was unable to fund itself.[62] It was a seductive scheme on paper but raised many questions. For example, what was the long-term effect on the construction of a national identity if ethnic governance—essentially through Bantustans—was formalized? Was there adequate protection for minority groups? What would happen if a local government failed because of incompetence, corruption, or a lack of resources? Could the scheme be implemented successfully, given the underdeveloped tax base and the high costs associated with the added layers of bureaucracy? Or would the government become, in essence, the business of the country?

These were legitimate questions on which the delegates did not fully deliberate because of the complex matters they raised or due to their distrust of the critics of this scheme of devolution. Many of the delegates acted according to their political sympathies, not the weight of the evidence. Besides, the majority were simply not competent to make critical and detailed decisions on such complicated questions of law and government. What's more, overpoliticization gave the conference a herd mentality, in which delegates would stampede toward particular positions based on the identity of the advocate, not the merits of the case. It did not help that the NAK side was woefully unprepared, extremely arrogant, and seemingly conspiratorial. Cabinet ministers did not speak with one voice on devolution or any other question. This incoherence, distrust, and the hatreds between political factions and parties irretrievably poisoned the conference and made it impossible to hold a rational dialogue on contentious matters, even though as illustrated in Table 10.1, the areas of convergence in the various draft constitutions far outweighed the contentious matters. The NAK government's defeat on devolution was one of the three major reasons the conference was stillborn.

The Structure of the Executive

The most important issue on which the National Constitutional Conference failed, however, was defining the post of a prime minister. It is on this question that the LDP and NAK completely deadlocked, creating a gargantuan crisis. The basic facts of the crisis were simple and straightforward, although Kenya's checkered history complicates them beyond comprehension. At the center of the storm was Raila Odinga, a seemingly indomitable political tactician, who sought political supremacy with a single mind. His immediate claim to the premiership was based on the MOU between NAK and LDP. Kibaki reneged on the promise to appoint Odinga premier once he was ensconced at State House. Odinga cried foul and devoted much of his considerable political energy and acumen to campaigning for the post at Bomas.

Few would contest the statement that Odinga was arguably the country's most exciting politician. Just like his father Oginga Odinga, Raila Odinga commanded a fanatical following among the Luo. He manipulated Luo politicians like minions, and those who failed to prostrate themselves before him were almost always ruined. *Odingaism* required political sycophancy, or damnation was virtually certain. Three important cases bear this point out. In 1997, Peter Anyang' Nyong'o, the prominent Luo academic and politician who was a key leader in the reform struggle, lost his parliamentary seat after he refused to run under the aegis of Odinga's National Development Party ticket. In 1992, Anyang Nyong'o had been elected with 91.1 percent of the vote when he ran under the Odinga-supported FORD-Kenya party, but was drubbed with a meager 19.7 percent when he contested the 1997 election

Table 10.1 Comparison of Draft Constitutions

Section	Draft Constitution (Bomas Draft)	CKRC Draft Constitution (Ghai Draft)	Proposed New Constitution (Wako Draft)	Proposal for a Model Constitution (KHRC, LSK, ICJ)
Executive	President as head of state President largely ceremonial Prime minister exercises executive power and is head of government	President head of state and symbol of nation Prime minister leader of cabinet Prime minister head of government	President as chief executive President appoints and dismisses prime minister Impeachment of president by 75% of MPs	President would not control Parliament President to declare wealth Provides for impeachment of president
Legislature	Independent legislature Provides for National Assembly and Senate (Parliament) Parliament determines its own calendar	Autonomous Parliament Approves constitutional appointments Creates two houses Elections through mixed member proportional representation (MMPR)	One house (Parliament) Independent One-third principle for women	Autonomous Parliament Cannot be dissolved until five-year term is over
Judiciary	Independent judiciary Judges appointed by president on approval by Parliament Provides directly for Kadhi courts	Independent judiciary Appointments of judges to be approved by upper house Establishes Kadhi courts	Provides for religious courts (Christian, Muslim, Hindu) Judges appointed by president and approved by Parliament Independent judiciary	Chief Kadhi elevated to High Court rank Independent judiciary
Bill of Rights	Expansive bill of rights Provides economic, social, and cultural rights Limits women's rights for Muslim family law Creates a gender commission	Comprehensive bill of rights, including economic, social, and cultural rights and no death penalty	Expansive bill of rights Restricts women's rights in Muslim courts Provides for economic, social, and cultural rights	Limited to core civil and political rights

continues

Table 10.1 Continued

Section	Draft Constitution (Bomas Draft)	CKRC Draft Constitution (Ghai Draft)	Proposed New Constitution (Wako Draft)	Proposal for a Model Constitution (KHRC, LSK, ICJ)
Gender	Entrenches one-third affirmative action principle for women for all elective and appointive offices Anti-abortion	No gender commission Strong on equal protection and antidiscrimination One-third principle for women Women can inherit land, but are not given direct control	Provides for gender equality Anti-abortion One-third principle	Calls for non-Kenyans married to Kenyans to be citizens regardless of gender
Devolution	Creates quasi-federal system Establishes strong regional governments	Creates strong regional governments District is focus of devolution	District are basic units of devolution District assembly elected	Election of local government officials
Land	Noncitizens entitled to leasehold tenure only	Noncitizens to own land on leasehold tenure for a maximum of 99 years	Limits noncitizens to 99-year leases	Creates land commission to oversee land matters
Citizenship	Dual citizenship	Dual citizenship	Dual citizenship	Dual citizenship

Section	Law Society of Kenya Draft Constitution	Ufungamano Draft Constitution	Model Proposals (Draft Constitution by Women's Coalition)	Official Constitution
Executive	President is chief executive President can be impeached President appoints prime minister	Provides for president as chief executive No prime minister	President as chief executive President appoints prime minister but only Parliament can dismiss prime minister	Imperial presidency Limited oversight by Parliament

continues

Table 10.1 Continued

Section	Law Society of Kenya Draft Constitution	Ufungamano Draft Constitution	Model Proposals (Draft Constitution by Women's Coalition)	Official Constitution
Legislative	Creates only one house (Parliament) President to dissolve Parliament	Provides for only one chamber	Establishes only one house of Parliament MPs elected through the MMPR system	Parliament is vibrant but lacks real authority to check president
Judiciary	Independent judiciary Provides for Kadhi courts President has broad powers to appoint judges	Independent judiciary No Kadhi courts Parliamentary approval for judges	Independent judiciary Provides for Kadhi courts Appointment of judges by president upon approval by Parliament	Judges and constitutional offices appointed by president with parliamentary approval
Bill of Rights	Many basic rights, including several economic and social rights Provides for human rights commission	Basic bill of rights Abolishes death penalty	No death penalty Expansive rights, including economic and social rights	Basic bill of rights, but rarely employed Permits death penalty
Gender	Equality for women Provides for one-third principle for women	One-third principle for women	Gender commission Provides for one-third principle Affirmative action Silent on abortion Engenders provisions on land	Patriarchal provisions Women are invisible
Devolution	No substantial devolution No regional governments	Unitary state with little devolution	Devolves power but retains strong center	Strong central government with provinces
Land	Creates national land commission No land tenure based on nationality	Basic provisions on land	Noncitizens limited (99-year leases)	A freehold tenure even for noncitizens
Citizenship	Dual citizenship	Dual citizenship	Dual citizenship	No dual citizenship

under the Social Democratic Party, led by Charity Ngilu, a Kamba, Kenya's first serious female presidential candidate.[63] Predictably, Anyang' Nyong'o was overwhelmingly elected in 2002 when he ran under the Odinga-dominated NARC. In 2002, James Orengo, arguably the most astute and national of Luo politicians, lost his Ugenya parliamentary seat when he ran on an SDP ticket instead of Odinga's NARC.[64] Another was Shem Ochuodho, a NARC rising star who was rigged out of the 2002 elections for being an outspoken rival of Odinga. The point is that Odinga was a formidable force, although most observers agreed that he was not electable to the presidency in a direct vote. That is why Odinga believed that the only way to power was through the premiership, a post to which he would not be elected but appointed by the president and confirmed by Parliament.

The struggle to restructure the executive did not have anything to do with Odinga. Yet he was the one person who was most associated with devolution of power within the executive. In fact, Kenyans blamed the failure of democracy on the concentration of personal and unchecked power in the executive. Both the civil society–led pro-democracy movement in the 1990s and the push for multipartyism were built on the demonization of the Moi presidency. Moi was the single most powerful symbol of dictatorship and all that was wrong with Kenya. It was no wonder the people told the CKRC that ending dictatorship was the most urgent business of the constitutional review process. The people's views could be summarized as antidictatorship, pro-democracy, and anti-Moi. As early as 1994, a KHRC-led effort had captured this growing national consensus in a model constitution.[65]

Why had the Kenyan state become so despotic? Part of the answer lay in the distrust of the ruling elites in the parliamentary system imposed on Kenya by the departing British. To consolidate power, Jomo Kenyatta and KANU dismantled the Westminster model in which the head of state is different from the head of government. Under this model, the head of state is either a constitutional monarch or a president, all of whom play largely ceremonial roles, although they are the symbols of the nation. It is a system in which real power lies with the cabinet and the head of government, usually a prime minister, formally appointed by the head of state from the party or coalition with the majority of seats in Parliament. The head of government plays other roles, such as formally authorizing the formation of government or dissolving Parliament so that new elections can be called. The prime minister picks his own cabinet and can sack its members, but in the classic iteration of this model, executive power lies collectively with the entire cabinet, not just the person of the prime minister. It is the contradiction within this system in an emergent state that creates dysfunction in postcolonial states.

Kenya is a perfect example of the inherent crises of the Westminster model for states in embryo. New ruling elites must consolidate power, usually fighting one another, in addition to the structures of the old order, to do so. But the checks and balances of the model, which cannot simply be imposed in a vacuum, can only work if the ruling faction is not threatened. That gives elites time to adapt to the system so that their political behavior can evolve to accommodate it. Unfortunately, the Kenyatta faction was impatient and did not permit norms and institutions to evolve within the model. First, he rolled the powers of the head of state with those of the head of government into a president and took over that new commanding position. KANU swallowed up KADU, and then Kenyatta expelled Odinga and his fellow dissenters, dismantled the bicameral legislature, ended regional autonomy, and created a powerful presidential system. In a stroke, Kenyatta had terminated the Westminster model. He abolished the parliamentary system and replaced it with a hybrid presidential system, but without the separation of powers and checks and balances. But in an oddity, he remained a member of Parliament and liable to a vote of no confidence. He could dissolve Parliament at will and veto legislation, powers that became gratuitous once Kenya became a one-party state. As H. W. O. Okoth-Ogendo has written, such a system boasts a constitution but lacks constitutionalism.[66] Moi perfected Kenyatta's autocratic state and increased public cynicism and alienation.

It was not surprising that the people told the CKRC that Kenya could not be reformed without dismantling the imperial presidency. In addition to devolving power to local authorities and Parliament, the majority of Kenyans wanted the executive broken up into two key offices—an executive prime minister and a ceremonial president. The president would "play the role of an Elder of the State serving as a symbol of unity and identity."[67] They also suggested that the president not be above the law, that his powers be sharply curtailed, and that the power to appoint senior officials be shared with Parliament.[68] The president would cease to be an MP, not have the power to determine election dates, and could be removed for misconduct.[69] Major political parties made similar recommendations, including the creation of a premiership. Speaking for the National Alliance for Change (NAC), the forerunner to NAK, Murungi decried the enormous powers of the president, whom he characterized as "an authoritarian imperial monarch exercising feudal powers."[70] He called for presidential powers to be "drastically reduced" through the creation of a prime minister as head of government upon appointment by the president and approval by Parliament.[71] KANU and DP also urged the creation of a premiership.[72]

From these recommendations, the CKRC proposed what it called a "modified form of parliamentary system."[73] Although it claimed that it was not "purely parliamentary," the proposed system made the prime minister the chief executive or head of government, and relegated the president to a largely ceremonial role without a direct hand in the running of the state.[74] Only the Parliament, not the president, could dismiss the prime minister.[75] The president would formally appoint ministers upon their nomination by the prime minister.[76] The president, who would be directly elected by the people, would be subordinate to the prime minister who had to be the leader of the majority party or the dominant coalition in Parliament.[77] Although it is true that the president under this model had more powers than in a pure Westminster parliamentary system, the office would no longer be the focus of power in Kenya. In effect, the Ghai Draft had taken a knife to the executive, carving it up into two offices and vesting the power of the state in the office of the prime minister. Without a doubt, the draft was a protest against Moi. It was not clear whether Ghai had merely transferred despotism from one office to another, even as he anticipated that line of attack.

> On balance, a modified form of parliamentary system is best able to achieve the principles of government . . . The aims of the modifications would be a more balanced Executive, with internal checks, to establish a collective form of government to facilitate coalition building across ethnic lines. It would cut across geographic areas and provide a basis for effective as well as accountable government through greater separation of powers.[78]

It is on this difference—whether to go parliamentary or presidential—that the national conference was immobilized. NAK, which had previously supported the creation of a prime minister, now opposed it, at least in the form provided for in the Ghai Draft. Popular commentary referred to the post as an *executive* prime minister, as opposed to a prime minister who would be the *chief executive* of government. This language deeply riled the NAK side, which saw the office as a direct threat to the Kibaki presidency. The office would, if created, strip Kibaki and his protégés of virtually all their power and vest it in Odinga, the presumptive prime minister. Murungi, the NAK mandarin, publicly ridiculed those advocating an "executive" prime minister. He dismissed calls for the office as a "political impossibility and a big joke."[79] He cited the Democratic Republic of Congo (formerly Zaire) as one country that had been plunged into chaos by competing offices within the executive. He flatly stated, "There can't be an executive president and an executive prime minister. There can't be two centers of power."[80] It was clear that NAK would not entertain a powerful premiership and was unlikely to even concede a less neutered office along the Tanzanian or Ugandan models. NAK's strategy was to offer the less appealing option to Odinga, hoping that he would reject it and be branded the obstructionist to the new constitution.[81] But the strategy backfired.

Odinga and the LDP had superior organizational skills at Bomas. They exploited NAK's incumbency for unpopularity, its incompetence at lobbying, and the fear it inspired in KANU to create a solid majority at the conference. Murungi came to personify the arrogance, bungling, and ineptness of the new regime. Muite, the NAK-friendly chair of the PSC, became deeply unpopular because of LDP's efforts to demonize him, but also due to suspicions that he was conspiring with NAK to derail the conference.[82] To make matters worse, NAK and Muite had completely alienated Ghai, effectively driving him into the arms of Odinga and the LDP. Odinga openly defended Ghai while Murungi and NAK called for his removal or resignation.[83] Various attempts to reconcile NAK and LDP and find common ground on the question of the premiership repeatedly failed. Mediation efforts, including one by the Coalition for National Unity, led by FORD-People leader Simeon Nyachae, and the consensus subcommittee chaired by Bishop Philip Sulumeti, failed to bear fruit. But the Sulumeti consensus was acceptable to NAK because it left intact many of the presidential powers and created a clearly subordinate prime minister.[84] It would revise the so-called Zero Draft,[85] the draft constitution produced by the CKRC after the reports of the technical committees.[86]

The Sulumeti agreement, which had been hashed out between LDP and NAK, was resoundingly defeated by a vote of 314 to 151.[87] Among the cabinet ministers, only Odinga voted against the agreement. The defeat prompted Moody Awori, the vice president, to lead the cabinet, except Odinga, Najib Balala, and Ochillo Ayacko, in a walkout from the conference. Only 138 delegates walked out, whereupon the remaining 327 "swiftly passed the Zero Draft version of the Executive section, which transfers power to the prime minister as head of government."[88] They then adopted the rest of the document and effectively passed the 2004 Draft Constitution. In a stunning theatrical finale, the long-running constitutional conference had completed its work. The draft's structure of the executive was a very close approximation of the Ghai Draft, with the prime minister at the center of executive authority.[89] The president was not completely ceremonial, although he would have virtually no say in the critical matters of the state. The 2004 Draft Constitution provided for a parliamentary system. It also gave Parliament wide latitude to impeach or remove the president.[90] It is obvious why Kibaki and Odinga had diametrically opposed feelings about the 2004 Draft Constitution.

There is little doubt that both LDP and NAK saw the National Constitutional Conference as a forum where power would either be won or lost, but not a conclave to reform the state. For NAK, all energies were geared toward preserving the executive authority that Kibaki now enjoyed as president and for which he had bitterly attacked Moi. For Odinga, the conference was a launching pad for an official, but peaceful, civilian coup d'état, a golden opportunity to write himself into the most powerful position in the state. That is why he orchestrated the defeat of the Sulumeti consensus after giving the impression that it was acceptable. He exposed Murungi and NAK as political greenhorns, even though he must have known that NAK would never forgive, trust, or accept him. At any rate, the "victory" by Odinga at Bomas was Pyrrhic, an empty maneuver. How could he now prevail upon the Kibaki state to implement the 2004 Draft Constitution against its own wishes and interests? But one thing was clear. He would surely use it as a political platform in the 2007 general and presidential elections against Kibaki. Once again, the political class had come close to a normative framework for state reformation, but was unable to act in the national interest. After the euphoric promise of the 2002 elections, Kenyans were again despondent. Many Kenyans felt betrayed by the NARC state, just as Murungi, then a leading oppositionist, had warned KANU they felt in 2000. His language was ironically prescient.

> Many Kenyans do not believe that there will be any meaningful comprehensive review of the constitution so long as KANU and Moi are in power. When they see the futility of peaceful legal struggles, they may take over from the bickering elite and introduce radical change through violence, like the Mau Mau did in the 1950s.[91]

Notes

1. "Fighting KANU with Fire," *Daily Nation*, November 25, 2002, editorial.

2. "Despite NARC's MPs' Retreat, Suspicion, Mistrust Persist," *Sunday Nation*, April 13, 2003.

3. "Constitution—NARC Should Not Renege," *East African Standard*, February 2, 2003, editorial.

4. "How Raila Lost Poll to Muite," *Sunday Nation*, March 23, 2003.

5. "Top NARC Leadership Divided over the Constitution," *Sunday Nation*, March 23, 2003, 12.

6. Frank Holmquist, "Kenya's Anti-Politics," *Current History: A Journal of Contemporary World Affairs* (May 2005): 212.

7. Ibid., 209.

8. Ibid., 210.

9. "MPs Gear Up to Raise Their Salaries, Allowances," *Daily Nation*, February 21, 2003.

10. Holmquist, "Kenya's Anti-Politics," 210.

11. US Central Intelligence Agency, *World Factbook,* 2005, at http://www.cia.gov/cia/publications/factbook/geos/ke.html#People, accessed May 24, 2005.

12. Muslim Task Force on Constitutional Review, "The Kenyan Muslim Position on the Constitutional Safeguard of the Kadhi's Courts," 2003, Jamia Mosque, Nairobi.

13. "Sharia Law Warning in Kadhi Court Row," *Daily Nation*, April 24, 2003.

14. Ibid.

15. Ibid.

16. Ibid.

17. FIDA, IED, KHRC, and League of Kenya Women Voters, *Safeguarding the Gains for Women in the Draft Constitution: Model Proposals, January 2005*.

18. Ibid., Article 159.

19. FIDA, IED, KHRC, and League of Kenya Women Voters, *Audit Report: The National Constitutional Conference of Kenya* (Nairobi: Kenya Human Rights Commission, 2004), 38.

20. Abdullahi Ahmed An-Na'im, "Human Rights in the Muslim World: Socio-Political Conditions and Scriptural Imperatives," *Harvard Human Rights Journal* 3 (1990): 37–46.

21. "Protect Chief Kadhi in Constitution, Says Don," *Daily Nation*, April 14, 2003.

22. "Bomas So Far: The Scorecard and Unfinished Business Ahead," *Sunday Nation*, October 5, 2003.

23. *The Constitution of Kenya Review Act*, Section 17, Chapter 3, 2001.

24. Constitution of Kenya Review Commission, *Report of the Constitution of Kenya Review Commission: The Main Report,* September 2002, 271 (hereinafter *Main Report*).

25. Ibid., 275.

26. Peter Okondo, *A Commentary on the Constitution of Kenya* (Nairobi: Phoenix Publishers, 1995).

27. Kiraitu Murungi, "Democratic Party of Kenya's Position on the Majimbo Debate," December 6, 2001, available at http://www.kenyaconstitution.org/docs/11d008 .htm, visited on May 27, 2005.

28. *Main Report*, 289–290.

29. Ibid., 286–289.

30. Ibid., 290.

31. Ibid., 289.

32. Murungi, "DP and Majimbo."

33. *Main Report*, 290.

34. Ibid.

35. Constitution of Kenya Review Commission, *The Draft Bill to Amend the Constitution,* 2002, Article 215 (hereinafter *Ghai Draft*).

36. Ibid., Article 220.

37. Ibid., Article 221.

38. Ibid., Article 226(1).

39. Ibid., Article 226(2).

40. Ibid., List II, Seventh Schedule.

41. Ibid., List I, Seventh Schedule.

42. Constitution of Kenya Review Commission, *The Report of the Rapporteur-General to the National Constitutional Conference on the General Debate Held Between April 28 and June 6, 2003 at the Bomas of Kenya,* 2003, 40 (hereinafter *Bomas Report I*).

43. "Clarify Power Sharing Plans," *Daily Nation*, May 24, 2003, editorial.

44. Constitution of Kenya Review Commission, *Bomas Report I*, 40.

45. Ibid.

46. Murungi, "DP and Majimbo."

47. "Fury over Official's Murder," *Daily Nation*, September 16, 2003.

48. Ibid.; "Ghai Receives Praise and Blame over His Position at the Conference," *Daily Nation*, September 28, 2003.

49. "Mayhem at Mbai's Funeral," *Daily Nation*, September 28, 2003.

50. "Ministers in Near Fistcuffs over the Murder of Mbai," *Daily Nation*, October 9, 2003.

51. "The Contentious Issues Facing Bomas III," *Daily Nation*, January 11, 2004.

52. Murungi, "DP and Majimbo."

53. *Model Proposals*, Articles 167–169.

54. "Malawian Suggests 3 Levels of Devolution," *Daily Nation*, January 27, 2004.

55. The National Constitutional Conference, *The Draft Constitution of Kenya* 2004, First Schedule (hereinafter *2004 Draft Constitution*).

56. Ibid., Articles 211–217.

57. Ibid., Articles 214, 221.

58. Ibid., Article 225.

59. Ibid., Fifth Schedule.

60. Ibid., Fourth Schedule.

61. Ibid., Article 239.

62. Ibid., Article 239(4).

63. Wambui Kimathi, "A Strategic Seclusion—Yet Again! The 1997 General Elections in Luo Nyanza," in *Out for the Count: The 1997 General Elections and Prospects for Democracy in Kenya*, ed. Marcel Rutten, Alamin Mazrui, and François Grignon (Kampala: Fountain Publishers, 2001), 495, 509.

64. Makau Mutua, "Raila Odinga: Nelson Mandela or Idi Amin?" *Sunday Nation*, May 6, 2007; "Orengo to Contest Ugenya Seat," *Daily Nation*, November 14, 2007.

65. Kenya Human Rights Commission, Law Society of Kenya, and International Commission of Jurists, *The Kenya We Want: Proposal for a Model Constitution* (1994).

66. H. W. O. Okoth-Ogendo, "Constitutions Without Constitutionalism: Reflections on the African Political Paradox," in *Constitutionalism and Democracy: Transitions in the Contemporary World*, ed. Douglas Greenberg, Stanley N. Katz, Melanie Beth Oliviero, and Steven C. Wheatley (New York: Oxford University Press, 1993). For a critique of Okoth-Ogendo, see also H. Kwasi Prempeh, "Marbury in Africa: Judicial Review and the Challenge of Constitutionalism in Contemporary Africa," *Tulane Law Review* 80 (2006): 1239.

67. *Main Report*, 243.

68. Ibid., 244.

69. Ibid.

70. National Alliance for Change, "Fundamental Principles to Be Considered in Making the New Constitution by the People of Kenya," March 7, 2003, available at http://www.kenyaconstitution.org/docs/11d009.htm, accessed May 27, 2005.

71. Ibid.

72. "Parties' Position on Prime Minister," *Saturday Nation*, September 13, 2003.

73. *Main Report*, 245.

74. *Ghai Draft,* Articles 150–152.

75. Ibid., Article 174.

76. Ibid., Article 175.

77. Ibid., Article 171.

78. *Main Report*, 245.

79. "Kiraitu Now Rules Out Executive PM," *Sunday Nation*, September 14, 2003.

80. "Kiraitu's Big Somersault over PM," *Daily Nation*, September 15, 2003.

81. "Let's Not Copy Other Countries, Says Raila," *Daily Nation*, August 19, 2003.

82. "Raila and Kiraitu in a New War of Words," *Sunday Nation*, December 7, 2003.

83. "Why Prof. Ghai Is in Deep Trouble," *Sunday Nation*, December 14, 2003; "Odinga: Ghai Is Being Used as an Excuse to Scuttle Bomas Process," *Sunday Nation*, December 7, 2003.

84. "President on Top in Bomas Power Deal," *Daily Nation*, March 13, 2004.

85. Constitution of Kenya Review Commission, *2004 Zero Draft of the National Constitutional Conference to Alter the Draft Bill,* February 14, 2004.

86. "Draft Gives PM More Powers," *Daily Nation*, February 18, 2004.

87. "VP Leads Bomas Walkout," *Daily Nation*, March 16, 2004.

88. Ibid.

89. *2004 Draft Constitution*, Chapter 12.

90. Ibid., Articles 163, 164.

91. Kiraitu Murungi, *In the Mud of Politics* (Nairobi: Acacia Stantex Publishers, 2000), 201.

11

The End Game

THE SWIFT ADOPTION in March 2004 of the draft constitution by the National Constitutional Conference was, even by the theatrical standards of the Kenyan constitution-making process, a politically titillating event. Most shocking perhaps was the humiliation Raila Odinga meted out to President Mwai Kibaki. The episode was an object lesson in the corruption of democracy by elites engaged in a zero-sum game for personal political power. To some, the adoption of the draft constitution could not have come sooner. It was the end of a national spectacle that displayed the worst proclivities of the country's deeply divided rulers. To others, it was a vindication of *wanjiku* (the female name and euphemism for the common Kenyan), of people power against an arrogant, hypocritical Kikuyu-dominated elite that had ascended to power on false promises. To KANU, the former ruling party that became an orphan after Moi relinquished control of it following the 2002 elections, the Bomas constitution was the death of the day of reckoning that the Kibaki regime may have initially planned for the corrupt lot. But for Raila Odinga, it was the pinnacle of his political power since the National Rainbow Coalition (NARC) had taken over in 2002. Objectively, however, the rancorous adoption of the 2004 Draft Constitution more likely marked the death, in the foreseeable future, of genuine constitutional reform of the state. Quite simply, the political landscape was so irreparably broken that the political class was unable to deliver a mutually acceptable constitution to radically redefine the Kenyan state.

The Broken Landscape

Every sector of society, including reformers, lost the moral high ground because of the Bomas debacle. No one could speak with authority about where the country ought to have gone from Bomas. Authoritative voices, even those that summoned the country to action in the past, had lost their effect. An air of deep cynicism and paralysis hung over the land. Ethnic fragmentation was at an all-time high, so soon after the 2002 elections that had united most communities against the Moi-KANU kleptocracy. What had gone awry? Why, particularly after Bomas, did it seem impossible for the review process to find a nationally acceptable stage for its completion? Ironically, those with the most at stake in the reform process—the majority of people at the bottom—became least likely to mobilize for change. They were fragmented and dazed by NARC's betrayal. What the nation saw was a sick elite, a collection of governors unable to lead in the national interest.[1]

Precisely because of its failure to agree on a broadly acceptable constitution, the *process* at Bomas opened up Kenya's deep wounds and left them unbound, abandoned to fester.[2] In the course of Bomas, the *process* continually poisoned the atmosphere, further contracted the sense of Kenyan-ness, and infected virtually every Kenyan with bile. Ethnic tensions, some of which had been sutured out of civility, now burst into the open. Every major institutional stakeholder at Bomas—civil society, the tribalized political parties, religious organizations, professional and trade groups, business interests, the Constitution of Kenya Review Commission (CKRC) itself, and rural delegates—was drawn into the maelstrom of petty politics. Bomas became an NAK-LDP snakepit, a living hell for anyone with a national reform agenda. These divisions were transferred to most living souls in the country. The few rational voices left bayed in the wilderness, unable to bring reason back to the reform processes. Some citizens despaired and called for Bomas to be terminated.[3] The review process, long a dream for the country, had now turned into a national nightmare.

In the aftermath of the passage of the 2004 Draft Constitution, key political actors adopted defiant tones.[4] The National Alliance Party of Kenya (NAK), the government side, announced through Moody Awori, the vice president, that the NARC government of which it was part had exited the review process.[5] The Liberal Democratic Party (LDP) and Kenya African National Union (KANU) formed an alliance to fight for the passage of the draft constitution by Parliament.[6] KANU MPs threatened a vote of no confidence in President Kibaki because his government had rejected the Bomas process.[7] The faiths-led Ufungamano Initiative indicated its displeasure with the draft constitution and attacked the legitimacy of the process through which it was adopted.[8] Civil society, the other major actor, came unstuck. Most civil society organizations had been sympathetic to NAK and supported the NARC government when it took power in 2003. The Kenya Human Rights Commission (KHRC), for example, endorsed Kibaki and NAK in the 2002 elections. Several prominent civil society leaders were appointed to senior positions in government and various reform bodies. For instance, Martha Koome, the leading Federation of Women Lawyers (FIDA) leader, was appointed to the judiciary; Makau Mutua, the chair of the KHRC, was appointed to head the Task Force on the Establishment of a Truth, Justice, and Reconciliation Commission; Kathurima M'Inoti, a thoughtful human rights lawyer long associated with the International Commission of Jurists and a former law partner to Murungi, was appointed head of the Law Reform Commission; Maina Kiai, the founding executive director of the KHRC, became chair of the Kenya National Commission on Human Rights, a statutory government watchdog; and John Githongo, the head of Transparency International–Kenya, was appointed by Kibaki as the anticorruption czar. Willy Mutunga, one of the key leaders in civil society, left the KHRC and went to work with the Ford Foundation, the US philanthropical organization, in Nairobi. But many other civil society leaders were close to the LDP. Many in civil society believed that NARC could still be salvaged. Because of these factors, civil society could not agree on a single coherent position and was wary of openly supporting either LDP or NAK. That is how its voice, long the standard in the reform agenda, was muffled. Frank Holmquist argues that the "shock of victory" was partially responsible for the paralysis in traditional reform sectors.

> Civil society then [after the 2002 NARC triumph] experienced the shock of victory. Organizations dependent on one or two leaders were "decapitated" when those leaders departed for government offices. Organizations were further hobbled when funding from some donors declined. Remaining civil society leaders and groups were uncertain about an appropriate role to play with the Kibaki state. Should civil society support a regime that included several of its friends and allies? Should it criticize the regime and implicitly give succor to opposition figures, many of whom were bitter enemies and oppressors of civil society in the not-so-distant past? Should civil society actively work with the new opposition, even though that might help opposition attempts to get back into office?[9]

The loss of a united, clear voice by civil society was arguably the biggest blow to the reform movement after Bomas. Many leaders in civil society found it difficult to embrace Odinga and support the 2004 Bomas Draft Constitution because they still remembered him as Moi's antireform advocate from 1998 until late 2002, when he decamped from KANU to join NAK and then form NARC. Most LDP legislators were KANU refugees and only converted to NARC to save their political skins. Except for Odinga, the LDP did not have a single proven reform advocate among its senior ranks.[10] And his credentials had been sullied by his alliance with Moi against the reform movement. To a person, no senior LDP leader was supportive of a truth commission, the Judicial Commission of Inquiry into the Goldenberg Affair, the purge of the judiciary, or any of the anticorruption and reform measures. Often, LDP sided with KANU to oppose or sabotage these efforts. Under these circumstances, a large number of civil society leaders could simply not bring themselves to support KANU or the LDP, even on the 2004 Draft Constitution. In fact, FIDA, the leading women's rights group, came in for some criticism when it organized capacity-building workshops for KANU, ostensibly to strengthen the opposition.[11] How on earth, wondered many in civil society, would you work to strengthen opponents of reform? The problem for civil society, however, was that its former friends and allies in NAK had also turned against the reform agenda.[12] These dilemmas were compounded by ethnic nativism, long the bugbear of Kenyan politics.

> As divisions within NARC, often along ethnic lines, became more evident, they also entered internal civil society relations more so than when opposition to the Moi regime had acted as glue binding them together. Division also seeped into church networks, which had long been the most impervious to ethnic division of any of the major institutions in Kenyan society.[13]

The paralysis within civil society and the church—the two most consistent reform advocates since the 1980s—left the reform movement adrift. Without their inspiration and leadership, the constitutional reform process would never have made it beyond 1997. Opposition political parties alone could not sustain the struggle. Experience had proven that political society was too fragmented and limited by short-term goals to remain steadfast. In the past, the Moi-KANU regime tricked political parties into sham agreements. In March 2004, political parties did it again. They denied the 2004 Draft Constitution legitimacy when they failed to agree on how power would be shared and devolved to lower levels. It was a classic case of failing to see the forest for the trees. NAK acted like a deer caught in the headlights. Instead of calling Odinga's bluff and proposing credible devolution and power-sharing arrangements, it became openly defensive and obstructionist. Even though the delegates were likely still to reject such proposals and vote with Odinga, standing on principle would have saved NAK public humiliation and loss of confidence by the populace. More importantly, it might have protected aspects of the reform agenda. Unfortunately, NAK conceded by its bungling at Bomas that it was no longer a force for change, but of politics as usual. The reform of the state stalled because of the bankruptcy of political parties and their lack of a coherent vision for change.

> Unlike the recent experience of historically left wing parties and social movements in Latin America, Kenya's political parties have failed to mobilize members or the population on reform. Kenya's parties are not internally democratic; they are not well organized on the ground; they have little autonomy from their top leader or leaders; and they rarely speak to the matter of mass poverty and material needs in policy terms. At the moment Kenya's political parties are in no condition to act as mobilizers of the populace for broad-based reform.[14]

In late 2004, there were positive stirrings from civil society. The euphoria that had defined the sector since January 2003 had quickly evaporated. Almost to a person, civil society had concluded that NARC had betrayed reform. The resignation in February 2005 by John Githongo, the anticorruption czar, further energized civil society. Nongovernmental organizations (NGOs) regrouped and met in multisectoral forums to reignite the reform agenda. Joined by the Ufungamano Initiative, the forums held several well-publicized meetings to think through the most contentious issues in the draft constitution and chart a way forward. Although it was the most significant development since Bomas by civil society and Ufungamano, the meetings did not capture the public imagination. But they were seen by many as an important step in the reconstruction of the nonstate lobby that had been responsible for engineering the public fervor for reforms. After the stillbirth of Bomas, no single individual or institution had the capacity or vision to craft a broadly acceptable process for the reform of the state.

Disparate Voices

Genuine reforms were possible only when leading voices acted in concert against the government of the day. The 1991 repeal of Section 2A of the constitution, the clause that prohibited plural politics, came only after civil society and reform advocates stood together. Similarly, KANU permitted constitutional review only after civil society led religious organizations and political parties to the precipice with the state.[15] Conversely, reforms have been most endangered when the voice for change fragments and cannot channel popular discontent into a coherent political agenda. But cooptation and evisceration of the drive for change have also taken place when political parties, civil society, and religious organizations collapse their efforts together with the state. That is precisely what happened in May 2001, when the Ufungamano Initiative merged with the process led by the Parliamentary Select Committee on Constitutional Review (PSC) to make the CKRC a joint institution. Moi attempted to kill the entire process when he dissolved Parliament in October 2002, just months away from the elections.[16] Moi hoped that Uhuru Kenyatta, his protégé, would win the elections and manipulate or scuttle the reform agenda altogether.

The state killed reform every time it was entrusted with its stewardship. As a matter of chronology, the failure of Bomas started even before it began in May 2001 when Ufungamano merged its initiative with the PSC process. Ironically, from that moment onward, key voices became more discordant because of their inability to agree on key issues in the "joint" process. Once Ufungamano was "inside," the government worked to smother the process. The state would destroy Ufungamano through an embrace and remove it as a threat to the KANU government. Key institutions of the review, such as the CKRC, the PSC, and Bomas itself, became forums for intrigue and disunity. Former allies could not act with a single purpose. The fragmentation of civil society and religious organizations, both historical allies in the struggle for reform, left a huge vacuum in the political arena. It was not just the rupture of the alliance between them, but also within each of them. The blissful alliances that had brought about the 1994 *The Kenya We Want: Proposal for a Model Constitution* were now a distant memory.[17] The Ufungamano happy days—before the merger—were now history. After the onset of Bomas in May 2003, these former allies would each pursue their own agendas and dissipate their once formidable joint capital.

Several key documents produced by nonstate reform actors—civil society and religious groups—pointed to a divergence of agendas and politics, even though there was a lot of common ground. The documents were motivated by the squabbles in NARC, institutional interests, and political orientation. But the groups could not come together and present a united front at Bomas or in the immediate aftermath. The documents, which were draft constitutions, were intended to influence the outcome at Bomas. There are no empirical data to demonstrate their impact, although media reports suggested that they might have further polarized the National Constitutional Conference. The most controversial was a draft released in January 2004 by the Ufungamano Initiative.[18] The faiths-led lobby had increasingly taken a dim view of Bomas after it became obvious that pro-LDP and KANU delegates dominated it. Mutava Musyimi, the Ufungamano head, virtually abandoned Bomas after some delegates accused him of hostility to the conference. The LDP, led by Odinga, ripped into the Ufungamano Draft, calling it "an unnecessary distraction."[19] Hastings Okoth-Ogendo, the vice chair of the CKRC, said the "document was badly and hurriedly done, a cut-and-paste job."[20] Ufungamano was even accused of a conspiracy with the Kibaki regime to scuttle the review process.[21] In February 2004, a frustrated Musyimi finally resigned his position as a delegate to the conference.[22] Because he was head of the NCCK, Mutava Musyimi's departure meant that Kenya's most influential religious organization had abandoned Bomas. It was the symbolic final divorce of the Ufungamano Initiative from the Ghai-led CKRC process.

The other key document, titled *Model Proposals*, was produced in January 2004 by the women's coalition, the collection of key NGOs formed to lobby for women's issues at Bomas.[23] The women's draft culminated a long, elaborate, and laborious process of advocacy and campaigns to promote women's rights and safeguard them in the Ghai Draft. Along the way, the campaign parted company with Ufungamano because of the latter's outright opposition to, or lack of support for, affirmative action, reproductive rights, and other women's rights. In addition, the coalition supported Kadhi courts, which Ufungamano vehemently opposed. The objective of the *Model Proposals* was to lobby women's rights to be mainstreamed in the draft constitution. The document was a gender agenda, even though it purported to offer suggestions on a range of questions. In *Yawezekana*, its own publication, the coalition took a shot at the Ufungamano Draft. It wrote, "Unlike the Ufungamano Draft, the Coalition's Proposals capture the recommendations contained in the Bomas Draft Constitution, deliberations at the Constitutional Conference and the views of the Coalition."[24] Its message to the delegates was clear: unlike Ufungamano, the coalition was an active participant in Bomas, whose views it deeply respected. Since Bomas had generally been receptive to women's issues, the coalition wanted to capitalize on its goodwill rather than antagonize it.

The other key nonstate actor to make proposals was the Law Society of Kenya (LSK), the bar association that had advocated for reform since the 1980s. In 1994, the LSK had teemed up with the KHRC and the International Commission of Jurists to produce *The Kenya We Want: Proposal for a Model Constitution*. The LSK became increasingly critical of both Yash Ghai and Bomas, accusing them of incompetence, bias, and overpoliticization. Abdullahi Ahmednasir, the outspoken chair of the LSK, called for Ghai's dismissal and the termination of Bomas.[25] The LSK Draft Constitution substantially differed from the Ghai Draft and the 2004 Draft Constitution.[26] It sharply edited or eliminated many of the radical proposals of the Ghai Draft. It provided for a weak prime minister under a powerful president. The prime minister was more like a chief minister, a senior aide to the president.[27] Its provisions on devolution, a highly emotive and volatile issue, were so curt as to be meaningless. It provided for devolution only to the district level but refused to define how powers would be divided, a task it left to Parliament.[28] It conceded the one-third principle on women, although it generally dealt with gender dismissively.[29] The LSK showed contempt for the Ghai Draft and was closer to NAK's more cautious view.

The *Model Proposals* by the women's coalition, the Ufungamano Draft, and the LSK Draft diverged on many key points, even though they converged on most. What is important, however, is not their convergence or divergence, but the fact that the organizations produced *three different* drafts. At Bomas, these organizations saw each other as opponents on a number of key issues. An attempt by the KHRC to forge a consensus on key issues with the potential to unite the erstwhile allies failed to bear fruit.[30] Even though Ufungamano in its draft finally supported affirmative action, it opposed Kadhi courts and the premiership, two key issues for which the women's coalition advocated. These two important questions drove the groups apart. There was no question, however, that both Ufungamano and the women's coalition had produced solid, important documents. But the LSK missed an opportunity to unite the groups, synthesize the various proposals, and produce a draft with a wider appeal. Its draft, much like the rest, contributed to the continued fragmentation and isolation of the forces that had traditionally fought for reform.

Calling for Experts

The subject of experts evokes bitter memories in Africa. Often, the word is code language for whites and a putdown for blacks. The term is a "racialized reference to the presumed skill, competence, and intelligence of Caucasians, or humans of white European ancestry."[31] In constitution making, the term had a rather odious smell in Kenya. In 1995, President Moi announced that he would invite foreign experts to write a new constitution for Kenya.[32] The Citizens' Coalition for Constitutional Change (4Cs), the main reform lobby, rejected Moi's proposal out of hand and accused him of denigrating Kenyans.[33] His statement declared, in essence, that Kenyans were unable to write their own constitution. Upon the rejection of this proposal, Moi argued that the KANU-controlled Parliament would drive constitutional change. That is how the Parliament became the birthplace for minimum reforms under the Inter-Parties Parliamentary Group (IPPG). Only the efforts of civil society and the Ufungamano Initiative forced the state to acquiesce to a CKRC-led participatory process under Ghai.

What was the meaning of the so-called people-driven process? By definition, constitution writing the world over has historically been exclusively an elite affair. It is only in the late 1980s that new constitutions have been written with some level of popular participation. The 1996 South African constitution is arguably the best example of this new genre of constitution making. Even there, the process was designed by elites, although it benefited from the large volume of contributions and views expressed by citizens from all walks of life. The South African Constituent Assembly received more than 1.7 million submissions before it wrote the constitution.[34] Perhaps this is the closest the process comes to being people-driven. Even then, it is important to realize that the South African constitution was a bargain struck between the elites in the African National Congress and the Nationalist Party to end formal apartheid and introduce black majority rule. To be sure, many ordinary people participated in the process, but it was the elites that designed the process, often with pressure from below.

Odinga and KANU, through the CKRC, initially drove the design of the Kenyan process. But civil society and Ufungamano forced the revision of the Constitution of Kenya Review Act to broaden the process as a condition to the merger of the CKRC and Ufungamano's People's Commission of Kenya (PCK). In fact, a number of advocacy organizations, in addition to the clergy, were the true forces that drove the reform agenda. Because of the predatory nature of the Kenyan state, it was impossible to mobilize a social movement for reform throughout the country. But civil society and clerics tapped into public discontent over KANU's misrule and corruption to organize frequent mass rallies and demonstrations in Nairobi. Government brutality at these peaceful rallies only heightened public resolve for change and increased mass support for the reform movement. But there should be no doubt that KANU mandarins negotiated the perimeters of reform with leaders of the clergy and civil society. Nor should one doubt that the PCK and later CKRC public hearings around the country were the most participatory phase of the review process. They allowed the largest number of Kenyans from the most diverse backgrounds and statuses to express their hopes and fears for a new constitution.

The National Constitutional Conference, in effect the second phase of the process, was remarkably less participatory, or people-driven. Only elites had access to Bomas, whether parliamentarians, the media, leaders of civil society, senior clerics, or the cream of the business and professional classes. Fully one-third of the conference was made up of MPs, an elite social group. The one-third drawn from the districts comprised rural elites—local politicians, businesspersons, professionals, and leading women. The final third were generally urban-based elites from civil society, the professions, business, political parties, and other special interests. The press incorrectly referred to delegates from the rural areas as "Wanjiku," or "the commoner." Rural delegates were as elitist as their urban-based counterparts. The so-called conflict between rural and urban delegates was more an intraclass quarrel than a true interclass struggle. *Wanjiku* had expressed herself at the constituency CKRC hearings but did not make it to Bomas. Neither Bomas nor the 2004 Draft Constitution could correctly be referred to as "people-driven." Even so, the draft constitution was the most participatory document ever produced in Kenya.[35]

It is important to understand the class character of Bomas to appreciate the angst over the call for experts in constitution making. The suggestion of experts was never intended to cut off the participation of ordinary Kenyans. It was meant to introduce a professional and technocratic group to produce a draft constitution that reflected the CKRC hearings and the deliberations at Bomas. These later calls for experts, unlike Moi's, were not racist and did not reflect a mistrust or disregard of the common people. On the contrary, it would have protected their views from mutilation by a myopic and corrupt elite. In 1999, Wangari Maathai, the respected environmentalist and 2004 Nobel Peace laureate, called for a committee of experts to draft the constitution consistent with the views of the people.[36] She argued that the political elite could not be trusted because they harbored hidden agendas at the "expense of the larger nation."[37] The intrigues played by KANU, LDP, and NAK at Bomas more than amply bore out this analysis.

As Bomas I drew to a close in May 2003, the conference was poisoned and deadlocked over schemes by political actors. It was in this climate of despair that the calls for experts were made.[38] The calls increased after the failure of Bomas II that fall. But a section of the media, KANU, and LDP read mischief in the calls and accused the government of attempting to derail the conference.[39] The country's leading daily acknowledged that "anyone who witnessed the power plays, name-calling and sheer venality and ineptitude by some delegates during Bomas I and Bomas II would agree that an unwieldy conference long ago got out of hand."[40] Even so, it opposed replacing delegates with experts so as not to subvert the will of the people.[41] As it turned out, experts were rejected and Bomas hurtled toward a doomed fate.

The Post-Bomas Legal Framework

The legal framework of the review process after the adoption of the 2004 Draft Constitution was simple and straightforward. The CKRC was required to prepare a final report and draft bill and submit them to the attorney general for presentation before the National Assembly.[42] Upon receipt of the documents, the attorney general had seven days to publish them in a bill to alter the constitution.[43] Two weeks later, Parliament had to enact the bill into law as the new constitution.[44] But no one in Kenya was under any illusion that the 2004 Draft Constitution would become the basic law of the land so quickly after its rejection by the Kibaki state. A series of maneuvers involving Amos Wako, the Moi-era attorney general not known for his independence, to put a spanner in the works of the draft constitution was hatched. What followed were vintage Kenyan postcolonial state actions. The Kibaki state found a way to recapture the process from the claws of the LDP-KANU alliance.

The failure of Parliament—and Ufungamano—to protect the constitutional reform process by entrenching it in the constitution gave the Kibaki regime an opportunity to escape the vise of the 2004 Draft Constitution. In 2001, KANU had rejected such protection because having it would make parliamentary approval of the constitution a mere rubber stamp.[45] It only agreed to support the merger on condition that the process would not be protected in the constitution. The entrenchment of the process would have required an amendment of the constitution by a vote of 65 percent of all the members of the National Assembly.[46] KANU could garner the support of the opposition to pass the change, but it believed that such a move would be suicidal. The opposition could not in the future be relied upon to support a reversal if KANU needed to remove the protection. Neither KANU nor the opposition could muster the parliamentary supermajority alone. An agreement to entrench the process in the constitution would have amounted to a death warrant for KANU, which had survived on its control of the legislature. Ironically, it was this loophole created by Odinga and Moi that Kibaki would later use to flummox Odinga.

The courts were the perfect foil. Delegates and citizens filed several suits when it seemed that NAK might lose at Bomas. The purpose of the suits, which were believed to have been either coordinated with the state or filed by individuals who had never supported Bomas, was to nullify the draft constitution. One suit, the *Gachuru wa Karenge* case, named for the plaintiff, sought to bar the attorney general from accepting the draft constitution from Bomas.[47] Timothy Njoya, a prominent cleric and reform advocate, filed the other.[48] The *Njoya* case was an assault on the CKRC-driven process by the National Convention Executive Council (NCEC), the executive arm of the National Convention Assembly, the civil society body that had brought the Moi-KANU state to the brink of elimination in 1997.[49] The "radical" NCEC had never accepted the merger of the CKRC and the PCK. Virtually its entire senior leadership—Gibson Kamau

Kuria, Timothy Njoya, Davinder Lamba, Kepta Ombati, and John Munuve—either declined to apply for or did not acquire delegate status at the National Constitutional Conference. Pheroze Nowrojee, a valued NCEC advisor, was not a delegate. Willy Mutunga, the other senior leader, became a delegate as executive director of the KHRC, and Kivutha Kibwana, its spokesperson, became a delegate as an NARC MP. Ironically, most of the NCEC leaders attended Bomas as observers, if only to check whether the process was not people-driven. Whether by design or happenstance, the *Njoya* suit would benefit NAK by giving it a reprieve from the draft constitution.

The Karenge suit spelled doom for the 2004 Draft Constitution. The applicants sought to bar the attorney general from receiving or accepting the draft constitution from the CKRC as required by the Review Act. That was important because upon receipt of the draft, the attorney general had to publish it within seven days for submission before the National Assembly. The publication would trigger the clock for the fourteen-day period by which Parliament had to enact the draft as the new constitution. The Review Act did not contemplate the alteration or revision of the draft by Parliament, although presumably it could refuse to enact it. Karenge also sought a declaration that the National Constitutional Conference had adopted five controversial chapters in violation of its own rules. In essence, Karenge wanted the High Court to declare the Bomas Draft a legal nullity and to bar Parliament from enacting it into the basic law of the land. On March 22, 2004, a day before Bomas endorsed the draft constitution and the conference officially closed, the court granted an injunction barring the attorney general from accepting the draft constitution.[50] The following day, Wako received a copy of the draft constitution as the conference closed, although he was quick to point out that he had received the document as a delegate, not the attorney general, and was therefore in compliance with the court order.[51] More significantly for the Kibaki regime, the clock for Wako to table the draft constitution before the National Assembly had been tripped.

But the *Njoya* suit was the more significant of the two cases. In that case, the applicants questioned the legal validity of the National Constitutional Conference, given its flawed representation and the role of Parliament in constitution making.[52] The court ruled that Parliament had no jurisdiction under the constitution to abrogate it and introduce a completely new one in its place; that the Review Act was unconstitutional in part because it failed to acknowledge the right of the people to exercise their constituent power through a referendum on the draft constitution; that the ratification of the draft constitution through a referendum was a fundamental and constitutional right of the people; that such constituent power derives from the people and their sovereignty; that the people of Kenya can use their constituent power to make a constitution in a legally constituted constituent assembly; and that the National Constitutional Conference was not competent to act as a constituent assembly because it did not have the people's mandate, which must be traced to a direct election.[53] In a nutshell, the ruling declared Bomas an improper body for constitution making and barred Parliament from enacting the draft constitution. Since Bomas had already concluded and adopted the draft, the most important part of the ruling for the Kibaki state concerned the role of the National Assembly in constitution making.

> That Parliament has no jurisdiction or power under any section of the Constitution to abrogate the existing constitution and enact a new one in its place. Parliament's power is limited to only alterations of the existing Constitution. The power to make a new constitution (the constituent power) belongs to the people of Kenya as a whole, including the Applicants. In the exercise of that power, the Applicants together with other Kenyans, are, in the circumstances of this case, entitled to have a referendum on any proposed new constitution.[54]

The fault of the Review Act was its provision for a referendum only on those matters not supported by two-thirds of the national conference.[55] Instead, the court argued that the entire 2004 Draft Constitution was subject to a referendum. The court, however, did not nullify the draft constitution and left the door open for it to be subjected to a national referendum. The court found fault with the logic of the Review Act that, since Parliament was granted power by Section 47 to amend one section of the constitution, it could amend not just several but all the others in a torrent to overhaul the entire constitution. It rejected this argument and held that Parliament only had the power to *alter*, not *enact*, a new constitution. The *Njoya* ruling effectively stopped the draft constitution in its tracks and bought the Kibaki regime time. The government could now further manipulate the review process to prevent a future constitution from transferring the enormous powers enjoyed by the Kibaki regime to a competing prime minister or autonomous local authorities.

However, the LDP, KANU, allied Bomas delegates, the CKRC, and many Kenyans received the *Njoya* ruling with anger. Some saw the case as an opportunistic reversal by Moi critics who had supported a people-driven constitution, only to call for the disbandment of Bomas.[56] Others read connivance by the court with the Kibaki state. Aaron Ringera, the High Court judge who delivered the majority opinion, was rumored to be in cahoots with Kiraitu Murungi, the minister for justice and constitutional affairs. It was not lost on Kenyans that both came from the Meru ethnic group and had been law partners.[57] At the time of the ruling, Ringera was under consideration for the highly paid head of the newly reconstituted Kenya Anti-Corruption Authority, a position to which he was later appointed.[58] Mary Kasango, the concurring judge, had just recently been elevated to the High Court by President Kibaki, presumably on the recommendation of Murungi. Only Benjamin Kubo, the dissenting judge, was thought to be independent of the Kibaki government, although his political sympathies were not publicly known. Although the impact of these relationships on the case was purely speculative, they hurt the government in the public's perception. But Ghai was scathing in his attack on the *Njoya* and *Karenge* opinions. He called the *Njoya* ruling "devoid of authority" and the *Karenge* opinion "a contravention of the law and without any legal justification."[59] However, the rulings dealt with novel questions in Kenyan constitutional law and seemed to be based on reasonable legal theories. It was difficult to dismiss the opinions, although their timing appeared to be evidence of collusion between the intrusive Kenyan state and a compliant judiciary.

Timothy Njoya, the cleric who had valiantly fought for a new constitution, successfully sabotaged the product of a process he thought unacceptable. The LDP-KANU brigades read in the ruling a Murungi plot to negate the Bomas decision. Every protagonist claimed the high moral ground. Subjectively, they all may have believed in the righteousness of their actions. Objectively, however, the case should be contextualized in the historical moment and interpreted in light of its impact on the major political struggles of the day. The *Karenge* and *Njoya* opinions were critical turning points in the review process. Put together, their significance was almost equal to the cancellation of the draft constitution. Its high rhetoric notwithstanding, the overall effect of the *Njoya* opinion was to give the Kibaki state control of the review process. In that sense, Kenya had come full circle. Kibaki now possessed what Moi had always craved: the opportunity to write a constitution to suit him. The use of the courts to stifle political initiatives was nothing new. Moi had always done it. The question was whether Kibaki had now become a mirror image of Moi. Ghai alluded to these maneuvers in an opinion article.

> A key minister told me [Ghai] several times before and during Bomas III that if his faction got from delegates what it wanted, he would ensure that litigation against the CKRC was stopped, legislative bills to amend the Review Act withdrawn, and section 47 issues dropped. But if he did not succeed, the whole panoply of state power would be used to derail the process. . . . The statement merely confirmed suspicions that litigation against the process is not now, and was not before, the manifestation of citizens' spontaneous outrage at an unfair process, but is engineered by those in high authority.[60]

For Kibaki and his NAK insiders, a strategy to revise the Bomas Draft became urgent. But for Odinga and his allies in LDP and KANU, the struggle was to protect the draft constitution from "mutilation" by the government. Ghai bitterly attacked Kibaki and his senior aides through the media.[61] He dismissed claims that the draft constitution was illegitimate and urged its enactment. He reminded its critics that the document "truly represents the views of Kenyans as submitted to the CKRC" and "follows closely the CKRC draft published in September 2002."[62] Elsewhere, he refuted claims by critics that in providing for both a prime minister and a president, the draft constitution had created inherently conflictual centers of power.[63] He argued that presidentialism was prone to despotism, a problem that devolution and a parliamentary system were more likely to cure. The LDP called for the enactment of the draft constitution without any alteration whatsoever.[64] Efforts to come to a consensus on what Parliament ought to do after the *Njoya* ruling came unstuck when NAK, KANU, and LDP attempted to sabotage each other's proposals. Meanwhile, Bomas Katiba Watch, a new lobby of former delegates headed by Martin Shikuku, the veteran politician, announced that it would mobilize citizens to demand the enactment of the draft constitution.[65] The lobby, named "Katiba," the Kiswahili word for constitution, sought to portray itself as the guardian of constitutionalism.

In alliance with LDP and KANU, Katiba Watch planned public protests and demonstrations, including a volatile one on July 3, 2004, on the grounds of the historic Uhuru Park.[66] Shikuku, the group's godfather, had enjoyed an illustrious career as a brave parliamentarian during the Kenyatta and Moi regimes and had been one of the leaders of the original FORD in 1991.[67] But since his ouster from Parliament in 1997, he had become theatrical and somewhat of a political nuisance.[68] However, the constitutional conference had given him a national platform as a delegate, a forum he used to great effect, taking the side of the LDP on the controversial questions of the premiership and devolution. But Katiba Watch failed to attract the support of the bulk of civil society, although it was buoyed by the refusal of the Kibaki regime to lead a new initiative beyond blocking the draft constitution. Efforts by the president to craft a parliamentary consensus failed miserably. Led by John Koech, a KANU-friendly Kalenjin MP, the government-sanctioned effort failed when the LDP refused to participate.[69] As a result, Kibaki failed to deliver a constitution by June 30, 2004, the date he had promised Kenyans.[70]

On July 3, 2004, President Kibaki reshuffled his eighteen-month-old cabinet in part to douse public protests by Katiba Watch and LDP. Kibaki brought into the cabinet Simeon Nyachae, the leader of FORD-People, and appointed John Koech and Njenga Karume, both KANU MPs, as ministers. He demoted Kalonzo Musyoka, a key Odinga ally, from the Ministry for Foreign Affairs to Environment and Natural Resources. Odinga was humiliated when housing was lopped off his Ministry of Roads, Public Works, and Housing. Kibaki also appointed other NAK-friendly MPs from LDP, KANU, FORD-Kenya, and FORD-People to the cabinet and gave new posts to ethnic groups, including the Kalenjin, Kisii, Somali, Maasai, Luhya, and coastal communities.[71] His strategy was clear: his regime would not be held hostage to the Odinga, Luo-dominated LDP. Kibaki reached across party and ethnic lines to broaden the base of his regime among elites from different groups. It was a time-honored tradition in Kenyan politics—both Kenyatta and Moi had consolidated absolute power by crafting "coalitions of the willing" among the elites of Kenya's ethnic collage. Even so, many of those Kibaki brought into the cabinet had been implicated in corruption or mass atrocities.[72] But this major realignment of the NARC state was intended to sideline the LDP, NAK's coalition partner. The reshuffle also sought to isolate the LDP in Parliament, where it had previously ganged up with KANU to defeat NAK initiatives.

But Kibaki's cabinet reshuffle did nothing to douse the fires of the Katiba Watch–LDP protests. Katiba Watch vowed to press ahead with its July rally. Kibaki's own lieutenants in NAK did not help matters when they planned a counter-rally on the same day.[73] Even though the government cancelled both rallies, the one by Katiba Watch went ahead but was violently broken up by security forces.[74] On July 7, police shot several pro-Bomas demonstrators, one fatally in Kisumu, the center of heavily Luo Nyanza Province and Odinga's ancestral region.[75] Kibaki accused Katiba Watch of obstruction, hypocrisy, and political greed.[76] The reshuffle did not give the Kibaki regime any reprieve in the short term, although in time Katiba Watch fizzled out.[77] Katiba Watch imploded for several reasons: it was a patently partisan pro-LDP front; except for Shikuku, its leadership had no reputable reformers, and he was a tired caricature of the former crusader; the leadership cut the image of a self-seeking crowd; broad sections of civil society, the traditional engine for reform, did not support it; and finally, the wrangling by the elites over the draft constitution had left the country too exhausted for mass action.

In July 2004, three events significant to the constitution-making process took place. First, Yash Ghai, the chair of the CKRC, resigned from the commission.[78] The end of his tumultuous reign came within days of Kibaki's cabinet reshuffle and signaled complete despair by Ghai over the fate of the draft constitution. Ghai had already unleashed a scathing attack on President Kibaki. In an open letter, he had charged "ethnic attempts had been made to sabotage the review, reviving tribalism while a few politicians have hijacked the review and your statement that the matter is now up to Parliament can be interpreted as an insult to the people."[79] In his resignation letter, however, Ghai avoided any caustic language and instead ironically thanked Kibaki for his support. He would have resigned earlier, although he had held out hope— in vain—that a new constitution could be enacted by June 30, the date Kibaki had promised to do so. For Ghai, it was a bitter personal and political disappointment for an internationally distinguished academic who had graciously agreed to serve his country, only to be consumed in the unforgiving pettiness and political dysfunction of its elites.

Second, William Ruto, a KANU stalwart, was elected to replace Paul Muite as chair of the Parliamentary Select Committee on Constitutional Review.[80] The election of Ruto, a hawk and powerful former minister in the KANU regime, was a strange irony even in the Byzantine world of Kenyan politics. A leading opponent of constitutional reform under Moi, he had advocated a scorched earth policy against reformers and human rights advocates. As the joint KANU-LDP candidate, he was elected unopposed when NAK failed to come up with its candidate and Muite declined to defend his seat. But his elevation may have been what NAK wanted all along—so that it could blame him for the gridlock on the constitution. It was inconceivable that such a vapid partisan—a supporter of Katiba Watch and an opponent of a more inclusive process at Bomas and thereafter—could be a successful arbiter. Ruto, like most of his KANU colleagues, had never been interested in a new democratic constitution and perhaps joined Odinga at Bomas to get back at NAK and Kibaki. It was remarkable that an opponent of democracy would shepherd Parliament through constitution making.

Third, Abida Ali-Aroni, a vice chair of the CKRC, was sworn in to replace Ghai.[81] Ali-Aroni did not have a distinguished resume, either as a lawyer or a reform advocate. The elevation of Ruto and Ali-Aroni to the two most important constitutional reform organs was a low point for the country. How could a nondescript and an antireformer succeed where more committed reformers had failed? That the constitution-making process was now under these two individuals marked a new low for such a noble exercise.

The task for Ruto and the PSC was to resolve the impasse between NAK and the LDP-KANU alliance. To do so, the parties had to agree on amendments to the act to comply with the *Njoya* ruling and chart the way forward. After protracted negotiations, the Consensus Bill, a law to revise the Constitution of Kenya Review Act, was agreed upon.[82] The bill would reopen the Bomas Draft Constitution for revision by Parliament to resolve contentious matters, provide for a national referendum to comply with *Njoya*, provide for the enactment of the constitution by presidential proclamation, and create a legislative framework for the completion of the constitution-writing project.[83] The bill provided that the Bomas Draft Constitution could only be revised by a two-thirds majority in Parliament, a fact that explains why Odinga and the LDP supported it, because no party could muster such numbers. That meant that the Bomas Draft would be adopted by Parliament without any changes once the bill became law. It would require 145 of the 222 MPs, or 65 percent of the legislature, to amend the Bomas Draft. Revealing why the LDP had supported the bill, an imprudent Odinga bragged that "it will not be possible for MPs to rubber stamp any change whatsoever."[84] Strangely, Murungi was the one who had moved for the passage of the bill.[85] However, once NAK realized its folly, it advised Kibaki to veto the bill, which he promptly did.[86] In December 2004, Parliament amended the bill to provide that only a simple majority would be required to amend the Bomas Draft. Kibaki then assented to the bill on December 29, 2004.[87]

The 2004 consensus review law created the framework—and a roadmap—for the completion of the constitutional review process. The National Assembly was required to debate and, if necessary, amend the Bomas Draft within ninety days of the date of the commencement of the law and was then required to submit it to the attorney general.[88] Within thirty days of receiving the draft, the attorney general would publish the proposed new constitution, including any changes approved by Parliament.[89] Ninety days after publication, the electoral commission would hold a national referendum on the draft constitution to be decided by a simple majority of the votes cast.[90] If the vote was affirmative as certified by the electoral commission, the president was compelled to "promulgate and publish the text of the new constitution" within fourteen days.[91] The law dissuaded court challenges to the referendum and its results by requiring that the applicant deposit 5 million Kenya shillings for a court action.[92]

There were several potentially explosive legal issues that the Constitution of Kenya Review (Amendment) Act of 2004 did not adequately address. Both related to the requirements imposed by the *Njoya* and *Karenge* opinions. The first was whether a valid draft constitution existed on which the people could vote in a referendum. The first question was whether the Bomas Draft, which according to *Njoya* was the fruit of a poisoned tree, was a validly adopted draft on which Kenyans could exercise their constituent power. How could Parliament construct a validly legal document on a product built on an illegality? Did Parliament have the power, in its capacity as the elected representatives of the Kenyan people, to cure the Bomas Draft? The second question was whether Parliament could, without amending Section 47 of the Constitution, make a constitution by amending the Bomas Draft and do so through a mere act of Parliament. Finally, the act did not resolve how the current constitution would be extinguished. Simeon Nyachae, the NAK-friendly FORD-People leader elected chair of the PSC in May 2005, essentially ignored these questions.[93] Nyachae, a NAK-friendly MP and head of FORD-People, replaced Ruto as chair of the PSC when parliamentary committees were reconstituted. The government hoped that he would turn the tide of constitutional review in its favor.

On July 21, 2005, by a vote of 102 to 61, the Kenyan Parliament approved a number of amendments to the Bomas Draft but rejected the so-called Kilifi Draft, a complete draft constitution prepared by the PSC.[94] Odinga immediately launched a campaign to have the draft constitution rejected at the referendum.[95] In response, President Kibaki announced that he would personally lead the campaign to ratify the draft constitution. On August 22, 2005, the attorney general published the proposed new constitution, also known as the Wako Draft.[96] The Electoral Commission of Kenya set November 21, 2005, as the referendum date on which Kenyans would vote to either accept or reject the proposed constitution.[97] If approved, the president would within fourteen days "promulgate and publish the text of the constitution."[98] If it were rejected, Kenya would continue to be governed under the extant constitution. In November 2005, just before the referendum, the judiciary rejected an opposition challenge to the review law, the process, and the vote.[99]

The Wako Draft and Contentious Issues

Kenyans wanted a state that was a servant, not a master. The only way to ensure a benign state is to make it accountable to the citizenry through the open political process. The Ghai, Bomas, and Wako drafts expanded political space and made political parties—the major vehicles for political participation—open, accountable, and inclusive vessels. The Wako Draft subjected the political process to gender equity and the principles of democracy and openness.[100] Although the Wako Draft kept the one-third principle for women in elective offices, it removed the elaborate and more unambiguous language of the Bomas Draft. Nevertheless, the Wako Draft was a major advance on the question of political participation and representation. Regrettably, although the Wako Draft kept most of the guarantees provided by the other drafts, it removed protections specific to marginalized groups and communities.[101] In an attempt to defuse the crisis over Kadhi courts, the Wako Draft provided for Christian, Hindu, and Kadhi courts.[102]

On women's rights, the Wako Draft steered a middle course between the Bomas Draft and the *Model Proposals*. Although it recognized women as a protected group, it nevertheless failed to fully guarantee their protection and even restricted some important rights.[103] It was retrogressive on reproductive rights, essentialized women, and adopted a backward construction of the family.[104] The Wako Draft did bend to popular will and provided for a gender commission.[105] But it failed to engender land. Even so, it gave a nod to the one-third principle in a victory for women.[106] Substantively, though, the Wako Draft did not represent a radical shift from the Bomas Draft on women's issues. The eventual rejection of the Wako Draft at the referendum was not because it did not largely reflect the wishes of Kenyans. It fell victim to a cluster of questions known as "contentious issues," a euphemism for power struggles within the elite.[107] These divisive issues were the Kadhi courts; devolution, including whether Kenya should have a second chamber; transitional arrangements; and the structure of the executive. What did they entail, and why were they so stubborn?

In theory, Kenya is a secular republic, although it has been dominated by Christian norms, politicians, and institutions. The state's legal, political, and philosophical templates are decidedly Eurocentric, which has left Islam and Muslims in a subordinate position. Islam and Christianity have historically been in a fierce competition for souls in Kenya. In the process, segments of either faith have engaged each other in religious brinkmanship. Scare-mongering and sleight of hand have characterized their relationship. These pathologies, which were played out over the review process, threatened to completely scuttle it. Competition between religions was a long-running theme throughout Bomas. In fact, it was one of the reasons the major churches refused to endorse the Wako Draft.

The crisis was provoked when the Ghai Draft gave prominent protection to Kadhi courts. The *Model Proposals* endorsed them, as did the LSK Draft.[108] Even the Ufungamano Draft obliquely recognized them as religious courts. The Bomas Draft sealed the deal when it unambiguously recognized them, sending Kenyan churches into a fury.[109] Not even the Wako Draft could deny protection to the Kadhi courts. So, even though this question was highly emotional—and became one of the pillars on which both the Bomas Draft and the Wako Draft fell—there was a large segment of the population that felt that Kadhi courts merited protection in the constitution. Perhaps that explains why in the end the churches did not openly oppose the Wako Draft in spite of its recognition of Kadhi courts.[110] Pressure from President Kibaki's government and NAK, to which the mainstream churches were sympathetic, may have forestalled an outright rejection of the Wako Draft by the major Christian clergy.

Devolution was another corrosive issue on which the constitution review process got hung up. This problem is a classic quandary for state building in postcolonial situations: how to forge a single coherent nation from disparate precolonial identities. Are equal protection norms, a bill of rights, antidiscrimination protections, and open political participation sufficient material to overcome subnationalism and tribal nativism? Or is a measure of autonomy and self-governance at the local level necessary for groups to buy into modern African postcolonial statehood? Devolution has been an immensely important question for Kenya since the dawn of independence in 1963. The British attempted to resolve it by creating a quasi-federal state in the Lancaster, also known as the Majimbo, Constitution. The issue haunted the constitutional review process at Bomas and undid the Wako Draft. The motives of the protagonists were complex, but all parties conceded that some form of devolution of power from the center to the regions was desirable and inevitable.

Devolution seeks to ensure that the political center does not suffocate the periphery. The trick for Kenya is to devolve power while at the same democratizing both the center and the periphery. Devolution without democratization would be a retrogressive step since it would only multiply the number of dictatorships to which Kenyans would be subject. Thus devolution should not simply empower people at the top of the local pyramid or create a feeding trough for local elites. Nor can it be a license to exclude and discriminate against Kenyans whose ancestry is not in the devolved unit. According to the CKRC, Kenyans wanted devolution so that they could exercise the democratic rights of citizenship. The CKRC reported that Kenyans felt that they were not citizens, but subjects, without a voice.[111] Populations in marginalized areas expressed a preference for a federal system of government, whereas larger ethnic groups favored simple devolution.[112] The Ghai Draft provided for an upper house, in addition to the lower house, and four tiers of devolved governments—the village, location, district, and provincial levels.[113] Most delegates wanted devolution structures that would create autonomous, regional, self-governing ethnic units, more akin to the formula of the Lancaster Constitution. The Bomas Draft did just that, and vested more powers in districts and regions. It granted local authorities a high degree of autonomy and reserved only the most "national" of functions to the center.[114] Unlike the Bomas and Ghai drafts, none of the other major drafts—Ufungamano, LSK, and *Model Proposals*—entertained the notion of an upper house, or Senate. The Wako Draft followed suit and only provided for a single chamber.[115]

Transitional arrangements governing a new constitution were a third contentious issue. The question was whether a new constitution would come into force in its entirety, or whether its implementation would be staggered according to the nature of certain sections. For instance, it would be rational to immediately bring into legal force the uncontested chapters that did not require laborious planning or enormous outlays of capital. This option would start the immediate renewal and democratization of the state. Sections on the bill of rights, judiciary, public service, land, and citizenship could, for instance, come into force at once. More complicated chapters, such as those on devolution, the legislature, the executive, and representation, could only be fully effected with new elections. Their complete implementation could wait until the 2007 general elections.[116] This issue was important because some argued that the sitting government should step aside once a new constitution was ratified. The Wako Draft provided a scheme under which various provisions of the new constitution would come into force, including legislative action by Parliament within a specified period.[117] In many instances, existing officeholders and structural arrangements would have remained in place until enabling laws were passed.

The structure of the executive was the most important single issue on which the making of a new Kenyan constitution floundered. On this issue, the LDP-KANU side and NAK were completely deadlocked. At the center of the problem was NAK's refusal to award Odinga a strong premiership in keeping with the pre-election MOU. In addition to devolution, Kenyans wanted the executive carved up in two—a powerful premier and a ceremonial president—in large measure a reaction to the way President Moi had exercised the powers granted him under the constitution.[118] Civil society and the opposition were then in accord about the creation of the office of the premier. The CKRC crafted a parliamentary system in which the prime minister was vested with the most important executive powers.[119] Once in power, Kibaki and NAK viewed this arrangement with alarm and vowed to reverse the roles of the president and the prime minister, vesting more powers in the former and turning the latter into a mere appointee of the president. But most Bomas delegates rejected NAK's position and adopted a parliamentary system with the prime minister as the chief executive of the state.[120] The presidency was relegated to largely ceremonial and symbolic roles.

As was expected, the Wako Draft provided for a prime minister who was appointed by the president but approved by Parliament with a bare majority.[121] The president could dismiss the prime minister without parliamentary oversight.[122] In fact, the premier was a third-tier official, after the deputy president, in the Wako Draft.[123] President Kibaki had finally gotten a draft that protected him from Odinga.[124] Predictably, the LDP-KANU clique vehemently rejected the Wako Draft's iteration of the office of prime minister. In a withering attack,

Odinga wrote that the Wako Draft had reduced the prime minister to a "mere errand boy."[125] Rather than bring consensus to the review process, the Wako Draft further split the political landscape, setting the stage for a bilious and costly referendum exercise.

Referendum Politics

Proponents of the Wako Draft argued that it was the best document under the circumstances. To them it democratized the state, curbed the executive, devolved power, erected an independent judiciary, and safeguarded the rights of all Kenyans.[126] However, opponents attacked it as oppressive, illegitimate, and a betrayal of the wishes of Kenyans.[127]

As Joel Ngugi correctly argued, the objections to the Wako Draft boiled down to two general tendencies. Proceduralists objected to what they saw as the illegitimacy of the process.[128] They claimed that since Bomas, the legality and constitutionality of the review process had been abrogated. As such, the Wako Draft, which was a product of that process, was null and void because Parliament passed the 2004 Consensus Act, an amendment to the Constitution of Kenya Review Act,[129] without amending Section 47 of the constitution. Further, the referendum itself was illegal because it was not explicitly contemplated by the constitution. James Orengo suggested that the promulgation of the Wako Draft after the referendum would amount to treason against the constitution and the state.[130] Proponents argued that the referendum was an exercise of the sovereign will of the people and would cure any deficiencies in the review process. In other words, the power to make the constitution vested in the people, Section 47 notwithstanding.

The substantialists attacked the Wako Draft in several ways: it strengthened the presidency, it was wrong to provide for religious courts, its devolution scheme was either unworkable or inadequate, the transitional arrangements were either problematic or dangerous, and the entire document was a shoddy work of draftsmanship.[131] The proceduralists and the substantialists were one and the same—drawn from the LDP-KANU alliance. In a kitchen-sink approach, they marshaled both arguments to strengthen their case against the Wako Draft.

On the one hand, the LDP-KANU alliance, which formed the Orange Democratic Movement (ODM), campaigned for a No vote, asking Kenyans to reject the proposed constitution on November 21, 2005. On the other, the NAK and allied parties, of which the major one was FORD-People, staked its future on a Yes vote, asking Kenyans to approve the Wako Draft at the referendum. Officially, an orange symbolized the No camp, whereas the Yes camp was represented by a banana.

The questions were valid. Unfortunately, political leaders were determined not to use these critiques to make a more acceptable and better constitution. Instead, they became material for battle in a referendum campaign that threatened to tear the country apart. Deadly violence, mayhem, and the most scurrilous attacks became commonplace.[132] Leading Kenyans, donors, and ordinary folks feared that the result of the referendum—no matter who won— would result in a more divided country.[133] The reason was that the Yes and No campaigns were waged on outright lies, misuse of state power, and nativist appeals to tribal hysteria. Kibaki and Odinga, the respective leaders of the Yes and No camps, ruled out any compromise, dialogue, or postponement.[134] The ODM and the state were headed for a collision. Odinga claimed that he was ashamed to be a member of the Kibaki cabinet.[135] In response, other ministers asked Odinga to resign from the government.[136]

Calls by the clergy, civil society, and other actors to postpone the vote were rejected. A small group of MPs calling itself the "Middle Ground Group" attempted to postpone the referendum until the issues were resolved, but their effort flopped.[137] A suggestion by Makau Mutua to reformulate the referendum and vote only on the contentious issues barely drew a public response.[138] I then recommended a boycott of the referendum to deny it legitimacy.[139] The Nation Media Group, the region's largest media group, and the publisher of the Nation Newspapers, issued an unusual plea in its flagship newspaper calling on rival factions to iron out the contentious issues before the vote.[140] An ODM lawsuit to stop the referendum and the Wako Draft was first postponed and then thrown out of court.[141] In the ruling, the court held that the referendum was constitutional and could not be stopped.[142] The judges stated that the process was not flawed and that the judiciary could not interfere with the people's right to make a constitution.[143]

The referendum campaigns were a replay of the 2002 general elections. Except for Nyachae's FORD-People and some NAK-friendly KANU legislators, the opposing political forces mirrored the political landscape before the rebel Rainbow Alliance broke away from KANU in 2002. The No campaign brought together political leaders who were in the new KANU, leaders from KANU and Odinga's NDP. NAK, which was a coalition of the Democratic Party (DP), FORD-Kenya, the National Party of Kenya, and other smaller parties, retained the same forces in the Yes camp, although it added FORD-People to its ranks. This chasm was solidified by Moi's open support for the No camp. The driving force in the ODM camp was Odinga, who cobbled an ethnic alliance of all the major groups except the Kikuyu, Meru, and Embu. The ODM drew wide support among the Luo, Moi's Kalenjin, Kalonzo Musyoka's Kamba, Musalia Mudavadi's Luhya, Najib Balala's coastal groups, and William Ole Ntimama's Maasai. Uhuru Kenyatta was the only prominent Kikuyu to support it. Billow Kerrow, an influential Somali legislator, called on the Northeastern Province to support the No vote.[144]

Kibaki and his coterie of advisers, however, counted on the solid support of the Kikuyu, Meru, and Embu groups in Central, Nairobi, parts of Eastern, and the Rift Valley provinces. He hoped to gain most of the Kisii vote where he was counting on FORD-People's Nyachae, and split with the No camp in the Coast and Northeastern provinces. He thought that Charity Ngilu and Kivutha Kibwana, two Kamba leaders, and Musikari Kombo, the leader of the Luhya-dominated FORD-Kenya, would help him carry Ukambani and Western provinces. It was clear that both sides were relying on the tribal card—ethnic arithmetic—to either make or break the proposed constitution. The fate of the new constitution became a contest between tribes. Whatever the outcome, there was little doubt that the country would be deeply divided after the referendum.[145] On November 20, the day before the vote, President Kibaki, the leader of the Banana/Yes camp, delivered a nationally televised speech and asked Kenyans to approve the draft constitution, a document he termed "one of the most modern and progressive in the world."[146]

The outcome of the referendum was as stunning as it was unpredictable. At the political level, the referendum campaigns were high theater, the likes of which Kenya had never really experienced. They signified a government divided against itself. It split the cabinet in two—with Odinga and Musyoka leading a group of rebel ministers against the Kibaki NAK faction. Even as vitriolic attacks were exchanged between the two sides, the rebel ministers refused to resign from government and President Kibaki declined to sack them. As demonstrated in Table 11.1, it proved to be a costly mistake for President Kibaki when the Orange/No, antireferendum, Odinga camp led the country in a resounding rejection of the Wako Draft by a vote of 57 percent to 42 percent.[147] President Kibaki's key allies, including Vice President Moody Awori and Ministers George Saitoti, Charity Ngilu, Simeon Nyachae, and Raphael Tuju lost the vote in their own constituencies.[148] Kivutha Kibwana and Norman Nyagah were the other important Banana leaders who lost in their own backyards.[149] The ODM swept every province, except Central and Eastern provinces, the two regions with large Kikuyu, Meru, and Embu residents.[150] But in Eastern Province, virtually the entire Kamba vote went to the No camp, a tribute to Musyoka's influence in the region.[151]

The vote was a rare repudiation of a democratically elected regime in an African country. Forty-eight hours later, President Kibaki accepted the referendum outcome and declared that there was no constitutional vacuum because the extant constitution was still in force.[152] He then immediately dissolved his cabinet.[153] Political analysts blamed President Kibaki's humiliating loss on a number of factors, including his hands-off style, corruption scandals, power struggles within NARC, a protest against perceived Kikuyu hegemony, and the government's failure to formulate an inclusive and consultative constitutional review process.[154] The defeat was also blamed on the patriarchy's opposition to the draft's inclusion of a broad range of women's rights, particularly the one-third principle on political participation.[155] This was the case even though the Wako Draft did not include the more detailed language on women's rights from the 2004 Bomas Draft Constitution. The vote was not viewed as

Table 11.1 Referendum Results on (Wako) Draft Constitution, 2005

	Yes Votes	No Votes	Rejected Ballots[a]	Total Votes	Registered Voters	Turnout
Nairobi Province	161,344 (42.51%)	211,805 (55.81%)	6,376 (1.68%)	379,525	961,295	39.48%
Coast Province	65,737 (19.63%)	265,537 (79.3%)	3,592 (1.07%)	334,866	964,518	34.72%
Northeastern Province	15,196 (26.23%)	42,217 (72.87%)	520 (0.9%)	57,933	237,321	24.41%
Eastern Province	557,504 (51.6%)	512,323 (47.41%)	10,701 (0.99%)	1,080,528	1,971,390	54.81%
Central Province	1,023,259 (92.32%)	74,296 (6.7%)	10,876 (0.98%)	1,108,431	1,791,817	61.86%
Rift Valley Province	422,457 (24.6%)	1,283,946 (74.78%)	10,603 (0.62%)	1,717,006	2,669,381	64.32%
Western Province	241,114 (38.98%)	365,686 (59.12%)	11,710 (1.89%)	618,510	1,322,604	46.76%
Nyanza Province	114,145 (11.99%)	828,394 (86.99%)	9,759 (1.02%)	952,298	1,664,725	57.2%
National Total	2,600,756 (41.62%)	3,584,204 (57.36%)	6,249,097 (1.03%)	64,137	11,583,051	53.95%

Source: Institute for Education in Democracy (Nairobi, Kenya).
Notes: a. Rejected ballots were spoiled ballots or those that were defective in some way.

an endorsement of the Orange leaders, but rather as a protest against the Kibaki government. President Kibaki fumbled as he tried to form a credible government. He even reportedly met Moi, his predecessor, in an attempt to split the ODM and bring leading KANU legislators into his new cabinet.[156] But these efforts bore no fruit as leading ODM leaders, including Odinga, roundly criticized Kibaki for failing to meet and consult with them.[157]

The new cabinet was a huge disappointment when Kibaki finally unveiled it on December 7, 2005. He took the opportunity to sack his most ardent critics, including Odinga, Musyoka, Peter Anyang' Nyong'o, Balala, ole Ntimama, Ochillo Ayacko, and Linah Jebii Kilimo—all ODM luminaries who had spearheaded the defeat of the Wako Draft.[158] Chris Murungaru, an NAK minister who had been linked to corruption in the defense sector, was the only key ally of Kibaki to be axed.[159] Most of those appointed were political cronies, tribal barons, or incompetent sycophants.[160] Kibaki was further weakened when some of his appointees declined their posts and others bargained for either more powerful positions or for the inclusion of their tribal cohorts.[161] It was not a credible way to legitimize the regime and the state after such a crushing electoral defeat. Kibaki was hardly in a position—either morally or politically—to lead the country toward a new constitution. For its part, the ODM, a movement of convenience brought together to defeat the Wako Draft, started to unravel because of the ambitions of its leading lights.[162] But the ODM grouping would later split into two political parties, one led by Odinga and the other by Musyoka, and front them as presidential challengers against Kibaki in the 2007 elections.

Politics After the Referendum

The defeat of the Wako Draft in the referendum postponed—but did not end—the struggle for a democratic constitution. The Wako Draft was defeated not because it was a draconian, undemocratic document. In fact, when measured by objective normative standards of constitutionalism, it was a progressive text. It was a more democratic document than the official constitution. It was defeated because of clumsy and unconsultative politics by Kibaki and his key aides. The persistent problem that haunted the process was the failure of NARC to share power between its two key factions—NAK and LDP. Had this political question been resolved, perhaps a new constitution would have been enacted. There is little doubt that had Kibaki and Odinga come to terms on a new constitution, their constituencies would have blessed the pact. In effect, the failure of the process was not about the democratic nature of the document, but an inability of key leaders to reach a political settlement.

No sooner had the referendum ended than the Kibaki regime was rocked by revelations of grand corruption. At the center of the storm was John Githongo, Kibaki's anticorruption czar, who had resigned in February 2005 and fled to exile in Britain. Githongo's revelations were contained in a dossier that identified cases of corruption and named those officials, including senior cabinet ministers, who were culpable. In addition to senior civil servants, the scandal involved Kibaki's most trusted aides—Kiraitu Murungi, David Mwiraria, Francis Muthaura, Alfred Getonga, and Chris Murungaru.[163] Vice President Awori was also implicated. The scandal created such a firestorm at home and abroad that in February 2006, Mwiraria and Murungi were forced to resign from the cabinet.[164] The scandal weakened an already besieged regime.

The constitution review process seemed all but dead. The Constitution of Kenya Review Commission wound up its activities in January 2006 after the process had cost the public purse an estimated KShs 10 billion, or more than US$140 million.[165] However, Kibaki knew that Kenyans would not be mollified without a new constitution. To stem the growing popularity of the opposition, in February 2006 he appointed the Committee of Eminent Persons to advise the government on how to jump-start the process.[166] Bethuel Kiplagat, a respected former diplomat, was appointed chair of the fifteen-member committee.[167] It was given until May 30, 2006, to present its findings to President Kibaki. However, the committee was bitterly attacked by a wide section of Kenyans, including the political opposition, civil society groups, and independent analysts. They termed it irrelevant, exclusive, and illegitimate.[168] Key leaders, such as Odinga, argued that the committee was irrelevant because only a political settlement could resolve the impasse over a new constitution.[169] The committee conducted public hearings and received testimony and submissions from a large number of individuals and organizations.[170] It wound up its public hearings on May 2, 2006, even as ODM leaders maintained that they would not accept its recommendations.[171]

On May 30, 2006, the Committee of Eminent Persons presented its report to President Kibaki at State House in Nairobi.[172] In his remarks, Kiplagat said that Kenyans "would like to see a people-driven review process devoid of political interference."[173] In response, President Kibaki pledged to "engage other stakeholders" in a dialogue—in "further and wider" talks—to produce a lasting document.[174] Within a week, Kibaki ordered the public release of the report and praised the committee for a job well done.[175] Opposition politicians in the ODM—KANU and LDP—dismissed the committee's report as irrelevant and inconsequential and called it a delaying tactic by the Kibaki regime.[176] As soon as the report was released to the public, the ODM made clear that it lacked political legitimacy. They rejected it out of hand, a fact that seemed to kill it.[177]

The Kiplagat report was a thoughtful document that carefully identified the social and political problems that had stalked the quest for a democratic constitution.[178] The committee's recommendations focused on charting a way forward in the review process. The state was called upon by Kenya's leading newspaper to embark on an inclusive process devoid of posturing by politicians and interest groups.[179] The committee recommended a roadmap and asked President Kibaki to lead the process.[180] It urged the president to hold consultations with all stakeholders, including the opposition.[181] However, the committee failed in its major charge: to make a single definitive recommendation on how to move forward. Instead the committee waffled and gave three options. It identified these as a constituent assembly, a committee of experts followed by a referendum, and a multisectoral forum backed by experts and a referendum.[182] Needless to say, there was nothing new or innovative in the recommendations. That is why some commentators concluded that the committee had been a waste of time and public resources.[183] The Committee of Eminent Persons, like other initiatives before it, was a victim of political struggles within the political class. The import of the larger national interest, in this case defined by the quest for a legitimate constitution, had eluded political leaders.[184]

IPPG II: Essential or Minimum Reforms

The prospects for a new constitution grew dim in spite of the Kiplagat report. Instead, opposition leaders resorted to calls for minimum reforms to level the playing field before elections.[185] Reminiscent of the 1997 IPPG package, these calls sought to increase the number of constituencies, put more opposition members on the electoral commission, and give leeway to ethnic-based political parties to entrench themselves in the 2007 elections.[186] They did not address the fundamental reform of the state—or any of the contentious issues that had deadlocked the process. On the whole, civil society was opposed to the proposed piecemeal reforms, just as it was in 1997.[187] Mwambi Mwasaru, the acting executive director of the Kenya Human Rights Commission, said that minimum reforms had no "credible references to vital issues of governance, accountability and human rights that have been the focal points of the long struggle for democratic reforms."[188] Instead, he called for a comprehensive constitution-making process and charged the political elite with the "misuse of the constitution-making process as a bargaining chip in the pursuit of their own machinations.[189] In a sharp rebuke to the political class, he said that the "proposed reforms seek only to resolve the problem of power-sharing in the run-up to, and after, the 2007 elections, while also facilitating an appropriate political and legal environment in which either faction can deploy its unique ethnic and regional support bases to dominate the state."[190]

Many sectors of civil society, including religious groups, denounced piecemeal reforms as hypocritical and selfish. Others, like Yash Ghai, pushed for a new constitution. Ghai produced a new draft constitution that sought to address some of the flaws in both the Wako and Bomas drafts.[191] Some critics likened the ODM to the ill-fated *Titanic* and dismissed its key leaders—Odinga, Musyoka, Ruto, Mudavadi, and Joseph Kamotho—as selfish, domineering, and a "part of the past we want to forget and so we must forget them as well."[192] Perhaps the most critical opposition came from the Kenya Episcopal Conference, the leadership of the Catholic Church, and the Supreme Council of Kenya Muslims (SUPKEM), the politically influential Muslim organization. SUPKEM said "the ODM is hoodwinking the public by calling for these reforms" and dismissed its leaders as self-seekers.[193] In a biting critique, Catholics accused legislators of being a "selfish dictatorship."[194] Their statement underscored a deep disappointment with Kenya's political class.

> The lessons of the historic referendum must inform the current debate about piecemeal amendments to the Constitution. We observe with surprise that the same people who championed the rejection of the proposed new constitution are now championing the minimum reforms comprising the same issues that were contained in the same document, which they campaigned against. *This is dishonesty and should be resisted by Kenyans.*[195] [emphasis added]

But as 2006 came to a close, it became clear that neither Kibaki nor the political opposition was keen on a new constitution. The government was vehemently opposed to the opposition calls for minimum reforms. ODM-Kenya (ODM-K), formed after ODM was denied its name on a legal technicality, teamed up with the Muite-led parliamentary Committee on the Administration of Justice and Legal Affairs to exert pressure on the government for minimum reforms. They combined with civil society and formed Muungano wa Katiba Mpya, a lobby for constitutional reforms. But civil society did not see the minimum reforms—now dubbed *essential* reforms—as an end in themselves. It thought that in return for its support for minimum reforms, the political actors could be bound to a date certain by which a new constitution had to be produced.[196] Muungano organized well-attended rallies to drum up public support for minimum reforms. In March 2007 President Kibaki finally succumbed to the demands and appointed a team to conduct the talks.[197] A joint government-opposition team led by Awori, the vice president, and Uhuru Kenyatta, the leader of the opposition, was launched.[198] But civil society abandoned the talks because they were not inclusive.[199] Instead, civil society launched its own parallel effort, which soon fizzled out.[200] As in 1997, the opposition and the government came together again at the exclusion of civil society to craft a minimum reforms package.

Muite's parliamentary committee had worked out the outline of the minimum reforms in December 2006.[201] The basic reforms sought to entrench the review in the constitution by providing for a referendum; enhance the independence of the Electoral Commission of Kenya; provide for judicial independence; entrench affirmative action in the constitution; require that the winning presidential candidate garner 50 percent plus one of the votes cast in addition to at least 25 percent of the vote in at least five of the eight provinces; increase parliamentary independence and authority; prohibit opposition MPs from joining the government without the permission of their party; require that holders of constitutional offices be vetted by Parliament; provide for dual citizenship; and set up a committee to oversee the distribution of national resources.[202] Many of these reforms would open up more political space, although a number were clearly designed to take away the advantages of incumbency enjoyed by Kibaki. The 50 percent plus one rule for the election of the president sought to make it difficult for Kibaki to win on the first round, especially if the opposition split its vote. The idea was to force a runoff with only one opposition candidate that would give Kibaki opponents a better chance.

In May 2007, the minimum reform talks achieved some success when the opposition and the government adopted most of the proposals of the Muite committee.[203] The more contentious proposals, such as the 50 percent plus one rule, affirmative action, and a committee on the equitable distribution of resources, were not adopted.[204] As history would have it, none of these measures, including the 50 percent plus one rule, saw the light of day as the Ninth Parliament expired at the end of 2007.[205] President Kibaki refused to give his nod to a proposal that would complicate his bid for a second term. In September 2007, Kibaki ordered Awori, the vice president, and Martha Karua, who had become minister for justice and constitutional affairs, to bring the minimum reforms bill to Parliament for enactment before its dissolution in advance of the 2007 elections.[206] As it turned out, in the stampede toward the elections, Parliament was sent home and the December 2007 vote was conducted without the passage of the minimum reforms.

Political Alliances and the 2007 Elections

Any doubt that NARC still existed as the ruling party after the rancorous 2005 referendum was removed soon thereafter. NAK and LDP went their separate ways after the referendum. Kibaki sacked the LDP leaders from his cabinet. NAK, a shell of its former self, appeared to have been initially replaced by NARC-Kenya, a new party that excluded Musikari Kombo's FORD-Kenya and Ngilu's National Party of Kenya.[207] Ngilu, the minister for health and the registered chair of NARC, refused to turn NARC over to Kibaki or his allies unless she was given a leading role in his reelection campaign. That is why most of Kibaki's allies fronted NARC-Kenya. In parliamentary by-elections in July 2006, President Kibaki and his political allies had campaigned for NARC-Kenya candidates, indicating that NARC was virtually dead.[208] FORD-Kenya announced that it would quit NARC over Kibaki's betrayal, but there was not really any NARC to quit.[209] Still, Kibaki refused to openly identify with NARC-Kenya or DP, his former party, although his allies in both parties kept on insisting that he would run for reelection under either of their auspices. Kibaki's reluctance to identify with NARC-Kenya was due to its image as the reincarnation of DP, which historically was a party of the Kikuyu and related communities in Eastern Province.

The ODM referendum camp was registered as ODM-Kenya, an alliance of KANU and LDP.[210] ODM was registered as ODM-Kenya because Mugambi Imanyara, a nondescript lawyer, ostensibly working in cahoots with the state, had in 2005 quickly registered a party known as ODM to deny Odinga the popular symbol of the group that had resoundingly won the referendum by defeating the government.[211] ODM-Kenya spent months attempting to coalesce as a political party and to define its identity.[212] But from the start, it was clear that Odinga intended to use it for his presidential bid. However, Musyoka was determined to become its nominee. What ensued was an open and fierce rivalry for supremacy within ODM-Kenya between Odinga and Musyoka and their allies.[213] The rivalry took overt tribal overtones because Odinga had the solid support of the Luo and Musyoka the full backing of the Kamba within ODM.[214] Typical of Kenyan political parties—which are personal vehicles for individual barons—ODM-Kenya failed to find a mechanism for resolving the competition for power between two strong-willed leaders. In July 2007, Musyoka defected from LDP to join Julia Ojiambo's Labor Party of Kenya (LPK).

Musyoka left LDP but also took ODM-K with him. Daniel Maanzo, the registered chairman of ODM-K and a Musyoka ally, turned the party over to Musyoka after refusing to step aside for Henry Kosgey and Peter Anyang' Nyong'o, who were Odinga's key supporters in ODM-K.[215] But in a strange twist, Odinga dug up Mugambi Imanyara, the registered chair of the original ODM, and prevailed upon him to hand the party over to him.[216] Odinga then installed Kosgey and Anyang' Nyong'o as the chair and secretary-general, respectively, of ODM. In effect, the ODM opposition movement was split into halves—one led by Musyoka, the other by Odinga. Each one of them had his own nomination vehicle for the presidency. Odinga's ODM took the lion's share of the leaders within the opposition. On his side were Musalia Mudavadi, the former vice president and a leading Luhya politician; William Ruto, a former KANU hawk who had emerged as the heir apparent to Moi in the Kalenjin Rift Valley; Najib Balala, a prominent leader from the Coast Province; Joseph Nyagah, a former minister under Moi from Embu; Anyang' Nyong'o, the party ideologue and a Luo; and Kosgey, a Kalenjin and former Moi crony.[217] In October, he picked up the support of Ngilu, the Kamba politician from Kitui Central in Eastern Province.[218] Several days later, Kibaki sacked her from the cabinet after she attended the launch of Odinga's presidential campaign and declared, if only with hyperbole, that Odinga was the "second Nelson Mandela of Africa."[219] Thus Odinga meant to assemble on his side as many tribal barons as possible to create an ethnic mass that would carry him to State House in the December elections. However, Odinga and ODM were bitterly opposed by Moi and Uhuru Kenyatta, who had been their allies during the referendum vote.[220] Musyoka, however, hoped to keep his support in Ukambani and make some inroads in the Rift Valley, Western, and Coast provinces, whence he drew some high-level support. But there was little doubt that in the split of ODM, Odinga had emerged as the main challenger to Kibaki.

In September 2007, both ODM and ODM-K carried out their presidential nominations. As expected, Musyoka was declared the nominee for ODM-K with token opposition from Ojiambo.[221] Similarly, Odinga overwhelmingly defeated Ruto, Mudavadi, and Nyagah for the ODM nomination.[222] In what appeared to be a rehearsed nomination exercise, Balala stepped down for Odinga, while the other contestants showered him with subservient praise. Odinga picked Mudavadi as his running mate, a move that was aimed at consolidating the Luhya vote. Musyoka, however, picked Ojiambo, a woman and a Luhya.[223] After a lot of dithering and false starts, Kibaki announced on September 30, 2007, that he would seek reelection on the Party of National Unity (PNU), a newly formed alliance of several regional and ethnic parties, including the Luhya-dominated FORD-Kenya, Ford-People of Simeon Nyachae, the Kisii baron, NARC-Kenya, DP, New FORD–Kenya, Paul Muite's Safina, Uhuru Kenyatta's KANU, and Shirikisho, a party of the coastal peoples.[224] He launched his reelection bid at a colorful and boisterous rally at the Nyayo National Stadium in Nairobi on September 30, 2007.[225] A week later, an estimated 400,000 people attended the launch of Odinga's presidential campaign at Uhuru Park.[226] Although Kibaki emphasized the achievements of his first term, the opposition accused him of aggravating tribalism, failing to tame corruption, and exacerbating economic inequality.[227] The presidential campaigns had finally kicked off in earnest.

As the 2007 elections approached, the political class divided into three formations, all personality-driven. Party defections reached a crescendo as politicians attempted to maximize their electability. Usually, defections were to the party of the baron who controlled the ethnic vote in a region. Some of the alliances appeared to be driven by intraclass struggles. For example, the Kenyatta, Moi, and Kibaki families came together because of their distrust of Odinga. In 2007, Kenyatta, Moi, and KANU supported Kibaki, even though he had run against them in 2002. Nicholas Biwott, the powerful Kalenjin minister under Moi and the man implicated in the Ouko murder as well as the looting of the public purse, became a Kibaki campaigner.[228] Nyachae, the FORD-People Kisii leader who had opposed him in 2002, joined Kibaki's PNU. Many senior Kibaki supporters were implicated in past economic crimes and gross human rights violations, as were many of those backing Odinga and Musyoka.[229] It is the complete suffocation of the political square by this political class that has made it difficult to reform the Kenyan state.

2007 Party Nominations

Historically, Kenyan political parties have not held proper primaries before national elections to nominate candidates for parliamentary and civic seats. The reasons for this deficit are many, but the most important is that political parties exist mainly on paper, and are therefore the virtual possessions of their leaders. Generally, parties have no memberships, membership lists, or structures, and rarely hold internal elections or formal party meetings. They are not based on ideologies or platforms to which the leaders or members, if they exist, are required to adhere.[230] This has been one of the most serious drawbacks to democratization in Kenya since it is impossible to develop a modern democracy without functioning, transparent, accountable, and internally democratic political parties.

Between 1964—the year of Kenya's independence—and 1991 when the legal prohibition on multipartyism was lifted, elections were held under conditions of either a de jure or de facto one-party state. Until 1991, the country had only known multipartyism for two brief periods: 1963–1964 when the Kenya African National Union swallowed the Kenya African Democratic Union (KADU) and 1966–1969 when the KANU government under Jomo Kenyatta permitted and then banned the Kenya People's Union (KPU). Needless to say, these two truncated experiments with democracy were insufficient to inculcate in the political class the culture of party democracy. National elections held between 1969 and 1988 suffered from the despotic culture of the one-party state under KANU.

In the 1969 elections, the first under a de facto one-party state, the KANU National Executive Committee approved the candidates for parliamentary seats on the recommendations of the KANU district branches.[231] Only those deemed loyal to KANU were allowed to contest the elections. In 1974, a contestant for that year's national elections was required to be a life member of KANU.[232] In the 1979 elections, all ex-KPU members were barred from the elections. In the 1983 and 1988 elections, KANU chose at the nominations stage only those in favor with the party. Only KANU members were allowed to vote at the nominations stage in the 1988 elections, which were conducted by queue voting, effectively abolishing the secret ballot.[233] These electoral malpractices assured Moi a rubber-stamp Parliament.

The 1992, 1997, and 2002 elections—all of which were held under the multiparty system—were not a model for internal party democracy or open competition for nominations. In 1992, for example, in spite of the rules laid down by all parties for nominations, the exercise was marred by incompetence, lack of party structures and resources, and the overbearing place of the party baron in the process. Parties failed to act according to their own rules, and in most cases candidates were picked by party leaders, rather than by the party's rank and file.[234] On the day that the successfully nominated candidates from the various parties were to present papers to the electoral officers for certification, there were bizarre "reports of kidnappings, blockades, actual beatings, abductions and snatchings of nomination documents from agents of certain candidates" by rivals from other parties.[235] Some of these malpractices would be repeated in 1997 and 2002, although to a lesser degree.

One would have thought that the experience of fifteen years—since 1992—with an open political process would have prepared political parties for nominations in the 2007 elections. However, the nominations for parliamentary and civic candidates for the 2007 elections—though the most competitive ever—were plagued by the same problems of the lack of preparedness, transparency, and internal democracy. Again, party bosses exercised control over the nomination process to a degree that is not acceptable in a democracy. Virtually all parties lacked party memberships or party lists by which party nominations could be conducted.[236] Since there was no way to track party identification, anybody could vote for a candidate for any party so long as they could produce a national identity card and an elector's card.[237] This allowed individuals to vote multiple times for multiple parties, possibly with the intent of influencing the nominations in rival parties.

In spite of the many flaws, the party nominations for the 2007 elections were the most dramatic in the country's history. There were the usual problems of party bosses giving favored candidates direct nominations. For example, the five most senior members of ODM—the so-called Pentagon of Raila Odinga, Musalia Mudavadi, William Ruto, Najib Balala, and Joe Nyagah—gave themselves direct nominations. They were not challenged for the party nominations in their constituencies.[238] PNU and ODM-K also did the same for some preferred candidates. The smaller parties, such as Safina, Sisi Kwa Sisi, Social Democratic Party (SDP), Kenya National Democratic Alliance (KENDA), which was taken over by Kamlesh Pattni, the notorious and pivotal player in the Goldenberg scandal, and others, liberally gave out nominations without any process.

The fringe parties became a receptacle for politicians who had failed to win the nominations of the three large parties. KENDA and Safina freely dished out nominations to candidates who defected to them after failing to clinch nominations elsewhere.[239] But even the winners of some of the big party nominations in ODM, PNU, KANU, and ODM-K were replaced by party brass for favored candidates or in situations where the party leadership felt that its interests would be better served by nominating a particular individual rather than going with the winner.[240] These defections and the override of voters' choices made a mockery of party democracy.

However, the nominations were high drama as a large number of established politicians were shown the door by the electorate at the nominations stage. Felled by the voters were such powerful individuals as Chris Murungaru, the Kieni MP and a former close aide of President Kibaki; David Mwenje, the Embakasi MP; Joseph Kamotho, the Mathioya MP; Norman Nyagah, the Kamukunji MP; and Wangari Maathai, the Tetu MP and the 2004 Nobel Peace laureate—all seeking a PNU ticket. From ODM, Luo Nyanza voters rejected sixteen of twenty-one MPs, all Odinga allies.[241] This was a particularly positive development for the region that had traditionally elected whoever was Odinga's fancy for the moment. It was a ray of hope that the long shadow that he cast over Luo Nyanza politics would be diminished to allow the populace a chance to exercise a more democratic choice.[242] In Ugenya, James Orengo, one of Kenya's storied reformers, received a direct nomination from ODM after Steve Mwanga, his challenger, was accused of violence.[243] But in Musyoka's ODM-K, Daudi Mwanzia, the Machakos Town MP and a close confidant of the party boss, was rejected by voters and had to seek the nomination of another party.[244] Even so, Musyoka was accused of running a chaotic nominations process and favoring his friends.

One positive sign was the high number of women candidates nominated for parliamentary seats—269 women. Women comprised roughly 10 percent of the total 2,548 candidates nominated to contest for the 210 parliamentary seats.[245] That was an astounding average of 12 candidates per constituency. Over 100 parties, out of over 300 registered, fielded candidates.[246] But the sad fact is that many of these were briefcase parties without any structural basis, ideological platforms, or memberships.[247] All in all, the nominations witnessed many rejected incumbents, probably a good sign for democratic development. However, due to the structural deficits, the nominations exercise resembled a circus.[248]

Those who are elected to Parliament after such sham processes without an ideological anchor cannot be stewards of a democracy in which competing national visions are worked out. That is why Kenya's Parliament has been turned into a lucrative job where MPs grant themselves pay raises that would make a member of the US Congress envious. Although the political class had from 2002—the date of the previous general elections—to get its house in order by creating and strengthening parties, it had chosen not to do so. Instead, Kenya's political elites treat political parties as instruments of inconvenience, whose bare frameworks are stood up once every five years as proxies for electoral processes, and then immediately ignored thereafter. Unless the political class comes to understand the central importance of political parties in a democracy, the country's political culture will remain retarded.

The 2007 General Elections

The 2007 general elections were the most hotly contested poll in Kenya's history. At the parliamentary level, the three main political parties were ODM, PNU, and ODM-K. These three were the parties with the most serious presidential contenders: Kibaki of PNU, Odinga of ODM, and Musyoka of ODM-K. KANU, the other party that could have fielded a serious presidential candidate, instead chose to back Kibaki. Uhuru Kenyatta, the KANU chairman, had decided to back Kibaki, a fellow Kikuyu, because he knew that the

Kikuyu would not support him over the incumbent. At any rate, he seems to have calculated that supporting Kibaki, who would be ineligible to run in 2012, would pay dividends in the future. Given the ethnic matrix of Kenyan politics, the youthful Kenyatta had a good chance of inheriting Kibaki's mantle among the Kikuyu in Central Province. In addition, Moi, the former KANU supremo and Kenyatta political mentor, had also decided to support Kibaki for the presidency.

Kibaki enjoyed all the advantages of incumbency. In addition, he had revived Kenya's economy. Raila Odinga, the son of Oginga Odinga, Kenya's first vice president, had vigorously been campaigning for the presidency since he fell out with Kibaki over the Bomas Draft Constitution in 2004. He conceived the Orange No campaign that led Kenyans in rejecting the Wako Draft Constitution in the 2005 referendum. In fact, the referendum was a proxy for the power struggle between the two men. It was a dress rehearsal for the 2007 elections. Since the referendum, Odinga had virtually spent all his enormous energy and political genius to create ODM, the political party that would face Kibaki at the polls.

Odinga assembled in ODM the largest collection of ethnic barons and baronesses in the land. He understood that in Kenya's broken ethnic landscape, the only way to craft a winning formula was to cobble a coalition of leaders of the major ethnic groups in the leadership of the party. This is the strategy that NARC had employed with great success against Moi and Uhuru Kenyatta in 2002. Ethnic groups were more likely to support Odinga if they saw one of their own in the leadership of the party. Building on the Orange No campaign, which had included William Ruto and the Moi family (Kalenjin), Kalonzo Musyoka (Kamba), Musalia Mudavadi (Luhya), William Ole Ntimama (Maasai), Uhuru Kenyatta (Kikuyu), Najib Balala (Coast), and Joe Nyagah (Embu), Odinga (Luo) felt that he would replicate the referendum victory in the 2007 elections. He figured that he would isolate Kibaki with this coalition of high-profile leaders from the country's major ethnic groups.

But Odinga lost some important leaders soon after the referendum. The first to bolt were Moi and Kenyatta. Then Odinga and Musyoka fought each other for the control of ODM and eventually split it in two—ODM and ODM-K. Still, Odinga held on to Mudavadi, Ruto, Balala, Ntimama, and Nyagah. He later added Charity Ngilu, the Kamba legislator, to his war chest. He named this top leadership group of ODM the Pentagon and embarked on nationwide campaigns. An indefatigable campaigner, Odinga crisscrossed the length and breadth of the country popularizing ODM. He drew large, ecstatic crowds wherever he went. A political showman, he became a national phenomenon and the most electrifying politician in the country.[249] Although he had been viewed as unelectable at one point, Odinga gained in popularity and in September 2007 was rated in opinion polls as the most popular choice for State House.[250] He had overtaken both Musyoka and Kibaki in the polls.

Musyoka took his show on the road as well, but, unlike Odinga, was unable to attract a large coterie of tribal barons across the land. Although he included in ODM-K Julia Ojiambo (Luhya) and minor figures from the Rift Valley and Coast provinces, ODM-K could not shake the perception that it was a regional Kamba party. But Musyoka persevered and refused to join either Kibaki's PNU or Odinga's ODM. Instead, he insisted that he would go all the way in his quest for the presidency.[251] His resilience, though baffling at the beginning, won him some admirers among the population, even if most Kenyans felt that he had no realistic shot at the presidency. But he counted on the populous Kamba vote to give him a respectable showing on election.

Of all the campaigns, Kibaki's was the most incoherent and chaotic, especially for an incumbent. He had waited until the last minute to pull together PNU, an empty vessel, as his reelection vehicle. He had invented PNU after failing to coax NARC out of Ngilu. But PNU was an unwieldy umbrella party of many regional and ethnic parties and KANU supporting his bid. It almost came unraveled during the party nominations when some of the affiliate parties decided to field candidates under their own name. Even so, Kibaki campaigned vigorously and admirably across the country. For a 76-year-old who had suffered a debilitating stroke several years earlier, Kibaki kept a surprisingly punishing pace. He visited every nook and cranny of the country, using all the tools of incumbency, including allocating resources, giving out land title deeds, commissioning hospitals, and creating new administrative units.[252]

All the candidates—Odinga, Kibaki, and Musyoka—tried to outdo each other in almost every respect. They competed on who would hold the largest public rallies. They produced manifestoes galore. They promised the creation of a more nurturing welfare state with better and more affordable services in key sectors such as health, education, water, electricity, infrastructure, and communications. They vowed to fight corruption, eradicate poverty, banish insecurity, introduce a new constitution, devolve power and resources from the center to the regions, strive for gender equity, protect religious freedom, grow the economy, and stand up to the US war on terror and the rendition program. But the promises were largely scanty slogans, and the candidates could not explain how all the programs would be paid for. It was populist presidential campaign rhetoric the likes of which Kenya had never seen before. It seemed to portend a positive future in which elections might be fought on issues, not personalities.

However, underneath the lofty campaign rhetoric were dangerous ethnic codes of incitement. Odinga's ODM campaign was a subtle appeal to anti-Kikuyu feelings. It was easy to demonize the Kikuyu in Kenya because they are the largest (although at 22 percent of the population still a minority) and most powerful ethnic group. Odinga frequently said in public rallies that Central Kenya (code for the Kikuyu and related peoples) should not isolate itself by refusing to support ODM. He had used similar language during the 2005 referendum. His support for Majimbo or federalism was also a calculated move to appeal to the Kalenjin, coastal peoples, Muslims, and Somalis in Northeastern Province, and to a lesser extent the Luhya, that they would be able to wrest control of their local affairs from the stereotype of the acquisitive and domineering Kikuyu.[253] He even signed a Memorandum of Understanding with Muslims promising them autonomy and better treatment under his administration.[254] But on the PNU side, there were equally odious nativist and tribalist sentiments against Odinga and the Luo. Some PNU supporters derided Odinga as unfit to rule because he was presumably uncircumcised, a rite of passage among Kikuyu males and other Bantu groups in Kenya.[255]

These stereotypes and appeals to base instincts were symptomatic of the underdevelopment of Kenya's democratic culture and the stunted growth of national consciousness. Demagogic politicians play to these fears to compete for power and the spoils of the state. The uneven development of the country by regions—and the commanding positions occupied by elites from some ethnic groups—have simply exacerbated these hatreds. In others, they have created a psychosis of victimhood. Odinga was able in his campaign to galvanize some of these primordial feelings against the Kikuyu. As a response, his popularity among groups outside Central Kenya soared. ODM, his party, was rated the most popular party in those areas.

The majority of opinion polls, which were a new phenomenon in Kenyan electoral politics, showed Odinga leading Kibaki and Musyoka for months before the elections. One of the polls before the election by the Steadman Group, a reputable firm, showed Odinga leading Kibaki 45 percent to 43 percent, with Musyoka a distant third at 10 percent.[256] Odinga led Kibaki in six of the country's eight provinces.[257] Other polls showed Odinga with wider leads over Kibaki.[258] But just before the election, Gallup put Kibaki ahead of Odinga 44 percent to 43 percent.[259] The polls, which had never been used so extensively in Kenya, created an air of both invincibility and victorious inevitability in Odinga and ODM. Their supporters came to believe that the election of Odinga as president and an ODM-dominated Parliament was a foregone conclusion. This would make it more difficult for Odinga and his fanatical supporters to swallow the bitter pill of defeat if he lost the election to Kibaki. Many analysts, including Joel D. Barkan, a US scholar, concluded that Kibaki could very well lose the election to Odinga.[260] Because several polls showed a statistical dead heat between Kibaki and Odinga, it was clear that the election would also be determined by voter turnout. Whichever candidate drove more of his supporters to the polls would most likely win it.

On December 27, 2007, Kenya went to the polls. The parliamentary results were the first to trickle out. Throughout the country, long-serving political heavyweights and established politicians were shown the door by voters.[261] Over twenty of Kibaki's cabinet ministers, including Moody Awori, the Luhya vice president who ran on a PNU ticket in Western Province, an ODM stronghold, were felled in the election.[262] Simeon Nyachae, long the undisputed baron of Kisii politics, was floored, as was David Mwiraria, the Meru confidant of Kibaki who had been implicated in the Anglo Leasing scams. Other significant casualties were Nicholas Biwott, once the most powerful man under Moi. Significantly, Moi's three sons—Gideon, Jonathan, and Raymond—were rejected by voters.[263] Also defeated were Ministers Kivutha Kibwana, Mutahi Kagwe, Musikari Kombo, the leader of FORD-Kenya, and Raphael Tuju, the Luo foreign minister and a critic of Odinga.[264] Paul Muite, the leader of Safina, lost his Kabete seat as did Wangari Maathai, the Nobel Peace laureate. But Ngilu retained her seat in Kitui Central, only one of several people to defy the Musyoka wave in Ukambani.[265]

As shown in Table 11.2, ODM came away with the lion's share of seats with a total of 99, PNU 43, ODM-K 16, KANU 14, Safina 5, and the rest shared among fringe parties.[266] As Table 11.3 shows, the voting was highly ethnic. ODM won most of its seats in Nyanza, Western, and Rift Valley provinces, the ethnic strongholds of its leaders. PNU took most of the seats in Central and Eastern provinces, except in Ukambani where Musyoka's ODM-K almost swept the board. These ethnic voting patterns have been the bane of Kenyan democracy.

ODM will have a strong presence in Parliament and may even be able to dictate the legislative agenda if it sticks together. The first sign of this was the election on January 15, 2008, of Kenneth Marende, an ODM MP from Emuhaya in Western Province, to the powerful post of Speaker of Parlia-

Table 11.2   Parliamentary Seats by Party, 2007

Party	Number of Elected Seats	Percentage of Elected Seats	Number of Nominated Seats (out of 12)
ODM	99	47.14	6
PNU	43	20.48	3
ODM-K	16	7.62	2
KANU	14	6.67	1
Safina	5	2.38	
NARC-K	4	1.90	
FORD-P	3	1.43	
NARC	3	1.43	
New FORD–Kenya	2	0.95	
CCU	2	0.95	
PICK	2	0.95	
DP	2	0.95	
Sisi Kwa Sisi	2	0.95	

Source: Saturday Nation, January 5, 2008.
Note: The following parties each were elected to one seat (each obtained 0.48 percent of the elected seats): Mazingira, UDM, PPK, FORD-A, KENDA, KADDU, NLP, KADU-Asili, PDP, FORD-K.

Table 11.3   Summary of Parliamentary Seats by Province, 2007

Province	Party Seats	Total	Province	Party Seats	Total
Nairobi	ODM: 5	7	Nyanza	ODM: 25	32
	PNU: 2			PDP: 1	
Central	PNU: 18	29		FORD-P: 1	
	PICK: 1			NLP: 1	
	KANU: 2			DP: 1	
	Safina: 3			KANU: 2	
	Sisi Kwa Sisi: 2			NARC: 1	
	FORD-A: 1		Coast	ODM: 12	21
	PPK: 1			ODM-K: 1	
	FORD-P: 1			PNU: 3	
Eastern	CCU: 2	36		KADU-Asili: 1	
	PNU: 7			NARC-K: 2	
	ODM-K: 14			FORD-P: 1	
	KANU: 4			KANU: 1	
	NARC-K: 1		Rift	ODM: 32	48
	PICK: 1		Valley	PNU: 11	
	NARC-K: 2			ODM-K: 1	
	DP: 1			NARC-K: 1	
	Safina: 1			KENDA: 1	
	ODM: 2			UDM: 1	
	Mazingira: 1			KANU: 1	
Western	ODM: 18	24	North-	ODM: 5	10
	PNU: 2		eastern	KANU: 4	
	New FORD–			Safina: 1	
	Kenya: 2				
	FORD-K: 1				
	KADDU: 1				

Source: Saturday Nation, January 5, 2008.

ment.[267] He received 105 votes to 101 for Francis Xavier Ole Kaparo, his PNU-backed predecessor.[268] There will be more women MPs, with the Rift Valley providing 6 for a total of 15, up from the 10 who served in the Ninth Parliament.[269] As in the Ninth Parliament, which had 8 nominated female MPs, a few more women were among the 12 slots allotted for nominations. The 12 nominations were to be shared by ODM with 6, PNU with 3, and ODM-K, KANU, and Safina with 1 each.[270] The ECK later revoked Safina's one-seat allocation, which would have gone to Muite, forcing the party to file an unsuccessful challenge in court.[271]

While the voters rejected some obviously terrible characters, they also elected or reelected other objectionable figures. These include Kiraitu Murungi, the South Imenti who was linked to the Anglo Leasing scams; Fred Gumo, who has been linked to human rights violations; Sally Kosgey, who served as the secretary to the cabinet under the repressive Moi regime; William

Ruto, the ODM Pentagon member who was implicated in gross abuses under the Moi government; and John Michuki, the Kibaki internal security minister known for his excessive tactics against dissenters. Parliamentary results from three constituencies were annulled because of irregularities. The ECK planned to conduct a rerun of those elections. But in sum, the electorate appeared to have voted for change, not reform.

In the presidential sweepstakes Kibaki edged out Odinga in a disputed election marred by allegations of rigging and fraud.[272] According to Table 11.4, Kibaki garnered 4,584,721 votes to Odinga's 4,352,993, a margin of 47 to 44 percent.[273] Musyoka finished third with 879,903 votes, or 9 percent of the tally. Kibaki was immediately sworn in at State House and asked his opponents to accept the results of the elections.[274] But Odinga and ODM vigorously rejected the results, which they termed a sham, and accused the Electoral Commission of Kenya (ECK) of complicity in the fraud. Odinga drew a dark parallel between Kenya and Côte d'Ivoire and hoped that Kenya would not descend into anarchy.[275] The announcement of the results came after a two-day delay as the ECK tried to gather and compute the returns. That delay was responsible for riots in ODM-dominated areas in Nairobi and other opposition strongholds incensed that the government was bent on stealing the election.

Kenya on the Brink

Violence escalated upon the announcement of the results and the hurried swearing-in of Kibaki.[276] Domestic and international leaders called for calm and asked the parties to either accept the election results, seek a political solution, or process their grievances through the courts and the ECK.[277] The country sat on a knife's edge as the opposition ODM threatened to swear in Odinga as the "people's president" but backed down. Allegations of rigging were

Table 11.4   Presidential Election Results, 2007

Candidate	Number of Votes	Percentage of Vote
Mwai Kibaki (PNU)	4,584,721	47
Raila Odinga (ODM)	4,352,993	44
Kalonzo Musyoka (ODM-K)	879,903	9
Nazlin Umar (Workers Congress Party)	48,789	0
Joseph Ngacha Karani (Kenya Patriotic Trust)	8,607	0
Pius Muiru (Kenya People's Party)	3,530	0
Kenneth Matiba (Saba Saba Asili)	3,039	0
David Waweru Ng'ethe (Chama Cha Umma)	2,602	0
Nixon Jeremiah Kukubo (Republican Party of Kenya)	2,466	0

Source: Republic of Kenya, Office of Government Spokesperson, at http://www.communication .go.ke/elections/default.asp, accessed January 8, 2008.

given credence by an admission by Samuel Kivuitu, the ECK chair, that he did not know whether Kibaki indeed won the election, and that he had been co-erced by PNU and ODM-K officials to prematurely declare the results.[278] A domestic and international consensus, based on the findings of election moni-tors, suggested serious flaws with the election, especially with the tallying of the presidential ballots. Although Kibaki had been hurriedly sworn in, his le-gitimacy remained tenuous, if not altogether absent.

Odinga and ODM refused to concede the election, and instead asked for Kibaki to resign, charging repeatedly that he had stolen the election. Kibaki would not budge. Severe violence, some of it bordering on anarchy and geno-cidal attacks, erupted in opposition strongholds in the Nairobi slums, where Odinga drew strong support, and the Rift Valley, Mombasa, Kisumu, and parts of Western Province, among others. In one particularly chilling incident, scores of Kikuyus were torched to death in Eldoret, in the Rift Valley, in scenes rem-iniscent of the 1994 Rwanda genocide.[279] Vigilantes set up roadblocks in the Rift Valley to trap members of other groups for attack. Gruesome scenes of vi-olence were reported in many parts of the country as it slid into despair and chaos. Hundreds of Kenyans were killed by their compatriots and several hun-dred thousand internally displaced, as others fled to Uganda and Tanzania.[280]

As grotesque scenes only witnessed in Kenya during the height of the so-called ethnic clashes of the 1990s were beamed across the globe, the country threatened to melt down completely. What was once unthinkable became prob-able: Kenya as a failed state. The world was stunned and political leaders in Kenya and around the world called on Odinga and Kibaki to come together and work out a resolution to the contested election to end the violence.[281] I called on behalf of the KHRC for a review of the vote under Archbishop Desmond Tutu to establish the true results.[282] Tutu and Jendayi Frazer, the US assistant secretary of state for Africa, met with Odinga and Kibaki to find a solution. Ali Mazrui, the internationally renowned professor, suggested three options to end the crisis: a rerun of the presidential vote, the creation of a post of prime min-ister for Odinga, or an international review of the vote.[283] The crisis abated somewhat in mid-January after intense international efforts to mediate between Odinga and Kibaki, including a pivotal effort by President John Kufuor of Ghana, the chair of the African Union, the continental body of African states.[284] But Kufuor's effort failed to bring the two sides together and violence resumed, even as a second mediation effort by Kofi Annan, the former UN secretary-gen-eral, was being planned.[285] At ODM protest rallies, police and security increas-ingly resorted to deadly force and scores of demonstrators were shot dead.[286] In February, Ban Ki-Moon, the UN Secretary General, traveled to Kenya to meet with Kibaki and Odinga to support Annan's mediation efforts. Annan's diplo-macy appeared to bear fruit as Kibaki and Odinga spoke of a resolution and a possible power-sharing deal to end the violence. The parties also appeared to agree on a truth commission to address Kenya's deep historical wounds and grievances.

Analysts may debate forever about if, and whether, Odinga lost the election, or Kibaki won it. To be sure, the contest was close, and one of the two could have won it. But perhaps the most important reason for the close outcome—and the contested Kibaki victory—was that the opposition split the vote. Reminiscent of the opposition defeats of 1992 and 1997, the opposition was split by the Odinga-Musyoka wrangles. Musyoka's nearly one million votes would have assured Odinga an unassailable victory against Kibaki. The truth is that Musyoka threw the election to Kibaki even without formally joining PNU.

The Implications and Aftermath of the 2007 Elections

The elections served to emphasize several important lessons for Kenya, and perhaps beyond. First, they shattered the myth of Luo unelectability. Odinga came within a whisker of being elected president, a fact that has enormous implications for the country's psychological health. Although he lost in a deeply flawed tallying process, he established that Kenyans of Luo origin are electable to the highest office in the land. But since the Luo are not a small group, his near triumph also showed that only members of large ethnic groups are probably electable.

Second, as shown in Figure 11.1, the elections served to illustrate the deep ethnic pattern of voting in Kenya. The three major candidates drew fanatical support from their ethnic strongholds; the Kikuyu overwhelmingly voted for Kibaki while the Luo did the same for Odinga, and the Kamba for Musyoka. Kibaki drew most of his votes from the Mount Kenya region, the home of the Kikuyu, Meru, and Embu. Odinga carried most of the vote in Western Province because of his promise that he would appoint Mudavadi, a Luhya, to the vice presidency. He also took virtually all the Kalenjin votes because they felt that Kibaki had mistreated the region, and because Odinga had promised to appoint Ruto to the post of prime minister. The 2007 elections proved that ethnic affiliation is still the most important variable in the choice for leaders.

Third, the elections were a testament to the subordinated place of women in Kenyan society. Although the nominations saw the highest number of women contestants ever, just a minute percentage were victorious. The political system will have to be reformed drastically to change this gender imbalance. Only a new constitutional structure and a political parties law can address the problem.

Fourth, the elections were proof that it is extremely difficult to unseat an incumbent in Kenya. No sitting Kenyan president has ever been voted out. In 2002, Kenyans rejected Kenyatta, Moi's protégé, not Moi himself. It would have been a testament to the power of the electorate and a leap for Kenyan democracy had Kibaki been voted out. Besides, it was not easy to unseat an incumbent who has led economic growth. But it was a positive development for Kenyan democracy that the incumbent had to fight extremely hard to retain his seat. Reelection, unlike in years past, was not a formality.

Figure 11.1   Presidential Votes by Province, 2007

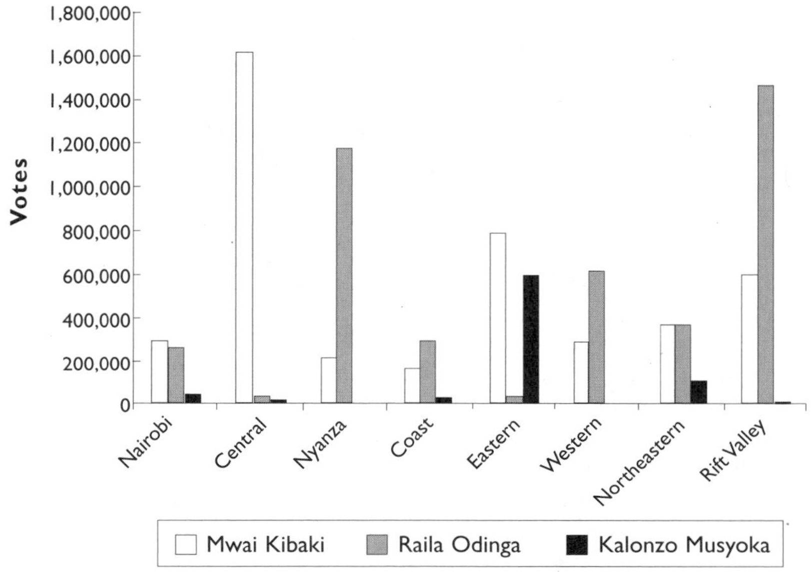

Source: Republic of Kenya, Office of Government Spokesperson, at http://www.communication
.gov.ke/elections/province.asp, accessed January 8, 2008.

Fifth, the chaos and near meltdown of Kenya in the aftermath of the Kibaki victory were an indication of the volatile nature of an ethnicized duel between Kikuyu and Luo candidates. Elites from these two communities have a historical rivalry that is manifested in their struggle to capture state power. It all started with the bitter conflict between Jomo Kenyatta and Oginga Odinga, a feud that was heightened by the killing of Tom Mboya. The Kibaki-Odinga conflict unwittingly represents that epic struggle.

Sixth, the credibility of the ECK and the country's electoral system, which had been restored by the 2002 elections, was shattered by its inability to run an efficient, fraud-free process. Rigging and fraudulent tallying of ballots were reported in several parts of the country—both PNU and ODM strongholds—and the ECK appeared to have been either complicit or unable to address the irregularities. Kivuitu, the chair of the ECK and long regarded as fair and evenhanded, came in for criticism. The lesson was that Kenya has to address its electoral system to make sure that such severe problems are minimized, and that elections are conducted freely and fairly. This will not be possible without an overhaul of the ECK and the entire electoral process.

Seventh, the elections gave the country a glimmer of hope that policies—not just tribes and their barons—could become important questions. The election campaigns forced candidates to address issues to distinguish themselves. Some, like Odinga, directly appealed to the poor and those left out of the economic boom created by Kibaki. Matters of the uneven development of regions and communities featured prominently. In short, the elections witnessed a slight departure from past elections that were fought largely on tribal lines.

Finally, the near collapse of Kenya following the election dispute signals the woeful fragility of the postcolonial state in Kenya, and how reversible the state is. What once looked like a stable state was threatened with catastrophe over a mere election in which the choice was not between saint and villain, but between two villains. If there was any doubt, the near collapse was confirmation that the project of nation building in Kenya will be long and arduous.

In early January 2007, Kibaki appointed his cabinet. He named Musyoka, the ODM-K leader, vice president.[287] In Musyoka, Kibaki sought to expand his base of support beyond the Kikuyu by securing the support of the Kamba, a closely related community, as a counterpoint against ODM's ethnic collage. However, the Kikuyu-Kamba coalition government was likely to be viewed as a Central-Eastern Kenya Bantu alliance against the Luo-Luhya-Kalenjin Western Kenya ODM group. These blocs divided Kenya in the middle, between the West and the Central-East.[288] But Kibaki's move also made sure that Musyoka's ODM-K would not join ODM in Parliament. Although the new cabinet was diverse, it still included some old names like Kiraitu Murungi, George Saitoti, Martha Karua, and Amos Kimunya. New faces included KANU's Uhuru Kenyatta, Naomi Shaban, Sam Ongeri, Asman Kamama, Samuel Lesuron Poghisio, and Yusuf Mohamed Haji.[289] It was not by any means a cabinet of reformers, although it drew from other parties beyond the PNU. ODM was not included. Many analysts, including from the Bush administration, thought that Kibaki's appointment of the cabinet was in bad faith in light of the reconciliation negotiations with Odinga and ODM.[290] It signaled his reluctance to accommodate any significant demands from Odinga.

Kibaki embarked on his second term in office a wounded man, lacking in legitimacy in several parts of the country, most notably in Luo Nyanza and large sections of Western and Rift Valley provinces.[291] It was an almost eerie replica of the red-blue state chasm in the United States after the victory by George W. Bush over Al Gore in the 2000 election. For the next five years, the country may have a divided government: the executive from one party and a Parliament dominated by ODM. This will be both an opportunity and a challenge for Kibaki to govern through inclusion, consultation, and dialogue. The arrogance of his first term, particularly among his senior aides, will not do. He must broaden his base of support in the country by making cross-ethnic appointments, carrying out development projects in marginalized areas and opposition strongholds, and tackling corruption. He must also finally deliver a new democratic constitution. A truth commission will be an indispensable vehicle to address historical injustices and heal the country. But this is all a tall order, and if history is any guide, there is little hope that Kibaki will rise to the challenge. Nor is there much hope that the opposition will be eager to carry out a true reformation of the state.

Notes

1. Makau Mutua, "After Bomas, Kibaki Must Take Lead," *Daily Nation*, April 7, 2004.

2. Lawrence Mute, "Delegates Have Greater Responsibility," *East African Standard*, February 20, 2004.

3. "Bomas Has Lost It; Let's Send Them Home," *Daily Nation*, March 9, 2004.

4. "Disharmony as Factions State Positions," *Daily Nation*, March 17, 2004.

5. "Draft Must Go to Parliament," *Daily Nation*, March 17, 2004.

6. "111 MPs Unite for Battle," *Daily Nation*, March 17, 2004.

7. "MPs Threaten to Move No-Confidence Motion," *Daily Nation*, March 22, 2004.

8. "Draft Must Go to Parliament," *Daily Nation*, March 17, 2004.

9. Frank Holmquist, "Kenya's Anti-Politics," *Current History: A Journal of Contemporary World Affairs* (May 2005): 212–213.

10. Makau Mutua, "A Spark of Hope in New Human Rights Watchdog," *Sunday Nation*, December 14, 2003.

11. L. Muthoni Wanyeki, "Civil Society Isn't Dead; It's Just Feeling Queasy," *East African Standard*, April 26, 2004.

12. Makau Mutua, "Setbacks in NARC Reform Agenda Stunning," *Daily Nation*, August 18, 2004.

13. Holmquist, "Kenya's Anti-Politics," 213.

14. Ibid., 214.

15. Willy Mutunga, *Constitution-Making from the Middle: Civil Society and Transition Politics in Kenya, 1992–1997* (Harare: MWENGO, 1999); Kiraitu Murungi, *In the Mud of Politics* (Nairobi: Acacia Stantex Publishers, 2000).

16. "Parliament Is Dissolved: Constitutional Process in Disarray," *East African Standard*, October 26, 2002.

17. Kenya Human Rights Commission, Law Society of Kenya, and International Commission of Jurists, *The Kenya We Want: Proposal for a Model Constitution* (1994).

18. Ufungamano Initiative, *Proposed Draft Constitution of the Republic of Kenya*, January 15, 2004; see also *Sunday Nation*, January 18, 2004.

19. "Raila Scoffs at Ufungamano Draft," *Daily Nation*, January 18, 2004.

20. "Ogendo: Ufungamano Just a Poor Replica of Bomas and a Ploy to Derail Bomas," *Daily Nation*, January 25, 2004.

21. "Raila Scoffs at Ufungamano Draft," *Daily Nation*, January 18, 2004.

22. "Musyimi Quits Constitution Review Talks," *Daily Nation*, February 8, 2004.

23. Federacion International d'abogadas (FIDA), Institute for Education in Democracy (IED), KHRC, and League of Kenya Women Voters (LKWV), *Model Proposals: Safeguarding the Gains for Women in the Draft Constitution,* January 25, 2004.

24. "Coalition Unveils Model Proposals," *Yawezekana: Bomas III*, January 28, 2004, 1.

25. Abdullahi Ahmednasir, "Dismiss the Ghai Team, and Bomas Too," *Daily Nation*, January 6, 2004.

26. Law Society of Kenya, *Draft Constitution of Kenya,* as edited by the Law Society of Kenya, March 16, 2004 (hereinafter *LSK Draft*).

27. Ibid., Article 77.

28. Ibid., Article 115.

29. Ibid., Article 55.

30. Makau Mutua and Willy Mutunga, "When Minds Meet: Points of Consensus," *Yawezekana: Bomas Agender*, May 22, 2003, 4.

31. Makau Mutua, "We Must Recognize Experts in Constitution Writing," *Sunday Nation*, December 7, 2003.

32. Mutunga, *Constitution-Making from the Middle,* 61.

33. Ibid.

34. United Nations High Commissioner for Human Rights, *Report of the Needs Assessment Mission to South Africa,* May 6–25, 1996. The mission included Jamal Benomar, Makau Mutua, Peter Rosenblum, and Alain Bockel.

35. Human Rights Watch, *World Report: Events of 2004* (New York: Human Rights Watch, 2005), 135.

36. "Leave Reforms to Experts, Says Prof. Maathai," *Daily Nation*, April 13, 1999.

37. Ibid.

38. "Sabotage Fears Stalk Delegates at Law Meeting," *Daily Nation*, May 24, 2003.

39. "What's Up with Bomas III?" *Saturday Nation*, November 15, 2003.

40. Ibid.

41. Ibid.

42. Republic of Kenya, *The Constitution of Kenya Review Act*, Section 28(1), (2), Chapter 3A, 2001 (hereinafter *Review Act*).

43. Ibid., Section 28(3).

44. Ibid., Section 28(4).

45. "Delay Review Bills: MPs Threaten Calls," *People Daily*, April 12, 2001.

46. Republic of Kenya, *The Constitution of Kenya* (1992) (1998), Article 47(2).

47. *Gachuru wa Karenge and Others v. Attorney General & Others* (High Court of Kenya, Nairobi, 2004).

48. *Timothy Njoya and Others v. Attorney General & Others*, No. 82 [2004] LLR 4788 (HCK) (hereinafter *Njoya* Case).

49. Peter Anyang' Nyong'o has written that the NCEC was planning a civilian coup through its national conventions. See Peter Anyang' Nyong'o, "Civil Society and the Transition Politics in Kenya: A Commentary," in Mutunga, *Constitution-Making from the Middle*, 282, 285.

50. "Bomas Draft Blocked," *Daily Nation*, March 23, 2004.

51. "At Last, Here's the Draft," *Daily Nation*, March 24, 2004.

52. "Njoya Goes to Court to Block Review Conference," *Daily Nation*, January 28, 2004.

53. *Njoya* Case, 27–28.

54. Ibid., 27.

55. *Review Act,* Section 27(7).

56. "How Radical Leaders Changed Their Stand on Wanjiku and Bomas Talks," *Daily Nation*, February 1, 2004.

57. "18 MPs Protest over Ringera," *Daily Nation*, January 15, 2004.

58. "Fresh Bid to Block Appointment of Anti-Graft Commission Chief," *Daily Nation*, February 4, 2004.

59. Yash Pal Ghai, "How Kenya's Future Is Being Betrayed," *Daily Nation*, May 7, 2004.

60. Ibid.

61. Yash Pal Ghai, "Consensus Not the Same Thing as Unanimity," *Daily Nation*, May 6, 2004, 9.

62. Ibid.

63. Yash Pal Ghai, "Provision on Executive Misunderstood," *Daily Nation*, May 25, 2004, 9.

64. "Little Hope for a New Constitution," *Sunday Nation*, May 9, 2004.

65. "Kibaki Falls Behind His Review Pledge Deadline," *Sunday Nation*, May 9, 2004.

66. "Kibaki Acts to Head Off July 3 Protests," *Daily Nation*, June 30, 2004.

67. "Calls for Mass Action Sounded as Groups Press for Kibaki's Promise," *Sunday Nation*, May 23, 2004.

68. "Moi Sacks Two Ministers," *Daily Nation*, March 1, 2001.

69. "Major Split over Talks on Bomas Draft Deal," *Daily Nation*, May 13, 2004; "Why 96 MPs Did Not Attend Mombasa Consensus Meeting," *Sunday Nation*, May 23, 2004; "Kibaki in Countdown to June 30 Deadline," *Daily Nation*, June 2, 2004.

70. "Broken Pledge: Big Day That Never Was," *Daily Nation*, June 30, 2004.

71. "Kibaki's Big Cabinet Shake-Up," *Daily Nation*, July 1, 2004.

72. Makau Mutua, "NARC Has Rejected the Path of Reforms," *East African Standard*, September 4, 2004.

73. "It Is Reckless Activism, Says FORD-Kenya," *Daily Nation*, June 30, 2004.

74. "Riots over Banned Rally," *Sunday Nation*, July 4, 2004.

75. "One Killed, 19 Injured as Riots Rock Kisumu," *Daily Nation*, July 8, 2004.

76. "Kibaki: Lobby Greedy for Power," *Daily Nation*, July 19, 2004.

77. "Reshuffling Cabinet Seems to Have Failed," *Daily Nation*, July 4, 2004; Kwamchetsi Makokha, "Cabinet Reshuffle Has Created More Tension," *East African Standard*, July 23, 2004.

78. "Ghai Resigns as CKRC Boss," *Daily Nation*, July 2, 2004.

79. Ibid.

80. "Ruto Now Boss of Constitution Team," *Daily Nation*, July 7, 2004.

81. "I'm Capable, Says Review Boss," *Daily Nation*, July 9, 2004.

82. *The Constitution of Kenya (Amendment) Bill*, No. 15 of 2004.

83. Ibid.

84. "Raila: Why We Backed Consensus Bill," *Daily Nation*, August 9, 2004; "'Review' Raila Reveals LDP 'Secret Weapon'—Why Party MPs Voted for Ruto's Consensus Bill," *Daily Nation*, August 9, 2004.

85. "Consensus Bill Opens Door to Review Talks," *Daily Nation*, August 6, 2004; Philip Ochieng', "Why They Didn't See the Catch," *Daily Nation*, August 10, 2004; "Now MPs Protest at How Review Law Was Passed," *Daily Nation*, August 10, 2004.

86. "Review Hitch as Kibaki Is Urged Not to Sign New Law," *Daily Nation*, August 12, 2004.

87. *The Constitution of Kenya Review (Amendment) Act*, 2004 (date of assent—December 29, 2004; date of commencement—April 22, 2005) (hereinafter *2004 Review Act*); "Kibaki Signs Review Law," *East African Standard*, January 25, 2005.

88. Section 27(1), *2004 Review Act*.

89. Ibid., Section 27(3).

90. Ibid., Section 28.

91. Ibid., Section 28A(4).

92. Ibid., Section 28B(4).

93. "Nyachae to Chair Review Team," *Daily Nation*, May 20, 2005.

94. Republic of Kenya, National Assembly, *Report of the Select Committee on the Review of the Constitution*, July 2005; "Govt Wins the Day but Four Ministers Rebel,"

East African Standard, July 22, 2005; "How MPs Voted on Review," *East African Standard*, July 23, 2005; "NARC Wins Crucial Vote to Change Bomas Draft," *Daily Nation*, July 22, 2005; Republic of Kenya, National Assembly, *The Draft Constitution of Kenya 2005,* July 2005; "Blow for State as Part of Kilifi Draft Rejected," *East African Standard*, July 23, 2005.

95. "Raila Asks Kenyans to Reject the MPs' New Draft at Referendum," *East African Standard*, July 25, 2005; "We Won't Surrender on Bomas Draft, Vows Raila," *Daily Nation*, July 25, 2005.

96. "AG Releases New Constitution Bill," *East African Standard*, August 23, 2005; "AG Releases Draft Constitution," *Daily Nation*, August 23, 2005; "Kenya's Proposed Constitution Unveiled," *Daily Nation*, August 24, 2005.

97. "D-Day for Historic Constitution Vote," *Daily Nation*, September 7, 2005.

98. *Review Act*, Section 28A(4).

99. "Court Throws Out Case Against Referendum," *Daily Nation*, November 15, 2005.

100. Republic of Kenya, *The Draft Constitution of Kenya* 2005 (Nairobi, 2005) [*Wako Draft*], Chapter 10.

101. See *Wako Draft*, Part II, Fundamental Rights and Freedoms.

102. *Wako Draft*, Article 195.

103. Ibid., Article 34(4).

104. Ibid., Articles 35, 38, 42.

105. Ibid., Article 76.

106. Ibid., Article 116.

107. Makau Mutua, "Treat Contentious Issues Differently," *Daily Nation*, August 25, 2005.

108. *LSK Draft*, Article 91.

109. The National Constitutional Conference, *The Draft Constitution of Kenya 2004* (Nairobi, 2004) (hereinafter *Bomas Draft*), Articles 198, 199.

110. *Wako Draft*, Article 195.

111. Constitution of Kenya Review Commission, *The Main Report of the Constitution of Kenya Review Commission,* September 18, 2002, 289–290 (hereinafter *Main Report*).

112. Ibid., 289.

113. Constitution of Kenya Review Commission, *The Draft Bill to Amend the Constitution,* 2002, Article 215 (hereinafter *Ghai Draft*).

114. *Bomas Draft,* Fourth Schedule, Fifth Schedule.

115. *Wako Draft,* Chapter 11, The Legislature.

116. Makau Mutua, "Treat Contentious Issues Differently."

117. *Wako Draft,* Fifth Schedule, Sixth Schedule.

118. *Main Report*, 243–244.

119. *Ghai Draft,* Articles 150–152.

120. *Bomas Draft,* Chapter 12.

121. *Wako Draft,* Articles 163, 164.

122. Ibid., Article 167(a).

123. Ibid., Article 158.

124. "A Powerful President to Appoint a Premier," *Daily Nation*, August 24, 2005.

125. Raila Odinga, "PM Reduced to Mere Errand Boy," *Daily Nation*, September 7, 2005.

126. "Kibaki Happy with Vote on Bomas Draft," *Daily Nation*, July 23, 2005; "Kiraitu's Relief," *Sunday Standard*, July 24, 2005; Simeon Nyachae, "Constitution: Take

Heed Not to Be Deceived by Politicians," *East African Standard*, July 26, 2005; "Powers of Executive Reduced," *Daily Nation*, August 25, 2005.

127. Odinga, "PM Reduced to Mere Errand Boy"; "Moi Says No to 'Divisive' Wako Draft," *Daily Nation*, August 29, 2005.

128. Ngugi, "The Search for a Perfect Constitution a Futile Effort."

129. *2004 Review Act*; "Kibaki Signs Review Law," *East African Standard*, January 25, 2005.

130. James Orengo, "Are We in the Throes of a Civilian Coup?" *Daily Nation*, September 8, 2005.

131. Joel Ngugi, "The Search for a Perfect Constitution a Futile Effort"; see also Pheroze Nowrojee, "This Is an Illegal Document," *Sunday Nation*, October 30, 2005; Wachira Maina, "Wako Did a Shoddy Job, Says Lawyer," *Daily Nation*, August 26, 2005; Wachira Maina, "AG's Cure for Bomas Excess Is Uncertainty," *Daily Nation*, August 27, 2005; Wachira Maina, "Transition Could Bring Uncertainty as Some Bodies Will Be Scrapped," *Daily Nation*, August 29, 2005.

132. "Outrage over Kisumu Chaos as Death Toll Rises to Four," *Daily Nation*, November 2, 2005; "Rethink Issue of Rallies," *Daily Nation*, November 1, 2005, Editorial; Macharia Gaitho, "Careless Talk a Recipe for Disaster," *Daily Nation*, October 31, 2005.

133. "Let's Save Our Country," *Daily Nation*, September 23, 2005; Makau Mutua, "To Save This Country, Don't Vote," *Daily Nation*, September 30, 2005; "Raila and Kalonzo Warn of Coup Peril," *Daily Nation*, October 28, 2005; "You Can't Trust Raila, Say 11 Yes Ministers," *East African Standard*, October 8, 2005.

134. "I Won't Stop the Referendum, Declares Kibaki," *Daily Nation*, September 19, 2005; "Awori: No Vote to Go On as Planned," *Sunday Nation*, September 18, 2005.

135. "Raila: I Am Ashamed of Serving in This Cabinet," *Sunday Standard*, November 6, 2005.

136. "Resign Now, Ministers Tell Raila," *East African Standard*, November 7, 2005.

137. "MPs Plea Motion to Call Off Vote," *East African Standard*, October 8, 2005.

138. Joel Ngugi, "The Search for a Perfect Constitution a Futile Effort"; Makau Mutua, "Treat Contentious Issues Differently."

139. Makau Mutua, "To Save This Country, Don't Vote."

140. "Let's Save Our Country."

141. "Case by LDP and KANU Is Postponed to October 28," *Daily Nation*, October 8, 2005; "Court Throws Out Case Against Referendum," *Daily Nation*, November 15, 2005.

142. "Why Judges Back the Vote," *Daily Nation*, November 16, 2005.

143. "Court Ruling a Landmark," *Daily Nation*, November 16, 2005, Editorial.

144. Billow Kerrow, "Forgotten Province Now Stirs Wide Awake," *East African Standard*, November 2, 2005.

145. Makau Mutua, "Which Way Forward After the Referendum?" *Daily Nation*, October 28, 2005.

146. "Kibaki's Televised Speech Causes a Stir," *East African Standard*, November 21, 2005; "Leaders Defy Ban on Campaign," *Daily Nation*, November 21, 2005.

147. The Orange side received 3,558,883 to Banana's 2,579,139 votes. "Referendum Results: How the Provinces Voted," *Daily Nation*, November 24, 2005; "Resounding No," *East African Standard*, November 23, 2005; "It's an Orange Win," *Daily Nation*, November 22, 2005.

148. "Resounding No," *East African Standard*, November 23, 2005.

149. Ibid.

150. "Orange Leads—Final Tally," *East African Standard*, November 23, 2005.

151. Ibid.

152. "Kibaki Accepts Referendum Outcome," *East African Standard*, November 23, 2005.

153. "Kibaki Sacks Entire Cabinet," *East African Standard*, November 24, 2005.

154. "Why President Kibaki Had It Coming," *Daily Nation*, November 23, 2005; "Ghai Explains What Went Wrong with the Constitution Review Process," *East African Standard*, December 29, 2005.

155. "Biased Men Caused Wako Draft Defeat," *Daily Nation*, May 8, 2006.

156. "Now Kibaki Calls in Moi for Crisis Talks," *Daily Nation*, November 29, 2005; "Why Kibaki Met Moi," *East African Standard*, November 29, 2005.

157. Raila Odinga, "President Kibaki Learnt Little from Poll," *Daily Nation*, December 6, 2005; Raila Odinga, "Kibaki Should Think Outside Circle of Rich Friends," *East African Standard*, December 6, 2005.

158. "Kibaki Drops Rebels in New Cabinet," *Daily Nation*, December 8, 2005.

159. "Kibaki Names New Cabinet," *East African Standard*, December 7, 2005.

160. Makau Mutua, "Cabinet Is One of Greatest Blunders in Kenya's History," *Sunday Standard*, December 11, 2005.

161. Macharia Gaitho, "Kibaki Rule Headed for Rough Time," *Daily Nation*, December 9, 2005; "Things Fall Apart," *East African Standard*, December 9, 2005.

162. "KANU Rocked by Split over ODM," *Sunday Standard*, May 28, 2006; "Now KANU Pulls Out of ODM," *Daily Nation*, May 24, 2006; "Moi: KANU Does Not Need Partner to Win," *East African Standard*, May 18, 2006; "Raila Cautions Uhuru Against Ditching Orange," *East African Standard*, May 16, 2006: "Uhuru Ditches Orange Team," *East African Standard*, May 15, 2006; "Let's Seek Moi's Backing, Kalonzo Urges ODM," *Daily Nation*, May 19, 2006; "Rift Widens in ODM as Moi Enters Debate," *Daily Nation*, May 18, 2006; "ODM Calls Crisis Talks over Uhuru," *Daily Nation*, May 17, 2006; "Leaders Break Ranks with Uhuru over ODM," *Daily Nation*, May 16, 2006; "LDP Candidate to Be Known Next Year, Says Raila," *East African Standard*, April 17, 2006; "Orange Will Nominate Me, Says Kalonzo," *East African Standard*, April 3, 2006; Makau Mutua, "ODM Is Not the Answer," *Sunday Standard*, December 18, 2005; "Why It Is Too Early to Write Off the Orange," *East African Standard*, December 20, 2005.

163. "Exclusive: The Anglo Leasing Truth," *Sunday Nation*, January 22, 2006.

164. "Saitoti and Kiraitu Resign," *Daily Nation*, February 14, 2006.

165. "Sh10bn Review Loss for Taxpayers," *Sunday Nation*, January 8, 2006.

166. Republic of Kenya, *Kenya Gazette,* Special Issue, February 24, 2006.

167. Apart from Kiplagat, the other members of the Committee of Eminent Persons were retired chief justice Abdul Majid Cockar; Peter Wambura, a former civil servant; Ole Moi Yoi, chairman of the Kenyatta University Council; Ng'ethe Njuguna; Karuti Kanyinga; Kaendi Munguti; Wanza Kioko; Kassim Farrah; Mwambi Mwasaru; Nemwel Nyamwaka Bosire; Jacinta Muteshi; Patricia Kameri Mbote; Richard Barasa; and Juma Mwachihi. "Kibaki Names New Review Team," *Saturday Nation*, February 25, 2006.

168. "Consult ODM on Law Review, Kibaki Told," *Sunday Standard*, February 26, 2006; "Kibaki Team on Laws Criticized," *Daily Nation*, February 27, 2006; "New Review Panel Must Be Disbanded," *Daily Nation*, March 1, 2006.

169. "Raila: Dialogue the Key on Constitution," *Sunday Nation*, April 30, 2006.

170. "Kiplagat Team on Wrong Path," *Sunday Nation*, March 19, 2006, Editorial.

171. "Review Team Winds Up Findings," *Daily Nation*, May 3, 2006; "Review Team to Compile Report," *East African Standard*, May 4, 2006.

172. "Committee Submits Report on Constitution Review to Kibaki," *East African Standard*, May 31, 2006.

173. "Constitution: Kibaki's Pledge on the Way Forward," *Daily Nation*, May 31, 2006.

174. Ibid.

175. "It Was a Job Well Done, Says Kibaki," *Daily Nation*, June 7, 2006.

176. "Reactions to Kiplagat Report Baffling," *Daily Nation*, June 9, 2006, Editorial; "LSK: Debate on Kiplagat Report Illegal," *East African Standard*, June 9, 2006.

177. "ODM Vows to Reject Kiplagat Review Plan," *Daily Nation*, July 8, 2006.

178. Republic of Kenya, *Report of the Committee of Eminent Persons,* May 30, 2006.

179. "Review: Let's Get On with It," *Daily Nation*, June 1, 2006, Editorial.

180. "Constitution: Kiplagat Team Urges Kibaki to Take the Lead," *East African Standard*, June 7, 2006.

181. Ibid.

182. Republic of Kenya, *Report of the Committee of Eminent Persons*, Paragraph 438.

183. "Kiplagat Team Did Not Have to Repeat the Obvious Tune," *East African Standard*, June 22, 2006.

184. Okech Kendo, "We Are Back Where Kenya Stumbled on Reform Request," *East African Standard*, May 4, 2006.

185. "MPs Push for New Reforms Before Elections," *Daily Nation*, August 10, 2006; "Law Review Before Polls a Must, Says House Team," *East African Standard*, August 10, 2006; "Raila Calls for Minimum Law Reforms Before Polls," *Daily Nation*, August 7, 2006.

186. Ibid.

187. "Piecemeal Reforms a Plot to Oppress People, Says Lobby," *East African Standard*, August 17, 2006; Joseph Mutua, "Piecemeal Reforms Won't Do," *Daily Nation*, August 18, 2006.

188. Kenya Human Rights Commission, "Kenya Human Rights Commission Against Minimum Constitutional Reforms," Press Release, August 15, 2006, available at http://www.khrc.or.ke/news, accessed August 18, 2006 (hereinafter "KHRC Against Minimum Reforms"). See also "Piecemeal Reforms Won't Do, Says Lobby," *East African Standard*, August 17, 2006.

189. "KHRC Against Minimum Reforms."

190. Ibid.

191. Yash Ghai, *An Alternative Draft of a New Constitution of the Republic of Kenya: Building on Bomas,* 2006.

192. Kibaara Wambugu, "ODM Is Like the Titanic, Don't Board it," *East African Standard*, August 18, 2006.

193. "Kibaki Rules Out Reforms Before 2007 Elections," *Daily Nation*, August 18, 2006.

194. "ODM Not Honest on Clamour for Reforms," Statement of the Kenya Episcopal Conference, *East African Standard*, August 18, 2007.

195. Ibid.

196. Makau Mutua, "Used and Dumped: That's Civil Society," *Sunday Nation*, April 15, 2007.

197. "Kibaki Names Team to Revive Talks," *Daily Nation*, March 20, 2007.

198. "Reforms: MPs Agree on Crucial Talks," *Daily Nation*, April 11, 2007.

199. "Lobby Groups Set Conditions," *Daily Nation*, April 10, 2007.

200. "Civil Societies Reject Call to Join Reform Talks," *East African Standard*, May 11, 2007; "Civil Society Launches Parallel Constitutional Review," *East African Standard*, April 25, 2007.

201. Kenya National Assembly, Departmental Committee on Administration of Justice and Legal Affairs, *Report on the Way Forward on the Constitutional Review Process,* December 2006.

202. Ibid.

203. "New Hopes Ignited in Push for New Talks," *East African Standard*, June 13, 2007.

204. "Review Team Adopts Bill to Cut President's Power," *East African Standard*, May 16, 2007.

205. "Ninth Parliament Has Failed in Law Reform," *East African Standard*, September 6, 2007; "House Autonomy Bill Adopted," *East African Standard*, May 28, 2007.

206. "Fast Track Reforms, Kibaki Orders," *Daily Nation*, September 12, 2007; Amina Abdallah, "Minimum Reforms: The Buck Stops with President Kibaki," *Daily Nation*, September 10, 2007.

207. "NARC-Kenya Unveils Its Vision," *Saturday Nation*, March 25, 2006.

208. "Spotlight on Kibaki over NARC-Kenya Campaigns," *Daily Nation*, July 24, 2006.

209. "FORD-Kenya Quits NARC over By-Elections Row," *Daily Nation*, July 27, 2006.

210. "Moi Defends Uhuru Stand Against ODM," *Daily Nation*, June 13, 2007; "Orange Group's Merger Deal for 2007 Elections," *Daily Nation*, August 17, 2006; "Report: Kenya Has 54 Political Parties," *East African Standard*, May 1, 2006.

211. "ODM Finally Splits," *Daily Nation*, August 15, 2007.

212. "It's Make or Break for Parties," *East African Standard*, May 20, 2007.

213. Makau Mutua, "How to Build the Kenyan Nation," *Sunday Nation*, July 15, 2007.

214. Makau Mutua, "Raila Is His Own Worst Enemy," *Sunday Nation*, July 8, 2007; Makau Mutua, "Kalonzo a Reformer? Give Me a Break!" *Sunday Nation*, August 19, 2007.

215. "ODM Finally Splits," *Daily Nation*, August 15, 2007.

216. Ibid.

217. "Final Fallout," *East African Standard*, August 15, 2007.

218. "Now Ngilu Declares Support for Raila," *Daily Nation*, October 6, 2007.

219. "Kibaki Kicks Ngilu Out of the Cabinet," *Sunday Nation*, October 7, 2007.

220. "What Moi-Kibaki Alliance Means," *East African Standard*, August 29, 2007; Makau Mutua, "Ethnicity the Bane of Kenyan Politics," *Sunday Nation*, September 23, 2007.

221. Makau Mutua, "Raila and Kalonzo Had No Opponents, Only Political Escorts," *Sunday Nation*, September 2, 2007.

222. Ibid.

223. "ODM-K Settles for Julia for VP," *East African Standard*, September 19, 2007.

224. "Kibaki to Seek Second Term Under PNU," *Daily Nation*, September 17, 2007.

225. "Kibaki's Pledge," *Daily Nation*, October 1, 2007.

226. "Aftershocks Follow Orange," *East African Standard*, October 8, 2007.

227. "I Have No Regrets, Ngilu Says as She Leaves Office," *Daily Nation*, October 9, 2007.

228. Kroll and Associates, *Project KTM: Consolidated Report* (*Kroll Report*), London, April 27, 2007.

229. Makau Mutua, "Cleansing the Country of Past Evils," *Sunday Nation*, September 30, 2007.

230. Michael Chege, *Political Parties in East Africa: Diversity in Political Party Systems* (Nairobi: International Institute for Democracy and Electoral Assistance [IDEA], 2007).

231. National Elections Monitoring Unit (NEMU), *The Multi-Party General Elections in Kenya, 29 December 1992* (Nairobi: General Printer, 1993), 8.

232. Ibid.

233. Ibid.

234. Ibid., 50.

235. Ibid., 51.

236. "Parties Suffer Credibility Crisis," *Daily Nation*, November 22, 2007.

237. Chege, *Political Parties in East Africa*.

238. "Direct Nominations Criticized," *Daily Nation*, November 29, 2007.

239. "Scores Defect as More MPs Lose," *Daily Nation*, November 19, 2007.

240. "Protests as Winners Are Replaced," *East African Standard*, November 19, 2007.

241. "Winds of Change as Voters Reject Former MPs," *East African Standard*, November 19, 2007.

242. Makau Mutua, "Raila Is His Own Worst Enemy," *Sunday Nation*, July 8, 2007.

243. "Protests as Winners Are Replaced," *East African Standard,* November 19, 2007.

244. Ibid.

245. The Gender and Governance Development Programme in Kenya website at www.genderandgovernance.org/news/women_in_circles.html, accessed December 30, 2007.

246. "2,600 Candidates in Battle for MPs' Seats," *Daily Nation,* November 29, 2007.

247. Makau Mutua, "Democracy or Theater of the Absurd," *Sunday Nation*, December 9, 2007.

248. Mutuma Mathiu, "Primaries Were Nothing Short of Blatant Rigging," *Sunday Nation*, November 25, 2007.

249. Makau Mutua, "Raila and Kalonzo Had No Opponents, Only Political Escorts," *Sunday Nation*, September 2, 2007.

250. Makau Mutua, "Opinion Polls and Democratic Practice," *Sunday Nation*, December 2, 2007.

251. Makau Mutua, "Kalonzo 'Strategic' Election Options," *Sunday Nation*, October 7, 2007.

252. Makau Mutua, "Agenda for the Next Government," *Sunday Nation*, December 23, 2007.

253. Makau Mutua, "Why Majimbo Spells Doom for Kenya," *Sunday Nation*, October 28, 2007.

254. "MOU Likely to Divide Muslims, Claims Group," *Daily Nation*, December 12, 2007.

255. "Tribalism Helps Shape Kenya's Election," *Boston Globe*, December 12, 2007.

256. "With Eight Days to Go, Race Too Close to Call," *Daily Nation*, December 19, 2007.

257. Ibid.

258. "Last Poll, Last Push," *East African Standard*, December 19, 2007.

259. "US Firm Puts Kibaki Ahead," *Daily Nation*, December 18, 2007.

260. Joel D. Barkan, "Too Close to Call: Why Kibaki Might Lose the 2007 Kenyan Election," Center for Strategic and International Studies (CSIS) Africa Policy Forum, December 4, 2007, posted at http://forums.csis.org/africa/?p=73, accessed January 7, 2008.

261. "Giants Fall by Way Side After ODM Wave," *Saturday Nation*, December 29, 2007.

262. "Newcomers Trounce Top Politicians," *Saturday Nation*, December 29, 2007.

263. "Moi's Sons Suffer Major Defeat," *East African Standard,* December 29, 2007.

264. "Newcomers Trounce Top Politicians, *Saturday Nation*, December 29, 2007.

265. "Mwau, Ngilu Upstage Kalonzo at His Game," *East African Standard*, December 29, 2007.

266. "How Parties Stand in the 10th Parliament," *Saturday Nation,* January 5, 2008.

267. "Marende Wins on Day of High Drama," *East African Standard*, January 16, 2008.

268. "ODM's Marende Is Speaker," *Daily Nation,* January 15, 2008.

269. Ibid., "Elections Propel More Women to the Tenth Parliament," *Saturday Nation*, December 29, 2007.

270. "The Sharing of 12 Nominee Seats in House," *Saturday Nation*, January 8, 2007.

271. "Safina's Attempt to Block the Nomination of 12 MPs Fails," *Daily Nation*, January 18, 2008; "Safina to Block Nomination of MPs in Court," *Daily Nation*, January 15, 2008.

272. "Kibaki Sworn in, ODM to Name Parallel Govt," *Sunday Nation*, December 30, 2007.

273. "Kibaki Declared Winner, Sworn In," *Sunday Standard*, December 30, 2007.

274. "Kibaki Asks His Opponents to Accept Results," *Daily Nation*, December 31, 2007.

275. "Raila Also Declared 'President,'" *Daily Nation*, December 31, 2007.

276. "Violence Erupts After Kibaki Is Sworn In," *Daily Nation*, December 31, 2007.

277. "US and Britain Call for Acceptance of Results," *Daily Nation*, December 31, 2007.

278. "I Acted Under Pressure, Says Kivuitu," *East African Standard*, January 2, 2008.

279. "Mob Sets Church on Fire, Killing Dozens," *New York Times*, January 2, 2008.

280. "Official Death Toll from Chaos Put at 486," *Daily Nation*, January 8, 2008; "Opposition Seeks New Vote as Violence Ebbs in Kenya," *New York Times*, January 5, 2008.

281. "Let Tutu Lead Vote Recount," *East African Standard*, January 5, 2008.

282. Ibid.

283. "Mazrui's Proposal over Poll Dispute," *East African Standard*, January 7, 2008.

284. "Hope as Kufuor Discusses Crisis with Kibaki and Odinga," *Daily Nation*, January 10, 2008; "Kibaki Holds Talks with Visiting Leader," *East African Standard*, January 10, 2008; "End of Turmoil in Sight as AU Boss Jets In," *Daily Nation*, January 8, 2008.

285. "Eight More Killed in Chaos," *Daily Nation*, January 18, 2008.

286. "Police Shoot Dead More Protesters in Day Two of Demos," *East African Standard*, January 18, 2008.

287. "Kalonzo Is New VP," *Daily Nation*, January 9, 2008.

288. Joel D. Barkan, "Kenya in Crisis," Center for Strategic and International Studies (CSIS), January 8, 2008, http://www.csis.org/media/csis/pubs/080108_kenya_crisis.pdf, accessed January 10, 2008.

289. "Kalonzo VP in Kibaki's New Cabinet," *East African Standard*, January 9, 2008.

290. "Bush Pushes for Peace Talks," *Daily Nation,* January 10, 2008; "Kibaki's Move Illegal, Declares Orange Group," *Daily Nation*, January 9, 2008.

291. Macharia Gaitho, "President Embarks on Second Term with Tarnished Mandate," *Daily Nation*, December 31, 2007.

12

What Must Be Done

CONSTITUTIONS HAVE BEEN a sham for much of the history of the African postcolonial state. Taken seriously, a constitution is the aggregate of all power in the state, nothing more and nothing less. Further, it is an allocation of that power—who can use it, when it can be used, and how it can be used. But it is also a limitation on that power—the freedoms and liberties that individuals, groups, and institutions can exercise without its hindrances. Yet, in the African context, as indeed in many others, there has often been a wide gulf between the power asserted by the text of the constitution and the authority it actually exerts.[1] To be effective, therefore, constitutions must regulate the exercise of state power and serve as the real and binding source of all state authority. But as argued by H. W. O. Okoth-Ogendo, this has rarely been the case in postcolonial Africa.[2] He refers to "constitutions without constitutionalism," a signature of the African state in which the constitution is a mere piece of paper, nothing more than a rhetorical tool. That has been true in the case of Kenya where successive postcolonial governments have clothed the constitution with legal formalism, only to use it to subvert the democratic regulation of state power.

Constitutional Order

The key question for Africa in this century is how to transform the constitution—as the basic instrument of state governance—from rhetoric to reality, from formalism to substance. The African state is doomed if this transformation is not undertaken or, for whatever reason, is aborted. History seems to demonstrate a clear relationship between the prosperity of states and the foresight and vision of their political elites. States have generally performed poorly where political elites have failed to forge and impose a national consensus on themselves and the nation at large. As a first step, it is imperative that elites internalize the fact that the nation is greater than any single individual or faction of its membership. That is why the design of the political state

263

in the constitution must emphasize institutions over individual offices. The basic idea of state re-creation ought to revolve around how norms and institutions of the state serve to catapult national—as opposed to personal—ambitions and interests to the fore. Unless a new constitutional order is implanted, the reformation of the state will remain a pipe dream. This is the most urgent task facing Kenya and other African states today.

But the inculcation of constitutionalism as the consciousness of the political class remains an elusive question. Intellectually, Kenyan elites seem to have arrived at a consensus that political democracy must guide government. However, they lack the cultural tools and the requisite normative political behavior to translate this intellectual consensus into the practice of politics. The place to start that process of translation is the introduction of a new democratic constitution that has wide acceptance and legitimacy among the elites and the general population. Although it is inevitable that the final constitution will be a creature of political compromise, it must arise out of basic, nonnegotiable principles that have the potential to re-create the state. In countrywide hearings, the Constitution of Kenya Review Commission (CKRC) established the gist of a democratic constitution for Kenya. It is those basic principles that should be used to negotiate a new constitution. Most of them were captured in the 2004 Draft Constitution and the Wako Draft. What needs to happen is a sober discussion on the contentious issues on which a new constitution has bogged down. In this exercise, key players should abandon political inflexibility, religious dogmatism and intolerance, and narrow personal and ethnic pursuits.

What ought to be the basic ingredients of a democratic constitution for Kenya? The most important value is the democratization of the state. It was dictatorship by a callous executive that spawned mass atrocities, corruption, economic deprivation, and the denial of basic rights across the board. Jomo Kenyatta was responsible for preserving the colonial state under the guise of an independent nation. His refusal to unshackle Kenyans by dismantling the colonial state deprived the young country of an opportunity to grow a culture of democracy. Instead, he erected state apparatuses that contracted political space and encouraged in the citizenry a culture of sycophancy, anti-intellectualism, and distaste for dissent. President Daniel arap Moi took the crude use of power to new highs. By the late 1970s, the country's life revolved around the person of the head of state, and nothing could be accomplished without his blessing or acquiescence. Under Moi, Kenyans viewed the success of every project as dependent on His Excellency.[3] The curse for Kenya, as elsewhere in Africa, was the rise of presidentialism without countervailing restraints on executive power.[4]

The challenge for Kenya, as indeed for other African countries, is to design the executive to make it virtually impossible for the head of state to overrun checks and balances. Kenyatta was able to quickly amass power at the expense of other institutions not only because the compromise in London lacked the allegiance of the elite, but also due to the novelty of independence and statecraft to the African elite and citizenry. The euphoria of independence and the awe in which Kenyatta, a dynamic symbol of African nationalism, was held made it easy for him to abuse his position and stampede dissenters. Within a few years, Kenyatta had custom-made the presidency and the state into a monolithic monster with himself at the helm. He snuffed out independent political spaces within the press, the legislature, civil society, and judiciary. By his death in 1978, he was an imperial president who ruled like a monarch. Kenyans knew that Kenyatta was a life president and that only death could vacate him from office. That is the omnipotent office that Moi took over. In spite of the reintroduction of open multipartyism in 1991, Moi left office in 2002 without fully internalizing the proper limits of executive power. Mwai Kibaki, his successor, was doubtless a more benign leader, but the enormous constitutional powers he enjoyed continued the tradition of autocracy in the executive. Under his watch, corruption continued unabated. This Westminster model was corrupted everywhere in Africa soon after independence.[5]

A new constitutional order must reform power at the top and democratize the institutions and structures of governance at every level of the state. That is why Kenyans ought to dispassionately debate the competing arguments for the reform of the executive. At Bomas, debate focused on whether Kenya ought to adopt a parliamentary or presidential system. In the end, the 2004 Draft Constitution opted for a parliamentary system in which most of the executive authority would vest in the prime minister.[6] The president, unlike the prime minister, would be directly elected, but real power would vest in the latter. The prime minister would be appointed by the president from the largest party, or coalition of parties, in the National Assembly.[7] That was one of the many devices meant to defang the executive presidency. Yash Ghai favored the parliamentary system as the antidote to African presidentialism because it would force political actors to seek coalitions across ethnic lines, reduce cronyism, and increase the accountability of the executive to Parliament.[8] In theory, Ghai's argument sounds reasonable, but it does not explain why the system failed so miserably soon after independence. Ironically, the parliamentary system may fail again in Kenya, given the country's charged ethnic arithmetic— the very sore that Ghai sought to cure.

The winner-take-all presidential system, in which parties play a zero-sum game for power, is a cause of state failure in fractious multiethnic societies, as was the case in Angola in 1994 or Congo (Brazzaville) in 1992.[9] In both cases, the losing candidate and party adopted putschist military campaigns against the winner. The argument was that the executive presidency was the only prize worth having, and once Jonas Savimbi, in the case of Angola, and Sassou Nguesso, in the case of Congo, lost the election, they inevitably resumed or resorted to armed struggle.[10] Although it is true that the winner-take-all system may discourage a national concord, it is an insufficient argument to explain the Angolan and Congolese cases. Nothing except the presidency would have mollified Savimbi, a freedom-fighter-turned-terrorist who would not be a part of the state unless he was at the head. Nguesso, a dictator who was ousted by mass protests, wanted nothing but his return to power. Besides, what type of a democrat accepts the results of an election only if he triumphs? Even if such leaders are elected by Parliament in a power-sharing arrangement, they are likely to seek absolute power over institutions of accountability. Elites have to be committed to nurturing a democracy, particularly at the outset, or following a prolonged national trauma, such as a civil war.

Kenya has almost been gutted by ethnic conflict, as long-simmering ethnic tensions, coupled with clumsy or brutal responses by the state, lit a powder keg that nearly incinerated a whole nation. The recent histories of Liberia, Somalia, Congo (Brazzaville), Rwanda, Uganda, Ethiopia, Togo, Côte d'Ivoire, Ghana, and Democratic Republic of Congo should serve as a warning to all postcolonial African states. Not a single state is immune. The fear—which is not unfounded—of creating a parliamentary system with an executive prime minister but a directly elected president is that there is real potential for conflict between the two offices. Apart from overrunning the parliamentary system, several African states have had a miserable time with it. In Nigeria, Zimbabwe, the Democratic Republic of Congo, and Uganda, the offices of the prime minister and the president came into conflict, with disastrous consequences for most of them. In a similar scenario in Kenya, the occupants of the two offices could engage in a power struggle for political supremacy and control of key institutions and decisionmaking. Two competing centers of power could emerge and send the body politic into convulsions.

The question for constitutional engineers was not just whether delegates at Bomas—or Kenyans at large—sought a parliamentary system. Constitutional thinkers had to ask themselves whether such a system was practicable. For what would be the purpose of creating a hydra in the executive when the office can be democratized through other devices? The fear was that the very creation of the two offices would seduce them into a costly, fatal duel.[11] Given the risk, the focus of constitution makers should have been the principle of democratization, not a fixation on the office of a prime minister. The office was proposed as a protest against the Moi presidency. The question ought to have been what constitutional arrangements, excluding the parliamentary system, could limit and tame executive power?

The premiership bogged down because it was personalized. Raila Odinga of the Liberal Democratic Party (LDP) was promised the post once the National Rainbow Coalition (NARC) he had joined assumed power and a new constitution was written.[12] But when Kibaki and his National Alliance Party of Kenya (NAK) used NARC to gain power and then reneged on the promise, Odinga went ballistic and worked tirelessly to frustrate the government. On several occasions, both sides softened their positions, with NAK proposing a less powerful premier, more like a chief minister. Odinga, a cunning politician, would indicate a willingness to talk but then quickly resume his filibuster of the Kibaki regime. In the end, the failure to agree on the post doomed the National Constitutional Conference at Bomas, when the state walked out as the conference adopted the parliamentary model advocated by Odinga. For its part, NAK was determined to keep key executive powers in the hands of President Kibaki. But key players at Bomas made several costly mistakes. First, a constitution, which is the charter of the nation, must never be written to benefit or punish a single individual. It is a document for the ages and through which the state binds itself to the people, not an individual. But both NAK and LDP held the process hostage because they saw Bomas as a venue to protect individual and factional ambitions, not national interests. Second, the constitution is not a contract between two individuals but a solemn pact between the people and the state. A national charter written for such perverted purposes is intellectually dishonest, ideologically faulty, and inherently unstable and, as such, cannot serve as the foundation of a democratic state.

On balance, it is apparent that the most viable and least problematic executive for Kenya should be presidential, but with powerful limitations on that power. Strong presidentialism has failed in Kenya not because of an inherent systemic defect, but due to the lack of enforceable checks on the unbridled power of the executive. Some devices to arrest despotism are obvious. The first is term limits, which limit presidents to two five-year terms. It must go without saying that real separation of powers—with an autonomous legislature and a substantively independent judiciary—must form the basis of the new constitution. The election of the president, a key feature of accountability, should be directly vested in the people. Some critics have attacked this model because it makes it difficult to remove the president, may result in the winner being elected on a minority vote, and could encourage a president elected with a wide mandate to seek the domination of Parliament.[13] But these potential problems, whose occurrence is more likely in postcolonial Africa because of its culture of autocracy, can be cured through a variety of devices. The president should not be a member of Parliament; nor should she have the power to dissolve it or control its calendar and business. This arrangement should make it possible for Parliament to pass a vote of no confidence on an incumbent president. That is the case in South Africa, although the president is elected by the legislature, not directly by the people.[14] An election of the president by a minority can be avoided with the requirement that she be elected by an absolute majority of the vote.

The independence of the legislature from the executive is essential in a presidential system. In addition to the parliamentary vote of no confidence, the legislature must control its own calendar. The power to prorogue, dismiss, or call Parliament into session must be provided for in the constitution and exercised by Parliament, not vested in the president. That allows the Parliament to free itself from presidential domination so that it can discharge its legislative and oversight duties without coercion or fear. In the constitution, the vice president ought to be protected from the caprice of the president and allocated constitutional duties, although it should be clear that the vice president is the president's deputy. The cabinet, whose maximum size should be fixed in the constitution to prevent its use by the president to reward cronies and bloat government, should be responsible to the Parliament, which must approve appointments but could also vote to dismiss a minister on specified grounds. The constitution should provide that executive power vests generally in the president and collectively with the cabinet in certain matters. That would force the president to consult the cabinet to make sure that it is not a mere rubber stamp. Finally, legislative power ought to be vested in the Parliament to insulate it from executive manipulation, although the president, who assents to bills, must also be able to veto them. In addition to constitutional commissions, which are semi-autonomous institutions within the state, the independence of the legislature should be a key building block for democracy.[15]

The major drawback in giving such absolute autonomy to Parliament in Kenya is the immaturity and vacuousness of political parties, the myopia of its leadership and the political class, and the corrupt ranks from which its MPs would be drawn. Although parliamentarians are popularly elected—many run on ethnic political parties—the majority are either openly corrupt or have questionable ethics. Although that is not the ideal crowd to entrust with the pillar of democracy, denying it autonomy is not the solution. Rather, internal oversight mechanisms and ethics rules should be formulated to ensure that corrupt elements are weeded out. In addition to wealth declarations for MPs, there should be strict enforcement of rules to regulate lobbyists and punish bribery. Campaign finance reform would stem some of the worst abuses, particularly of the state funded parties. Such a normative and structural framework ought to contain executive excesses and help implant a culture of official accountability. This is a scheme that avoids the enormous risks of the parliamentary system by providing a series of techniques and structures that contain the imperial president. Going the parliamentary route opens a Pandora's box. In all likelihood, the prime minister and the president would not be members of the same ethnic group. The real possibility of "tribalizing" the offices exists so that two sources of state authority, each belonging to a different "tribe," would be created. Students of the Kenyan state know that this would have meant two statelets within the state—one by Odinga for the Luo, and the other by Kibaki for the Kikuyu.

The other contested question, which is essential for democracy and one that Kenyans must resolve in a new constitution, is that of the devolution of power to local authorities from the central government. Devolution of power has been one of the central demands on the Kenyan state, even before independence in 1963. But it is a potentially explosive issue that needs careful deliberation. Historically, the key purposes for devolution of power from the center to the periphery have been twofold. First, it responds to the aspirations of groups with a shared identity to exercise some control over their lives. Second, it brings the remote citizen closer to public power so that she can meaningfully influence policy. With autonomy regimes for minorities and other self-government mechanisms, more states are devolving power to regions and local authorities.[16] Increasingly, there is recognition that internal self-determination for groups and regions can be an essential feature of democratic government.[17] In fact, the liberal project, which lies at the center of the democratic constitution, is driven by diversity, pluralism, multinationalism, and tolerance—values that are meant to deepen popular participation of the citizenry in their own government. Perhaps no other arrangement brings government closer to the people than devolution.

The crux of devolution is the right of a people to self-determination. But that right has been the subject of vigorous debate among jurists. What does it mean and entail? Who can exercise it and under what conditions? This problem of definition is critical for multinational states that are inhabited by more than one large group, or even minority communities. Early in the life of international law, the principle of self-determination applied only to select European powers that regarded themselves as "civilized nations."[18] At the Treaty of Versailles after World War I, the victorious powers again redefined the principle of self-determination and redrew the map of Europe largely along ethnic lines, creating nation-states. But the principle was not universalized because of its racist bias.[19] It left out some European groups and was not applied to colonies in Africa, Asia, the Middle East, and the Caribbean and Pacific.[20] After World War II, decolonization movements deployed the principle of self-determination to coalesce the right, by colonial territories, to break away from the colonial, metropolitan European powers and form independent sovereign states.[21]

The extension of the principle of self-determination to colonial territories did not, however, apply to individual groups within those territories, but rather to the territory itself.[22] International law did not extend the right of self-determination to the "peoples" within the former colonies, but rather to the territory as a single unit. Newly independent African states quickly adopted the principle of *uti possidetis*, developed first in Latin America, to sanctify the inviolability of their colonially established borders.[23] The 1963 charter of the Organization of African Unity validated the colonial state as the basic unit for self-determination.[24] States in Asia, the Middle East, and other regions adopted the same rigid view of self-determination. They rejected the secessionist proclivities of national subgroups within their borders. But did this rejection amount to *opinio juris*, a customary rule of international law, or are there circumstances under which secession and separation of national subgroups is permitted?

Scholars are divided on whether and under what circumstances national subgroups, including minorities and indigenous peoples, can exercise the right to self-determination, understood as secession from existing sovereign states. The practice, however, would seem to point to the existence of a limited right to secession under certain circumstances. Even Justice Rosalyn Higgins of the International Court of Justice, who reads the right to self-determination more strictly than most jurists, reluctantly concedes that there could be some exceptions. But she rejects the notion that the right of self-determination, as used in Article 1 of the UN Charter,[25] should properly be understood to apply only to "peoples."[26] According to her, minorities are not "peoples" in the language of the UN Charter. Higgins contends that minorities possess only *minority rights* that are granted under Article 27 of the International Covenant on Civil and Political Rights.[27] She argues that Quebec, for example, has no right to secede from Canada on the ground that it is a linguistic minority. But she concedes what she calls a "perceived need to secede" where minority rights are suppressed.[28]

Higgins believes that societies ought to live with their differences, even where the situation is horrible. That view leads her to reject what she calls illiberal "uninational and unicultural states that constitute postmodern tribalism."[29] To be sure, an open-ended right to self-determination, understood as the right to separate, could be problematic. One could imagine the explosion of minitribal states—or states in embryo—with no real chance at viability. But such a suggestion ignores genuine cases that should be recognized. Situations of extreme exploitation and repression come to mind. It would be unconscionable to deny ethnic, cultural, racial, religious, or linguistic groups the right to exit where they were subject to genocidal, nativist, racist, and religious ruling classes or majorities and where the state was so repressive that there was no possibility of freedom or respect for human rights. The cases of black Africans in the south of Sudan, or its Darfur region in the west, most poignantly come to mind. Alan Buchanan has identified three bases under which the right to secession should be allowed as a remedy of last resort: persistent and serious violations of human rights, historically unjust and unaddressed seizures of territory like annexation, and discriminatory redistribution through internal colonialism or regional exploitation.[30]

In spite of the views of some traditional jurists, international law now treats subnational groups, including minorities and indigenous peoples, as "peoples." The Supreme Court of Canada declared in the 1998 Quebec secession case that "it is clear that a 'people' may include only a portion of the population of an existing state" who could exercise the right to self-determination.[31] The opinion suggests that groups can secede as a last resort if the government does not represent all the people on the basis of equality and nondiscrimination.[32] Thus, "when a people is blocked from meaningful exercise of its right to self-determination internally, it is entitled, as a last resort, to exercise it by secession."[33] The point is that groups must be granted adequate rights within the borders of the state if they are to enjoy the right to *internal self-determination* as part of the body politic. Otherwise, international law may recognize their right to separate, or *external self-determination*, if they are impermissibly repressed within the unitary state. For African postcolonial states, in which their peoples were forcibly lumped together willy-nilly, that is a radical suggestion. But rather than shut their eyes to one of the continent's enduring problems, African states are better advised to craft political and constitutional arrangements that permit their "peoples" meaningful participation in governance. To ensure that groups and regions are, and feel, fully included, the state must go beyond majoritarian devices, such as concepts of *equality in law*, and introduce measures that will bring about those values *in fact*.

Devolution of power from the center to the regions is at the core of the right to internal self-determination. Yet the Kenyan state has been allergic to the concept, despite strong demands by the people, particularly those who have felt neglected or outside the orbit of central authority. The CKRC found that most groups and individuals advocated a form of devolution.[34] In a poor state like Kenya, the general writ of central authority thins out the farther out one goes from Nairobi. In particular, the capacity of the state to deliver social services and act as a spur to economic development fades as one leaves the center. In most parts of the country, state power is only used to hold territory, not govern it. Government officials at provincial outposts are rarely local, which alienates the people who live there. These debilitating conditions cannot be overcome if the central government refuses to devolve power to local authorities. The global trend is away from total central control.

> The shift towards devolution is largely a reflection of the political evolution towards more democratic and participatory forms of government that seek to improve the responsiveness and accountability of political leaders to their electorates. It is premised on the fundamental belief that once they are entrusted with their own destiny through the medium of local democratic institutions, human beings can govern themselves in peace and dignity in pursuit of their collective well-being.[35]

The 2004 Draft Constitution's devolution chapter was unacceptable to the Kibaki regime and other powerful constituencies. Typical devolution structures provide three levels—national, regional, and local—but the draft constitution provided four levels: national, regional, district, and location governments.[36] They were top-heavy with bureaucracies and legislatures, but they were also granted extensive powers to regulate most economic, social, and cultural activities in their areas of jurisdiction. If implemented, they would have amounted to a quasi-federal system. In the rush to reclaim autonomy from central control, the draft constitution succumbed to an antiregime stampede. The result was an overconcentration of local governments shielded from the guidance of the central government. The costs to administer such a system would have drained the economy. Its design replicated the bloated central government that officials have historically treated as no more than a personal piggy bank. It is more likely that many rural delegates saw local governments as a feeding trough, machinery for them to "eat," a Kenyan euphemism for unjust enrichment. The defeated Wako Draft rejected this radical scheme and instead provided a devolution system with more central control.

The other extremely problematic design was the draft constitution's imagination of devolution along ethnic lines. Almost all the regions and districts were ethnotribal, unicultural enclaves that were drawn on the basis of tribalist considerations.[37] For example, in this devolution scheme, the Kamba, Meru, Kisii, Luo, Luhya, Kalenjin, Kikuyu, Somali, Maasai, and other groups were each allocated their own regions and districts. Kenya is ethnically polarized, and political demagoguery has undermined the project of Kenyan-ness by promoting ethnic cleansing of "foreigners" by pogroms and threats of atrocities.[38] The structures of devolution in the draft constitution were more likely to heighten ethnic consciousness and promote tribal exceptionalism. On this issue, the Wako Draft was not different; it used ethnicity to create administrative units. Yet, this is a complex issue because precolonial ethnic identities—even though they were sharpened and mutated by colonial policies of divide, conquer, and rule—still have a legitimate claim to survival.[39] Herein lies the paradox of self-determination, postcolonialism, and modern nationalism.[40] If precolonial ethnic identities are in fact "peoples" in the language of international law, how can they be denied self-governance within the postcolonial state?

Indeed, as demands for internal self-determination increase, the sovereignty of the center, the state, may be diminished as the commitment of the citizen to colonial borders is weakened.[41] It is this distress of the state that has broken what Ali A. Mazrui called the "three post-colonial taboos": the taboo of recolonization, such as the UN tutelage to reestablish the Somali state, or more recently international efforts to reinvent Liberia; the taboo of sanctioned secession, as was the case with Eritrea and almost in Sudan before the peace pact with the south; and the taboo of retribalization, with the creation of a "federal" system in Ethiopia based on precolonial ethnicities.[42] Mazrui's argument is that the rise of ethnic consciousness and the "politicized tribal identity" in the context of multipartyism will force federalist structures on states. Otherwise, postcolonial states will fail. That may be true for many African states, but irredentist and separatist claims are not likely to threaten Kenya now. Except for the Somali—and even their separatist claims died out—no community has shown an urge to exit the state. But Kenya, like other African states, must guard against nativism in designing a devolution scheme.

> There are, however, political dangers in the devolution of power to subnational units. For example, wrongly structured sub-national entities such as regions can provide an opportunity for political mobilization on the divisive base of ethnicity or religion, with potential consequences of political oppression, intolerance and, at the extreme, secessionist movements. A related danger is that a regional system might frustrate the task of "nation-building."[43]

These dangers were not sufficiently considered by delegates at Bomas. Given the fact that Kenya's political parties are tribal, the devolution structures that carve out ethnically pure districts and regions only magnify the problem and coalesce exclusivist political structures. The natural tendency then will be for groups to produce their own "tribal" barons and baronesses, who then negotiate with their counterparts for the "national spoils." Such a system only constitutionalizes postmodern tribalism in the guise of devolution. In the end, it defeats the purpose of political democracy, which is to create a society based on ideals and principles, not tribal membership. Granted, if Kenya were threatened with extinction, as was the case in Nigeria unless it allocated power to groups in tribal federal units, then political necessity would require such a solution. But Kenyan communities and elites understand that none can survive alone nor is there a ready neighboring state, a receptacle to which they could flee. Kenyan Somalis abandoned their separatist aspirations once Somalia collapsed, making the dream of a greater Somalia fictitious. The key is to design accommodative arrangements that permit greater ethnocultural and linguistic autonomy and structures of devolution that deepen democracy without increasing the dangers of tribalization.

Economically, devolution can be "exorbitantly expensive" by "unnecessarily multiplying government departments," which could lead to costly, inefficient, and lethargic units.[44] Devolution must be designed in such a way that it does not widen the development gulfs between regions and cause more resentment within the state. In Kenya, the Northeastern Province, one of the most underdeveloped regions, could be further alienated unless the devolution system requires an equitable redistribution of national resources with a built-in bias for poor areas. With regard to distortions and regional imbalances, the relationship between the central government and the devolved units is critical. The center must make sure that services in education, health, and other key areas meet a national standard, the tax base of a region notwithstanding. Even so, devolved units must be able to largely support themselves by raising and controlling taxes on a wide variety of services. There must be a clear division of powers between the units and the center to avoid competition and duplication in the fiscal, political, and bureaucratic arenas. The center and the units must complement each other, not work at cross-purposes or engender tension.[45]

Kadhi, or Muslim, courts were the last key issue that was a stumbling block to a new constitution. Although Kenya is a deeply religious society, the 2004 Draft Constitution unambiguously provided that the state would be secular.[46] Even so, it took several openly religious positions, such as the right to life, which it defined as beginning at conception.[47] Another was a general prohibition on abortion unless the life of the mother was in danger.[48] The draft constitution exempted Muslim personal law from compliance with the equal rights and antidiscrimination norms of the bill of rights.[49] In defiance of the church, the Bomas Draft provided for the establishment of Kadhi courts, an act that cloaked them in the steel blanket of the constitution. The church, led by the Ufungamano Initiative, fought tooth and nail to exclude Kadhi courts, even though they would only be applicable when both parties professed the Islamic faith in a writ limited to Muslim personal law.[50] In an attempt to avoid this problem, the Wako Draft provided for religious courts and Muslim, Christian, and other faith-based tribunals.

The Civic Revolution

The reform of the Kenyan state has stalled because of the inability and unwillingness of the political class, the fraction of society that would lead the exercise, to embrace a new political culture. This reluctance or incapacity for reform is a result of the relationship between the political class and the state itself. Kenya's political class is a direct creation of the state and has no other independent origin. That is why it is virtually impossible for it to clean up the state, since it is an integral part of the culture and institutions of the state. Political parties run by this political elite are conservative; they are meant to preserve the power and the institutions of the status quo. Whether the party is the Party of National Unity (PNU), the Orange Democratic Movement (ODM), ODM-Kenya, NARC, NARC-Kenya, the Kenya African National Union (KANU), or the Forum for the Restoration of Democracy–People (FORD-People), its primary function is to capture and husband the power of the state, not to change the way and the purpose for which it is practiced. This conclusion is unlikely to change unless there is an overhaul of the culture and leadership of current political parties. But one thing is certain: the current political class is unlikely to transform its raison d'être. New political players will have to seize the platform for reform. "For broad and sustainable reform, Kenyans with the greatest material interest in reform—and they are not in the political class—must become a larger physical and ideological presence in the political process. Broad movement on reform should be seen as part of a project to deepen democracy."[51]

To empower the nonpolitical class, the reform movement cannot be located in the traditional parties that, in any case, rarely mobilize citizens. When they do, it is not for the fundamental reform of the state. What Kenya needs is a social movement, articulating the debilitating challenges of poverty, to take command of the political process. The vast majority of Kenyans are woefully impoverished, but no party has ever politicized poverty and powerlessness to the average Kenyan. No politician has been able to explain to Kenyans why they are poor and oppressed and how they can overcome those dire economic shackles. For the current political class to mobilize the people on this platform would be tantamount to committing suicide. That is why the country needs new vehicles and leadership, not part of the current political class, to transform the calculus of the political debate. Reform will not be possible unless the political discourse is purged of the myopia and corruption of the governing class.

It is encouraging, however, that the political space created by the democratic struggles since the late 1980s makes mass mobilization a possibility. It is this opening that new political actors must seize to transform the nature of politics in Kenya.

Since Kenya's "political parties are in no condition to act as mobilizers of the populace for broad-based reform," leadership must emerge from other sectors.[52] Since the late 1980s, the mantle for reform leadership has unquestionably belonged to civil society. Within this sector, churches have been critical leaders in the struggle to open up the political process, guarantee fair play, and protect basic rights.[53] But Kenya's political and economic fortunes are unlikely to change unless a new coalition of social forces emerges to direct politics. What is needed is a civic revolution, a reformist social movement that must bring together the key actors of civil society—nongovernmental organizations (NGOs), professional associations, religious organizations, business, and labor. With secular leadership drawn from NGOs, civil society must mobilize the citizenry for a popular democratic renaissance. The coalition of these groups must exploit religious organizations and tap into their deep reservoirs of social conscience and advocacy for social justice, and those tendencies to mobilize people at the grassroots.

Each one of the fractions of civil society has enormous potential for renewing politics. Kenyan organized labor, one of the most developed on the African continent, can be an indispensable partner in reform.[54] Although labor played key roles in the struggle for independence, it soon became moribund as a force for democratic reform. Some of the country's most prominent independence political leaders were drawn from it.[55] Tom Mboya, Pio Gama Pinto, Makhan Singh, and Fred Kubai played key roles in Kenya's independence struggle.[56] But Kenyatta's drive for absolute power was made possible by shackling the Central Organization of Trade Unions (COTU), the labor union, to the KANU party-state. Strikes were largely prohibited, depriving workers of their most potent weapon. The leadership of the labor movement was sanctioned by the state throughout the Kenyatta and Moi regimes. The hostility of the state to workers has continued into the Kibaki era as 9,000 striking workers, demanding better pay, were sacked in June 2005.[57] The government dismissed the workers to fulfill a pledge to Western donors to trim the workforce by 21,000 as a condition for assistance.[58]

The potential of the labor movement to play a key role in reform makes its recruitment an urgent priority. But that will not be possible unless COTU is reconstructed and delinked from the state. A hopeful sign is that COTU's rank and file is estranged from its corrupt leadership. Objectively, the conditions of workers have worsened due to globalization and the connivance of the state with investors to weaken labor laws. The culture of the export-processing zone has put Kenya in the thick of the race to the bottom.[59] Kenya's disenfranchised workers—in agriculture, service sectors, manufacturing, retail, and the lower and middle echelons of the public service—have a large stake in the reform of the state and must be an integral part of the social movement to capture political power and remake the state.

Businesses and professional associations have often borne the brunt of public corruption, the collapse of infrastructure, and lack of security. Professional and trade classes in law, medicine, accounting, the media and information services, engineering and construction, real estate, banking, finance, and insurance seek an environment that is conducive to business, entrepreneurship, innovation, and development. They seek a state free of frustrating red tape. Many business concerns in manufacturing, retail, transportation, agriculture, and other key sectors are hampered by an inefficient, extortionist, and corrupt state bureaucracy. These critical players—both corporate and individual—must become part of the reform agenda to broaden its pragmatic appeal.

Civil society only seeks to influence, not capture, power. Generally, civil society should be nonpartisan, although that does not entail keeping silent or refusing to take sides in the face of tyranny or betrayal.[60] That is why, for example, the Kenya Human Rights Commission (KHRC) endorsed Kibaki and NAK in 2002 against Uhuru Kenyatta and the Moi-led KANU party-state.[61] The KHRC rejected the narrow interpretation of political partisanship that Western international human rights groups, such as Amnesty International and Human Rights Watch, have adopted in their advocacy.[62] Local human rights organizations, unlike international ones, cannot be aloof from local politics.[63] In fact, the work of human rights is deeply political.[64] Civil society constitutes the people's watchdog and must always be there to police the exercise of state power, but there is no internal logic or principle that would disqualify its leadership from entering direct politics.

The historical experiences of Eastern and Central Europe and South Africa—not to mention the roles played by the KHRC, the Citizens' Coalition for Constitutional Change, and the National Convention Executive Council in Kenya's struggle for democracy in the 1990s—show the indispensability of civil society in leading political transitions. Poland's Solidarity movement is perhaps the best-known example of a civil society–led revolution in the former Soviet bloc.[65] It transformed itself from a civil society organization to a sociopolitical movement that eventually captured state power.[66] In South Africa, the United Democratic Front (UDF), which was launched in 1983, affiliated 600 organizations, including trade unions, youth groups, student movements, women's organizations, civic groups, political parties, and professional organizations, and played a decisive role in ending formal apartheid.[67] The UDF effectively mobilized township populations by an appeal to "people power" and mass political participation in the struggle against apartheid. The UDF remained relevant until the African National Congress assumed formal leadership of the struggle.[68] Both Solidarity and the UDF offer useful lessons for Kenya's civil society.

But there are hurdles that Kenyan civil society will have to overcome. In the wake of the 2002 elections, a thick layer of the most able civil society leadership was decimated by inclusion in the state. The remaining cadres were thrown into disarray by the Kibaki victory and the wrangles over constitution making. Never a monolith, civil society has always been fragmented by organizational rivalries, conflicting political visions, and competing interests. But in its golden age—from 1990 until 2002—civil society led a broad reform agenda that was responsible for the country's first regime change in four decades. Even then, civil society did not penetrate society at its lowest levels to mobilize the poor for reform. The question is whether in the wake of the betrayal and implosion of NARC and the outcome of the 2007 elections, civil society can launch afresh another reform agenda. The new language of change, which must be premised on the organization of a social movement, requires an astute, young, and untainted leadership. That is the challenge that civil society must meet to recapture the initiative for political discourse and chart a path to the country's renaissance.

The Betrayer Class

Kenya's elite, like that of other African states, is a tiny percentage of the population. Much of the elite—political, business, intelligentsia, professional, civil society—is concentrated in urban areas, most visibly in Nairobi. Its lifestyle and values are at a great remove from those of the average Kenyan. The elite occupies an insular cultural, social, and economic world that is driven by gossip, intrigue, and the culture of the imitation of the West. Its universe revolves around Kenya's two major media houses, the Nation Media Group and the Standard Group, which together dominate most of the print and electronic markets, even though the Kenya Broadcasting Corporation, the anemic state media, has the widest national reach. Although this elite is fractionalized by many cleavages, and different factions have controlled the state in turn, it is a resilient group that selectively reproduces itself. Its business, real estate, and financial interests are intertwined with foreign interests. It has expanded over the years, but it remains very small relative to Kenya's population surge. This class, the gatekeepers of the political state, is largely responsible for the failure of reform in Kenya. Early in the life of the Kenyan postcolonial state, Kenyatta established the benchmark for the elite's political morality in a publicly humiliating harangue of Bildad Kaggia in 1965. In the dressing-down, Kenyatta showed his disdain for the politics of his former fellow Kapenguria Trial detainee.

> We were together with Paul Ngei in Jail. If you go to Ngei's home, he has planted a lot of coffee and other crops. What have you done for yourself? If you go to Kubai's home, he has a big house and has a nice shamba [farm]. Kaggia,

what have you done for yourself? We were together with Kung'u Karumba in jail, now he is running his own buses. What have you done for yourself?[69]

Kenyatta's *what-have-you-done-for-yourself* speech outlined the morality of the new state. Greed and theft from the public became the purpose of leadership. But Kenyatta's brazen admission was most shocking. Kenyatta's speech ended the challenge posed by Oginga Odinga and Kaggia within KANU to adopt reformist and redistributive policies, as opposed to the more market-oriented and conservative politics advocated by Kenyatta and Tom Mboya. Kenyatta's outburst came after a test of wills between him and the critics of his pro-settler, antireform government. In April 1964, Kenyatta, then prime minister, wrote to Kaggia, a junior minister, demanding that he either stop the attacks on the government's land policies or resign as parliamentary secretary in the Ministry of Education.[70] Kenyatta ended by stating, "I shall be glad to receive your personal assurance that incidents of the type to which I have referred will not recur."[71] That moment of rapture foretold the end of any possibility of land reforms by KANU. Kaggia's response was swift and determined.

> As a representative of the people I found it very difficult to forget the people who elected me on the basis of definite pledges, or to forget the freedom fighters that gave all they had, for the independence we are enjoying . . . I, therefore, decided not to give the assurance required of me . . . I felt that to give such an assurance and to be prepared to remain muzzled I was betraying my innermost convictions for the sake of a salary and a position . . . It is my firm conviction that the answer in this struggle of resettling our landless Africans, without endangering agricultural production, is cooperative farming.[72]

When Bildad Kaggia died in March 2005, he was a pauper living on the margins of society.[73] His life of sacrifice to the people was the antithesis of the morality of the elite and the Kenyan state they control. He was said to "have committed political suicide by choosing the nationalist route."[74] He was eulogized as "a man who worked his heart out for a thankless system that often idolized deceit and which had no room for the principled, especially those who crusade for the poor."[75] What transpired on the eve of independence laid the foundation for the continuation of the status quo in Kenya. Public records indicate that Kenyatta was determined to pursue an accommodationist course in league with the European settlers and their African collaborators. He set this course early, in his first speech, when he accepted the instruments of power on December 12, 1963. It was a bitter irony that the man who had spent years in detention on charges of leading the Mau Mau refused even to acknowledge their contribution to Kenya's independence.

> Kenyatta's speech [on December 12, 1963] inexplicably made no mention of the people who had laid down their lives in the struggle, the fighters of the

forests and the camps who have been in danger in Kenya of becoming the forgotten men of the freedom fight because it suits the ambitions of the self-seeking politicians to divert our people from the real freedom aims of the people . . . Without the forest fighters in the so-called "Mau Mau" period, Kenya's independence would still be a dream.[76]

Over the years, Kenya's elite has closely followed in Kenyatta's footsteps in forging a deeply conservative state. In 2002, as the KANU state disintegrated under popular pressure, the elite galvanized under the banner of NARC to perpetuate its control over society. The proof was in NARC's nonchalance over the contradiction between its election pledges and the deliberate failure to fulfill them. For reformers, the question must remain, how can control of the state be wrested from this ubiquitous elite? Can the elite be transformed if a direct takeover of the state is not possible? In a word, how does the reform movement deal with the betrayer class, a cabal that has ruled Kenya since its inception and that seems incapable of political growth, of a grander imagination, a more robust vision for the nation?

Two critical variables are a prerequisite for genuine reform within Kenya. First, the new civil society–led social movement cannot permit itself to be hijacked by the current political class. Its leadership cannot be drawn from among the political elite that has run Kenya into the ground and is incapable of a larger national vision. That elite is a "political class that is bereft of elementary morality, and which suffers from acute intellectual bankruptcy."[77] No good can come of a political class that has morally and intellectually atrophied. Indeed, the "only way to reverse what appears to be Kenya's decline into a failed state is the immediate cultivation of new political leadership, a fresh cadre that has not been swimming in the same dirty pool for the last several decades."[78] There is little doubt that members of the political class will attempt to capture any viable reform movement, particularly if it is broad-based. The only way to avoid this problem is to guard the stratum of leadership jealously. It cannot be an open receptacle, a pit latrine, at the ready to accept any refuse. Without a doubt, Kenyans across the board must be welcome to join the movement, but those with dubious pasts and corrupt reputations, part of the current political class, should not be allowed to either control or become part of the movement's leadership. Such open-door policies have been the ruin of genuine reform efforts in the past.

Second, the reform movement should compile a list of members of the country's elite whom it would exclude from vying for elective or appointive offices under its aegis. The list of exclusion would be part of the code of ethics of the new social movement. Several thousand members of the elite who have been implicated in gross official misconduct and atrocities, including political murder, corruption, and other abuses of public office, have ruined Kenya's politics. The culprits are drawn from virtually every sector of society, including politics, judiciary, public service, business, agriculture, the security forces, the professions, religious organizations, and the intelligentsia. Many of these individuals have been identified in public inquiry reports and investigations.[79] Their names would be published as a form of lustration, a truth commission device of ceremonial purification that would bar them from holding office.[80] It is virtually impossible to reform the state unless a large number of those culpable among the elite are taken out of public circulation. Lustration, to be enforced first within the reform movement, would be given official state sanction once reformers capture power.

Finally, the reform movement will also have to contend with the donor community, which is largely Western. Since the early 1990s, donors have been the critical supporters of the emergent activist civil society. In fact, the African human rights movement, an elite, urban-based clique that lacks a social base among the poor majorities, would not be possible without donor support.[81] It is a discomfiting fact that Western donors fund all leading Kenyan NGOs almost fully. That encourages dependency and parasitism and distorts the priorities and ideological allegiances of the NGOs. How can a foreign-funded sector be accountable to constituencies in which it has no base? This lamentable state of affairs not only severely limits the political maneuver of NGOs but also sharply curtails their vision.[82] Donors become nervous whenever NGOs galvanize wide support among the poor on sensitive political or economic issues that could threaten the status quo. Even so, Kenyan NGOs must assert their independence from donor control to play a more active role in popular mass mobilization. Civil society ought to be prepared for the inevitable clash with donors in case of popular mobilization.

> But popular mobilization makes donors nervous because they are committed to political stability. During the constitutional reform mobilization in 1997, some donors were uneasy with the radical public action of reform activists. In cases like these, donors may oppose civil society mobilizations to bring a wider array of people and interests into the political arena. Organizations' dependence on donor financial support may have a dampening effect on mobilization.[83]

External Factors

To the vast majority of Kenyans, their country is a badly governed, often brutal place. Most live under conditions so horrible that they haunt the human conscience. Such a horrid existence is not just the lot of Kenyans who live in grinding poverty and a fatalism that defy description. But within this vast desert of despair, there are some oases, most notably in choice enclaves in Nairobi where the local elite hobnobs as though it were in any prosperous American or European city. That is what the African postcolonial state has become: a cog that deceptively holds a place in the international state system but has little to show for it. All is well as long as the local elite can collaborate with the West, international finance, and business to maintain stability. The key is to prevent a descent into anarchy or disintegration, as was the case in Somalia, Liberia, and elsewhere. This desperate state, which was made up by the West, cannot be fully reformed unless it is reformulated. The simple reason for this conclusion is the phenomenon called globalization.

Since 1945, the United Nations has played a key role in preserving the global order, which the West dominates. Today, the UN is the exclusive preserve of the United States and Europe, and in particular Britain and France, the two most voracious colonial powers. It is not an exaggeration to state that the global political agenda has been narrowed to the interests of these three powers. In the area of international trade, the World Trade Organization, formerly the General Agreement on Tariffs and Trade (GATT), now fuels globalization.[84] The adverse effects of globalization, which disproportionately and negatively affect the Third World, have forged an unjust economic and political order. Small, weak states like Kenya, which are ruled by elites that lack basic morality, have become easy pickings for a free market system gone amok.[85] Yet globalization cannot be reversed. However, it can be tamed and managed, even by weaker states, if the political will exists. It can happen in emergent democratic states where the populace can express itself meaningfully in the formulation of foreign policy. Gone should be the days when Cold War autocrats secretly mortgaged their countries for a penny to the West. Empowered legislatures must scrutinize all treaty obligations, especially in controversial matters relating to terror, trade, human rights, and security.

Africans cannot simply reinvent history to create a new beginning that is more to their liking. First, they have to rewrite the internal structures of their societies. To do so, they must abandon the culture and consciousness of fatalism that has been acquired due to centuries of brutalization. They must create more legitimate states out of the present colonial derivations. But no matter what Africans do within Africa, it will not suffice unless they can find partners abroad, not just in the West but also elsewhere in the global South. Key to Africa's assertion of its sovereignty, and in particular its freedom of maneuver from the West, is the diversification of economic and political relationships among its own states and with the global South. Globalization—both its positive and negative dimensions—makes impossible the development of any state or society in isolation from the rest of the world. Thus Africa's revival is inextricably linked to the global economy, which the West dominates. Africa must therefore demand that the West, and the United States in particular, radically revise its relationship with the continent. But that will require an enlightened and astute leadership, one that understands the nuances of international relations and how they can be exploited to the advantage of poor states.

There are important lessons that African states can learn from other Third World nations, particularly in Latin America, which is turning away from the worst excesses of neoliberalism, and the so-called Washington Consensus.[86]

The term *Washington Consensus* was coined by John Williamson to refer to neoliberal, market fundamentalist policies that the Bretton Woods institutions—the World Bank, the International Monetary Fund, and the GATT—imposed on Latin America in the late 1980s.[87] This "market fundamentalism," as termed by George Soros, the philanthropist, put democratic reform at the service of the market, and international capitalism in particular.[88] Unbridled markets, not people, are placed at the center of reform. It is a formula that opens up the Third World to global Western capital, weakens or even overrides sovereignty, and turns democracy into a sham. Most of Latin America has concluded that the free market reforms of the 1990s do not work.[89] As a result, recent electoral changes in the region have produced left-leaning leaders in three-quarters of its states, most notably in Bolivia, Venezuela, Brazil, and Uruguay. Led by Brazil, these states are politely distancing themselves from the United States as a pragmatic, leftist consensus emerges.[90] The inability of both Ghana and Uganda, the two Bretton Woods darlings in Africa, to make the Washington Consensus work should be an object lesson to the rest of the continent as it retools its relationship with the West.

Fundamental to this new relationship with the West must be Africa's place in the global economy. Even with utopian democracies, African states will not develop unless they are freed from crushing debts that were advanced by the West to benefit corrupt and wasteful Cold War despots. The debts must be fully forgiven if African economies are to be jump-started, human capital developed, and infrastructure built. Only then can fair trade and equitable investments make a difference. Equally important is the significance of Africa's voice in multilateral organizations such as the World Bank, the World Trade Organization, and the International Monetary Fund. These institutions of global governance cannot continue to be opaque and undemocratic to Third World states, particularly toward Africa. Africa needs the West, with whom it largely has had a tragic history, to revive its economy, but it cannot approach its long-term tormentor on bended knee. Projects like the New Partnership for Africa's Development (NEPAD) and former British prime minister Tony Blair's Africa Commission—the supposed tools for the reformulation of Africa's relationship with the West—must avoid the fate of the panaceas of the past. NEPAD must not simply open up Africa for the worst excesses of globalization. It must pursue regional political and economic integration with urgency to set up strategic blocs that help African countries in dealing with dominant Western players. Trade and political blocs, such as the proposed East African Federation, can create regional synergy and a more viable voice to address external questions.

Kenya's four-decade history surprisingly yields no clues about an independent Kenyan foreign policy. Any internal reformation of the state cannot succeed unless it pivots on a principled, defined, and self-interested foreign policy agenda. The basic maxim is that a nation's foreign policy should be a reflection of its domestic policy. But a country becomes a nation—a political society with a defined identity—when it forges irreducible values and interests. At a bare minimum, Kenya must be a liberal democratic state. It is these values that should guide the formulation of Kenya's foreign policy. But small and medium-sized emergent states like Kenya are particularly vulnerable in this era of globalization. Is there any wiggle room for such countries, or is Kenya condemned to irrelevance, unable to craft a specific foreign policy that caters to its national interests and values?

Two classic interests must guide Kenya's foreign policy. First, and most important, is the commercial and economic interest. Kenya's foreign policy must primarily be driven by the country's economic fortunes. It will require that contacts with other countries, international institutions, and foreign corporations be crafted to extract preferential benefits for the country. Favorable trade terms, not aid or assistance, ought to be the primary goal. Reliance on trade—as opposed to dependency on funds from donors—will enhance the country's ability to act more independently, both internally and externally. A case in point was the insistence by the United States that Kenya sign the bilateral immunity or nonsurrender agreement to shield US soldiers from the International Criminal Court or lose military assistance.[91] As a beggar nation, Kenya is hard-pressed to resist such bully tactics. But it can improve its bargaining position if it diversifies its foreign policy relationships and strengthens its economy to reduce dependence on donor funds in general and any one donor in particular.

The second classic foreign policy interest that Kenya must pursue is support for democracy, human rights, peace building, and the reconstruction of failed or dysfunctional states. This is an agenda that Kenya must pursue in the larger East African region, at the continental level, and internationally. So far, Kenya has only focused on conflict resolution in Somalia, where it has tried to put Humpty Dumpty back together, and Sudan, where it has pushed for a negotiated solution to the north's genocidal war against the south. But Kenya needs to imagine a bigger role in Africa, beyond Somalia and Sudan. Africa is littered with many a failed and dysfunctional state, a description that Kenya narrowly escaped in December 2002 when the KANU kleptocracy lost power to NARC. In addition to forging peace in these countries, Kenya must catalyze the formulation of broad Africanist policies on major global issues. Kenya needs to understand that it is one of four key states in Africa, the others being South Africa, Nigeria, and Egypt. A reformist government cannot succeed at home unless it pursues these strategic interests abroad.

Practical Challenges and Theoretical Lessons

Even with the violence following the 2007 election, Kenya remains one of the more hopeful states on the African continent. However, the country continues to fall behind many Third World states in a number of statistical indices.[92] Nevertheless, Kenya offers a glimmer of hope that the African postcolonial state may be tamed with a combination of tools and projects. Even the stalled, drawn-out constitution-making process was a window of hope for the possibilities of popular participation. At the very least, the process came up with a fairly detailed outline of what a democratic constitution might look like. The question that remains is, what can be done to effect political reform and national transformation? Put differently, what lessons does Kenyan history teach the country, Africa, and even the world about democratic reform? What could have been done differently to move away from political despotism? What might be done now to incubate legitimacy in the state and cultivate democracy?

A key lesson from Kenya has been the limits of open electoral politics as the antidote to the illegitimacy of the state and the incubation of a democratic culture.[93] What analysts should realize is that democracy is more than electoral processes.[94] Assessments of the 2002 regime change that brought NARC and Kibaki to power put too much weight on that historic election. As the first years of the Kibaki regime demonstrated, the gains of the election did not reform the state. Many of the pathologies of the postcolonial state reared their ugly heads anew: negative ethnicity, corruption, rejection of reforms, and a clawing back of basic freedoms. But there were some gains in the economy, civil society remained autonomous, the press became vibrant, and Parliament grew lively and raucous. What these rays of hope signaled is a dormant reservoir that can be tapped for a renaissance. The Kenyan experience makes it abundantly clear that elections must be followed with the reform of institutions to deepen democratic practices.[95] The failure by the Kibaki regime to carry out a broad range of institutional and normative reforms—passing a new constitution, purging the judiciary, establishing transitional justice mechanisms through a truth commission, and creating a viable political party culture—arrested the reconstruction of the state.

The Kenyan experience demonstrates the importance of abiding by pacts among elites in fractious multiethnic societies. Political leaders who derive their power from an ethnic base—as has been the case in Kenya—cannot be ignored or marginalized without serious repercussions to the reform process. One of the decisive factors in the early collapse of the reform agenda in Kenya was the failure of the Memorandum of Understanding between NAK and LDP. Although NARC may have eventually abandoned the reform agenda because of its class character and the interests of its key leaders, that moment did not have to come so soon after the elections. But the refusal by Kibaki and his aides to reward his coalition partners in LDP, particularly Raila Odinga, Kalonzo Musyoka, and their allies, with more senior positions hastened the collapse of reforms.[96] The wrangles over the constitution became a forum for power struggles and a battleground for succession politics. Those conflicts within NARC provided the opportunity for KANU to reemerge by playing

NAK and LDP against each other and cutting deals with both to protect itself against a purge.[97] Kibaki's decision to play Machiavellian politics gave anti-reformers in KANU and within NARC leverage and marginalized the few reform-minded members of the government.[98]

It is impossible to underestimate the importance of decisions taken by the government in the early months of a political transition from an authoritarian regime to a more open society. John Githongo, Kenya's former anticorruption czar, repeatedly warned that the reform agenda would die unless it was effected within the first twenty-four months of the transition.[99] That is one of the most important lessons to emerge from Kenya's stalled 2002 transition. Immediately after KANU was defeated in 2002, the party hierarchy was shell-shocked. From Moi on down, they seemed unable to grapple with their loss of power after forty years of uninterrupted rule.[100] Blunt talk by NARC's ministers about ending corruption and punishing the perpetrators of past atrocities put the squeeze on KANU.[101] In the first six months in power, the government took several reformist steps. These efforts gave hope that genuine reforms might be implemented. But then the state abandoned many of these initiatives when infighting started in NARC. The last straw came in February 2005, when Githongo resigned and went into exile. Kibaki did not provide access to reformist advisers or grant them real power, particularly when NARC started to implode. The vital lesson is that reformers must put their imprint on the state at the beginning of the transition and remain vigilant at the center of policymaking.

Political transitions to consolidate democratic electoral gains and regime change depend on many highly uncertain factors.[102] There are no straight paths to a stable democracy. In Kenya's case, the hand of fate may have been a little cruel. Kibaki's incapacitation by a road accident just before the election in 2002 and a stroke in early 2003 that diminished his capacity to make critical decisions may have adversely affected the course of NARC.[103] During his long convalescence, a cabal of Kikuyu courtiers antagonized his allies within NARC and earned the derided label of "Mount Kenya Mafia," a cabal of politicians that had thrown a cordon around Kibaki.[104] No advance planning could have anticipated some of these problems. For that reason, it is important to focus attention on structural factors that can be controlled; political planning and activism on the ground to transform social realities are indispensable. It is in this context that Kenyan reformers—and there are more than a few—must consciously organize themselves, mobilize the public at the grassroots, and create alliances in the private sector, the professions, and even within the state bureaucracy with those who desire and seek a modern, clean, and accountable state. Public sentiment in Kenya, filtered through the media, suggests that this reservoir of goodwill and expectant talent is open to mobilization. The only drawback has been the lack of credible leadership. It is this opportunity that needs to be seized.

Finally, one must contemplate Kenya's missed opportunities and what might have been. There are several pivotal moments when, had they played out differently, Kenya might have escaped some of the worst excesses of the last several decades. The first important event was the 1964 merger of KANU and the Kenya African Democratic Union (KADU). It killed the opposition, an important lever in an emergent democracy, and made it easier for Kenyatta to centralize power, create an oppressive executive, subjugate Parliament, and end democratization. But it also led to the purge of dissent within the party and of any possibility of policies to transform the economy and restructure the state. Ultimately, Kenyatta banned the opposition Kenya People's Union (KPU) and made Kenya a de facto one-party state.

The second important event was the 1969 assassination of Tom Mboya, the popular labor leader and likely successor to Kenyatta. In all likelihood, Mboya's ascendancy would have spared Kenya the ruinous twenty-four-year rule by Moi. An astute leader, Mboya would have steered Kenya's economy toward faster economic growth, even though he probably would not have fundamentally restructured social relations to tackle poverty and create a more equitable society. Importantly, his presidency would have avoided the vitriolic Kikuyu-Luo polarization, a problem that was exacerbated by Odinga's marginalization and that still stalks the country to date.

Mboya's assassination spurred a third turning point in the character of the state. Until then, political assassinations were a novel idea. Leaving aside the political killings of the colonial era, the assassination of Pio Gama Pinto in 1965 was the dry run for the killing of Mboya in 1969. Pinto's killing appears to have convinced the Kenyatta state that political opponents could be physically terminated. The fact that Pinto's death passed without any major disruption to the security of the regime seems to have confirmed this view. Even though Mboya's assassination led to some violence, it did not threaten the regime. From that moment forward, the state adopted political killings of opponents or likely successors as an instrument of maintaining power. Over the years, other prominent killings would include those of J. M. Kariuki under Kenyatta, and Robert Ouko, the urban foreign minister, under Moi. Later, the state under Moi widely used extrajudicial killings, including the so-called ethnic clashes of the 1990s, to silence dissent.

The banning of the KPU in 1969 and the detention of its key leaders was the fourth important moment in Kenyan history. Until then, Kenya had been learning how to practice competitive politics in a fragile multiparty democracy. The first decade of independence was a crucial period for many a postcolonial state in Africa because it was formative in fundamental ways. The political culture and the practices of that first decade have deeply determined how states later evolved. The banning of the KPU inevitably led the state toward despotism and implanted in the political class a culture of intolerance for dissent. It gave rise to political sycophancy, cronyism, and mediocrity in the bureaucracy. More importantly, outlawing the KPU removed from Kenya's official public discourse the politics of redistribution and the fundamental reform of the state, and abandoned any attempts to confront the inequitable and distorted legacy of colonialism. As a government-in-waiting, the KPU would have continued to present Kenyans with an alternative vision of the state. It would have given Kenyans an option to elect to power a party with a competing ideological outlook.

Three additional events have been critical turning points. First, at the advent of multipartyism, the Forum for the Restoration of Democracy (FORD) had the potential to bring about regime change in the early 1990s. It was because of FORD's implosion that Kenya missed the wave of regime change that swept Africa in the first five years of that decade. FORD's success would have ended Moi's rule and spared Kenya at least a decade of one-party rule in the guise of an illiberal democracy. There was a good chance that a FORD regime would have written a democratic constitution, given the preponderance among its leaders of young idealistic reformers. But FORD was derailed by a combination of factors, the most important of which was the irreconcilable ambitions of Kenneth Matiba, a Kikuyu, and Oginga Odinga, a Luo. This ethnic chasm split the opposition and allowed Moi to win with a minority vote.

Second, the refusal by Kibaki to honor the MOU between NAK and LDP fundamentally altered the course of politics. Although it is not certain that a united NARC would have restructured the state, chances are that the experiment in reforms could have lasted a little longer. The watershed event would have been an agreement on a new democratic constitution to fundamentally reform the state.

Finally, the December 2007 elections offered yet another chance for Kenyans to remake the state. Since 2002, when KANU was kicked out of power, the Kibaki government had reversed the country's dim economic fortunes, but also failed to tackle corruption and tamp down seething ethnic divisions. Opposition political parties could have articulated a reformist agenda and strengthened party structures. Instead, those seeking to depose Kibaki at the ballot box organized around ethnic themes and codes. The opposition parties, much like Kibaki's Party of National Unity (PNU), played on ethnic fears and hopes to galvanize support. In this respect, both the Orange Democratic Movement (ODM) of Raila Odinga and the Orange Democratic Movement–Kenya (ODM-K) of Kalonzo Musyoka, the two main opposition parties, became havens for leaders linked to gross human rights violations and egregious economic crimes. None of the parties in the 2007 elections had the vision or leadership for genuine reform. In fact, the elections turned out to be a flashpoint that almost saw the collapse of the state.

What these moments of hope suggest is that a wrong turn here or there—or a different decision—could have fundamentally affected the character of the state. In all these cases, the country took the wrong turn because the political class or individual leaders lacked the vision, courage, or will to make the right choice. There is no doubt that the postcolonial state is an ogre, but it can be tamed, as the experiment in Tanzania and several postcolonial states in Africa indicates. The task of taming this leviathan is enormous, and cannot be entrusted to a political class that is bereft of vision and commitment to the democratic project. Even so, throughout Kenyan history, there have been encouraging signs of citizen participation and a yearning for real change. The short history of the country is a testament to the resilience of the human spirit and the insatiable desire for reform in the face of great odds. The fact that Kenya was able to pull back from the brink and not become a failed state after the disputed 2007 elections speaks to this resilience and a commitment to build one nation. That is why there is hope for Kenya, even though its history is replete with one betrayal after another. The immediate task is for reformers to reengage politics and seek state power for reformist purposes.

Notes

1. Walter F. Murphy, "Constitutions, Constitutionalism, and Democracy," in *Constitutionalism and Democracy: Transitions in the Contemporary World*, ed. Douglas Greenberg, Stanley M. Katz, Melanie Beth Oliviero, and Steven Wheatley (New York: Oxford University Press, 1993).

2. H. W. O. Okoth-Ogendo, "Constitutions Without Constitutionalism," in *Constitutionalism and Democracy*. For a critique, see also H. Kwasi Prempeh, "Marbury in Africa: Judicial Review and the Challenge of Constitutionalism in Contemporary Africa," *Tulane Law Review* 80 (2006): 1239.

3. Mugambi Kiai, "Presidential Directives vis-à-vis Democracy, Human Rights, and the Rule of Law: A Paradox," in *In Search of Freedom and Prosperity: Constitutional Reform in East Africa*, ed. K. Kibwana, Chris Maina, and Joseph Oloka-Onyango (Nairobi: Claripress, 1996), 267.

4. B. O. Nwabueze, *Presidentialism in Commonwealth Africa* (New York: St. Martin's Press, 1974).

5. John Hatchard, Muna Ndulo, and Peter Slinn, *Comparative Constitutionalism and Good Governance in the Commonwealth: An Eastern and Southern Perspective* (New York: Cambridge University Press, 2004), 58–59.

6. *The Draft Constitution of Kenya 2004,* Chapter 12 (hereinafter *2004 Draft Constitution*).

7. Ibid., Article 173.

8. Yash Pal Ghai, "Provision on Executive Misunderstood," *Daily Nation*, May 25, 2004.

9. Hatchard, Ndulo, and Slinn, *Comparative Constitutionalism in the Commonwealth*, 62–63.

10. *2004 Draft Constitution,* Article 173.

11. Makau Mutua, "Kenya Does Not Need a Prime Minister," *Sunday Nation*, September 14, 2003.

12. Mwenda Njoka, "NARC Crisis: The Story Behind the Intrigues," *Sunday Standard*, March 23, 2003; Njeri Rugene and David Mugonyi, "It's All Together Now," *Daily Nation*, October 22, 2003.

13. M. Shugart and J. Cary, *Presidents and Assemblies: Constitutional Design and Electoral Dynamics* (New York: Cambridge University Press, 1992), 28–43.

14. *Constitution of the Republic of South Africa,* 1996, Section 102(2).

15. Hatchard, Ndulo, and Slinn, *Comparative Constitutionalism in the Commonwealth,* 78.

16. Hurst Hannum, "Contemporary Developments in the International Protection of the Rights of Minorities," *Notre Dame Law Review* 66 (1991): 1431; Hurst Hannum, *Autonomy, Sovereignty, and Self-Determination* (Philadelphia: University of Pennsylvania Press, 1990).

17. Rosalyn Higgins, "Comments," in *Peoples and Minorities in International Law*, ed. Catherine Brolman, R. Lefeber, and M. Ziek (Boston: M. Nijhoff, 1993), 30.

18. Diane Orentlicher, "Separation Anxiety: International Responses to Ethno-Separatist Claims," *Yale Journal of International Law* 23 (1998): 1.

19. James Thuo Gathii, "International Law and Eurocentricity," *European International Law Journal* 9 (1998): 184.

20. Antony Anghie, "Finding the Peripheries: Sovereignty and Colonialism in Nineteenth Century International Law," *Harvard International Law Journal* 40 (1999): 1.

21. See, for example, Declaration on the Granting of Independence to Colonial Countries and Peoples, General Assembly Res. 1514 (XV), December 14, 1960; Declaration on Principles of International Law Concerning Friendly Relations and Co-operation Among States in Accordance with the Charter of the United Nations, General Assembly Res. 2625 (XXV), December 24, 1970.

22. Makau wa Mutua, "Why Redraw the Map of Africa? A Moral and Legal Inquiry," *Michigan Journal of International Law* 16 (1995): 1113.

23. Orentlicher, "Separation Anxiety."

24. Charter of the Organization of African Unity, Articles I–II, signed May 25, 1963, 479 U.N.T.S. 39, entered into force September 13, 1963.

25. UN Charter, Article 1(2), provides that one of the purposes of the world body is to "develop friendly relations among nations based on respect for the principle of equal rights and self-determination of peoples." *Charter of the United Nations*, June 26, 1945, 59 Stat. 1031, T.S. 993, 3 Bevans 1153, entered into force October 24, 1945.

26. Higgins, "Comments."

27. International Covenant on Civil and Political Rights, Article 27, opened for signature December 19, 1966, 999 U.N.T.S. 171, entered into force March 23, 1976.

28. Higgins, "Comments."

29. Ibid.

30. Alan Buchanan, "Self-Determination, Secession, and the Rule of Law," in *The Morality of Nationalism*, ed. Robert McKim and J. McMahan (New York: Oxford University Press, 1997), 301, 310.

31. Reference re Secession of Quebec, Supreme Court of Canada, (1998) 2 S.C.R. 217, Para 124; 37 I.L.M. 1342 (1998).

32. Ibid., Para 130.

33. Ibid., Para. 134; see also Abdullahi A. An-Na'im and Francis Deng, "Self-Determination and Unity: The Case of Sudan," *Law and Policy* 18 (July–October 1995): 205.

34. Constitution of Kenya Review Commission, *The Main Report of the Constitution of Kenya Review Commission,* September 18, 2002, 183.

35. Hatchard, Ndulo, and Slinn, *Comparative Constitutionalism in the Commonwealth*, 183.

36. *2004 Draft Constitution,* Chapter 14.

37. Ibid., First Schedule.

38. "Ntimama Back on the Warpath," *Sunday Nation*, July 2, 2006; "There Is No Room for Bantustans," *Sunday Nation*, July 2, 2006, Editorial.

39. Makau wa Mutua, "Why Redraw the Map of Africa?"

40. Ali A. Mazrui, "The Bondage of Boundaries," *Economist*, September 11, 1993, 28.

41. Jeffrey Herbst, "Challenges to Africa's Boundaries in the New World Order," *Journal of International Affairs* no. 46 (1992): 24–25.

42. Mazrui, "The Bondage of Boundaries."

43. Hatchard, Ndulo, and Slinn, *Comparative Constitutionalism in the Common-wealth*, 188.

44. Ibid., 189.

45. Ibid.

46. *2004 Draft Constitution,* Article 9.

47. Ibid., Article 34(2).

48. Ibid., Article 34(3).

49. Ibid., Article 33(4).

50. Ibid., Articles 198, 199.

51. Frank Holmquist, "Kenya's Anti-Politics," *Current History: A Journal of Contemporary World Affairs* (May 2005): 215.

52. Ibid., 214.

53. Africa Watch, *Taking Liberties* (New York: Africa Watch, 1991), 217–236.

54. Makhan Singh, *Kenya's Trade Unions, 1952–1956* (Nairobi: Uzima Press, 1980).

55. Colin Leys, *Underdevelopment in Kenya* (London: Heinemann, 1978).

56. Oginga Odinga, *Not Yet Uhuru: The Autobiography of Oginga Odinga* (New York: Hill and Wang, 1967), 108–109.

57. "9,000 Civil Servants to Get Sack Letters," *Daily Nation*, June 5, 2005.

58. "Kenya: Thousands Fired from Government Jobs," *New York Times*, June 7, 2005, A8.

59. Kenya Human Rights Commission, *Manufacture of Poverty: The Untold Story of EPZs in Kenya* (Nairobi: Kenya Human Rights Commission, 2004).

60. Willy Mutunga, "So, What Really Is Non-Partisanship?" in *Eyes on the Prize*, ed. Athena Mutua (Nairobi: Kenya Human Rights Commission, 2003), 31.

61. Kenya Human Rights Commission, "Why and How to Bring About Regime Change in Kenya," in *Eyes on the Prize*, ed. Athena Mutua (Nairobi: Kenya Human Rights Commission, 2003), 25.

62. Makau Mutua, "Civil Society's Relevance in the Age of NARC," *Sunday Nation*, January 4, 2004.

63. Makau Mutua, *Human Rights: A Political and Cultural Critique* (Philadelphia: University of Pennsylvania Press, 2002), 47–56.

64. See, generally, Claude E. Welch, *NGOs and Human Rights: Promise and Performance* (Philadelphia: University of Pennsylvania Press, 2001); Makau wa Mutua, "Politics and Human Rights: An Essential Symbiosis," in *The Role of Law in International Politics: Essays in International Relations and International Law*, ed. Michael Byers (New York: Oxford University Press, 2000), 149; David Kennedy, "The International Human Rights Movement: Part of the Problem?" *Harvard Human Rights Journal* no. 15 (2002): 101; Peter Rosenblum, "Teaching Human Rights Activism: Ambivalent Activism, Multiple Discourses, and Lingering Dilemmas," *Harvard Human Rights Journal* 15 (2002): 301; Kwadwo Appiagyei-Atua, "The Role of NGOs in the Current Democratic Dispensation in Africa: The Lessons of the Ghanaian Experience," in *Legitimate Governance in Africa: International and Domestic Legal Perspectives*, ed. Edward Kofi Quashigah and Obiora Chinedu Okafor (Boston: Kluwer Law International, 1999), 309; Kenya Human Rights Commission, *Human Rights as Politics* (Nairobi: Kenya Human Rights Commission, 2003).

65. Z. A. Pelczyniski, "Solidarity and 'Rebirth of Civil Society' in Poland, 1976–81," in *Civil Society and the State: New European Perspectives,* ed. John Keane (New York: Verso, 1988).

66. Lech Walesa, Franklin Philip, and Helen Mahut, eds., *The Struggle and the Triumph: An Autobiography* (New York: Arcade Publishing, 1993); Timothy Garton Ash, *The Polish Revolution: Solidarity* (New Haven: Yale University Press, 2002).

67. M. Swilling, "The United Democratic Front and Township Revolt," in *Popular Struggles in South Africa,* ed. W. Cobbett and R. Cohen (Trenton, NJ: Africa World Press, 1988), 90–113.

68. J. Seekings, *The UDF: A History of the United Democratic Front in South Africa 1983–1991* (Athens: Ohio University Press, 2000), 271–284.

69. See Ngugi wa Thiong'o, *Ngugi Detained: A Writer's Prison Diary* (Nairobi: Heinemann, 1981), 89.

70. Letter from Kenyatta to Kaggia, dated May 22, 1964, reproduced in Oginga Odinga, *Not Yet Uhuru: The Autobiography of Oginga Odinga* (New York: Hill and Wang, 1967), 265–267.

71. Ibid., 266.

72. Statement by Kaggia, dated June 1964, reproduced in Odinga, *Not Yet Uhuru: The Autobiography of Oginga Odinga* (New York: Hill and Wang, 1967), 266–267.

73. "Kaggia Burial Tomorrow," *Daily Nation,* March 18, 2005.

74. Kilemi Mwiria, "What Kaggia Stood for Is Slowly Dying," *Daily Nation,* March 21, 2005.

75. Ibid.

76. Odinga, *Not Yet Uhuru,* 254–255.

77. Makau Mutua, "NARC Has Rejected the Path of Reforms," *East African Standard,* September 4, 2004, 4.

78. Ibid.

79. See National Council of Churches of Kenya, *The Cursed Arrow: A Report on Organized Violence Against Democracy in Kenya* (Nairobi: National Council of Churches of Kenya, 1992); Kenya National Assembly, *The Report of the Parliamentary Select Committee to Investigate Ethnic Clashes in Western and Other Parts of Kenya* (Nairobi: National Assembly of Kenya, 1992); Africa Watch, *Divide and Rule: State Sponsored Ethnic Violence in Kenya* (New York: Human Rights Watch, 1993); Law Society of Kenya, *Impunity: Report of the Law Society of Kenya on the Judicial Commission of Inquiry into Ethnic Clashes in Kenya* (Nairobi: Law Society of Kenya, 2000); Republic of Kenya, *Report of the Judicial Commission of Inquiry into Ethnic Clashes in Kenya* (Akiwumi Report) (Nairobi, 2002); Republic of Kenya, *Report of the Commission of Inquiry into Illegal/Irregular Allocation of Public Land* (Nairobi: Government Printer, 2003); James Orengo, "Only Keen Vigilance Will Halt Graft," *Daily Nation,* June 10, 2005.

80. Republic of Kenya, *Report of the Task Force on the Establishment of a Truth, Justice and Reconciliation Commission* (Nairobi: Government Printer, 2003), 25.

81. Chidi Anselm Odinkalu, "Why More Africans Don't Use the Human Rights Language," *Human Rights Dialogue* 4 (Winter 2000).

82. Makau Mutua, "African Human Rights Organizations: Questions of Context and Legitimacy," in *Human Rights, the Rule of Law, and Development in Africa,* ed. Paul Tiyambe Zeleza and Philip J. McConnaughay (Philadelphia: University of Pennsylvania Press, 2004), 191.

83. Holmquist, "Kenya's Anti-Politics," 215.

84. Marrakesh Agreement Establishing the World Trade Agreement, signed on April 15, 1994, 33 I.L.M. 13 (1994); General Agreement on Tariffs and Trade, October 30, 1947, 61 Stat. A-11, 55 U.N.T.S. 194.

85. Robin L. Cowling, "Pic, Pops, and the Mai Apocalypse: Our Environmental Future as a Function of Investors' Rights and Chemical Management Initiatives," *Houston Journal of International Law* 21 (1999): 231.

86. John Williamson, "What Should the World Bank Think About the Washington Consensus?" *World Bank Research Observer* 15 (August 2000): 251.

87. John Williamson, "What Washington Means by Policy Reform," in *Latin American Adjustment: How Much Has Happened*, ed. John Williamson (Washington, DC: Institute for International Economics, 1990).

88. George Soros, *The Crisis of Global Capitalism: Open Society Endangered* (New York: Public Affairs, 1998).

89. Larry Rotter, "With New Chief, Uruguay Veers Left, in a Latin Pattern," *New York Times*, March 1, 2005.

90. Ibid.

91. "Kenya to Say No to the US on Treaty on the Military," *Daily Nation*, June 8, 2005.

92. United Nations Development Programme, *UNDP Annual Report 2006: Global Partnership for Development* (New York: UNDP, 2006); UNDP, *Human Development Report 2005: International Cooperation at a Crossroads: Aid, Trade, and Security in an Unequal World* (New York: UNDP, 2005).

93. Larry Diamond, *Developing Democracy: Toward Consolidation* (Baltimore: Johns Hopkins University Press, 1999); Larry Diamond and Richard Gunther, eds., *Political Parties and Democracy* (Baltimore: Johns Hopkins University Press, 2001); Peter W. Galbraith, *The End of Iraq: American Incompetence Created a War Without End* (New York: Simon and Schuster, 2006).

94. Edward D. Mansfield and Jack Snyder, *Electing to Fight: Why Emerging Democracies Go to War* (Cambridge, MA: MIT Press, 2005).

95. Stephen Brown, "Theorising Kenya's Protracted Transition to Democracy," *Journal of Contemporary African Studies* 22 (September 2004): 337.

96. Joel D. Barkan, "Kenya After Moi," *Foreign Affairs* 83 (2004): 93.

97. Makau Mutua, "End of Reforms in Kenya," *Boston Globe*, August 14, 2004.

98. Makau Mutua, "NARC Has Rejected the Path of Reforms, *East African Standard*, September 4, 2004.

99. "Kenya Fights Losing War on Graft," *Cape Times*, August 4, 2004.

100. "Former Ruling Party MPs on Unfamiliar Territory Now," *Daily Nation*, January 10, 2003.

101. "Ministers Talk Tough on Graft," *Daily Nation*, January 11, 2003.

102. G. O'Donnell and P. Schmitter, *Transitions from Authoritarian Rule: Tentative Conclusions About Uncertain Democracies* (Baltimore: Johns Hopkins University Press, 1986).

103. Author's interview with David Kibaki (son of President Mwai Kibaki), Nairobi, Kenya, December 2007; Barkan, "Kenya After Moi," 92.

104. L. Muthoni Wanyeki, "Oh No, It's the Old Boy's Network—Again," *East African*, March 31, 2003; "Q&A: Kenya Referendum," *BBC Online*, November 22, 2005.

Acronyms

4Cs	Citizens' Coalition for Constitutional Change
ABAKO	Alliances des Bakongo
CBOs	community-based organizations
CCF	constituency constitutional forum
CKRC	Constitution of Kenya Review Commission
CNC	Coalition for a National Convention
COTU	Central Organization of Trade Unions
DP	Democratic Party
ECK	Electoral Commission of Kenya
FIDA	Federation of Women Lawyers (Federacion International d'abogadas)
FORD	Forum for the Restoration of Democracy
FPTP	first-past-the-post system
GEMA	Gikuyu, Embu, and Meru Association
ICCPR	International Covenant on Civil and Political Rights
ICESCR	International Covenant on Economic, Social and Cultural Rights
ICJ	International Commission of Jurists
IEA	Institute for Economic Affairs
IED	Institute for Education in Democracy
IMF	International Monetary Fund
IPK	Islamic Party of Kenya
IPPC	Inter-Parties Parliamentary Committee
IPPG	Inter-Parties Parliamentary Group
KADU	Kenya African Democratic Union
KANU	Kenya African National Union
KASA	Kenya African Socialist Alliance
KCA	Kikuyu Central Association
KENDA	Kenya National Democratic Alliance

KHRC	Kenya Human Rights Commission
KLFA/Mau Mau	Kenya Land and Freedom Army
KNC	Kenya National Congress
KPC	Kenya People's Coalition
KPU	Kenya People's Union
KSC	Kenya Social Congress
KShs	Kenya shillings
LDP	Liberal Democratic Party
LEGCO	Legislative Council
LPK	Labor Party of Kenya
LSK	Law Society of Kenya
MMPR	mixed member proportional representation
MNC	Mouvement National Congolais
MOU	Memorandum of Understanding
NAC	National Alliance for Change
NAK	National Alliance Party of Kenya
NARC	National Rainbow Coalition
NARC-K	NARC-Kenya
NCA	National Convention Assembly
NCC	National Constitutional Conference
NCCK	National Council of Churches of Kenya
NCEC	National Convention Executive Council
NDP	National Development Party
NEMU	National Elections Monitoring Unit
NEPAD	New Partnership for Africa's Development
NGOs	nongovernmental organizations
NPK	National Party of Kenya
ODM	Orange Democratic Movement
ODM-K	ODM-Kenya
PCK	People's Commission of Kenya
PICK	Party of Independent Candidates of Kenya
PNU	Party of National Unity
PPSA	Preservation of the Public Security Act
PR	proportional representation
PSC	Parliamentary Select Committee on Constitutional Review
RPP	Release Political Prisoners
SDP	Social Democratic Party
SUPKEM	Supreme Council of Kenya Muslims
TWGs	technical working groups
UDF	United Democratic Front
UDHR	Universal Declaration of Human Rights
UPD	Uganda People's Congress

Bibliography

Achebe, Chinua. *Things Fall Apart*. New York: Ballantine Books, 1959.

Africa Watch. *Kenya: Taking Liberties*. New York: Africa Watch, 1991.

———. *Divide and Rule: State-Sponsored Ethnic Violence in Kenya*. New York: Human Rights Watch (Africa Watch), 1993.

Ake, Claude. *A Political Economy of Africa*. New York: Longman, 1981.

———. "Rethinking African Democracy." *Journal of Democracy* 2 (1991): 32.

———. *Democracy and Development in Africa*. Washington, DC: Brookings Institution, 1996.

Anderson, David. *Histories of the Hanged: The Dirty War in Kenya and the End of Empire*. New York: W. W. Norton, 2005.

Anene, Joseph C. *The International Boundaries of Nigeria, 1885–1960: The Framework of an Emergent African Nation*. New York: Humanities Press, 1970.

Anghie, Antony. "Finding the Peripheries: Sovereignty and Colonialism in Nineteenth-Century International Law." *Harvard International Law Journal* 1, no. 40 (1999).

An-Na'im, Abdullahi Ahmed. "The Rights of Women and International Law in the Muslim Context." *Whittier Law Review* 9 (1987): 491.

———. "Human Rights in the Muslim World: Socio-Political Conditions and Scriptural Imperative." *Harvard Human Rights Journal* 3 (1990): 13.

———. "The National Question, Secession, and Constitutionalism: The Mediation of Competing Claims to Self-Determination." In *State and Constitutionalism: An African Debate on Democracy,* ed. Issa Shivji. Harare: SAPES Trust, 1991.

———, ed. *Proselytization and Communal Self-Determination in Africa*. Maryknoll: Orbis Books, 1999.

Appiagyei-Atua, Kwadwo. "The Role of NGOs in the Current Democratic Dispensation in Africa: The Lessons of the Ghanaian Experience." In *Legitimate Governance in Africa: International and Domestic Legal Perspectives*, ed. Edward Kofi Quashigah and Obiora Chinedu Okafor. Boston: Kluwer Law International, 1999.

Appiah, Kwame Anthony. *In My Father's House: Africa in the Philosophy of Culture*. London: Methuen, 1992.

Archer, Jules. *African Firebrand: Kenyatta and Kenya*. New York: J. Messner, 1969.

Atieno, E. S., and John Lonsdale, eds. *Mau Mau and Nationhood: Arms, Authority, and Narration*. Athens: Ohio University Press, 2003.

Avirgan, Tony, and Martha Honey. *War in Uganda: The Legacy of Idi Amin*. Westport: L. Hill, 1982.

Ayittey, George B. N. *Africa in Chaos.* New York: St. Martin's Press, 1998.

Badejo, Babafemi A. *Raila Odinga: An Enigma in Kenyan Politics.* Nairobi: Yintab Books, 2006.

Baldwin, W. W. *Mau Mau Manhunt: The Adventures of the Only American Who Has Fought the Terrorists in Kenya.* New York: Dutton, 1957.

Bannon, Alicia L. "Designing a Constitution-Drafting Process: Lessons from Kenya." *Yale Law Journal* 116 (2007): 1824.

Barbour, Kenneth. "A Geographical Analysis of Boundaries in Inter-Tropical Africa." In *Essays on African Population* 30, ed. Kenneth M. Barbour and R. M. Protero. New York: Praeger Publishers, 1961.

Barkan, Joel D. "Kenya: Lessons from a Flawed Election." *Journal of Democracy* 4 (1993): 85.

———, ed. *Beyond Capitalism vs. Socialism in Kenya and Tanzania.* Boulder: Lynne Rienner Publishers, 1994.

———. "Kenya After Moi." *Foreign Affairs* 83 (January–February 2004): 87.

Barnett, Don, and Karari Njama. *Mau Mau from Within: Autobiography and Analysis of Kenya's Peasant Revolt.* New York: Monthly Review Press, 1966.

Bayart, Jean-François. *The State in Africa: Politics of the Belly.* London: Longman, 1993.

Bennett, George. *Kenya, a Political History: The Colonial Period.* London: Oxford University Press, 1963.

Berman, Bruce J. *Control and Crisis in Colonial Kenya: The Dialectic of Domination.* Athens: Ohio University Press, 1999.

Black Man's Land: Images of Colonialism and Independence in Kenya, VHS, directed by David Koff and Anthony Howarth. 1979.

Bratton, Michael. "Beyond the State: Civil Society and Associational Life in Africa." *World Politics* 407, no. 41 (1989).

Bratton, Michael, and Nicholas van de Walle. *Democratic Experiments in Africa: Regime Transitions in Comparative Perspective.* New York: Cambridge University Press, 1997.

Brown, Stephen. "Theorising Kenya's Protracted Transition to Democracy." *Journal of Contemporary African Studies* 22 (September 2004): 325.

Brownlie, Ian. *African Boundaries: A Legal and Diplomatic Encyclopedia.* London: C. Hurst for the Royal Institute of International Affairs, 1979.

Buchanan, Alan. "Self-Determination, Secession, and the Rule of Law." In *The Morality of Nationalism*, ed. Robert McKim and J. McMahan. New York: Oxford University Press, 1997.

Carothers, Thomas. *Aiding Democracy Abroad: The Learning Curve.* Washington, DC: Carnegie Endowment for International Peace, 1999.

———. *Critical Mission: Essays on Democracy Promotion.* Washington, DC: Carnegie Endowment for International Peace, 2004.

———, ed. *Promoting the Rule of Law Abroad: In Search of Knowledge.* Washington, DC: Carnegie Endowment for International Peace, 2006.

Carson, J. B. *The Administration of Kenya Colony and Protectorate: Its History and Development.* Nairobi: Noia Kuu Press, 1945.

Chabal, Patrick. "Introduction." In *Political Domination in Africa: Reflections on the Limits of Power,* ed. Patrick Chabal et al. Cambridge: Cambridge University Press, 1986.

Chazan, Naomi, John W. Harbeson, and Donald Rothchild, eds. *Civil Society and the State in Africa.* Boulder: Lynne Rienner Publishers, 1994.

Chazan, Naomi, Robert Mortimer, John Ravenhill, and Donald Rothchild. *Politics and Society in Contemporary Africa.* Boulder: Lynne Rienner Publishers, 1988.

Chege, Michael. "Between Africa's Extremes." *Journal of Democracy* 44, no. 6 (1995).

Clayton, Antony. *Counter-Insurgency in Kenya, 1952–1960: A Study of Military Operations Against the Mau Mau.* Nairobi: Transafrica Publishers, 1976.

Cohen, Jean L., and Andrew Arato. *Civil Society and Political Theory.* Cambridge, MA: MIT Press, 1992.

Committee to Protect Journalists. *Attacks on the Press.* New York: Committee to Protect Journalists, 1992.

Constitution of Kenya Review Commission. *The Constitutional Review Process in Kenya: Issues and Questions for Public Hearing.* 2001.

———. *General Regulations.* 2001.

———. *Reviewing the Constitution.* 2001.

———. *Curriculum for Civic Education.* 2002, available at http://www.kenyaconstitution .org/docs/04d001.htm, accessed April 28, 2005.

———. *Draft Bill to Amend the Constitution of Kenya Review Commission.* September 18, 2002.

———. *The Main Report of the Constitution of Kenya Review Commission.* September 18, 2002.

———. *The People's Choice: The Report of the Constitution of Kenya Review Commission, Short Version.* September 2002.

———. *The Constitution of Kenya Review (National Constitutional Conference Procedure) Regulations.* 2003.

———. *National Constitutional Conference: Information Handbook for Delegates.* 2003.

———. *The Report of the Rapporteur-General to the National Constitutional Conference on the General Debate Held Between April 28–June 6, 2003 at the Bomas of Kenya.* 2003.

———. *2004 Zero Draft of the National Constitutional Conference to Alter the Draft Bill.* February 14, 2004.

Cowling, Robin L. "Pic, Pops, and the Mai Apocalypse: Our Environmental Future as a Function of Investors' Rights and Chemical Management Initiatives." *Houston Journal of International Law* 21 (1999): 231.

Crowe, S. E. *The Berlin West African Conference.* Westport: Negro Universities Press, 1970.

Dahl, Robert. *A Preface to Democratic Theory.* Chicago: University of Chicago Press, 1956.

Davidson, Basil. *Can Africa Survive? Arguments Against Growth Without Development.* London: Heinemann, 1975.

———. *Africa in Modern History: The Search for a New Society.* London: Allen Lane, 1978.

———. *Africa in History: Themes and Outlines.* New York: Collier Books, 1991.

Days, Drew S. *Justice Enjoined: The State of the Judiciary in Kenya.* New York: Robert F. Kennedy Memorial Center for Human Rights, 1992.

Diamond, Larry, and Richard Gunther, eds. *Political Parties and Democracy.* Baltimore: Johns Hopkins University Press, 2001.

Diamond, Larry A. Kirk-Greene, and O. Oyediran, eds. *Democracy in Developing Countries: Africa*, vol. 2. London: Adamantine Press, 1988.

Dianga, James. *Kenya 1982: The Attempted Coup: The Consequence of a One-Party Dictatorship.* London: Pen Press, 2002.

Dilley, M. *British Colonial Policy in Kenya.* London: Frank Cass Publishers, 1967.

Dudziak, Mary L. "Working Toward Democracy: Thurgood Marshall and the Constitution of Kenya." *Duke Law Journal* 56 (2006): 721.

Edgerton, Robert B. *Mau Mau: An African Crucible*. New York: Free Press, 1990.

Eleazu, Uma O. *Federalism and Nation-Building*. Illfracombe: Stockwell, 1977.

Elias, T. O. *Africa and the Development of International Law*. Dobbs Ferry, NY: Oceana Publications, 1988.

Elkins, Caroline. *Imperial Reckoning: The Untold Story of Britain's Gulag in Kenya*. New York: Henry Holt, 2005.

Englebert, Pierre. *State Legitimacy and Development in Africa*. Boulder: Lynne Rienner Publishers, 2000.

Fatton, Robert. *Predatory Rule: State and Civil Society in Africa*. Boulder: Lynne Rienner Publishers, 1992.

Faure, A. M., and Jan-Erik Lane, eds. *South Africa: Designing New Political Institutions*. London: Sage, 1996.

Federacion International d'abogadas or Federation of Women Lawyers (FIDA), Institute for Education in Democracy (IED), Kenya Human Rights Commission (KHRC), and League of Kenya Women Voters (LKWV). *Safeguarding Women's Gains Under the Draft Constitution: Parliamentary Handbook 1*, 2003.

———. *Audit Report: The National Constitutional Conference*. Nairobi: Kenya Human Rights Commission, 2004.

———. *Model Proposals: Safeguarding the Gains for Women in the Draft Constitution*. January 25, 2004.

Federacion International d'abogadas (FIDA-Kenya). *Step-by-Step: Backwards or Forwards?* Annual Report, 2003.

Fowler, Alan. "The Role of NGOs in Changing State-Society Relations: Perspectives from Eastern and Southern Africa." *Development Policy Review* 9 (1991): 80.

French, Howard W. *A Continent for the Taking: The Tragedy and Hope in Africa*. New York: Vintage, 2005.

Freund, Bill. *The Making of Contemporary Africa*. Boulder: Lynne Rienner Publishers, 1984.

Furedi, Frank. *The Mau Mau War in Perspective*. London: James Currey, 1989.

Galbraith, Peter W. *The End of Iraq: American Incompetence Created a War Without End*. New York: Simon and Schuster, 2006.

Garton Ash, Timothy. *The Polish Revolution: Solidarity*. New Haven: Yale University Press, 2002.

Gathii, James Thuo. "International Law and Eurocentricity." *European International Law Journal* 9 (1998): 184.

———. "Imperialism, Colonialism, and International Law." *Buffalo Law Review* 54 (2007): 1013.

Ghai, Yash P. "Constitutions and Governance in Africa: A Prolegomenon." In *Law and Crisis in the Third World*, ed. Sammy Adelman and Abdul Paliwala. London: H. Zell, 1993.

———. *An Alternative Draft of a New Constitution of the Republic of Kenya: Building on Bomas*. Kampala: Kituo Cha Katiba, 2006.

Ghai, Yash P., and J. P. W. B. McAuslan. *Public Law and Political Change in Kenya*. Nairobi: Oxford University Press, 1970.

Gillies, David, and Makau wa Mutua. *A Long Road to Uhuru: Human Rights and Political Participation in Kenya*. London: Westminster Foundation for Democracy, 1993.

Gimode, Edward. *Tom Mboya*. Nairobi: East African Educational Publishers, 1996.

Gloppen, Siri. *South Africa: The Battle over the Constitution: Law, Social Change, and Development*. Aldershot: Ashgate, 1997.

Gourevitch, Peter. *We Wish to Inform You That Tomorrow We Will Be Killed with Our Families: Stories from Rwanda.* New York: Picador, 1998.

Gramsci, Antonio. *The Modern Prince.* London: Lawrence and Wishart, 1957.

Hannum, Hurst. *Autonomy, Sovereignty, and Self-Determination.* Philadelphia: University of Pennsylvania Press, 1990.

―――. "Contemporary Developments in the International Protection of the Rights of Minorities." *Notre Dame Law Review* 66 (1991): 1431.

Hansen, Art. "African Refugees: Defining and Defending Their Human Rights." In *Human Rights and Governance in Africa,* ed. Ronald Cohen, Goran Hyden, and Winston P. Nagan. Gainesville: University of Florida Press, 1993.

Harbeson, John W. *The Kenya Little General Election: A Study in Problems of Urban Political Integration.* Nairobi: Institute for Development Studies, University College, 1967.

―――. *Land Resettlement and Development Strategy in Kenya.* Nairobi: Institute for Development Studies, University College, 1967.

―――. *The European Factor in Kenya Nation Building.* 1970.

―――. *Nation Building in Kenya: The Role of Land Reform.* Evanston, IL: Northwestern University Press, 1974.

―――. "Guest Editor's Introduction: Political Crisis and Renewal in Kenya: Prospects for Democratic Consolidation." *Africa Today* 45 (1998): 161–184.

Harbeson, John, Donald Rothchild, and Naomi Chazan, eds. *Africa in World Politics.* Boulder: Westview Press, 1991.

―――, eds. *Civil Society and the State in Africa.* Boulder: Lynne Rienner, 1994.

Harris, Eddy L. *Native Stranger: A Black American's Journey into the Heart of Africa.* London: Viking, 1992.

Hatchard, John Muna Ndulo, and Peter Slinn. *Comparative Constitutionalism and Good Governance in the Commonwealth: An Eastern and Southern Perspective.* New York: Cambridge University Press, 2004.

Haugerud, Angelique. *The Culture of Politics in Modern Kenya.* Cambridge: Cambridge University Press, 1995.

Hempstone, Smith. *Rogue Ambassador: An African Memoir.* Sewanee, TN: University of the South Press, 1997.

Henderson, Ian, and Philip Goodhart. *The Hunt for Kimathi.* London: H. Hamilton, 1958.

Henkin, Louis. *The Age of Rights.* New York: Columbia University Press, 1991.

Herbst, Jeffrey. "Challenges to Africa's Boundaries in the New World Order." *Journal of International Affairs* 46 (1992): 24–25.

―――. *States and Power in Africa: Comparative Lessons in Authority and Control.* Princeton: Princeton University Press, 2000.

Higgins, Rosalyn. "Comments." In *Peoples and Minorities in International Law,* ed. Catherine Brolman, R. Lefeber, and M. Ziek. Boston: M. Nijhoff, 1993.

Hochschild, Adam. *King Leopold's Ghost: A Story of Greed, Terror, and Heroism in Africa.* New York: Mariner Books, 1999.

Holmquist, Frank. "Kenya's Anti-Politics." *Current History: A Journal of Contemporary World Affairs* (April 2005): 209.

Holmquist, Frank, and Michael Ford. "Kenya: State and Civil Society the First Year After the Election." *Africa Today* 5, no. 41 (1994): 7–8.

―――. "Kenyan Politics: Towards a Second Transition?" *Africa Today* 45 (1998): 22–58.

Hornsby, Charles. "Election Day and the Results." In *Out for the Count: The 1997 General Elections and the Prospects for Democracy in Kenya,* ed. Marcel Rutten, Alamin Mazrui, and François Grignon. Kampala: Fountain Publishers, 2001.

Hughes, Lotte. *Moving the Maasai: A Colonial Misadventure.* New York: Palgrave Macmillan, 2006.

Human Rights Watch. *Divide and Rule: State-Sponsored Violence in Kenya.* New York: Human Rights Watch, 1993.

———. *World Report 2000: Events of 1999.* New York: Human Rights Watch, 2000.

———. *Tanzania: "The Bullets Were Raining": The January 2001 Attack on Peaceful Demonstrators in Zanzibar.* New York: Human Rights Watch, April 2001.

———. *Playing with Fire: Weapons Proliferation, Political Violence, and Human Rights in Kenya.* New York: Human Rights Watch, 2002.

———. *Testing Democracy: Political Violence in Nigeria.* New York: Human Rights Watch, 2003.

———. 2005 *World Report: Events of 2004.* New York: Human Rights Watch, 2004.

———. *"They Do Not Own This Place": Government Discrimination Against "Non-Indigenes" in Nigeria.* New York: Human Rights Watch, 2006.

Huntington, Samuel. *The Third Wave: Democratization in the Late Twentieth Century,* 6th ed. Norman: University of Oklahoma Press, 1990.

Huxley, Elspeth. *White Man's Country: Lord Delamere and the Making of Kenya.* London: Macmillan, 1935.

Ibrahim, Jibrin. *Democratic Transition in Anglophone West Africa.* Dakar: CODESRIA Books, 2004.

Ihonvbere, Julius. *Towards a New Constitutionalism in Africa.* London: Center for Democracy and Development, 2000.

Ijalaye, David. "Was Biafra at Any Time a State in International Law?" *American Journal of International Law* 65 (1971): 551.

Ingham, Kenneth. *The Making of Modern Uganda.* London: George Allen and Unwin, 1958.

Institute for Economic Affairs. *The Little Fact Book: The Socio-Economic and Political Profiles of Kenya's Districts.* Nairobi: Institute for Economic Affairs, 2002.

Institute for Education in Democracy. *Enhancing the Electoral Process in Kenya: A Report on the Transition General Elections 2002.* Nairobi: Institute for Education in Democracy, 2003.

Institute for Education in Democracy, Catholic Justice and Peace Commission, and National Council of the Churches of Kenya. *Report on the 1997 General Elections in Kenya: 29–30 December 1997.* Nairobi: Institute for Education in Democracy.

International Commission of Jurists. *Democratization and the Rule of Law in Kenya: ICJ Mission Report.* 1997.

International Human Rights Law Group. *Failing the Pluralist Challenge: Human Rights and Democratization in Kenya's December 1992 Multi-Party Elections.* Washington DC, November 1992.

Isichei, Elizabeth. *A History of Christianity in Africa: From Antiquity to the Present.* Grand Rapids: Eerdman's Publishing, 1995.

Itote, Waruhiu. *"Mau Mau" General.* Nairobi: East African Institute Press, 1967.

Jackson, Robert H. "Juridical Statehood in Sub-Saharan Africa." *Journal of International Affairs* 46 (1992): 1.

Jackson, Robert H., and Carl Rosberg. *Personal Rule in Black Africa: Prince, Autocrat, Prophet, Tyrant.* Berkeley: University of California Press, 1982.

———. "Why Africa's Weak States Persist." *World Politics* 35 (1982): 1.

Jackson, Vicki, and Mark Tushnet. *Comparative Constitutional Law.* New York: Foundation Press, 1999.

Jeal, Tim. *Stanley: The Impossible Life of Africa's Greatest Explorer.* London: Faber and Faber, 2007.

Joseph, Richard A., ed. *The Democratic Challenge in Africa.* Atlanta: Carter Center, 1994.

———. "Africa: The Rebirth of Political Freedom." *Journal of Democracy* 2 (1995): 11.

———, ed. *State, Conflict, and Democracy in Africa.* Boulder: Lynne Rienner Publishers, 1999.

Journal of African Marxists. *Independent Kenya.* London: Zed Books, 1982.

Juma, Laurence. "Ethnic Politics and the Constitutional Review Process in Kenya." *Tulsa Journal of Comparative and International Law* 9 (2002): 471.

Kaggia, Bildad. *Roots of Freedom, 1921–1963: The Autobiography of Bildad Kaggia.* Nairobi: East African Publishing House, 1975.

Kahiga, Samuel. *Dedan Kimathi: The Real Story.* Nairobi: Longman, 1990.

Kanogo, Tabitha. *Squatters and the Roots of Mau Mau, 1906–1963.* Athens: Ohio University Press, 1987.

———. *Dedan Kimathi: A Biography.* Nairobi: East African Educational Publishers, 1992.

Kanyinga, Karuti. "The Socio-Political Context of the Growth of NGOs in Kenya." In *Economic Liberalization and Social Change in Africa,* ed. Peter Gibbon. Uppsala: Nordic African Institute, 1993.

Karimi, John, and Philip Ochieng. *The Kenyatta Succession.* Nairobi: Kenyatta Succession, 1980.

Kariuki, Josiah Mwangi. *"Mau Mau" Detainee: The Account by a Kenya African of His Experience in Detention Camps, 1953–1960.* New York: Oxford University Press, 1963.

Kasfir, Nelson. "Cultural Sub-Nationalism in Uganda." In *The Politics of Cultural Sub-Nationalism in Africa,* ed. Victor A. Olorunsola. New York: Anchor Books, 1972.

———. *State and Class in Africa.* London: Cass, 1984.

———. "Explaining Ethnic Political Participation." In *The State and Development in the Third World,* ed. Atul Kohli. Princeton: Princeton University Press, 1986.

Katumanga, Musambayi. *Cascading Donor Interest and the Democratic Transition in Kenya.* Nairobi: IPAR, 1998.

Keane, John, ed. *Civil Society and the State.* London: Verso, 1988.

Kennedy, David. "The International Human Rights Movement: Part of the Problem?" *Harvard Human Rights Journal* 15 (2002): 101.

"Kenya." In *The World FactBook,* available at https://www.cia.gov/cia/publications/factbook/geos/ke.html, accessed August 1, 2006.

Kenya Church. *A Gathering Storm: Critical Concerns on the Draft Constitution.* Nairobi: Kenya Church, 2003.

Kenya Constitutional Conference: Report on the Conference. *Kenya Gazette,* February 25, 1960.

Kenya Human Rights Commission. *Human Rights as Politics.* Nairobi: Kenya Human Rights Commission, 2003.

———. "Why and How to Bring About Regime Change in Kenya." In *Eyes on the Prize,* ed. Athena Mutua. Nairobi: Kenya Human Rights Commission, 2003.

———. *Manufacture of Poverty: The Untold Story of EPZs in Kenya.* Nairobi: Kenya Human Rights Commission, 2004.

————. "Kenya Human Rights Commission Against Minimum Constitutional Reforms." Press Release, August 15, 2006, available at http://www.khrc.or.ke/news, accessed August 18, 2006.

Kenya Human Rights Commission, International Commission of Jurists, and Law Society of Kenya. *The Kenya We Want [Kenya Tuitakayo]: Proposal for a Model Constitution.* Nairobi, 1994.

Kenya National Assembly. The Departmental Committee on Administration of Justice and Legal Affairs. *Report on the Way Forward on the Constitutional Review Process.* December 2006.

Kenyatta, Jomo. *Suffering Without Bitterness.* Nairobi: East African Publishing House, 1968.

Kiai, Maina. *The Legitimization of Repressive Laws and Practices in Kenya.* Nairobi: Kenya Human Rights Commission, 1994.

Kiai, Mugambi. "Presidential Directives vis-à-vis Democracy, Human Rights, and the Rule of Law: A Paradox." In *In Search of Freedom and Prosperity: Constitutional Reform in East Africa,* ed. K. Kibwana, Chris Maina, and Joseph Oloka-Onyango. Nairobi: Claripress, 1996.

Kiano, Julius G. "The Emergent East African Federation." In *Federalism and the New Nations of Africa,* ed. David P. Currie. Chicago: University of Chicago Press, 1964.

Kibaki, Mwai. Speech During the Opening of Kenya Review National Constitutional Conference at Bomas of Kenya on April 30, 2003, available at http://www.kenya constitution.org/docs/12d006.htm, accessed May 11, 2005.

Kibwana, Kivutha, ed. *Law and the Administration of Justice in Kenya.* Nairobi: International Commission of Jurists, Kenya Section, 1992.

————, ed. *Readings in Constitutional Law and Politics in Africa: A Case Study for Kenya.* Nairobi: Claripress, 1998.

Kimathi, Wambui. "A Strategic Seclusion—Yet Again! The 1997 General Elections in Luo Nyanza." In *Out for the Count: The 1997 General Elections and Prospects for Democracy in Kenya,* ed. Marcel Rutten, Alamin Mazrui, and François Grignon. Kampala: Fountain Publishers, 2001.

Kimunya, Amos, Minister for Finance. *Kenya Budget for Fiscal Year 2006/2007,* Nairobi, June 15, 2007.

King, Noel. *Christian and Muslim in Africa.* New York: Harper and Row, 1971.

Kinyatti, Maina wa. *Kenya's Freedom Struggle: The Kimathi Papers.* London: Zed Books, 1988.

Kiteme, Kamuti. *We, the Panafrikans: Essays on the Global Black Experience.* New York: Edward W. Blyden Press, 1992.

Klug, Heinz. *Constituting Democracy: Law, Globalism, and South Africa's Political Reconstruction.* Cambridge: Cambridge University Press, 2000.

Kyle, Keith. *The Politics of the Independence of Kenya.* New York: St. Martin's Press, 1999.

Law Society of Kenya. *Impunity: Report of the Law Society of Kenya on the Judicial Commission of Inquiry into Ethnic Clashes in Kenya.* Nairobi: Law Society of Kenya, 2000.

————. *Draft Constitution of Kenya,* as edited by the Law Society of Kenya, March 16, 2004.

Layachi, Azzedine. "Algeria: Reinstating the State or Instating a Civil Society." In *Collapsed States: The Disintegration and Restoration of Legitimate Authority,* ed. I. William Zartman. Boulder: Lynne Rienner Publishers, 1995.

Leakey, Louis S. B. *Mau Mau and the Kikuyu.* London: Methuen, 1953.

————. *Defeating Mau Mau.* London: Methuen, 1954.

Leys, Colin. *Underdevelopment in Kenya: The Political Economy of Neo-Colonialism.* Berkeley: University of California Press, 1975.

Locke, John. *Two Treatises of Civil Government.* London: J. M. Dent and Sons, 1955.

Maathai, Wangari. *Unbowed: A Memoir.* New York: Alfred A. Knopf, 2006.

Magnusson, Bruce A. "Testing Democracy in Benin: Experiments in Institutional Reform." In *State, Conflict, and Democracy in Africa.* Boulder: Lynne Rienner Publishers, 1999.

Maina, Wachira. "Kenya: The State, Donors and the Politics of Democratization." In *Civil Society and the Aid Industry,* ed. Alison Van Rooy. London: Earthscan Publications, 1998.

Maloba, Wunyabari O. *Mau Mau and Kenya: An Analysis of a Peasant Revolt.* Bloomington: Indiana University Press, 1998.

Mamdani, Mahmood. "Social Movements and Constitutionalism: The African Context." In *Constitutionalism and Democracy: Transitions in the Contemporary World,* ed. Douglas Greenberg, Stanley M. Katz, Melanie Beth Oliviero, and Steven C. Wheatley. New York: Oxford University Press, 1993.

———. *Citizen and Subject: Contemporary Africa and the Legacy of Late Colonialism.* London: Fountain Publishers, 1996.

Mamdani, Mahmood, and Ernest Wamba dia Wamba, eds. *African Studies in Social Movements and Democracy.* Dakar: CODESRIA Books, 1995.

Mansfield, Edward D., and Jack Snyder. *Electing to Fight: Why Emerging Democracies Go to War.* Cambridge, MA: MIT Press, 2005.

Marais, Hein. *South Africa: Limits to Change: The Political Economy of Transition.* New York: Palgrave Macmillan, 2001.

Marrakesh Agreement Establishing the World Trade Agreement, World Trade Organization, signed on April 15, 1994, 33 I.L.M. 13. 1994.

Marx, Karl. *The German Ideology.* New York: International Publishers, 1970.

Mazrui, Alamin. "Rights Integration in an Institutional Context: The Experience of the Kenya Human Rights Commission." *Buffalo Law Review* 8 (2002): 123.

Mazrui, Ali A. *The African Condition: The Reith Lectures.* London: Heinemann, 1979.

———. *The Africans: A Triple Heritage.* London: Little, Brown, 1986.

———. "The Bondage of Boundaries." *Economist,* September 11, 1993.

———. "The African State as a Political Refugee: Institutional Collapse and Human Displacement." *International Journal of Refugee Law* (July 1995): 21, Special Issue.

Mbaku, John Mukum, and Julius Omozuanvbo Ihonvbere, eds. *The Transition to Democratic Governance in Africa: The Continuing Struggle.* Westport: Praeger Publishers, 2003.

Mbiti, John S. *African Religions and Philosophy.* London: Heinemann, 1969.

Mboya, Tom. *Freedom and After.* Boston: Little, Brown, 1963.

———. *Challenge of Nationhood.* New York: Praeger Publishers, 1970.

Mburugu, E. K., and F. Ojany. "The Land and the People." In *Kenya: An Official Handbook,* ed. Richard Ndirango. Nairobi: Ministry of Information, 1988.

Mkandawire, P. Thandika. *African Intellectuals: Rethinking Politics, Language, Gender, and Development.* Dakar: CODESRIA, 2006.

Morton, Andrew. *Moi: The Making of a Statesman.* London: Michael O'Mara, 1998.

Moyo, Ambrose. "Religion in Africa." In *Understanding Contemporary Africa,* ed. April A. Gordon and Donald L. Gordon. Boulder: Lynne Rienner, 1996.

Mudimbe, V. Y. *The Invention of Africa: Gnosis, Philosophy, and the Order of Knowledge.* Bloomington: Indiana University Press, 1988.

Mugi-Ndua, Elizabeth. *Mekatilili wa Menza: Woman Warrior.* Nairobi: Sasa Sema Publications, 2000.

Muigai, Githu. "Ethnicity and the Renewal of Competitive Politics in Kenya." In *Ethnic Conflict and Democratization in Africa,* ed. Harvey Glickman. Atlanta: African Studies Association Press, 1995.

Murphy, Walter F. "Constitutions, Constitutionalism, and Democracy." In *Constitutionalism and Democracy: Transitions in the Contemporary World,* ed. Douglas Greenberg, Stanley M. Katz, Melanie Beth Oliviero, and Steven Wheatley. New York: Oxford University Press, 1993.

Murray-Brown, Jeremy. *Kenyatta.* New York: Dutton, 1979.

Murunga, Godwin R., and Shadrack W. Nasong'o, eds. *Kenya: The Struggle for Democracy.* London: Zed Books, 2007.

Murungi, Kiraitu. *In the Mud of Politics.* Nairobi: Acacia Stantex Publishers, 2000.

———. "Democratic Party of Kenya's Position on the Majimbo Debate." December 6, 2001, available at http://www.kenyaconstitution.org/docs/11d008.htm, accessed May 27, 2005.

Muslim Task Force on Constitution Review. "The Kenyan Muslim Position on the Constitutional Safeguard of the Kadhi's Courts." Jamia Mosque, Nairobi, 2003.

Muthien, Yvonne, and Gregory Houston. "Transforming South African State and Society: The Challenge of Constructing a Developmental State." In *The African State: Reconsiderations,* ed. Abdi Ismail Samatar and Ahmed I. Samatar. Portsmouth: Heinemann, 2002.

Mutua, Athena, ed. *Eyes on the Prize.* Nairobi: Kenya Human Rights Commission, 2003.

———. "Gender Equality and Women's Solidarity Across Religious, Ethnic, and Class Difference in the Kenya Constitutional Review Process." *William and Mary Journal of Women and Law* 13 (2006): 1.

Mutua, Makau. "A Call for a National Dialogue." *Nairobi Law Monthly* (September 1991).

———. "Democracy in Africa: No Easy Walk to Freedom." *Reconstruction* 2 (1992): 39.

———. "The Regionalization Controversy." *Africa Report* (September–October 1993).

———. "Putting Humpty Dumpty Back Together Again: The Dilemmas of the Post-Colonial African State." *Brooklyn Journal of International Law* 21 (1995): 505.

———. "Why Redraw the Map of Africa? A Moral and Legal Inquiry." *Michigan Journal of International Law* 16 (1995): 1113.

———. "The Ideology of Human Rights." *Virginia Journal of International Law* 36 (1996): 589.

———. "Limitations of Religious Rights: Problematizing Religious Freedom in the African Context." In *Religious Human Rights in Global Perspective: Legal Perspective,* ed. Johan D. van der Vyver and John Witte, Jr. The Hague: Martinus Nijhoff, 1996.

———. "Returning to My Roots: African 'Religions' and the State." In *Proselytization and Communal Self-Determination in Africa,* ed. Abdullahi Ahmed An-Na'im. Maryknoll: Orbis Books, 1999.

———. "Politics and Human Rights: An Essential Symbiosis." In *The Role of Law in International Politics: Essays in International Relations and International Law,* ed. Michael Byers. New York: Oxford University Press, 2000.

———. "Justice Under Siege: The Rule of Law and Judicial Subservience in Kenya." *Human Rights Quarterly* 23 (2001): 96.

———. *Human Rights: A Political and Cultural Critique.* Philadelphia: University of Pennsylvania Press, 2002.

———. "African Human Rights Organizations: Questions of Legitimacy and Context." In *Human Rights, the Rule of Law, and Development in Africa*, ed. Paul Tiyambe Zeleza and Philip J. McConnaughay. Philadelphia: University of Pennsylvania Press, 2004.

———. "Proselytism and Cultural Integrity." In *Facilitating Freedom of Religion or Belief: A Deskbook,* ed. Tore Lindholm, W. Cole Durham, Jr., and Bahia G. Tahzib-Lie. Leiden: Martinus Nijhoff Publishers, 2004.

———, ed. *Human Rights NGOs in East Africa: Political and Normative Tensions.* Philadelphia: University of Pennsylvania Press, forthcoming 2008.

Mutua, Makau wa, and Willy Mutunga. "Why and How to Bring About Regime Change in Kenya." Kenya Human Rights Commission, October 2, 2002.

———. "When Minds Meet: Points of Consensus." *Yawazekana: Bomas Agender,* May 22, 2003.

Mutua, Makau wa, and Peter Rosenblum. *Zaire: Repression as Policy.* Lawyers Committee for Human Rights (now Human Rights First), 1990.

Mutunga, Willy. *Constitution-Making from the Middle: Civil Society and Transition Politics in Kenya, 1992–1997.* Harare: MWENGO, 1999.

———. "So, What Is Non-Partisanship?" In *Eyes on the Prize,* ed. Athena D. Mutua. Nairobi: Kenya Human Rights Commission, 2003.

Mutunga, Willy, and Alamin Mazrui. "Rights Integration in an Institutional Context: The Experience of the Kenya Human Rights Commission." *Buffalo Law Review* 8 (2002): 123.

Mwangi, Paul. *The Black Bar: Corruption and Political Intrigue Within Kenya's Legal Fraternity.* Nairobi: Oakland Media Services, 2001.

Nasong'o, Shadrack Wanjala. "Political Transition Without Transformation: The Dialectic of Liberalization Without Democratization in Kenya and Zambia." *African Studies Review* 50 (April 2007): 83.

National Alliance for Change (NAC). "Fundamental Principles to Be Considered in Making the New Constitution by the People of Kenya, March 7, 2003," available at http://www.kenyaconstitution.org/docs/11d009.htm, accessed May 27, 2005.

National Assembly. *The Report of the Parliamentary Select Committee to Investigate Ethnic Clashes in Western and Other Parts of Kenya.* Nairobi: National Assembly of Kenya, 1992.

National Council of Churches of Kenya (NCCK). *The Cursed Arrow: A Report on Organized Violence Against Democracy in Kenya.* Nairobi: National Council of Churches of Kenya, 1992.

National Elections Monitoring Unit (NEMU). *The Multi-Party General Elections in Kenya, 29 December 1992.* Nairobi: NEMU, 1993.

Ndegwa, Duncan. *Walking in Kenyatta's Struggles: My Story.* Nairobi: Kenya Leadership Institute, 2006.

Ndegwa, Stephen. *The Two Faces of Civil Society: NGOs and Politics in Africa.* Bloomfield, CT: Kumarian Press, 1996.

———. *A Decade of Democracy in Africa.* Leiden: Brill Academic Publishers, 2001.

Neuberger, Benjamin. "Federalism in Africa: Experience and Prospects." In *Federalism and Political Integration,* ed. Daniel Judah Elazar. Lanham, MD: University Press of America, 1979.

Ngunyi, Mutahi. "Civil Society and the Challenge of Multiple Transitions in Kenya." In *Civil Society and Democratic Development in Africa: Perspectives from Eastern and Southern Africa,* ed. Julius Nyang'oro. Harare: MWENGO, 1999.

———. "Comparative Constitution Making in Africa: A Critique of the Kenyan Process from Seven Countries." In *Constitution-Making from the Middle: Civil*

Society and the Politics of Transition in Kenya, 1992–1997, ed. Willy Mutunga Harare: MWENGO, 1999.

———. *Democracy and the Aid Industry in Kenya: An Assessment of Grantmaking to the DG Sector of Civil Society in Kenya.* Leeds: University of Leeds/SAREAT, 1999.

Nkrumah, Kwame. *Neo-Colonialism: The Last Stage of Imperialism.* New York: International Publishers, 1965.

———. *The Challenge of the Congo.* New York: International Publishers, 1967.

———. *Africa Must Unite.* Los Angeles: International Publishers, 1970.

Nowrojee, Eruch. "Kenya: Political Pluralism, Government Resistance, and United States Responses." *Harvard Human Rights Journal* 5 (1992): 149, 156.

Nwabueze, B. O. *Presidentialism in Commonwealth Africa.* New York: St. Martin's Press, 1974.

Nyong'o, Peter Anyang', ed. *Thirty Years of African Independence: The Lost Decades?* Nairobi: Academy Science Publishers, 1992.

Nzomo, Maria. "Women, Democracy, and Development in Africa." In *Democratic Theory and Practice in Africa,* ed. Walter O. Oyugi, Afrifa K. Gitonga, Atieno Adhiambo, and Michael Chege. Nairobi: East African Educational Publishers, 1988.

———. "Civil Society in the Kenyan Political Transition: 1992–2002." In *The Politics of Transition in Kenya: From KANU to NARC,* ed. Oyugi Walter, Peter Wanyande, and C. Odhiambo-Mbai. Nairobi: Heinrich Böll Foundation, 2003.

Nzongola-Ntalaja, Georges. *The Congo from Leopold to Kabila: A People's History.* London: Zed Books, 2002.

Odinga, Oginga. *Not Yet Uhuru: The Autobiography of Oginga Odinga.* New York: Hill and Wang, 1967.

Odinkalu, Anselm Chidi. "Why More Africans Don't Use the Human Rights Language." *Human Rights Dialogue* 4 (Winter 2000).

O'Donnell, G., and P. Schmitter. *Transitions from Authoritarian Rule: Tentative Conclusions About Uncertain Democracies.* Baltimore: Johns Hopkins University Press, 1986.

Ogot, B. A., and W. R. Ochieng', eds. *Decolonization and Independence in Kenya, 1940–93.* Athens: Ohio University Press, 1995.

Ojo, Bamidele A. *Contemporary African Politics: A Comparative Study of Political Transition to Democratic Legitimacy.* Lanham, MD: University Press of America, 1999.

Okondo, Peter J. "Prospects of Federalism in East Africa." In *Federalism and the New Nations of Africa,* ed. David P. Currie. Chicago: University of Chicago Press, 1964.

———. *A Commentary on the Constitution of Kenya.* Nairobi: Phoenix Publishers, 1995.

Okoth-Ogendo, H. W. O. "Constitutions Without Constitutionalism: Reflections on an African Political Paradox." In *Constitutionalism and Democracy: Transitions in the Contemporary World,* ed. Douglas Greenberg, Stanley M. Katz, Melanie Beth Oliviero, and Steven C. Wheatley. New York: Oxford University Press, 1993.

Okullu, Bishop H. "Church, State and Society in East Africa." In *Thirty Years of Independence in Africa: The Lost Decades,* ed. Peter Anyang' Nyong'o. Nairobi: Academy Science Publishers, 1992.

Okumu, Washington A. J. *The African Renaissance: History, Significance, and Strategy.* Trenton, NJ: African World Press, 2002.

Oliver, Roland. *The African Experience.* New York: Icon-Harper Publishers, 1991.

Oloka-Onyango, Joseph, ed. *Constitutionalism in Africa: Creating Opportunities, Facing Challenges.* Kampala: Fountain Publishers, 2001.

Onalo, P. L. Agweli. *Constitution-Making in Kenya: An African Appraisal.* Nairobi: Transafrica Press, 2003.

Opiata, Odindo. "Of Phrase-Mongering and Political Debate." *Nairobi Law Monthly* (September 1991).

Orentlicher, Diane. "Separation Anxiety: International Responses to Ethno-Separatist Claims." *Yale Journal of International Law* 23 (1998): 1.

Ottaway, Marina, ed. *Democracy in Africa: The Hard Road Ahead.* Boulder: Lynne Rienner Publishers, 1997.

Patel, Zarina. *Unquiet: The Life and Times of Makhan Singh.* Nairobi: Zand Graphics, 2006.

Pelczyniski, Z. A. *The State and Civil Society: Studies in Hegel's Political Philosophy.* New York: Cambridge University Press, 1984.

———, ed. "Solidarity and 'Rebirth of Civil Society' in Poland, 1976–81." In *Civil Society and the State: New European Perspectives,* ed. John Keane. New York: Verso, 1988.

Peter, Chris M. "The Proposed African Court of Justice—Jurisprudential, Procedural, Enforcement Problems and Beyond." *East African Journal of Peace and Human Rights* 117, no. 1 (1993).

Peterson, Scott. *Me Against My Brother: At War in Somalia, Sudan, and Rwanda.* New York: Routledge, 2002.

Pobee, John S. "Africa's Search for Religious Human Rights Through Returning to the Wells of Living Water." In *Religious Human Rights in Global Perspective: Legal Perspective,* ed. Johan D. van der Vyver and John Witte, Jr. The Hague: Martinus Nijhoff, 1996.

Prempeh, H. Kwasi. "Marbury in Africa: Judicial Review and the Challenge of Constitutionalism in Contemporary Africa." *Tulane Law Review* 80 (2006): 1239.

"President Moi Defends Kenya's Human Rights Record." FBIS-AFR-93-189, October 1, 1993, at 3, from Kenya Broadcasting Corporation Television, September 29, 1993.

"Protection of Fundamental Rights and Freedoms of the Individual." Chapter 2 in *Kenya Independence Constitution.* 1963.

Republic of Kenya. *African Socialism and Its Application to Planning in Kenya.* Sessional Paper 10. 1965.

———. *Report of the Administration of Justice: Summary of Recommendations* (Kwach Report). 1998.

———. *Report of the Judicial Commission of Inquiry into Ethnic Clashes in Kenya* (Akiwumi Report). Nairobi: Law Society of Kenya, 2002.

———. *Report of the Task Force on the Establishment of a Truth, Justice, and Reconciliation Commission.* Nairobi: Government Printer, 2003.

———. *Report of the Judicial Commission of Inquiry into the Goldenberg Affair* (Bosire Report). Nairobi: Government Printer, October 2005.

———. *Kenya Gazette,* Special Issue, February 24, 2006.

———. *Report of the Committee of Eminent Persons,* May 30, 2006.

Republic of Kenya, State House. "His Highness the Aga Khan Commends Kenya's Economic Growth." August 13, 2007, available at http://www.statehousekenya .go.ke/.

Richburg, Keith. *Out of America: A Black Man Confronts Africa.* London: Harper-Collins, 1997.

Rivkin, Arnold. *Nation Building in Africa.* New Brunswick: Rutgers University Press, 1969.

Rodney, Walter. *How Europe Underdeveloped Africa.* Dar-es-Salaam: Tanzanian Publishing House, 1973.

Roseberg, Carl, and John Nottingham. *The Myth of the "Mau Mau": Nationalism in Kenya.* New York: Praeger, 1966, published for the Hoover Institution on War, Revolution, and Peace, Stanford, CA.

Rosenblum, Peter. "Teaching Human Rights Activism: Ambivalent Activism, Multiple Discourses, and Lingering Dilemmas." *Harvard Human Rights Journal* 15 (2002): 301.

Rothchild, Donald. *Managing Ethnic Conflict in Africa: Pressures and Incentives for Cooperation.* Washington, DC: Brookings Institution Press, 1997.

Salim, A. I., and K. K. Janmohamed. "Historical Development." In *Kenya: An Official Handbook,* ed. Richard Ndirango. Nairobi: Ministry of Information, 1988.

Samatar, Ahmed I. "Somalia: Statelessness as Homelessness." In *The African State: Reconsiderations,* ed. Abdi Ismail Samatar and Ahmed I. Samatar. Portsmouth: Heinemann, 2002.

Sanneh, Lamin. *Encountering the West: Christianity and the Global Cultural Process: The African Dimension.* Maryknoll: Orbis Books, 1993.

Schumpeter, J. *Capitalism, Socialism, and Democracy,* 3rd ed. New York: Harper and Row, 1950.

Seekings, J. *The UDF: A History of the United Democratic Front in South Africa 1983–1991.* Athens: Ohio University Press, 2000.

Selassie, Bereket Habte. *The Making of the Eritrean Constitution: The Dialectic of Process and Substance.* Trenton: Red Sea Press, 2003.

Shivji, Issa G., ed. *State and Constitutionalism: An African Debate on Democracy.* Harare: Sapes Trust, 1991.

Shropshire, Denys. *The Church and Primitive Peoples.* New York: Macmillan, 1938.

Shugart, M., and J. Cary. *Presidents and Assemblies: Constitutional Design and Electoral Dynamics.* New York: Cambridge University Press, 1992.

Singh, Makhan. *Kenya's Trade Unions, 1952–1956.* Nairobi: Uzima Press, 1980.

Slater, Montagu. *The Trial of Jomo Kenyatta.* London: Secker and Warburg, 1965.

Solomon, Joel A., and James Silk. *Failing the Democratic Challenge: Freedom of Expression in Multiparty Kenya.* Washington, DC: Robert F. Kennedy Memorial Center for Human Rights, 1993.

Soros, George. *The Crisis of Global Capitalism: Open Society Endangered.* New York: Public Affairs, 1998.

Soyinka, Wole. *The Open Sore of a Continent: A Personal Narrative of the Nigerian Crisis.* New York: Oxford University Press, 1996.

Steiner, Henry J. "Political Participation as a Human Right." *Harvard Human Rights Yearbook* 1 (1988): 77.

Steiner, Henry J., and Philip Alston. *International Human Rights in Context: Law, Politics, Morals.* New York: Oxford University Press, 2000.

Strayer, Robert W. *The Making of Mission Communities in East Africa: Anglicans and Africans in Colonial Kenya, 1875–1935.* Albany: State University of New York Press, 1978.

Stropshire, Denys. *The Church and Primitive Peoples.* New York: Macmillan, 1938.

Swilling, M. "The United Democratic Front and Township Revolt." In *Popular Struggles in South Africa,* ed. W. Cobbett and R. Cohen. Trenton, NJ: Africa World Press, 1988.

Thiong'o, Ngugi wa. *Ngugi Detained: A Writer's Prison Diary.* Nairobi: Heinemann, 1981.

————. *Barrel of a Pen: Resistance to Repression in Neo-Colonial Kenya.* Trenton, NJ: Africa World Press, 1988.

————. *A Grain of Wheat.* London: Heinemann, 1988.

————. *The River Between.* London: Heinemann, 1990.

Thiong'o, Ngugi wa, and Micere Mugo. *The Trial of Dedan Kimathi.* London: Heinemann, 1977.

Throup, David. *Economic and Social Origins of the Mau Mau.* Athens: Ohio University Press, 1988.

Throup, David W., and Charles Hornsby. *Multiparty Politics in Kenya: The Kenyatta and Moi States and the Triumph of the System in the 1992 Election.* Athens: Ohio University Press, 1998.

Tignor, R. L. *The Colonial Transformation of Kenya: The Kamba, Kikuyu, and Maasai from 1900 to 1939.* Princeton: Princeton University Press, 1976.

Tocqueville, Alexis de. *Democracy in America.* New York: Library of America, 2004.

Umozurike, U. O. "International Law and Colonialism in Africa." *East African Law Review* 3 (1970): 47.

United Nations Development Programme (UNDP). *Human Development Report 2005: International Cooperation at a Crossroads: Aid, Trade, and Security in an Unequal World.* New York: UNDP, 2005.

————. *UNDP Annual Report 2006: Global Partnership for Development.* New York: UNDP, 2006.

United Nations General Assembly. Universal Declaration of Human Rights, G.A. Res. 217A, U.N. Doc. A/810, at 71. 1948.

————. Eritrea: Report of the United Nations Commission on Eritrea. Resolution 390(V) UN GAOR, UN Doc. A/1605. December 2, 1950.

United Nations High Commissioner for Human Rights. *Report of the Needs Assessment Mission to South Africa.* New York, May 6–25, 1996.

US Central Intelligence Agency. *CIA World Factbook.* 2005. http://www.cia.gov/cia/publications/factbook/geos/ke.html#People, accessed May 24, 2005.

US Department of State. Bureau of African Affairs. *Background Note: Kenya,* available at http://www.state.gov/r/pa/ei/bgn/2962.htm, accessed August 2, 2006.

Villalón, Leonardo A., and Philip A. Huxtable, eds. *The African State at a Critical Juncture: Between Disintegration and Reconfiguration.* Boulder: Lynne Rienner Publishers, 1998.

Walesa, Lech, Franklin Philip, and Helen Mahut, eds. *The Struggle and the Triumph: An Autobiography.* New York: Arcade Publishing, 1993.

Wamwere, Koigi wa. *Conscience on Trial: Why I Was Detained: Notes of a Political Prisoner.* Trenton, NJ: Africa World Press, 1993.

————. *I Refuse to Die: My Journey for Freedom.* New York: Seven Stories Press, 2002.

Wandabba, Simiyu. *Masinde Muliro.* Nairobi: East African Educational Publishers, 1996.

Wanjau, Gakaara wa. *Mau Mau Author in Detention.* Nairobi: Heinemann Kenya, 1988.

Weisbord, Robert. *African Zion: The Attempt to Establish a Jewish Colony in the East Africa Protectorate, 1930–1905.* Philadelphia: Jewish Publication Society of America, 1968.

Weissman, Stephen. "The CIA and US Policy in Zaire and Angola." In *American Policy in Southern Africa,* ed. René Lemarchand. Washington, DC: University Press of America, 1978.

Welch, Claude E. *Protecting Human Rights in Africa: Strategies and Roles of Non-Governmental Organizations.* Philadelphia: University of Pennsylvania Press, 1995.

———. *NGOS and Human Rights: Promise and Performance.* Philadelphia: University of Pennsylvania Press, 2001.

Widner, Jennifer A. *The Rise of a Party-State in Kenya: From Harambee to Nyayo!* Berkeley: University of California Press, 1992.

———, ed. *Economic Change and Political Liberalization in Sub-Saharan Africa.* Baltimore: Johns Hopkins University Press, 1994.

Williams, Juan. *Thurgood Marshall: American Revolutionary.* New York: Times Press, 1998.

Williamson, John. "What Washington Means by Policy Reform." In *Latin American Adjustment: How Much Has Happened,* ed. John Williamson. Washington, DC: Institute for International Economics, 1990.

———. "What Should the World Bank Think About the Washington Consensus?" *World Bank Research Observer* 15 (August 2000): 251.

Young, Crawford. *Ideology and Development in Africa.* New Haven: Yale University Press, 1982.

———. *The African Colonial State in Comparative Perspective.* New Haven: Yale University Press, 1994.

———. "The Heritage of Colonialism." In *Africa in World Politics,* ed. John W. Harbeson and Donald Rothchild. Boulder: Westview Press, 1995.

———. "The Third Wave of Democratization in Africa: Ambiguities and Contradictions." In *State, Conflict, and Democracy,* ed. Richard Joseph. Boulder: Lynne Rienner Publishers, 1995.

Zartman, I. William, ed. *Collapsed States: The Disintegration and Restoration of Legitimate Authority.* Boulder: Lynne Rienner Publishers, 1995.

Zeleza, Paul Tiyambe. "Introduction: The Struggle for Human Rights in Africa." In *Human Rights, the Rule of Law, and Development in Africa,* ed. Paul Tiyambe Zeleza and Philip J. McConnaughay. Philadelphia: University of Pennsylvania Press, 2004.

Zeleza, Paul Tiyambe, and Philip J. McConnaughay. *Human Rights, the Rule of Law, and Development in Africa.* Philadelphia: University of Pennsylvania Press, 2004.

Index

311

About the Book

TRACING THE TRAJECTORY of postcolonial politics, Makau Mutua maps the political forces that have shaped contemporary Kenya. He also critically explores efforts on the part of both civil society and the political opposition to reform the state. Analyzing the tortuous efforts since independence to create a sustainable, democratic state, he uses the struggle over constitutional reform as a window for understanding the larger struggles confronting Kenyan society.

Makau Mutua is SUNY Distinguished Professor, Floyd H. and Hilda L. Hurst Faculty Scholar, and interim dean at the State University of New York at Buffalo Law School.